W9-ACR-950

A CITIZEN'S DISSENT

Rush to Judgment

A Citizen's Dissent

MARK LANE

A CITIZEN'S DISSENT

Mark Lane Replies

HOLT, RINEHART AND WINSTON
NEW YORK CHICAGO
SAN FRANCISCO

Published simultaneously in Canada by Holt, Rinehart
and Winston of Canada, Limited.

Library of Congress Catalog Card Number: 68-13044

First Edition

Designer: Ernst Reichl
8686958
Printed in the United States of America

To Vickie Martin

Contents

Introduction

DURING my trips to Europe following the death of President Kennedy, I became aware of an area of concern that prevailed when knowledgeable Continental sophisticates discussed the subject. None believed the Warren Report, yet many were puzzled by the obvious endorsement of the document by the American press. Chief Justice Warren's reputation was largely national; and while Americans asked how his findings could be doubted, or even examined, Europeans, even those well known in the legal profession and judiciary, with the exception of some Londoners, were less than fully acquainted with his image of integrity. Instead, they asked how the independent American newspapermen had been silenced or cajoled into supporting the Report.

Hollywood has played a large part in convincing the world that the old-fashioned reporter is still at large; that his spiritual inheritance flows from the man of unshakable independence who set type by hand out West somewhere, while his wary wife and beautiful daughter fretted, because he exposed the corrupt established power in town. Half a century later the same character, often played by the same actor, drank coffee at his desk, whiskey in the saloon and in between dashed unimpeded about the metropolis in search of the scoop—letting the chips fall where they may. His honest white-haired boss, the publisher, always backed him up and, while a trifle disconcerted by his occasional drinking, often encouraged him to take on the biggest and most evil forces in the power structure.

The assignment we have undertaken precludes the possibility of exploring the validity of such stereotypes, but it seems doubtful that the movie-script accolades were ever universally merited. How do the American media act when a matter of historic dimensions occurs and when the Government takes the very firm position that that which is demonstrably false is true? How does organized society respond?

The Report of the President's Commission on the Assassination of President Kennedy (the Warren Commission Report) provides an admirable laboratory for research, for the subject with which it is concerned and the Report itself are both not without historical significance. In concluding the CBS-TV four-hour documentary defense of the Report's conclusions, Walter Cronkite stated that "there has been a loss of morale, a loss of confidence among the American people toward their own government and the men who serve it."[1] Cronkite's presentation here is accurate, for the most respected polls had indicated that two-thirds of the American people did not believe the Warren Commission.[2]

Cronkite continued: "The damage that Lee Harvey Oswald did the United States . . . did not end when the shots were fired from the Texas School Book Depository. The most grievous wounds persist and there is little reason to believe that they will soon be healed."[3]

The lack of confidence by the American people in an important governmental finding and in the media for their many efforts to endorse the Report is a matter of some concern. Since the Report is without merit, the response to it by a biddable press is indicative that wounds persist which may not soon be healed. We must examine this response in an entirely different light from that which illuminated Mr. Cronkite's assessment. So conscious was I of that circumstance that I concluded *Rush to Judgment* with these words: "As long as we rely for information upon men blinded by the fear of what they might see, the precedent of the Warren Commission Report will continue to imperil the life of the law and dishonor those who wrote it little more than those who praise it."[4]

The list of those who have praised the finding that Lee Harvey Oswald was the lone assassin has grown since those words were written. This book is about them, the powerful, the influential men and forces who have been enlisted in the sad cause of saving the unsalvable. If they appear desperate on occasion, bitter and humorless almost throughout, it is understandable, since the burden they have assumed is without adequate compensation. And so we observe the *modus operandi* of the Establishment. No giant conspiracy, save the conspiracy of life and all its complications, brought J. Edgar Hoover, Earl Warren and a couple of otherwise reputable law professors to the same crusade. Yet, lemming-like, they are there, marching toward oblivion under the banner, "Save us and what we believe in," while the Associated Press, *Newsweek*, *Time*, CBS, NBC and many others provide the almost pathetic and consistent accompaniment. The organized liberals, if those two terms not be mutually exclusive, are in the forefront, although armed with the tools of yesterday. This army may well be motivated not at all by greed or avarice, but by a genuine desire to insure the stability of its country. Almost any motive save that one could be endured.

Rush to Judgment was a difficult book to write. First, because writing is hard work for me, and also because in the Commission's work there was a plethora of witnesses, exhibits and questions that had been raised for which solutions were not forthcoming. It was only after many months of sifting through the verbiage, the superfluity of often inconsequential documents with which the Commission burdened its record, that I was to determine that the evidence bore little relation to the Commission's conclusions. Since that determination was made before I began to write, the conclusions that flowed from the writing did not surprise me at all.

This work has been more difficult, for its conclusions proved to be somewhat startling. An analysis of the Warren Report called into question the integrity of a local police force and of the Federal police agencies. An *ad hoc* committee, admittedly comprised of important men, was shown to have issued an invalid document. Surely not for the first time and not for the last had such an event taken place. The full significance of that act and of the circumstances that surrounded it and subsequently flowed from it offers a view far more frightening.

If *Rush to Judgment* and other critical works helped to isolate a symptom, then this volume seeks to take the full measure of the disease. If a numerically insignificant segment of society was discovered in that episode to have been involved in corrupt practices, then a phalanx of patricians are here found to be their associates, their accessories after the fact. The ease with which the princes of the networks, who share a Government-created monopoly, at first accepted and, when that was proven to be insufficient, then embraced the conclusion that Lee Harvey Oswald alone assassinated President Kennedy suggests a closer than arm's length relationship between the media and the Government.

The difficulty of presenting a dissenting view in the face of such constraint is predictable. The draconic power of those who would negate reasonable disagreement is our subject. In pursuing it we will meet police directors, television commentators, Pulitzer Prize winners, doctors, lawyers and FBI chiefs—the makers of public opinion, except perhaps in this instance. Then we may better know why the freedoms we cherish and speak of have become more and more illusory and why our nation moves, imperceptibly to those who will not observe the phenomenon, but nonetheless significantly, toward the strictures of a closed society.

Author's Note

SHOULD a book review the reviews? Should an author criticize critics? There are numberless possibilities concomitant with the initiation of such a process. However intriguing their potential, I believe that the book reviewers should have the last word. Once an author submits his work for publication he invites critical assessment, and he can hardly expect that all of it will be favorable or even fair. His solace flows from the knowledge that the integrity of the work, if ever present, will survive a hostile press. The work is indestructible if it has been so constructed, and although temporal rewards may elude him, if his was so expedient an objective, the work may well have been flawed at the outset.

Accordingly, I eschew the task of reviewing the legitimate book reviews of *Rush to Judgment*. I do so reluctantly, for the vast majority of the hundreds of reviews were objective, the majority favorable and, with a handful of exceptions, all were fair; and to ignore them while discussing the writings of the Commission's defenders is to present a less than balanced picture of the total response to the book. This note is intended to place the reader in a position to view the defenders in proper perspective and to salute the reviewers for remaining, by and large, independent of those forces which have so directly affected other responses. May the luminiferous quality of the book pages one day reach into and illuminate the dark confines of the editorial offices.

The antonym for "legitimate" as employed here assuredly is not "illegitimate," just as so pejorative an appellation could not fairly be applied to off-Broadway theater productions, films or other similar endeavors that escape the classification "legitimate theater." Exempt from comment herein, for the reasons already stated, are those analyses of *Rush to Judgment* that appeared in the ordinary course of events in newspapers and magazines or which were broadcast as book reviews by radio or television stations.

M.L.

December 1967

PART ONE: THE DISSENT

I · The Death

1 THE FIRST QUESTION

WHILE I had met President Kennedy on several occasions and he had been kind enough to endorse me when I was a candidate for the New York State Assembly, my interest in the charges against Lee Harvey Oswald probably was related more to my professional discipline than to my personal attachment to the victim. I had been a defense trial lawyer for more than a decade and the question of pre-trial publicity designed to make a fair trial an impossibility was a matter of serious concern to me. The police and prosecutors, using the press, radio and television, had developed the concept of instant guilt in the hours following the assassination.

I was interested in knowing who killed the President, and I was not confident that I could ever discover the answer by reading the police accounts in the newspapers. I had had the experience of reading police accounts of various of my clients' exploits in the past, and I knew how difficult it was on occasion to reconcile the facts with the police view.

I learned that the President had been shot through radio reports, as did millions of other Americans. I was stimulated to enter the discussion tentatively by what appeared to be prejudicial and questionable announcements then being made by local and Federal prosecuting and investigatory agencies. Perhaps I was sufficiently challenged to participate fully in the debate, indeed to initiate it, primarily by the craven attitude of the leading mass and intellectual periodicals.

On Friday morning, I traveled by subway to the Criminal Court Building located in lower Manhattan. My calendar reminded me that I had several motions to make, a prisoner awaiting trial to visit, and perhaps a case to try. The judge did, in fact, insist that the case be tried and the prosecutor began to present his evidence. At one o'clock, as is the custom, the judge adjourned the trial for a luncheon recess of one hour. Lunch consisted of Chinese pastries in nearby Chinatown and last-minute preparations for the afternoon session.

As I walked back toward the courthouse, I saw a group of men and women clustered around a small grocery store. They appeared to be listening to a radio. The scene was immediately reminiscent of newsreels taken in European capitals when news of war was broadcast. The tone was heavy with tragedy. "What happened? What is it?" "The President's been shot. Maybe killed." I ran to the press room in the courthouse, where the same sense of tragedy prevailed.

Lawyers, clerks, reporters and courtroom attendants stood or sat in silence as the radio offered suspense-filled and sometimes contradictory bulletins. "It is thought that a Negro was involved in the assassination," the radio charged. A Negro attendant shifted his weight from one foot to another and looked away from those who covertly glanced in his direction. Jack Roth, the *New York Times* criminal court reporter, entered a phone booth, spoke briefly with his office, and then re-entered the room with tears in his eyes. "He's dead," he said to me quietly.

I went to the trial courtroom to learn the adjourned date of the case and to move for the continuation of bail for my client. The judge was annoyed that I was late. I said that the President had just died. "Yes," he replied, "I know. There's nothing we can do about that here. Let's move along with this trial."

At the end of the day, as I left the building, I met an old trial judge slowly walking down the massive stone steps.

"Well, Lane, do you think he did it alone?" he asked.

"Who, sir? Did what?"

"Do you think this Oswald killed the President?" he asked.

"I'm afraid that I don't know anything about it. I just heard that the President was killed. I haven't heard any of the details."

The judge proceeded with caution down the next few steps, then stopped and looked at me.

"He couldn't very well shoot him from the back and cause an entrance wound in his throat, could he? The doctors said the throat wound was an entrance wound. It'll be an interesting trial. I want to see how they answer that question."

I forgot the judge's observation as I searched the streets for a taxi to take me to my office in midtown Manhattan. Now, years after the event and years after the publication of the Warren Report, it seems that the judge's question remains without satisfactory answer. And there was no trial.

There was no trial, but offerings of Oswald's guilt were not lacking as Federal and local police and prosecutors held impromptu press conferences in the Dallas courthouse. With few exceptions, the relevant question was not asked. Some reporters sought to ingratiate themselves by avoiding the difficult questions, by failing to point up evident contradictions. Most, however, were ill-equipped for the task. They were not courtroom reporters but part of the President's entourage. The questions that the reporters failed to ask, Americans began to ask themselves. When two days after the assassination Oswald was murdered in the basement of the Dallas Police and Courts Building while being guarded by some seventy police officers, the persistent doubts multiplied and intensified.

It was to still those doubts that Henry Wade, the Dallas prosecutor, called a press conference soon after Oswald's death was announced. Wade said that he was convinced beyond any doubt that Oswald was guilty of assassinating the President. He was equally sure that Oswald did it alone and that he alone killed Dallas Police Officer J. D. Tippit. Wade then proceeded to present some fifteen assertions—some mere conclusions, some with the source not revealed, some buttressed by documentation of sorts. Many of the assertions contravened the facts known even then. Some assertions contradicted others. Yet the press in general reported the conference as if nothing were amiss.

When the *New York Times* published the text of the press conference two days later, I was able to study the allegations more leisurely. The weaknesses were blatant, and yet no one seemed concerned. I sat down to analyze the charges and to place them alongside what was then known about the case. When I was finished, I had written a ten-thousand-word article which began with this plea for a rational examination of the evidence:

> In all likelihood there does not exist a single American community where reside 12 men or women, good and true, who presume that Lee Harvey Oswald did not assassinate President Kennedy. No more savage comment can be made in reference to the breakdown of the Anglo-Saxon system of jurisprudence. At the very foundation of our judicial operation lies a cornerstone which shelters the innocent and guilty alike against group hysteria, manufactured evidence, overzealous law enforcement officials, in short, against those factors which militate for an automated, prejudged, neatly packaged verdict of guilty. It is the sacred right of every citizen accused of committing a crime to the presumption of innocence.
>
> This presumption, it has been written, is a cloak donned by the accused when the initial charge is made, and worn by him continuously. It is worn throughout the entire case presented against him, and not taken from the defendant until after he has had an opportunity to

> cross-examine hostile witnesses, present his own witnesses and to testify himself.
>
> Oswald did not testify. Indeed, there will be no case, no trial, and Oswald, murdered while in police custody, still has no lawyer. Under such circumstances the development of a possible defense is difficult, almost impossible. Under such circumstances, the development of such a defense is obligatory.
>
> There will be an investigation. No investigation, however soundly motivated, can serve as an adequate substitute for trial. Law enforcement officials investigate every criminal case before it is presented to a jury. The investigation in almost all such cases results in the firm conviction by the investigator that the accused is guilty. A jury often finds the defendant innocent, notwithstanding.
>
> That which intervenes between the zealous investigator and the jury is due process of law, developed at great cost in human life and liberty over the years. It is the right to have irrelevant testimony barred. It is the right to have facts, not hopes or thoughts or wishes or prejudicial opinions, presented. It is the right to test by cross-examination the veracity of every witness and the value of his testimony. It is, perhaps above all, the right to counsel of one's own choice, so that all the other rights may be protected. In this defense, Oswald has forfeited all rights along with his life.
>
> The reader, inundated at the outset with 48 solid television, radio and newspaper hours devoted to proving the guilt of the accused and much additional "evidence" since then, cannot now examine this case without bringing to it certain preconceived ideas. We ask, instead, only for a temporary suspension of certainty.[1]

The suspension of certainty that Oswald was the assassin was long in coming to America—it required almost three years. An analysis of Wade's fifteen assertions comprised the bulk of the article. I concluded not that Oswald was innocent or even that if guilty he could not have been alone, but only that there should be "a fair consideration of the evidence."

My first call was to Carey McWilliams, the editor of *The Nation*. I told him I had an article for him. He seemed pleased, expecting, I suspect, an article on New York politics, as I had been active in the Democratic Party, a founder of the reform Democratic movement and a member of the New York State Legislature. In the past, at his own request, McWilliams had conducted a brain-picking session or two with John Harrington, a very wise young political leader, and myself. I told him that I felt that Oswald's guilt had not yet been established and that the article that I had written suggested the need for dispassionate study of the evidence. There was a moment's silence and then he began: "We cannot take it. We don't want it. I am sorry but we have decided not to touch that subject."

I explained that I did not state that Oswald was innocent or that others were involved—only that there appeared to be unanswered questions which required serious examination. I said that I would send the article to him so that he might make an informed decision about it. "No. Don't send it. We won't print it," he replied. "We have already discussed the subject and decided not to touch it." I said I'd send a copy anyway on the chance that he might be persuaded. "No, please don't send it," were his final words.

In the course of the following days I offered my analysis, gratis, to almost every periodical in the United States, including *Fact*, the magazine of controversy, where I was informed that the subject was too controversial; *The Reporter; Look; Life;* the *Saturday Evening Post;* and on and on. An editor at *The New Republic* said that they were considering a similar article. No one was willing to read it, let alone consider publishing it. I then took the article to James Wechsler, one of the editors of the liberal New York *Post*. I had known Jimmy for some time, and he had in fact been a speaker at a then recent major campaign dinner for me when I was a candidate for public office.

Without a great deal of enthusiasm, but rather in the spirit of helping a friend out, he suggested that I contact *The Progressive*, a magazine which published him regularly. "I don't know if Rubin will run your article, but I am sure that he will at least read it." I called Morris Rubin, the editor of the publication, and he did agree to read the article, although he informed me that he had just put the magazine to bed and that no new article could be published for at least a month. "I presume that by then the subject may be forgotten," he said.

The next day I received a telephone call from James Aronson, the editor of the *National Guardian*, a publication of the left. Aronson told me that he had heard that I had written an article on the assassination and that he would like very much to see it. I told him that I would be happy to send a copy to him but that I was not authorizing him to publish it. He called again that day, after having read the piece. "We consider it to be a very important document and we want to publish it," he said. When I informed him that I was still seeking a broader publisher, he chided me for being unrealistic and unfair.

I called Wechsler to tell him that *The Progressive* seemed out and of the offer from the *National Guardian*. "Don't let them publish it," he advised. "They'll turn it into a political issue." I explained that my choice seemed to be between the *National Guardian* and my file drawer, unless he had an alternative. He said that he could not help me as he could think of no other periodical that might even consider it. I called Aronson and said that it was theirs if they still wanted it.

It was published in the *National Guardian* on December 19, 1963, less than one month after the assassination. At about the same time an article written by Staughton Lynd and Jack Minnis which raised similar questions appeared in *The New Republic*.[2] My article, referred to as a "brief," covered five pages in the tabloid-sized *National Guardian*. Additional press runs were unable to keep the newsstands supplied, and the *Guardian* announced that the demand was so heavy that a special pamphlet reprint was required. The *New York Times* published a major story about the points made in the brief,[3] but no other newspaper in New York, or to my knowledge elsewhere in the country, published a line about it. The *Guardian* later reported: "Abroad the reaction was quite different. In Rome the Lane brief was scheduled to be printed in full in *Paese Sera*, the largest in the evening field, and in *Liberation* in Paris. *Oggi*, an Italian magazine with a circulation of one million, sought permission to reprint. The Japanese press and news agencies also were on top of the story. Several Mexican papers picked it up, too."[4]

Advance proof sheets were sent to the United Press International (UPI) by the *Guardian*. The UPI responded that they "wouldn't touch it."[5]

In view of subsequent developments, it now appears that the most important person to read the brief was a housewife in Hominy, Oklahoma.

2 THE CALL

Shirley Martin lived in Hominy, Oklahoma, with her husband, four children and several dogs and cats. She was deeply moved by John F. Kennedy's presence in the White House. Mrs. Martin felt that the President had willed an important new spirit into the nation and that the country was indeed moving forward again. His sudden death came to her, as to many others, as a very personal blow. She wondered why he had been killed. She could not ascribe a motive to Lee Harvey Oswald. As she read the accounts of the assassination closely, she became less convinced of the validity of the charges against Oswald. She sent money to Marina Oswald, the widow, as did many other Americans. She wrote to Marguerite Oswald, the mother. She read the brief published in the *National Guardian* and sent that to Marguerite Oswald as well.

Mrs. Oswald had not known Mrs. Martin. I had known neither.

Yet a grieving mother asked me to appear as counsel for her son's interests before the President's Commission on the Assassination of President Kennedy because a housewife in Hominy read an article I had written. When we met, Mrs. Oswald said that no other lawyer had even suggested that her son was entitled to a trial before being condemned as a murderer. She asked me to appear before the Commission so that I might cross-examine the witnesses and perhaps even find witnesses the Commission had overlooked.

That I was interested was obvious, yet there were problems which appeared insurmountable. My law practice consisted to a very large extent of representing persons charged with crimes. Many were indigent or nearly so. My one corporate client, which made the remainder of my work possible, had informed me that sufficient corporate embarrassment had already been suffered as a result of my article and that any future similar activity would result in the reluctant, but certain, termination of my services. Mrs. Oswald was unable to pay any fee or even to undertake my expenses. My total income from the world-wide publication of my brief was a $100 check from the *National Guardian*, which I had not even expected.

To complicate the matter further, Mrs. Oswald told me that she believed that it was not unlikely that her son had been an intelligence agent of the United States and that she intended to make her feelings on that subject known. I saw no evidence at that time to support her assertion, and I expected that she would suffer considerable public ridicule if she made that unsupported charge. She did so, and the personal attacks upon her mounted. More than three years later, the New Orleans District Attorney investigating all aspects of the case reached the same conclusion, and six months after that, CBS, while defending the conclusions of the Warren Commission, conceded that Oswald may have been an agent of an American intelligence organization.[1] However, at the time, influenced no doubt by the hysteria of the period, I was reluctant to be associated with what I considered to be a possibly unfounded and certainly an unprovable and inflammatory charge.

Mrs. Oswald then turned my own argument toward me. She reminded me that I had said that her son and the country were entitled to a fair and critical analysis of the evidence. "He's being tried by the Warren Commission. He has no lawyer. Will you represent his interests or didn't you mean what you wrote?" I agreed to conduct an independent investigation—one independent of Mrs. Oswald as well. We agreed that to insure my freedom of action I would not serve as her attorney when she appeared before the Commission. We stipulated in writing that if I reached the conclusion that her son had been the assassin I would be free to state so publicly, a condition that would be quite improper were he still alive.

With a modicum of reluctance and a generous amount of apprehension, I approached a task that I never really sought. My resignation as counsel for the corporate client was accepted. The press hostility was almost universal, but nothing quite so painfully indicated that I had embarked upon a lonely journey as the public attack by James Wechsler in the New York *Post*. He asked aloud why I had given my article to a left-wing periodical, broadly implying that it could have been published elsewhere. When I called to ask him about his comment, he refused to speak with me.

Today, when David Susskind, Louis Nizer and other terribly comfortable men who devote most of their lives to making money charge that my interest in the subject was motivated by financial considerations, I think back to the desolate days of December 1963 and the equally desolate five hundred days that followed.

3 REPORTS FROM DALLAS

The controversy surrounding the official governmental explanation of the assassination of John F. Kennedy has spilled over into every form of communication in a complicated society. Books, films, radio and television interviews, panels, debates, documentaries, newspaper and magazine articles and analyses, phonograph records and the stage have all played a part in placing the question high on the American agenda of unfinished domestic business. It therefore requires considerable concentration to go back to the public origins of the dispute in order to realize that soon after the shots were fired in Dealey Plaza dissent from the official findings was proscribed. The consequences of the proscription were not immediate, but the process was initiated not many hours after the assassination, with effects that varied, often in inverse ratio to the independence and dedication of the reporter.

Reporters were on the scene as quickly as were the Federal and local police. What they discovered, in most instances, they filed, and thus it was that important witnesses and their viewpoints were known to the American people on the very day of the assassination. Jean Hill and Mary Moorman, two of the spectators closest to the Presidential limousine when the shots were fired, were interviewed on the scene by reporters before they were discovered by the police.[1] Charles Brehm was approximately twenty feet from the limousine when the fatal shot shattered the President's head.[2] He too was questioned on the spot by reporters and within a short period of time was broadcasting his observations via WFAA-TV in Dallas.[3] Mr. and Mrs. William Newman, also close eyewitnesses, were interviewed in the Dallas television studio of WFAA even before that station was able to broadcast news of the President's death.[4]

Most of what these witnesses said was inconvenient, not to say entirely incompatible, with the Commission's subsequent conclusions. Jean Hill stated that the shots originated at the grassy knoll area; indeed, apparently she was the witness who gave that area the name by which it has since been known.[5] She also said that she heard between four and six shots, while the Commission maintained that only three were fired.[6] Her friend, Mary Moorman, took two photographs, one of which evidently revealed the sixth floor of the Book Depository approximately at the time when the shots were fired.[7] Charles Brehm said that he witnessed the effect that the fatal shot had upon the President's head: "That which appeared to be a portion of the President's skull went flying slightly to the rear of the President's car and directly to its left."[8] This phenomenon should not have ordinarily resulted from a bullet fired from behind. The Newmans said that the shots originated from the knoll area.[9]

The journalists in Dealey Plaza went about their tasks with an energy that at least equaled that demonstrated by the Federal and local police and far surpassed the efforts of the Presidential Commission. Jean Hill was questioned by counsel only because I had previously interviewed her and had given her name to the Commission.[10] I had learned of her through Shirley Martin, who had become a devoted volunteer investigator and who had read Mrs. Hill's statements in the press. None of the other witnesses mentioned above was questioned by the Commission or even by Commission lawyers, and the potentially important photograph was not published by the Commission in its Report or in the twenty-six volumes of evidence that it later released.[11]

Reporters were everywhere in Dallas that day. The answers given to the questions they asked comprise a record that still remains inexplicable in terms of the Commission's assertions. Two reporters at Parkland Hospital noticed a mark at the center of the windshield of the President's limousine while it was parked outside the hospital.[12] They were not permitted to take a closer look, and the vehicle was dispatched to Washington, where it was kept under lock and key and made unavailable to those members of the press who sought to see it.

Reporters, hearing of Oswald's remarkable shooting, discovered that in the Marine Corps Oswald had been something less than expert with a rifle. Within a short period, witnesses began to report that they had been advised by local and Federal authorities not to talk to journalists. Until that time some of the press corps representatives had begun to resemble their mythical Hollywood antecedents. In the confusion that followed the announcement of the President's death, a reporter who stood idly by awaiting official handouts faced the probability of being scooped by more enterprising journalists.

In addition to the intrinsic excellence of some reporters, one other factor worked against the efficiency of the Federal Government in quashing inconvenient reports. Reporters from foreign countries arrived on the scene. They and the publications for which they worked were less concerned with the wishes of the American police and the forces they represented, and they therefore were able to make interesting discoveries and provide serious competition for their American colleagues. For example, representatives of three of Italy's leading newspapers arranged for a rifle test from the sixth floor of the Book Depository. With a camera fitted to a Mannlicher-Carcano carbine, Dallas rifle experts were asked to "fire" at another reporter who was driven past the building in a convertible. When the developed film showed that the local experts had not been as proficient as Oswald, the order came to seal off the Book Depository to all media representatives and nongovernmental investigators. The American public was thus spared the possibility of exposure to future tests while at the same time the American media declined to publish the results of the Italian test. In this fashion foreign enterprise was rendered less competitive.

In short order it became obvious that the dissenting view was not to be adequately presented in the United States at that time. America tended to accept the early findings of the authorities, while in Europe, where conflicting evidence was available, the Government's case and subsequently the Report itself were widely rejected. Governed no doubt by the spirit of self-defense, the American media were constrained to explain this evident disparity. It became popular for newscasters to nod wisely, although in the case of radio commentators this was difficult to discern, and lament the historical developments that had left Europeans so conspiracy-minded by nature. Later, much later, when the American people, themselves then armed with the facts, rejected the Commission's Report, it appeared that the media might be hoist by their own petard. Not so. Without apparent embarrassment, CBS brought forth Eric Sevareid and Henry Steele Commager to explain that Americans, unlike others, were conspiracy-minded.[13]

It would be unfortunate to leave the impression that all of the

American press representatives were paralyzed by the firmness of the official position. Among those few reporters who continued to serve their profession and their nation were Peter Kihss of the *New York Times*, Thayer Waldo of the Fort Worth *Star-Telegram*, Richard Dudman of the St. Louis *Post-Dispatch* and the late Dorothy Kilgallen of the now defunct New York *Journal-American*.

However, even the most devoted American journalists had difficulty securing the facts in the face of the instructions given to witnesses by agents of the FBI, the Secret Service and the local police. Witness after witness declined to grant interviews, some explaining that they were forbidden to do so. Witnesses who were also Government employees—the military physicians who performed the autopsy upon the President's body, for example—flatly stated that they had been ordered not to discuss the case.[14] In the instance of one important witness, an admonition not to talk was evidently considered inadequate and she, Marina Oswald, was held almost incommunicado for months.[15] The basic evidence was suppressed while inaccurate reports were made as to the meaning of the evidence. Gordon Shanklin, the FBI agent in charge at Dallas, said, according to the *New York Times*, that the paraffin test "showed that particles of gunpowder from a weapon, probably a rifle, remained on Oswald's cheek and hands,"[16] while the test report revealed the absence of any particles upon the face.[17] Thus the evidence, then unavailable, was consistent with innocence, while the official statement, all that was then available, was consistent with guilt.

Approximately three years after the assassination, I was invited to address the convention of the Associated Press Managing Editors in San Diego, California.[18] Some of the editors appeared to bridle at the import of my remarks, for I said that they had played a part in denying access to the facts to the public. After the formal portion of the affair had been concluded, I met with executives of the association and with other members. Some of those present indicated to me that they never had accepted the Commission's Report but were powerless to act, since the Government had wanted only one side presented.

"Why, the witnesses were ordered not to talk. We weren't allowed to see the evidence. What could we do?" exclaimed one executive.

"Well, for one thing," was the reply, "you might have written about your complaints instead of saving them for three years for me."

"Now you, of all people, know better than that. If we had told the story, you know what would have happened."

Of course I did not and do not know what would have resulted from full disclosure of the facts, but it seemed plain that the editors felt it might have been something unpleasant.

The reports of responsible journalists regarding the witnesses' reluctance to talk receive corroboration from the witnesses and from an additional and unexpected source as well. The interservice rivalry between the FBI and Secret Service was very much in evidence in the hours following the President's death. FBI agents, in an effort to trace the alleged assassination weapon, arrived at Klein's Sporting Goods in Chicago, conducted their interviews and left before the Secret Service agents located the store. When the special agents of the Secret Service called upon Klein's, they were at first unable to secure any information, for the relevant witness informed them that he had been instructed by the FBI agents not to talk to anyone.[19] The Secret Service agents were called upon to explain that they had priority and that the FBI agents could not have expected their injunction to apply to Secret Service interviews. Very few journalists, even if they had wished to pursue the investigation, could have been as persuasive as the somewhat beleaguered investigators from the Secret Service.

Governmental initiative designed to prevent the publication of a contrary view does not end with an effort to silence witnesses. Indeed, it may begin there, for journalists, being less naïve than most and no more selfless in their dedication to the truth, are clearly given to understand what is expected of them by the authorities. To the extraordinary reporter the scent of censorship is a challenge, not an obstacle, but by definition he is neither average nor available in large quantities. A reporter's courage and initiative do not guarantee the publication of his findings, for the ultimate decision to publish or suppress is not always his. A number of important stories on the subject written and submitted by a leading *New York Times* reporter were killed, as was the original *New York Times* decision to conduct its own investigation.

Just prior to the issuance of the Warren Report, Walter Cronkite's news program decided to film portions of a lecture that I had been delivering in New York City on a daily basis. At the request of the producer, I met with him, the director and the entire camera and sound crew hours before the lecture was to begin. Substantial portions of the lecture were filmed, as were numerous random interviews with members of the audience. The following day I was told by a CBS representative that it had been reduced to nine minutes and that it represented "about the finest nine minutes of television viewing that I have ever seen." "It will be shown tomorrow evening or the next evening," he told me. That was three years ago, and it has not yet been televised.

After the press reported that I had doubts about the official case, Dorothy Kilgallen called and invited me to meet with her at her Manhattan town house. She was the one reporter of my acquaintance who told me that she did not believe that Oswald was the sole murderer and who said that she was going to persevere until she discovered who was involved. We exchanged information and agreed to meet again. Miss Kilgallen told me that she believed that her telephone was being tapped and that she was quite certain that mine was. She suggested that future telephone calls be made from public telephones and that we use other names for telephone calls: Miss Parker for her, Mr. Robinson for me.

Since this suggestion appeared to be a condition for future meetings, I acquiesced, although I was somewhat surprised that a reporter whom I had considered an Establishment fixture was so suspicious of her Government. I voiced that feeling. Miss Kilgallen said that she was seriously committed to the case and that the Government was seriously committed to preventing the truth from being known. She told me that she had secured the transcript of Jack Ruby's testimony before the Warren Commission while it was a classified secret document and that her own newspaper had at first declined to take advantage of what was a world-wide exclusive. For four days the *Journal-American* refused to publish the transcript, until Miss Kilgallen persuaded the editors and publisher by agreeing to take full responsibility for the document.

The transcript was at last published, in serial form, and within three hours after the first article was available at the newsstands, two FBI agents were at Miss Kilgallen's home: "They were very polite and I think a little embarrassed about having to ask me where I got the transcript from. They knew that I just was not going to tell them that. While they were here, though, I asked them why they came so quickly when it took the Chief Justice so long to get around to questioning some important witness like Jack Ruby. And Jackie (Mrs. John F. Kennedy) wasn't questioned for months. Why, Warren knows Jackie very well; kisses her when they meet. No one can say that she couldn't see him. She had been seeing Marlon."

Miss Kilgallen told me that she did tell the FBI agents that a man, not a woman, gave her the transcript, since she had heard that some innocent secretary was under investigation by the Chief Justice. She added, "And I told the men that I did not get the transcript from John Daly." Mr. Daly, now director of the Voice of America, was then moderator of the television game program on which Miss Kilgallen appeared each week. He was also the Chief Justice's son-in-law.

I asked Miss Kilgallen why, in her view, her newspaper was so reluctant to publish an exclusive series of articles. "Well, no one has to be told that the Administration won't like it. That's clear. Some newspapers own radio and television stations and they are regulated by the Government. But in the case of our paper, I think the publisher is just afraid that he won't be invited to White House cocktail parties if he makes Lyndon mad."

"Doesn't that concern you?" I asked.

She answered, "Oh, Lyndon is a bore. Who even wants to go to his parties? When Kennedy was President, it was a different matter."

While many reporters may be as aware of the predilections of their employers as was Miss Kilgallen, not as many may wish to ignore those preferences. After a lecture in San Francisco, I was interviewed by a reporter for the *Chronicle*. I suggested that he might earn a Pulitzer Prize by going to Dallas and conducting a series of interviews. I offered him the names and addresses of the most relevant witnesses upon the condition that he agree to write whatever he discovered. The naïveté on my part can be demonstrated by the fact that a Pulitzer Prize was awarded to Merriman Smith for writing a series of highly inaccurate articles about the assassination. One of Smith's most recent pieces on the subject reveals that, unlike most Americans in or out of Dallas that day, he, an eyewitness, does not even remember where he was when the shots were fired.[20]

The reporter seemed enthusiastic at first, then, over a beer, thought a bit more and declined the offer with obvious reluctance. When I asked him if he thought that his paper might not print his conclusions, he quickly denied that that was the trouble. "No," he said. "In the years that I have been with the *Chronicle* they have never censored a single article that I have written." I asked if that was exceptional or if he was fortunate. He drank his beer, paused and then replied, "Well, I just know what they want, and I know what they don't want."

Among those most *au courant* regarding the employer's commitment was the reporter in charge of the Associated Press desk in Pittsburgh. I was in that city the day that President Johnson, in answer to a reporter's question, voiced his faith in the Commission's conclusions and then proceeded to offer some unkind remarks of a general nature about the Commission's critics.[21] I had never been referred to before during a Presidential press conference, and I felt justified in calling the local AP desk to file my reply. The reporter at the other end of the telephone listened a short while and then said, "No, we are not going to run an answer. We are going along with the President on this one." I tried to explain that the reporter's endorsement of my position was a matter of the utmost unconcern to me. Very likely he had not even read the Warren Report, much less the volumes of evidence or the material on file in the National Archives. His opinion regarding the controversy was no doubt based more upon prejudice than evidence. All I wished was that he be kind enough to send my reply out on the AP wire. "Sorry, cannot do. We are going along with the President on this one."

Subsequently I called the New York office of the Associated Press, filed my reply there and was assured that it would be dispatched. Clearly no giant conspiracy controlled the Associated Press that day. Just as clearly the feeling that the press services are to be used with discretion, not to say discrimination, predominated in at least one AP branch office that day.

II · The Great Silence

4 THE POLICE ARE INTERESTED—IN ME

UPON completion of the article which was subsequently published by the *National Guardian*, I sent it together with a covering letter to Earl Warren, who had just been appointed chairman of the Commission.[1]* I urged the Chief Justice to "give consideration to the appointment of defense counsel in order that in your inquiry an advocate zealously protecting his client's rights may be present."[2] Two weeks later, a most cordial undated letter from J. Lee Rankin thanked me for the article and stated that "the views contained in your letter will be given appropriate consideration by the Commission prior to the preparation of any final report."[3]†

However, the Commission did not agree to appoint counsel to represent Oswald's interest, and when Marguerite Oswald subsequently asked me to undertake that task, and I agreed, I sent a telegram, followed by affidavits executed by Mrs. Oswald, to the Commission.[4] Rankin wrote to "acknowledge receipt of your recent telegram informing the Commission that you have been retained by Mrs. Marguerite C. Oswald to represent her deceased son."[5]‡ He added: "The Commission does not believe that it would be useful or desirable to permit an attorney representing Lee Harvey Oswald to have access to the investigative materials within the possession of the Commission or to participate in any hearings to be conducted by the Commission."[6]

Later the Commission was to appear to reverse its position with the appointment of Walter E. Craig, the president of the American Bar Association, as Oswald's lawyer.[7] Although Craig specifically rejected that role, stating, "We are not counsel for Lee Harvey Os-

* This letter is reproduced as Appendix I.

† This letter is reproduced as Appendix II.

‡ This letter is reproduced as Appendix III.

wald," the press editorially hailed the appointment.[8] Said the liberal New York *Post,* "The Warren Commission's appointment of the president of the American Bar Assn. to represent the interests of Lee H. Oswald, President Kennedy's accused assassin, is a welcome development."[9] Although Craig had rejected the assignment, the *Post* continued, "His willingness to undertake the assignment is consistent with a long legal tradition in which men of conservative backgrounds have entered the arena of controversy and undertaken to defend the least popular causes."[10]

Years later, the Commission's most stalwart defenders conceded that the Craig appointment was of significance only in that it provided softer public relations for the Commission in its decision to deny counsel to the deceased accused. Professor John Kaplan, writing in defense of the Commission, said, "The Commission did appoint a lawyer to 'represent' Oswald but neither this attorney—the then President of the American Bar Association—nor the Commission took the appointment in any way seriously."[11] Kaplan subsequently referred to "the lack of counsel for Oswald on the issue of his own guilt."[12] Marcus Raskin, whose review in the *Yale Law Journal* was generally critical of the Commission, wrote, "In effect, Judge Craig and his associates were counsels to the Commission and its staff."[13] In retrospect, the Craig appointment was clearly without substance, yet at the time it was seized upon by an acquiescent press.

The Commission decided to call me before it to offer testimony. During the brief period in which I had served as counsel for the interests of Oswald I had begun an investigation. I had conducted and tape-recorded interviews with witnesses to the assassination and to the murder of Officer J. D. Tippit. When I appeared before the Commission, Chief Justice Warren said, "The Commission has been informed that Mr. Lane has collected numerous materials relevant to the Commission's work. The Commission proposes to question Mr. Lane on all matters of which he has knowledge concerning the assassination of President Kennedy and the subsequent killing of Lee Harvey Oswald."[14]

Of course, my voluminous correspondence with the Commission had previously made the members aware of the fact that I had no "knowledge" of the events. I had been retained to act as counsel; I had not been present when the shots were fired. Very little, if any, of my testimony could have been properly accepted by a trial court, since it was comprised of hearsay. I suggested to the Commission that I had come across some evidence and that I wished to present the evidence by presenting the witnesses who could properly offer it.[15] I renewed my request that "I be permitted to, at the request of Lee

Oswald's mother, who survives him—to function before this Commission as counsel on his behalf."[16] Warren replied that "the Commission, as you already know, has considered your request and has denied it. It does not consider you as the attorney for Lee Oswald. Now, this is not for any discussion. We are not going to argue it."[17]

The Commission declined the evidence; it insisted upon hearsay. Consequently, I answered all the questions that the Commission put to me, on rare occasions declining to reveal sources which I was not at liberty to divulge. Later, one of the Commission lawyers, Joseph A. Ball, was to complain at a bar association meeting that I had come before the Commission to testify and offered nothing but hearsay.

At the public session I made reference to a meeting which allegedly took place eight days before the assassination.[18] I had been informed that Tippit and Bernard Weissman, a sponsor of a vehement anti-Kennedy advertisement that was published on the morning of the assassination in the *Dallas Morning News*, had met with a third person on November 14, 1963.[19] I testified, "I have been informed that Mr. Weissman and Officer Tippit and a third person were present there. I have been given the name of the third person. But for matters which I will make plain to the Commission, I will be pleased to give you the name of the third person as given to me, but not in the presence of the press. I would rather do that in executive session—that one piece of testimony."[20]

Shortly thereafter the Commission went into executive session and I continued, "The person that I was informed was there, the third person, is named Jack Ruby. It was my feeling, of course, while his case was pending it would not be proper to comment on that in the presence of the press."[21]

The Commission evidently agreed with me that the matter should not be divulged, since it classified that portion of my testimony that had been taken in executive session "Top Secret." When a copy of that portion of the transcript was sent to me by registered mail, the outer envelope stated that it was to be delivered to the addressee only, while the inner envelope warned that the contents were highly classified and that I alone was to open the envelope. Accordingly, I was astonished when I received a letter the following month from Rankin. It had been sent by regular mail, was unclassified, and the envelope did not even indicate that it was personal. In the normal course of events it had been opened by my secretary and was lying on my desk. The first sentence read, "You will recall that during the course of your testimony before the Commission on March 4, 1964, you stated that you had information concerning an alleged meeting involving Bernard Weissman, Jack Ruby and Officer Tippit."[22]

I was to become exposed, but never fully acclimated, to other odd activities of the Federal Government. One morning, as I was leaving the apartment building in Manhattan where I then resided, two men approached me. It was raining slightly and the men surrounded me, as well as two men can surround one. One stood directly in front of me, preventing my forward progress. The first one to speak told me that he had been informed that I had in my possession certain files which I had illegally removed from the offices of the FBI. I asked him who he was, and he replied by flashing a dark, simulated-leather card case which appeared to contain a green card. He then put the case back into his pocket. When I informed him that I was unable to read that quickly and that I did not intend to hold a conversation with someone who had not properly identified himself, he retrieved the case from his pocket. His name, which I copied into my notebook, was Special Agent of the Federal Bureau of Investigation William E. Folkner, serial number 5954. His colleague was Special Agent of the Federal Bureau of Investigation John P. Di Marchi, serial number 4256, facts which I secured only by repeating the ritual.[23]

Folkner then informed me that "we have confidential information that you have illegally obtained FBI reports." When I asked, "Oh, are you missing some files?" he replied that "this was no time for levity." I was inclined to agree, since the rain was becoming heavier, I was dressed in a suit and had no umbrella. Both Folkner and Di Marchi were wearing trench coats. I pointed out to the agents that I had made that information which I possessed available to the Warren Commission. Folkner said that they had nothing to do with the Warren Commission and that they intended to secure those documents from me directly.

He said he took my answer to be an admission that I did have documents illegally obtained from the files of the FBI in my possession, and as he stepped even closer to me he said in a loud and firm voice, "I now demand that you give me all of the documents in your possession which you have illegally obtained from the files of the FBI." His colleague moved toward my attaché case. I held the case more securely than before and informed the two agents that I did not like to be accosted in front of my house, particularly when it was raining, and that they might inform Mr. Hoover, or whoever it might be that they were on speaking terms with in the Bureau, that if he wished to secure any information from me directly it would be wise to send a letter. I asked to be excused. The agents did not move. Using just the slight amount of body contact necessary to push one of them aside, I exited from the impromptu conclave and hailed a taxi.

I never did hear from Hoover or any of his associates, and to this day I have no idea what his agents were making reference to. I sent a letter to the Commission regarding the apparent excesses of the FBI agents, but the Commission evidently ignored the matter.[24]

On June 19, 1964, Rankin wrote, asking that I return from London to Washington to testify before the Commission once more.[25] I agreed, made reservations for the first available flight and arrived at the John F. Kennedy Airport in New York. I showed my passport to the agent of the Immigration and Naturalization Service, as did others entering the country. The agent read my name and in routine fashion checked my name against the list contained in his "lookout book." He stopped for a moment and checked the list again. As I glanced down at the book on his desk to see what it was that had attracted and held his attention, I saw my name: "Lane, Mark G-15." He took my passport and said that he would return shortly. After a short while he did return, offered the passport to me and said that I might enter.

I had just returned from a tour of a dozen European countries, and I had experienced nothing but kindness and courtesy in contacts with foreign passport officials. My first unpleasant encounter with immigration authorities took place in the city of my birth. I knew that my name had not been on the proscribed list several months earlier, and it seemed quite clear that my question about the official version of the assassination was the reason that I had been listed along with narcotics importers and gold smugglers. I inquired why my name was listed and I was asked, "You've been to Cuba, haven't you?" I said that I had never been to Cuba. "Well, then I can't tell you why your name is there."

I asked to see a supervisor. That gentleman invited me into his office. "Care for a drink?" he asked. I replied in the negative, stating that I just wanted to know why my name was on his list. He offered me a cigarette, which I declined, stating that I was interested in knowing why my name was in his book. He settled back in his chair, threw one leg over his desk, stared at me for a moment and said, "So you think your name is in our book, do you?" I said that I did. I asked him if he would care to know on what basis I had reached that conclusion. He said, "Yes, tell me, why do you think it's there?" I told him that I thought it was there because I had seen it there just a few minutes before. "I assure you, Mr. Lane," he replied, "your name is not there." I assured him that it was, and just as he was about to reassure me I suggested that our dilemma was not without a solution.

I suggested that we examine one of the "lookout books" and see if I was listed alphabetically. "No can do," he replied. "That's secret. You can't look there." I told him that I just had looked there a few minutes earlier. "Well, you can't look again," he answered. When I contacted the director of the Immigration and Naturalization Service for the port of Kennedy Airport and placed my question before him, he replied, "I'm not going to tell you a goddamned thing."

I called Rankin and told him of my experience with the immigration officials, and he said that he could assure me that the Commission did not order the immigration authorities to list me. I informed him that I was less concerned with the mechanics of my being listed than in the reason for it. I explained that I had never been charged with a crime, had been honorably discharged from the United States Army, had served as a member of the New York State Legislature and as an executive assistant to a United States Congressman and was a member of the bar of the State of New York. The only conduct which I could conceive of the authorities considering untoward might be my refusal to accept the Government's view that Oswald was the lone assassin of the President. I suggested that the Chief Justice should not permit efforts to intimidate dissenters.

When I appeared before the Commission, I raised the matter directly with Warren, stating that "I am deeply concerned."[26] Rankin said, "And I told you at that time on the telephone, didn't I, that the Commission had nothing to do with that? Is that right?"[27] I said, "You did tell me that," but added that I had asked him "to find out if my name was listed in relationship to the inquiry which I have conducted, and the testimony that I have given to this Commission."[28]

The Commission never did respond to that request, for Warren broke in to ask, "Were you prevented from entering the United States?"[29] The answer to that question seemed rather obvious. I replied, "No; I am here now, Mr. Chief Justice, but I was stopped."[30] Warren then surprised me by indicating that temporary interference with the rights of a citizen seemed inconsequential.[31] Shortly thereafter Warren demanded that I reveal to him the names of all those who had assisted me in my endeavors.[32]

The true flavor of the session can best, perhaps only, be appreciated by reading the published transcript.[33] It was my definite impression at the time that Warren, Rankin and Ford considered me to be a defendant and themselves to be alternating prosecuting attorneys. In rereading the transcript, that original impression is strengthened. Writing in the *Yale Law Journal*, Marcus Raskin observed, "Reading through the Commission Report and its record gives one the impression that Lane was put on continuous trial."[34] He added, "He was followed on various occasions. In the Archive files there are a number of references to FBI reports about Lane, some still secret."[35]

After I had delivered a lecture at a university in New York, a young man approached me. I had referred to the airport incident, and he told me that he was employed by the immigration authorities. He said that he was entirely sympathetic to efforts to understand what had happened in Dealey Plaza and very disturbed about the Government's effort to bury the facts. He said that he would find out if my name was on the list and why. He returned the next day with a page that he had torn out of the "lookout book." My name and the designation "G-15" were there. When I asked what "G-15" meant, he said it was a coded reference to another document. The reference work, he said, was "top secret." He then produced that as well. Under category "G-15" was the statement that the Federal Bureau of Investigation and the United States Department of Justice were to be notified "immediately and telephonically" when a person so characterized sought to enter the country. A note stated that the traveler was to be detained until the notification had taken place. I thanked the young man for the documents and subsequently had slides made of them so that they might be displayed at lectures.

Later I visited Europe again and returned, this time via Los Angeles. Again I was delayed, and again I asked to see a superior officer. He was very kind, offered me his hand and said that he had just read *Rush to Judgment* and that "it really made you think."

"I'm awfully sorry that they put your name in here," he said, indicating the lookout book. "I just don't know why you're classified F-9."

"F-9?" I asked. "I used to be G-15."

"Really?" he asked. "Well, I guess you've been promoted."

5 BANNED FOR LIFE

My encounters with the Commission and with various agencies of Government led me to conclude that the official version of the events might be related more to what some conceived to be the best interest of the nation than to the facts alone. I was convinced that in those circumstances an independent force was required. Accordingly, an organization—the Citizens' Committee of Inquiry—was formed with offices in New York. It was my hope that such a force might, in focusing upon the Commission's strange procedures, help to reform them. If that was our primary goal, it may be said with little qualification that it was not attained.*

We considered the necessity of keeping minds and options open and as many persons as possible acquainted with the then known facts, for an informed public might better be able to assess accurately the forthcoming Report. In this effort we were more successful, although our efforts were severely hampered by a press reluctant to publish the facts and radio and television stations unwilling to permit question or debate. It was during this period that the great silence descended upon the country, with not a single dissenting voice permitted on network radio or television programs broadcast within the United States.†

On occasion there were those who conducted discussion programs on a less than network basis who, although not in agreement with the nonofficial position, were inclined to believe that it should not be suppressed. In New York, Barry Gray was among the first to permit a dissenting view to be presented. In Boston it was Jerry Williams, and when he moved to Chicago his program there was available as well. There are others, but the honor roll is a short one, for those who served the concept of their profession well can be counted on the fingers of one hand. Self-censorship, I am convinced, played a large part in inhibiting those producers and performers who otherwise sought the unusual or controversial. Just as it was not necessary to inform the reporter for the San Francisco *Chronicle* what it was that his employers might not wish to read, therefore what he should not write, apparently radio and television interviewers were also sufficiently clued in to what was happening. Yet there is evidence to suggest that the Federal Government was prepared to offer a reminder to a communicator who was without the requisite self-discipline.

* Various documents do indicate that the Commission was not unaware of our activity. For example, a memorandum filed by Wesley J. Liebeler, one of the Commission's lawyers, reveals conflict among the staff regarding the weight to be assigned to an unconvincing witness.[1] Liebeler charged that in crediting the testimony, the Commission "played into Lane's hands."[2] Documents on file in the National Archives also reveal that Commission personnel—more often than not Rankin's assistant, Norman Redlich—were in the habit of requesting FBI reports upon my activity.

† During that period I was able to broadcast to more than one American city at a time only through the courtesy of the Canadian Broadcasting Company. I appeared on two discussion programs, one in Toronto and one in Montreal. I am informed that some American border cities were able to receive the broadcasts.

During February 1964 I was interviewed by Murray Burnett on his late-night "Contact" program broadcast by radio station WINS in New York.[3] After 1:00 A.M., when I left the studio, two agents of the FBI questioned Burnett.[4] FBI agents also questioned his secretary, Linda Priestly.[5] According to an FBI report, Burnett was questioned again by an agent half a year later regarding my appearance on his program.[6] FBI agents demanded a copy of the tape recording of the program, which was then, according to another FBI report, "monitored on July 7, 1964, at the New York Office of the Federal Bureau of Investigation (FBI)."[7] Later, when I saw Burnett again, he told me of his concern about the questioning. He had been asked, he told me, why he had permitted me to be interviewed and how well he knew me.

Not long afterward I was interviewed by a radio commentator in Philadelphia. More than two years later, in a subsequent interview, he told me that as I departed from the room at the conclusion of the first interview, two FBI agents approached him and proceeded to question him about me. The FBI agents neither directed the two men not to interview me again nor stated that they should not have interviewed me previously, but both of the radio men understood that an unspoken complaint had been issued.

In New York City, WOR presented a late-night, or, more accurately, early-morning, program called "The Randy Show." Randy took over the airwaves at midnight and did not relinquish them until 5:00 A.M. He invited me, along with another New York lawyer who was critical of the Commission, Florynce Kennedy, to debate with two other attorneys who supported the Commission's efforts. We talked for five hours, kept awake, if not alert, by huge quantities of coffee. I wondered what it was that was supposed to keep the audience awake during the same period, for the program was dulled by the failure of the defenders to demonstrate the slightest familiarity with the facts.

Toward dawn, Randy announced that it had been one of his most exciting broadcasts and invited us to return for five more hours the next day. Wearily, I agreed, having been excluded from so many other programs. The second broadcast (it went for five and a half hours) did offer an innovation. The listening audience was encouraged to become a jury. Randy urged his listeners to write to WOR and to vote upon Oswald's guilt or innocence. On the air, he invited me to return when the Commission's Report was released. I agreed to do so.

I do not recall at this time whether the critics' viewpoint had been effectively or poorly presented, but, with a view toward assessing the verdict in context, it must be said that the Government's spokesmen were ill-equipped with the facts. Of course the media in general had shown no reluctance to publish the official view and that side was not entirely unknown before the two broadcasts. Randy later wrote to me, stating that the audience response had been unprecedented in WOR's history, to his knowledge. He said that his staff was unable to open the letters, they arrived so quickly and in such bulk. The final calculation, he said, showed that Oswald had been acquitted by a seven-to-one ratio.

Randy was opposed by Long John Nebel, who occupied a similar time period on a rival radio station. Evidently some energetic listeners tuned back and forth between the two programs, and accordingly many callers asked Long John when he would invite me to discuss the case. Then I was called by listeners, who informed me that Nebel had explained that he had no sympathy for my view and implied that he would demolish my arguments in the near future. He assured his listeners, I was told, that he was trying to convince me to appear on his program but that I constantly excused myself by stating that I was traveling. I called Nebel to explain that I was there in New York and available for an appearance at his convenience. His office explained that Nebel would not permit me to be on his program.

As the date for the issuance of the Report approached, I called Randy to arrange for the third program. Randy said that he could not permit me to appear ever again: "WOR has banned you for life." Two years later, when *Rush to Judgment* was published and our cause respectable, booking agents for the publisher sought to arrange an interview for me with a dialogist who was broadcast by WOR. They were informed that the ban was still in effect. During 1967, WOR radio presented what was widely advertised as "The Warren Report." It was to be a "two-hour uninterrupted discussion" with the four leading critics and defenders of the Report. I was not invited to participate.

Nebel, however, invited me to appear for a serious debate with quasi-official defenders, whose names at that time he could not reveal. When I arrived at the station, I met Roy Cohn, a former assistant to the late Senator Joseph McCarthy, and his colleague, a local aspiring right-wing politician, who were there to attack my book, which they had not read, and to defend the Report, with which they appeared to be unfamiliar.

They began by alleging that since I had been counsel for the Fair Play for Cuba Committee, I had been biased at the outset. Since I had never been counsel for that organization, the point was lost. So was the evening, for the two defenders had inadequate information upon which to base a defense. Later, in London, Dick Gregory commented that my experience with Nebel was much like that of his cousin in Alabama. He had sat in at a lunch counter for two years, and when the effort succeeded and he had been handed a menu, he discovered that there was nothing there that he wanted.

David Susskind's office called to invite me to appear as a participant in a television program that he hosted. Dorothy Kilgallen was also to be a guest and the proposed subject was the Warren Report. I had known David just slightly; at a small luncheon in my honor a few years back, at the request of Eleanor Roosevelt, he had made a not inconsiderable financial contribution to my campaign for public office. I was pleased with the invitation and accepted at once. A warm letter followed, saying that David was very much looking forward to the program. A few days later his producer called. She said that the program had been canceled and that officially she was to inform me that the reason was that there were just too many "political programs that week" and that "the program would be rescheduled." She said that she was furious because that was not the real reason. WPIX is owned by the *Daily News*, she said, and "David has a terrible contract with the station. He cannot control the programs." She added that David had been ordered to cancel my appearance and in doing so he "was just following orders." She urged me to do something about it, to publicize the cancellation as widely as I could, without making specific reference to her.

I thanked her for the information and assured her that I would tell my family about it. "Why not call a press conference?" she asked. I explained that I had uncovered evidence of some importance which cast doubt upon the Government's claims about the death of the President. I was unable to secure publication of those facts. In those circumstances, it seemed unlikely that the media would show greater concern with the cancellation of a local program. She concluded by stating that David would later invite me to appear on his "Open End" program, over which presumably he has more control, but that invitation has not been forthcoming.

David did appear as a surprise guest on the Merv Griffin program when I was being interviewed. He interrupted the interview to shout that those who doubted the Warren Report did so only to make money and that all of Europe had been convinced by me that there had been a conspiracy in Dallas. Peter Lind Hayes, an actor, indicated that he was in agreement with David and suggested that the President's "immortal soul" should be "left to rest in peace"—

the curious theory being, evidently, that the soul of the deceased may be comfortable only when one's murderers are permitted to walk freely about. Later David was heard to state that he had "hurt" his image through his outburst and felt that perhaps he should not have commented upon a subject about which he knew little. However, that thought contemplated such a sharp change of direction in his professional life that he apparently abandoned it.

During the two-year period, commencing with the assassination, in which the national media kept the public fairly well insulated from the facts, I found it possible to reach numbers of people primarily from the lecture platform. I spoke at many of the major universities, approximately eighty-five schools in all, and for weeks I delivered a daily lecture at a New York theater. The funds thus realized were collected by and used by the Citizens' Committee of Inquiry to further the independent investigation.

Researchers and volunteer investigators were sent to Dallas, and some uncovered information that escaped the Commission. Some of the investigators were students, one was a professor, one a lawyer, one a scientist and one a dancer. Many wrote to volunteer their services, some approached me at lectures and one with a note left in my box at the Chelsea Hotel in New York, where I was then staying. It read: "We are two Follies Bergère showgirls living at your hotel. We are very anxious to meet with you to discuss the Warren Report. Please call. Our room number is . . ." and the numerals followed. Naturally I too was anxious to explore the matter, and I did contact them.

They were very interested in and knowledgeable about the case. One, Margo Hamilton, later volunteered to go to Dallas and make contact with the world of Jack Ruby. She did in fact go there, spent some time in the nightclub milieu and secured information of value from Marina Oswald's former attorney. However, ethical considerations prevent full disclosure of her information at this time.

During this period I lectured at Cornell University in response to a request from Professor Andrew Hacker. After the lecture, he offered his services to our endeavor. I asked if he would serve as a member of the CCI, and he agreed, adding that he was quite willing to do more than lend his name to the cause. He was an excellent host; I spent the night at his home and he invited one of his students who had been at the lecture the previous evening and who had expressed an interest in meeting me to join us for breakfast the next morning. The student, Edward J. Epstein, said that he would like to help also.

Later, after I had returned to my office, I thought of a task which might fully utilize Hacker's not inconsiderable talents. I wrote to him, suggesting that he undertake to write an article for the *New York Times Magazine*, where he had been frequently published in the past, regarding the making of the Warren Report. I suggested that he might interview the various members of the Commission and the Commission lawyers and prepare a document that would illuminate the areas that the Commission had ignored: Who wrote the various chapters? How often had the members met? On what basis was it decided to call certain witnesses and ignore others? Was the Report unanimously arrived at, or were there conflicts among the staff and members on substantive issues?

I said that while I felt that the *Times* might be unwilling to publish material critical of the Commission, an objective study of the Commission's working methods might have more appeal. He agreed, but subsequently I learned the *Times* rejected the offer, stating that "the case is closed." Much later the *Times* was to call editorially for a reopening of the matter; but that was much later.[8]

One day a young man called and asked for an appointment. He explained that he was Ed Epstein from Cornell and that Professor Hacker had suggested that he contact me. I remembered him from our breakfast, and we arranged for a meeting. He told me that when the *Times* rejected the article, Hacker, his professor, suggested that Epstein might devote his thesis to the subject. Epstein agreed when Hacker said that he would contact some of the Commission members on Epstein's behalf. Epstein told me that he was not fully familiar with the facts but that he was anxious to learn the details. We spent hours together that day, as I made all my files available to him and then dictated a series of questions to my secretary which he might put to those he interviewed. We agreed to meet on occasion, and Epstein said that he would share all his information with me as he secured it.

ABC-TV was experimenting with an evening network entertainment and interview program hosted by Les Crane, and he decided to present a discussion of the assassination controversy. He invited Melvin Belli, the colorful San Francisco lawyer, who had represented Jack Ruby, to support the official version. Crane, his producer and I met early one morning in an East Side Manhattan late-night bistro where they decided, upon interviewing me, to invite me to represent the other side in the debate. The following day those volunteers who labored at the Citizens' Committee of Inquiry were in a jubilant mood. They were confident that this first nationally televised discussion of the events would place the matter on the agenda for America, and that once there it could no longer be exclusively relegated to off-Broadway theaters and college campuses. I was less sanguine, for, although I was confident in my knowledge of the facts, Belli's almost legendary oratorical accomplishments had preceded him to the East Coast.

With some trepidation, I began to assemble my notes for the meeting. These preparations were interrupted by a telephone call from Crane's producer. "Mark, I'm awfully sorry," he said, "but we can't get you on the program." I asked what had happened, and he said, "It's not Les's fault. It's the ABC brass. They have just said no. Period. They say you have the facts and the affidavits and that would just confuse the audience." Incredulously, I asked if that was the basis for the cancellation of the program. "Oh, it's not canceled," he said. "It's just that we can't have you on. There's going to be a debate anyway. We're getting Oswald's mother."

And so it came to pass that the first network broadcast presenting both sides of the controversy found splendiferous Melvin Belli, conqueror of a thousand juries, opposed to a poorly educated widow. Mrs. Oswald's visceral responses were meritorious, but her lack of command over the facts, together with Belli's bullying tactics, reduced the program to the low level of entertainment that the network apparently sought. The evidence being absent, the provinces did not suffer the confusion that the network palatines had feared.

I had almost abandoned hope of ever reaching large numbers of my fellow citizens, but not quite the determination to keep trying anyway, when I received an unsolicited telephone call from a man who described himself as a literary agent. He introduced himself as Oscar Collier, and suggested that I write a book about the case. He said that he was confident that he could find a publisher. A book may be the only avenue available to you to express your view, he advised me. I told him that I appreciated his call and that I would consider his suggestion. If I did decide to write a book, I said, I would certainly call him. I did give the matter serious thought. There are but three networks, but many book publishers, and it appeared that the full presentation of the dissenting view could best be presented in a volume. I was concerned that I was not sufficiently disciplined to write a book on a part-time basis, but that it would be necessary for me to give up my other activities and isolate myself somewhere until the work was done. I was not sure that the CCI could weather the defection of its chairman and main fund-raiser.

I decided to write the book, and I called Collier. A few days later he said that he had found a publisher, Grove Press. I was to meet the president of the company and some of the editors at lunch.

We met, talked, signed contracts for a very modest advance, much of which was required to assist the Committee through a particularly difficult period.

Not long afterward, Emile de Antonio called. He said that he had directed the documentary film *Point of Order*. I had seen the film long before and I had heard de Antonio in a radio interview at that time. I was impressed with the film and with his candid approach in discussing the difficulties that had been involved in putting it together. He said that he wanted to meet with me to consider the possibility of a documentary film on the Warren Report. We met on many occasions and we both became committed to the project. We were prevented from beginning by the absence of two factors that, in the case of documentary films, are *sine qua nons*. We had no money, de Antonio estimated that approximately $60,000 was required and the networks and local stations had refused to make any film footage available.

De Antonio's efforts to raise funds were frustrated by a general feeling among those whom he approached that the subject was not commercial and that since Oswald was the lone assassin the subject was not current. In addition, de Antonio could not state to prospective investors that funds, once secured, could be used to buy the necessary footage. While no progress was made toward the realization of the film, de Antonio and I became close friends. I shall not forget the summer of 1965, when, completely devoid of funds, I worked away on the manuscript. De Antonio noticed my gradual loss of weight and consequently invited me to dine with him for lunch and dinner almost every day.

6 THE DEBATES THAT NEVER OCCURRED

The uncritical commitment to the Report evidenced by the panegyrical articles appearing in the press, together with what was tantamount to the suppression of a dissenting view by the networks, left the critics with an insurmountable communications problem. The ordinary methods for reaching our fellow countrymen having been foreclosed, we looked about for other methods, pending completion of the book.

The matter was under discussion one day in the fall of 1964 when Renée Taylor, a talented and attractive actress and a friend of the Committee, suggested that I debate Melvin Belli on a stage since no television platform was available. Belli was in New York at that time, and a telephone request by Miss Taylor for an appointment to discuss the subject was granted. Several hours later she arrived at Belli's hotel. Later she emerged with Belli's agreement to debate, "if Lane meets one demand." The condition—that we both wear tuxedos.

Formal papers were drawn and signed providing for three debates. The proceeds were to be shared by the sponsor (the Citizens' Committee), Mr. Belli and myself, with my share to be given to the Committee. The first debate was to be held in San Francisco, the second in New York and the third at a university in the West. The agreement required that both participants be formally attired and that advertisements announcing the event give top billing to Belli.

I gathered my papers together, secured a copy of Belli's then just available book about the Ruby trial and flew to San Francisco.[1] I read the book on the plane and was struck by one story that Belli had recounted. He wrote that he was before the trial judge, Joe B. Brown, making motions for the release of Ruby on bail pending trial, when a curious incident occurred. He said, "When I cited a series of cases to show that bail could be granted for Ruby under Texas precedents, he obligingly filled me in on Texas social mores. In tones too low for the court reporter to catch he said helpfully, 'Mel, them's nigger cases. Don't cite them.' "[2]

I met Belli in his opulent office, where he asked if I had brought my tuxedo and informed me that his friend Jake Ehrlich would serve as moderator. I explained that I did not own formal clothing, but in reply to his worried look I assured him that I was about to rent or buy one at once. He suggested that we might consider a debate in Dallas as well, since he was so well liked there. "I sent copies of my book to all of them, from Joe Brown on down," he said.

I thought that his was an excellent suggestion, but I wondered aloud about the reception he might be given after the disclosures in his book about what appeared to be a confidential bit of advice given to him by the trial judge. "What are you talking about?" he asked. I referred him to the passage in his book. He replied, "My God, was that left in there!"

That evening we debated before a capacity audience in an auditorium seating 2,500.[3] We were all, participants and moderator, formally attired, unless the fact that Belli and Ehrlich wore boots detracts from the accuracy of that assessment. Belli removed his handsome black cape with a flourish, revealing its lining, a refulgent exorbitance of red silk.

At the outset a polite audience was agitated by the moderator's repeated reference to his friendship with and great respect for Earl Warren. Whatever that man put his name to must be considered to be the truth, they were informed. Belli was introduced and spoke of his certainty that Oswald had done it alone. When my turn to speak came, Ehrlich interjected a question. "How do you explain the chicken bones and Oswald's prints on the bag they were in?" he challenged. The audience moaned. The chicken bone question and Oswald's related fingerprints had been withdrawn shortly after its debut on November 22, since Bonnie Ray Williams, another Book Depository employee, had identified the remains of the lunch as his.[4]

Belli's main argument flowed from what appeared to be the necessity of accepting the Report as valid. He said, "If we cannot trust the FBI, the CIA and Earl Warren, then God pity us!"[5] He accused me of "hurting our national image" and demanded that I explain each of Oswald's movements after the assassination.[6] I replied that I was more concerned with the nation's substance and that as to the details of Oswald's movements, "I'm at a disadvantage there. Your client killed my client before he could tell his story."[7]

In San Francisco, if Belli's office is burglarized or if he agrees to represent a topless dancer, he is on the front page of the newspapers and may be seen repeatedly on television screens. Ehrlich was the criminal lawyer whose life story was depicted, or glamorized, in the television series "Sam Benedict," and his movements are also well publicized. Perhaps those assembled that evening constituted the largest paying audience to witness a debate in many years in San Francisco. Yet not one word appeared in any of the three daily newspapers the morning after the debate. A journalist for a left periodical published on the West Coast said that she called the three dailies—the *Chronicle*, the *Examiner* and the *News Call-Bulletin*—and also the Oakland *Tribune* and secured "practically identical replies from the city desks: 'No, we did not send anyone to cover the Warren Report debate last night.' "[8] She wrote: "A silence-boycott was clamped down last weekend by every daily newspaper in the Bay area on one of the most controversial issues in the country."[9]

When I returned to New York for the second of the three scheduled debates, I was determined to establish optimum conditions for press coverage. The largest hall then available was chosen for the debate.[10] The midtown Manhattan Center was contracted for, and almost four thousand chairs were jammed into every available space. Press notices advised the media that it was expected that the hall might be filled, making the event unprecedented. Public debates where admission is charged rarely occur, and they are sparsely attended when they do take place, the latter condition no doubt influencing the former.

More than half of the tickets were sold in advance, and traffic was tied up in midtown Manhattan as a veritable multitude converged upon the hall on the evening of the debate. The demand persisted long after all the tickets had been sold, and as a result many hundreds were turned away. One hundred and seven representatives of the press were present. Radio reporters and entire television crews were on hand. Many of the delegations at the United Nations had requested tickets and many were represented. I was interviewed by two reporters from the *New York Times* before and after the debate, and the proceedings were punctuated by exploding flashbulbs as photographer after photographer took picture after picture. William Kunstler, a noted New York lawyer, moderated with estimable fairness and charm.

Belli cried that Oswald had had his trial already: "He has been tried in the Dallas police station and been found guilty." The sophisticated and at the outset impartial audience (if one can judge from the welcome afforded to each of the participants) began to jeer Belli. That I had "won" the debate was not open to question, nor is it a matter of pride. Belli was ill-prepared and misinformed regarding the facts, and his not inconsiderable oratorical gifts were squandered as he pleaded with the audience to have faith in the nation's Federal police force and political leaders. Those present evidently came to hear the facts, and subsequently I was scolded by many for having agreed to a debate with a man who appeared to be so lacking in specific knowledge of the subject matter. In a sense the criticism was justified, but the assumption that one of America's best-known lawyers, who was himself deeply submerged in a related trial, would be knowledgeable seemed a reasonable one when the agreement was signed.

In a joint interview that evening, the reporter asked Belli where the funds for the three debates were going. He said he was keeping his share and that he was canceling the third debate. He added that he was sorry he ever became involved in the debates in the first place. Volunteers for the Citizens' Committee who had been monitoring the television stations in New York that night and the next day reported that the portion of the interview referred to above constituted the only mention of the debate on television. Not one daily newspaper in New York, and possibly in the nation, even mentioned that the event had occurred. At that time there were half a dozen important daily newspapers published in New York. The customary fillers appeared in each of them the next day—cats in trees rescued by firemen, allegations that the Pacific Ocean is saltier than the Atlantic and that the world's record for demolishing an upright piano and passing the wreckage through a ring nine inches in diameter was established in Detroit. I wondered what prompted the news world to be so heavily in attendance the previous evening, what their hopes and expectations had been and what coverage might have resulted had Belli triumphed.

The *New York Times* refers to itself as a newspaper of record. That which is not found within its many pages ostensibly did not happen. For this reason the Belli encounter in New York is known to some as the debate that never occurred.

Still, we had perceived a slight but noticeable improvement in the atmosphere. Earlier in the year the *National Guardian* had rented Town Hall, a public meeting hall in New York owned by New York University, for the purpose of discussing the assassination. After the contract had been signed, a hostile newspaper story appeared. The proprietor canceled the contract at once, and if not for the intervention of Edward Ennis, a distinguished attorney, who was also counsel for the American Civil Liberties Union, and the agreement by the sponsor to post a huge bond, the Town Hall meeting would have been prohibited. While the press did, with frightening effectiveness, suppress any news of the Belli debate, even here some improvement could be discerned. Earlier, the liberal New York *Post* had refused to accept advertisements for a meeting sponsored by the Militant Labor Forum at which I was to lecture on the case. They had accepted advertisements for the Belli debate.

III · The Response

7 THE MAKING OF A BOOK

MY STUDY of the Commission's evidence took place during long periods in which I absented myself from the office of the Citizens' Committee. During this period I also made several trips to Dallas and intermittently accepted university lecture invitations. The leadership of the Committee was assumed by Deirdre Griswold, its executive secretary, who also arranged the lecture engagements so that they constituted cohesive tours. In that fashion, I crisscrossed the United States three or four times and spoke at scores of colleges.

During the early part of 1964 I had met a young Danish fashion designer, Anne-Lise Dabelsteen, following a lecture given in Copenhagen. At the very end of 1964, we were married in a small town in Denmark. I decided to remain in Denmark to finish the book, with the knowledge that my prolonged absence from the Committee, particularly my abandonment of fund-raising responsibilities, might pose serious difficulties for the Committee. Miss Griswold and the other officers accepted that decision and carried on with the work as long as was possible. Before my return, however, the funds had been exhausted, and even the modest monthly rental of $80, together with telephone and other standard office expenses, was beyond the capacity of the office staff. The only full-time employee had long since become a volunteer, and rather than incur additional debts the office was closed.

My wife and I moved into a very small summer house consisting of two and a half rooms. It was on the Baltic Sea at Ulslev Strand and was adequately equipped for the summer months. We were there, however, in January and February. My wife's grandfather located an English-speaking stenographer who was employed at a bank in nearby Nykøbing. The bank made its dictaphone available to me, and the final draft of the book was completed in that manner. When I was finally satisfied with the work, I returned to the United States.

In the interim, Grove Press had changed its mind. The contract was canceled, I was informed, and no substantive reason was offered. I was sufficiently insecure about the writing style of my initial effort that I was quite prepared to accept editorial suggestions. However, no one at Grove had ever seen the manuscript when I was informed that the book would not be published. My many efforts to reach the president of the company were unsuccessful; he was not in when I called, and he declined to return the calls. An editor there informed me that Grove was convinced that the book was not commercially viable, and might well be a financial loss for the publisher. I asked how many copies must be sold in order that the publisher be insured against loss, and he responded that approximately five thousand hard-cover sales constituted the break-even point. I calculated the possibility of borrowing the requisite sum from a bank and reselling the books through the Citizens' Committee of Inquiry. The plan appeared to be feasible, and I offered to purchase the first five thousand copies. The offer was rejected, leaving me with the impression that the fear of financial loss, although the only stated factor, may well have been only one among the factors that caused the publisher to reject the manuscript it had commissioned but never examined.

In the interim, my literary agent had become an editor at another publishing house, and at his own suggestion he relinquished his interest in *Rush to Judgment*. He explained that he did not have the time to try to place the manuscript elsewhere, and implicit in his comments was the determination that his present employer was not interested in reading the manuscript. I took the work to a friend in the industry, who read it and said he liked it but was sure the publisher for which he worked would not accept it due to its controversial nature. He did not submit it for formal consideration. Although not one publisher had formally considered the manuscript, it had been rejected on behalf of three firms.

During the following months I submitted the manuscript to most of the leading publishers in the United States. Simon & Schuster was the only firm to reject it twice; the others rejected the work just once each. One of the leading editors at Simon & Schuster was particularly enthusiastic. He said that the other editors there felt that it should be published. I was informed that since a policy decision was involved, the approval of top management was required. I was advised that publication seemed certain. Somebody evidently disagreed with that evaluation, for I was informed later that the work had been reluctantly rejected. In due course, Bertrand Russell was kind enough to read the manuscript and urge Simon & Schuster, at that time his publishers, to reconsider. I submitted the manuscript again, but the result was the same.

Random House had at one time agreed to publish Leo Sauvage's analysis of the Warren Report, but subsequently declined to do so. Later it was to sign a contract with Mrs. Joseph Field to publish her analysis, but subsequently it broke that contract as well. *Rush to Judgment* was rejected at the outset and never made it to the secondary stage of a signed contract. If it were not for Random House's vacillation, nothing else would mark it as being consistent in this area. Long afterward, just after Holt, Rinehart and Winston had agreed to publish the book, Random House decided to submit a bid for it.

These were the bitter and difficult months. I had but one copy of the manuscript, some of it typed, portions handwritten, and I was possessed of neither the time nor the funds to have other copies made. Each publisher required from one week to three weeks to make a decision. A month might well be spent awaiting two rejections. It was necessary during this period to stand by so that I might be available to the publisher then considering the work should questions arise. There were many hopeful moments when it seemed that the document would at last be accepted. But each of these was followed by substantially longer periods of dejection.

George Brockway, the head of W. W. Norton, discussed the book one day with Emile de Antonio at a social affair. Brockway was on his way to Europe, but he told de Antonio that Norton would certainly publish the work if it met but two criteria: if the work raised questions in the mind of the reasonable reader that the Commission might have been wrong and if the allegations contained in the work were susceptible of verification. My wife and I celebrated, tentatively, that evening, for we were convinced that the Norton response seemed reasonable and the criteria easily attainable.

The next day I delivered the manuscript to an editor at Norton and talked with him about it. He repeated Brockway's criteria and said that he would read it first but that other editors would read it as well. He promised to call when a decision had been reached. About two weeks later he called. At his office I was informed that the book had been rejected. They were satisfied, he said, as to the accuracy of the statements in the manuscript. However, he added, the book not only convinced the reader that the Commission had been in error but offered very convincing evidence that indicated that there had been a willful disregard of the facts by the members of the Commission, its staff and the police agencies. I said that the book did not make that specific charge, although I was personally inclined to agree that the Commission's erroneous conclusions were willful. He replied that the implication was not in my words, which could be edited by Norton to soften their impact, but in the facts which I had presented. I agreed that the facts could not be altered to provide a nicer book.

Regarding the ending, he said that, although this was not his view nor the view of the majority of the editors, one editor did feel that the ending was not satisfactory. I asked what he meant, fearing, but not really believing, that he might say that had I found the assassin we would have had a tidy conclusion. He began by again dissociating himself from the view he offered, and then said: you just say Oswald probably did not do it alone, but you do not say who did; in fact, you don't even guess. I tried for a moment to frame an answer, but then decided that the effort would be wasted. I took the manuscript, used my conserved effort to try to say good-bye, if not politely, at least with civility, and left.

Before I decided to try for a publisher in England, the better part of a year and a list of fifteen publishers had been exhausted. In London I submitted the manuscript to James Michie at The Bodley Head, a venerable and highly respected publishing house. I later discovered that on the very day of my arrival The Bodley Head had received in the post a copy of a book written by a Commission member, Congressman Gerald R. Ford. It purported to be a psychological study of Lee Harvey Oswald and was called *Portrait of the Assassin.* It had been sent by Simon & Schuster. The Bodley Head decided that it could not publish both works, although some American publishing houses take a very different view of their responsibilities.*

My manuscript was sent to Hugh Trevor-Roper, the Regius Professor of Modern History at Oxford University, for evaluation. Ford's book was sent to the legal correspondent of one of London's most important newspapers. I had met that gentleman, and he had told me at that time that he was quite satisfied with the Commission's conclusions. He reported that the Ford book was without substantial value and that in its treatment of me it was inaccurate and unnecessarily hostile. He said he could not recommend its publication. Trevor-Roper recommended that *Rush to Judgment* be published.

Michie called me with the news. He began to say that The Bodley Head was "willing to publish," but corrected himself in mid-sentence to say that his firm was "honored to publish *Rush to Judgment.*" Anne-Lise and I celebrated the occasion with a rare treat for us,

* For example, Dell published two critical assessments of the Warren Report by Harold Weisberg and a book condemning Weisberg for being a scavenger for having written about the case.

dinner at Stone's Chop House in Piccadilly. Our happiness was tempered only by the fact that the first publication of my work on the death of an American President was not to take place in my own country.

When Michie and I met to discuss terms for the contract, he said that he expected that the book would do moderately well in England and that he hoped that it would be published in America as well. Since the latter was not a certainty, we agreed upon an advance of two thousand pounds ($5,600) for world rights for the book in hardcover and paperback and all subsidiary rights.* I had worked for more than two years on the project, having abandoned my law practice for the investigation. No doubt the estimable Louis Nizer was paid more for writing the introduction to a commercially published edition of the Warren Report. Yet later he was to condemn those who disagreed with him, me in particular, as scavengers.

Before leaving for England, I had introduced de Antonio to Epstein, for Epstein had given me some valuable information and I wished de Antonio to serve as liaison in my absence. Epstein had informed me of his trip to Vermont to visit Wesley J. Liebeler, a Commission lawyer. Epstein introduced himself as a student at work on a thesis involving the Commission's work. He refrained from revealing his friendship with me when meeting with Commission personnel, and he did not inform them that he was reporting back to me regarding the information he came upon. At the same time, he declined to tape-record the statements of those he interviewed, despite my suggestion that he do so. He said that if he used a recorder that was visible the interviewee would probably become inhibited and that a hidden recorder would be improper and might be discovered. Since he was offering his material to me to be used, if I wished, in one chapter of my book, I told him that I was eager to learn what he had uncovered but that I would be reluctant to utilize his interviews if they could not be verified.

Epstein said that Liebeler had shown him a number of documents, which he described. They were, in my view, of varying degrees of relevance, with one being of genuine significance. It was the then unavailable FBI report of December 9, 1963, stating that "medical examination of the President's body revealed that one of the bullets had entered just below his shoulder to the right of the spinal column at an angle of 45 to 60 degrees downward, that there was no point of exit, and that the bullet was not in the body."[1]

* Later, when it appeared that a documentary film was feasible, I purchased rights to make the film from my publisher for $750, thereby reducing the advance to $4,850.

I explained to Epstein that for the first time in a known FBI report serious doubt was cast upon the theory that a bullet struck the President in the neck and exited from the throat. Since the document appeared to confirm an autopsy diagram prepared contemporaneously by one of the pathologists, it received corroboration.[2] I urged Epstein to try to secure a copy of the report, but he declined to do so at that time, saying that he could not think of a valid excuse to give to Liebeler as to why he wanted to see him again in Vermont. I asked Epstein if he would object if I called Liebeler. He said that he would not, but specifically enjoined me from revealing anything to Liebeler that might reveal our most recent conversation.

Liebeler agreed to a luncheon meeting, which we drank at the Pan Am Building. He said that he had been the choice of the Goldwater movement in the Tenth Assembly District in New York to run against me when I sought re-election for the state legislature. His plans had been altered, he said, when I decided not to seek re-election. I learned a bit about his life and ambitions but very little about the Warren Report. He said that he would make no documents available to me.

In London I received a telephone call from de Antonio. He reported that Epstein had told him he had secured a copy of the FBI report and that he had added, "I have my own book now." De Antonio said that Epstein had decided to share no more information with me. I wrote several letters to Epstein, but he responded to none of them.

The Bodley Head became engaged in two tasks. It sought to secure publication of the book in the United States and in other countries, and it subjected the manuscript to the most minute examination of a leading firm of libel solicitors in London. Plaintiffs in defamation actions in England enjoy far more advantages than their counterparts would in an American court. Nevertheless only a few trifling changes were made regarding the substance, while the style was considerably improved due to the careful editing of Benjamin Sonnenberg, Jr., an American then residing in England.

At one time it appeared that the New American Library was certain to publish the work, but at the last moment it declined. Viking Press indicated great interest, and Michie suggested that I meet the president of the company, Thomas Guinzburg. I flew to New York and met with him and two of his associates. One editor appeared to be enthusiastic, another interested and Guinzburg at first noncommittal. As our discussion progressed, Guinzburg's fears were articulated. He asked if I knew of anything that might be done to guarantee Viking immunity from "unfair attack." The curious phrase was repeated several times during the conversation, and more than a year later it reappeared in a conversation with the publicity director at Viking, who informed me that his company had refused to publish the book due to its concern about "unfair attack."

I told Guinzburg that no work is ever invulnerable to that type of criticism but that I thought that *Rush to Judgment* was thoroughly cited with accurate references and could withstand hostile, but fair, evaluation.

Despite the fact that my optimism vis-à-vis American publishing firms had suffered considerably, I left the offices with the distinct impression that Viking would publish the book. I subsequently discovered that Epstein's book *Inquest* had also been submitted to Viking. At Viking it was determined that it was safe from unfair attack and would sell more copies than would *Rush to Judgment*. In due course, I was informed that my book had been rejected again.*

With the serenity that enhances retrospect, it now appears that among the most disturbing aspects of my unsuccessful odyssey into the publishing industry was the discovery that executives at important publishers declined to take responsibility for a controversial work. Just as Susskind was following orders, and thus avoided confronting his own obligations, publishers achieved the same result, but of necessity by different means. At New American Library and Viking Press, as examples, this was accomplished by asking those unconnected with the firm to read and recommend. Hacker read *Rush to Judgment* for one publisher, and I should not like to think that it was with his student's work in mind that he damned it with faint praise and hoped against hope in his report that another work might come along instead.

Dwight Macdonald, who carries his own independence carefully in both hands as if afraid that it might wither or, worse, escape observation, urged one publisher who was considering publishing it not to do so. The great dissenter, who had embraced many a popular unpopular cause, lent his voice to those who sought to suppress a

* *Rush to Judgment* appeared on the best-seller lists published by the *New York Times* and *Time* magazine every week for more than six months. During a considerable period of the time it occupied the number one position on the list. Subsequently, when published in paperback by Fawcett Publications, it became the number one paperback best-seller and for a time appeared simultaneously on both the hardcover and paperback lists. *Inquest* has appeared on neither of the lists, at the outset was subjected to extremely unfair criticism, and the majority of the lawyers and members of the Commission quoted in the work have reportedly denied the accuracy of the statements ascribed to them.

dissenting view. The reasons he gave revealed nothing more than his peculiar notion of the facts of the assassination.

In *Rush to Judgment* I described the scene just after the shots were fired. A Dallas deputy constable, Seymour Weitzman, had testified that he heard the shots and raced up the grassy knoll that was in front of and to the right of the limousine.[3] He said that he climbed over the fence at the top of the hill.[4] I wrote:

> He described the confusion behind the fence, with other law enforcement officers arriving, and he testified that he had encountered a very important witness there—a railroad employee: 'I asked a yardman if he had seen or heard anything during the passing of the President. He said he thought he saw somebody throw something through a bush.' Weitzman added that he asked the yardman where he thought the noise came from and the yardman 'pointed out the wall section where there was a bunch of shrubbery'.
>
> The Commission would appear to have been informed about a most important eyewitness to the event—a railroad employee who thought the shots came from the area behind the fence and who thought he saw a man throw something into the bushes when the President's car had passed. However, just after Weitzman gave that information, Commission counsel said, 'I think that's all', and Weitzman was dismissed. He was not asked for the name or description of the employee. He was not asked if he looked into the bushes or if he found anything there. Nothing in the 26 volumes of evidence or in the Report indicates that the Commission or its investigators made any effort to locate or identify the railroad employee.[5]

Macdonald wrote that the section was invalid, for there was no need for counsel to have inquired as to what it was that Weitzman had found in the bushes, since Weitzman, according to Macdonald, had testified that he had discovered a piece of the President's skull in the bushes. Weitzman, however, testified that after he had spoken with the yardman "I went back over the fence and that's when I found the portion of the skull."[6] He had previously located the skull more precisely in his testimony: "I would say 8 to 12 inches from the curb" on the south side of Elm Street.[7]

Thus my original criticism stands. Macdonald, who apparently had read the testimony quickly and selectively, might be excused for his error, which in large measure was responsible for the rejection of my book by a leading publisher, were it not that he had pretended to be expert in an area in which he evidently had no real knowledge. The bushes on the knoll were located some seventy-five yards from and well above the limousine. Macdonald could hardly have imagined that the skull portion was driven that distance. While apparently completely innocent of the physical environs in which the assassination took place, he was willing to pose as an expert on the subject long enough to play a vital role in the rejection of the book.

We had just about run out of publishers when Michie informed me that Arthur A. Cohen, editor-in-chief of the General Book Division at Holt, Rinehart and Winston, wanted to read it. I had not previously submitted the manuscript there, since Holt, Rinehart and Winston published the works of J. Edgar Hoover and a portion of the stock was owned by conservative Texas interests.

I was not sanguine about the manuscript's chances there, but I was more than willing to meet Arthur Cohen and discuss the possibility. When I did meet him, I knew that I had found a man in publishing—actually he had found me—who relied upon his own judgment and the advice of his colleagues. This man was not about to shift his responsibilities elsewhere.

8 THE ELECTRONIC REVERSAL

Arthur Cohen had heard about the manuscript and had asked The Bodley Head to send him a copy of the proofs. When one copy arrived, he read it, decided it should be published, had seven additional copies made through a photographic process and sent them to officers and editors at Holt, Rinehart and Winston. This transpired on a Thursday afternoon. Cohen asked for a decision from his colleagues by Monday. With his strong endorsement, the vote was unanimous for publication.

On one occasion I asked Cohen why he had accepted a book that no other publisher was willing to print.* He said that the book had upset him, for if it appears that the Government has not fully disclosed the facts about a subject of such great domestic concern, one must examine all similar pronouncements in a new light and with considerable caution. That, however, cannot be done when dissent is suppressed, when but one view is available. At long last there was a publisher.

The proofs were submitted to the law firm retained by Holt, Rinehart and Winston to ferret out possible libel, sometimes furtively secreted in odd corners of a manuscript. I was amused to note that one of the Warren Commission's lawyers was a partner in the firm.

* Just after Holt, Rinehart and Winston agreed to publish, Random House indicated that it was willing to bid for the book. The Bodley Head was quite satisfied that the former would publish the book well and so informed Random House.

The lawyer's report came back with a number of questions and several exclamations, such as "I can hardly believe that to be true." Consequently, I carried the Commission's volumes of evidence in an old suitcase to the offices of the distinguished firm, and point by point together we examined every question or doubt that they had raised. I left the office of the partner in charge many hours later with the almost certain feeling that I had just tried my most important case. In the face of the evidence, his doubts had been dispelled.

My wife and I had by then moved into a small walk-up flat in the southern portion of Greenwich Village to await publication. Viking rushed through Epstein's book, and mine, having been considerably delayed by its long confinement at publishers' offices, was published much later that same summer. One newspaper, *The Village Voice*, conducted a prepublication interview with me. Later, the *East Village Other* also published an interview. Epstein's book received national attention even before publication. *Look* magazine paid him a considerable sum for an exclusive interview and the right to review the book before the other reviewers did. Quite naturally, in the publishing industry the books were viewed as natural rivals. Yet, the father of one, I felt close to the other as well. I had been there at the moment of conception—even before its author.

Less personal and of greater significance was the fact that the two complemented each other. Together they assessed the Commission's work, pointed out its errors and revealed some of the apparent causes for the Commission's failings. The sparks of rivalry, given the circumstances, were always present, although had principle alone prevailed they would have been ignored.

Guinzburg evidently noticed a certain reluctance on the part of the booksellers to accept large quantities of *Inquest*. Perhaps he reasoned that this was caused by the imminent publication of *Rush to Judgment*. In any event, he stated he had read and rejected *Rush to Judgment* and that it was in his view an inferior work. I was less than pleased with that comment, and I so informed him. He denied making such a statement. Nevertheless, when *Look* utilized its exclusivity to attack *Inquest* unfairly, I called an editor at Viking, after having discussed the matter with Cohen, and offered to send a letter of protest to *Look*. The spirit of cooperation never did fully succeed. Epstein, perhaps reluctant to meet with me, rejected numerous opportunities to appear on radio and television panels to discuss the case, the grounds he offered often being that "Lane will be there."*

* I did meet Epstein in London in September 1966, when both books were being published there. I informed him that the past had been forgotten and

Some reviewers have commented that Epstein approached his task as an objective student while I assumed the role of counsel, and was therefore presumably biased. Of course, they are incorrect in both respects. Epstein had a very decided view before he began his interviews, and I was under no legal or ethical constraint that would interfere with the exercise of my own judgment. While I never fully sought to publicize the origins of Epstein's work, I do admit that I was on occasion sufficiently rankled to write a correction to a reviewer.

Before August 15, the publication date for *Rush to Judgment*, a schedule of radio and television appearances had been arranged by my publisher to commence on the sixteenth. We agreed to a three-week tour of some of the major cities in the country, my requests being that I not be scheduled to appear at book-signing affairs at stores and that every broadcast that appeared possible be arranged, even if it might interfere with a good night's sleep. A major press conference was arranged for August 15 at a midtown hotel in New York.

Evidently the publication of the book was not newsworthy, for the press ignored the event. That evening, however, while watching television, I was surprised to observe Edwin Newman review the book. In measured tones he said that it raised important and profoundly disturbing questions, did so persuasively and should be read. The next morning the "Today" program devoted one hour to the subject. The first half of the period was a fair and precise summary of the points raised by *Rush to Judgment*, the second half a confrontation between Albert Jenner, a Commission lawyer, and myself. The "Today" program was an auspicious start. Its script could not have been put together more accurately or with more scrupulous fairness. The interviews were conducted by Barbara Walters and Hugh Downs, both of whom seemed well acquainted with the facts.

The three-week tour was the most exhausting period of my life as a civilian. I discovered that some radio stations never go to bed, and my request to disregard my sleeping requirements was honored. In one city I appeared on interview programs for twenty-five consecutive hours, with just enough time budgeted into the schedule so that I might rush from one studio to another. The book did well in each city that I visited, and at my request the tour was extended.

---

that I preferred a joint approach to the Commission's transgressions. He agreed, and we appeared on several programs together, first in England and later in the United States. The CCI in Los Angeles later invited him to address the students at UCLA, and he did speak there.

Before the tours were completed, I had appeared on approximately five hundred radio and television programs or news interviews and the book was in its sixth printing.

In New York City, WNEW-TV showed the greatest interest in the subject, and ingenuity as well. Alan Burke, who often ridicules the views expressed by his guest, was among the first to invite me to appear. One of the critics had declined a similar invitation, no doubt due to fear of Burke's caustic wit. I too approached the program with real concern, but, as it developed, without reason; Burke provided a serious format for a two-hour discussion of the Warren Report. His questions were fair and revealed a knowledge of the facts. When the dignity of the program seemed threatened for a moment by a persistent member of the audience, Burke interceded.

Mel Baily and Paul Noble at the same station approached me regarding a special program. They conceived of a number of the leading critics involved in an open-ended discussion of the Report. Props and films were to be placed at the disposal of the participants. When Epstein refused to appear, the program was slightly altered so that a Commission defender was added. The program was syndicated and was therefore shown in a number of other cities. Subsequently, the same team produced another discussion program designed as an answer to the first. They invited me to meet with Louis Nizer and two Commission attorneys. That program too was broadcast in other cities.

I discovered that perhaps my appearance on the Mike Douglas program aroused the greatest national interest. The interview was pleasant; Douglas was equipped with the facts and generous in terms of time. I presume that the very substantial reaction to the program, if my mail is any barometer, is an indication not that anything untoward occurred but that he has an extremely large audience.

Once the previously forbidden subject was permitted to be aired, its wide acceptance as a matter for debate appeared unprecedented. I was invited to appear on almost every interview program in almost every major city in the country. In Chicago, as an example, I appeared twice on the Kupcinet program, which dominates its area probably as no other television show does elsewhere, and on twenty-eight other programs as well in a three-day interval. The response to the Jerry Williams radio program originating in that city was unequaled by that of any other radio discussion program.

In some cities the subject was discussed so frequently and so expertly by the various guests and by the hosts that there came a time when little more could be said. In Philadelphia, the home of a Commission critic, Vincent Salandria, the radio program conducted by Jack McKinney presented such intricate details so precisely that I feared that McKinney was talking over the heads of the members of his audience. Yet the questions called in by listeners at home showed that McKinney was understood. In the previous months he had educated a sizable portion of the city.

In the Bay area on the West Coast, a similar situation prevails with the Joe Dolan two-way radio program. Dolan surely is among the most articulate and generally well-informed of America's radio hosts and particularly up to date regarding the facts surrounding the assassination. In Denver, it is the morning television program with Jack Wilson. In Chicago it is Williams' radio show.

These few, together with others previously mentioned, and a few more, constitute the lonely outposts in a vast network of local radio programs devoted to rock and roll, farm and country, and, when intellectually inclined, to unidentified flying objects. Little of the moment touches them. Their more affluent counterparts in the television studios are primarily concerned with soap operas, horse operas and examination of the criminal law through the endeavors of Perry Mason. The stations seek to entertain, not inform, and even in that narrow pursuit the objective eludes them. For every Joe Dolan or Jack McKinney, there were five announcers who inquired on the air, with variations: "Well, I haven't read your book, but I have heard about it. Isn't it about the Warren Court and do you come out for it or against it?"

My ego permits me to understand that the majority of my fellow citizens have not read *Rush to Judgment* and will not read these words either. I am not offended by that state of affairs. I am concerned that the airwaves, a vital means for communication and education, are in the hands of those who would put an author on the air and not have the faintest notion what he has written or will speak about. With each occupation there is a responsibility. In the media, the individual's obligation to think and to decide has been taken from him in large part. That which is left he squanders.

A less than casual approach marks the efforts of Joe Pyne. He is fully prepared. When I appeared on his program, it was a local Los Angeles show. His own very vocal audience appeared handpicked—certainly homogeneous. He was made up with layers of pancake. The lights were excessively bright. His guests were afforded no makeup at all, causing the audience to marvel that Joe looked so much cooler than his guests. Pyne is equipped with the "Facts"—not always the facts that the guest is invited to discuss and not always facts at all. The persistent guest who manages to carry Joe, kicking and screaming all the way, back to the stated subject matter finds that he has transformed the otherwise lively show into a rather dull one, for Joe appears incapable of a serious discussion of a serious subject. He is the David Susskind of the right and, although a bit more crude, essentially less offensive.

On the other extreme—I speak not politically now—is William Buckley. He is well informed, the last word in urbanity, and a delight to duel with, even to lose points to. His producer offered me twenty-five tickets to the program, more if requested. The tiny studio in which the broadcast is taped accommodates few more than twenty-five—he had offered us control of the studio audience. I arrived on time and was expertly made up by a technician. Buckley was late and therefore received a patchwork job. His shirt was rumpled; no doubt he had just arrived from another engagement. His questions were incisive but not unfair. The program ended with his producer asking us each a question or two. The questions put to me were relevant and fair. Of Buckley the producer asked the unanswerable: How could he possibly make up his mind to accept the Warren Report if he had not read all the evidence?

When I returned to the West Coast, Pyne's producer invited me to appear on his syndicated television program. I accepted. Later, when he learned that I had been invited to appear on the Mort Sahl program as well, he informed me that since Sahl's program was aired first and since Pyne is the most important man on the Coast, I would have to cancel the Sahl program. I incredulously asked him to repeat his observation, and he said, "Well, you cannot do them both. You got to choose one or the other." No choice was ever less complicated. I called Sahl and told him I had canceled the Pyne program.

In the following months, I appeared on Sahl's television program six times and innumerable times on his radio program. He was fired from both programs for dwelling on the subject of the assassination. A massive popular response—including thousands of letters and a picket line at the studio—caused the station to rehire him, but he was fired again after he played recordings of exclusive interviews with Jim Garrison. In another time he might have been awarded a Pulitzer Prize or some similar honor for his work.

The subject could now be discussed, but advocates were still not to be tolerated. I found that the reporters who had ignored my efforts to discuss serious flaws in the Government's case suddenly became anxious to report every word I offered. I yielded my resolve not to sign books in stores, perhaps in favor of crass commercialism, as has been suggested, perhaps to assist the bookstore owners who had made the book available and who had played such a large part in making it a well-read document.

The night before an autographing appearance in a large downtown department store, I had worked a full night's sleep into the schedule and was feeling practically ebullient as I arrived. A local reporter asked how all was going, and feeling that no one was listening anyway, perhaps in reaction to my previous circumstances, I replied that all was going very well. "In fact," I added jocularly, "the store has now placed all the remaining copies of the Warren Report in the fiction department." The following day, the store came under fire in the reporter's column and felt called upon to issue denials.

Not long afterward I spoke at Loretto Heights College, a Catholic women's college in Denver. The following morning—I spent the night on campus as a guest of the college—a sister informed me that two men known to her to be agents of the Federal Bureau of Investigation had been in the audience. As I looked back, not without some degree of nostalgia, upon the great silence, I realized that although others were now beginning to listen, during the difficult days the men of the FBI were my most loyal followers.

9 THE MAKING OF A FILM

When three principals in an English film company—Tony Richardson, John Osborne and Oscar Lewenstein—agreed to invest funds in a film about the assassination, and when ABC-TV agreed to make its film clips available, the documentary film became a possibility. A West Coast film crew was hastily assembled, and de Antonio, assistant director Richard Stark, my wife and I were ready to depart for Dallas from New York almost at once. The budget provided for no luxuries, and a few essentials, such as air transportation, were considered beyond our means as well. Accordingly, we rented a terrible little automobile for under $70 a week, no mileage charge, and began our drive to Dallas.

I drove the first shift and my wife the second. De Antonio took over as we retired to the rear seat for a nap. I awoke at about dawn and saw a familiar skyline in the distance. I observed, half to myself, that it certainly looked a great deal like Chicago, but since that city hardly lies between New York and Dallas, I dismissed the thought until a road sign welcomed us to Chicago a few minutes later. De Antonio took it calmly, saying that he probably had made one wrong turn in the night.

We arrived in Dallas thirty-four hours after leaving New York, which, de Antonio observed, very likely established a record for nonstop driving from New York to Dallas by way of Chicago. It is a record that may remain unchallenged for some time.

We moved into the Tower Motel, not far from the downtown

area of Dallas, where we met the film crew, consisting of a cameraman, a sound technician and an assistant. De Antonio was to direct the project, I was to find and then interview the witnesses, Stark was to keep the records and see to it that the exposed film was mailed safely to a New York laboratory each day, and Anne-Lise was to cook for all seven of us.

We called S. M. Holland, a railroad employee who had witnessed the assassination from the vantage point of the railroad bridge just above Elm Street.[1] He agreed to see us that evening, but he expressed reservations about being filmed. De Antonio and I arrived at his house in nearby Irving, Texas, that evening, leaving the crew and the equipment in the car parked not far away. I was aware of Holland's reluctance to speak, since three separate and unsuccessful visits had been paid him by volunteers for the CCI, and I had just reread their reports in preparation for the interview.

He was personable and friendly when we discussed the weather and similar subjects. When the conversation turned toward the assassination, he spoke with more caution but with conviction. At one point, he turned to me and asked, "Do you believe the Warren Report?" It should be said here that he did not know who I was, since I had employed a pseudonym, Robert Blake, for my short film career. We were prepared to pay small sums to those who agreed to grant interviews, and I thought it important that the witness have no idea as to my own firm position on the case so that it might not be said that he was unfairly influenced. In addition, my name was known in Dallas, and I thought it best to attract as little attention as possible in order that our project not be interfered with by the authorities.

Although I was not above some pretense when the occasion demanded it, I was reluctant to mislead Holland, whose obvious sincerity practically precluded it. I replied, "No, I do not believe the Report." There was more than a moment's silence, in which I considered the possibility that I had just wiped out the trip to Dallas by naïvely responding to the question put by the man who was very likely the most important witness we were to find. Holland then said, "All right, bring in the camera. I'll tell you what I know." He explained that some young people, "students, I guess, have come by over the last couple of years to ask me questions." He was, I believe, making reference to our volunteers. "But they believed that Report, so there was no sense in telling them anything. The Report is what the Commission wanted the whole world to believe, that Oswald did it alone. But it just did not happen that way."

Holland's discussion of the events was enough to shake the most fervent Commission supporter; it even convinced one of the crew members who had been inclined to accept the Report. Holland concluded by stating that he had been a Dallas deputy sheriff for seventeen years and had worked for the railroad companies for longer. "I might even get fired for this interview," he said. I asked him why he had granted it, and he answered, "When the time comes that an American can't tell the truth because the Government doesn't, that's the time to give the country back to the Indians—if they'll take it."

I spoke of a fee for the interview, but he refused to accept any money. He said that one day America might know what actually happened that day and that he would like to have a copy of the interview to give to his grandchild. Holland gave us the names of other railroad men who were on the underpass that day, and he agreed to meet us on the underpass for additional filming.

We called one of the other men, and he agreed to an interview the next afternoon. We arrived at his home and filmed his responses. As we left he told us that he had just brought his wife back from the doctor minutes before we arrived and that he had learned that she was dying of cancer. He said he thought that he should go through with the interview anyway, for it was also a matter of real concern to him to find out why the President had been killed.

Shirley Martin and her two daughters arrived, and together with my wife they looked for various witnesses: Wilma Tice, who had seen Ruby at Parkland Memorial Hospital when the President's death was announced there;[2] Ruth Paine, with whom Marina Oswald had lived;[3] Eva Grant, Jack Ruby's sister (who demanded $2,000 for an interview);[4] and Dial Ryder, the Irving gunsmith who had affixed a telescopic sight to a rifle not the alleged assassination weapon for a man who said his name was Oswald (he was afraid to be interviewed).[5]

I joined the Martins for a visit to Acquilla Clemons, a witness to an aspect of the murder of J. D. Tippit, whose evidence indicates that two men may have been involved in that crime.[6] Mrs. Clemons was reluctant to talk for fear that the man who had warned her not to talk—a man she believed to be a Dallas police officer—might pay her another visit. We were able to persuade Mrs. Tice and Mrs. Clemons, but we could not overcome Ryder's fear or meet Mrs. Grant's price.

We spent an entire day trying to locate Domingo Benavides, the closest eyewitness to the Tippit murder.[7] He had not been interviewed since his testimony before counsel for the Warren Commission, and that attorney had failed to ask the relevant questions.[8] We located his place of employment, a garage in a town near Dallas, and I talked with him there about the murder. He gave a description of the murderer that differed from Oswald's and agreed to meet the next morning at our motel for a filmed interview. I agreed to pay him $100, which was to cover his loss of a day's wages and transportation to and from the motel, the remainder constituting a fee.

We continued our quest for other witnesses and subsequently returned to the motel early in the evening. The crew was silent, while one member was preparing to leave. De Antonio explained that two men who identified themselves as detectives attached to the homicide squad had been there asking for "Robert Blake." Unable to find me, they questioned de Antonio. They demanded to know why "Blake offered that Mexican boy $100." They left, after frightening, not to say intimidating, the crew and indicating that they had begun an investigation of our efforts. They also indicated that Benavides would not keep his appointment. He did not.

Long afterward, immediately following a lecture that I gave at Michigan State University, I met Earl Ruby and his attorney, Alan S. Adelson, who had driven from Detroit to talk with me. In a long and, for me, very enlightening conversation, they told me that the Dallas authorities had told them that they had frightened us out of Dallas when we had been making a film. They said that the police authorities had sent two officers to convey the impression that we were not welcome in Dallas.

At the advice of Penn Jones, Jr., the editor of the Midlothian, Texas, *Mirror* in nearby Midlothian, we vacated the premises we had been occupying and moved to a motel in Arlington, about twenty miles away. Theoretically, we reasoned, we would be beyond the jurisdiction of the Dallas police and we might drive into Dallas for the interviews. This compromise kept the crew intact—and in Texas.

De Antonio had heard of Harold Williams through Warren Leslie, who, after having written about Dallas, was himself encouraged to leave the city. Williams had been Leslie's chef and evidently in possession of valuable information linking Tippit to Ruby, a connection that the Commission said did not exist.[9] We located Williams, who was not the first witness we interviewed who had been invisible to the Commission.[10] I questioned him in a room at our Arlington motel. During the interview, he told of the close relationship between Ruby and the officer. He also said that he had been warned by the Dallas police of the consequences of ever telling what he knew about the case. He concluded, "Well, they say this is a free country." He looked around, as if in search of agreement, shrugged his shoulders and added, "I hope it is."

Another important witness was due shortly. James Tague, the only person other than the President and Governor Connally known to have been injured in Dealey Plaza as a result of the shots fired, was to arrive in ten minutes.[11] Williams asked to be taken back to the Negro section of Dallas. Three of us were required for the Tague interview. Either of the two remaining members of the crew were at liberty to make the trip. De Antonio asked one of them to go. He refused, stating frankly that he was afraid to. The other, when asked, made the same answer. Anne-Lise said that she would drive Williams back to Dallas, and she did so. For a day or so, the crew members appeared a bit sheepish; but afterward they were less reluctant to drive to Dallas.

We called Holland again and asked if he would meet us at the underpass in Dealey Plaza for some on-site filming. He agreed, and later that day we assembled near the Texas School Book Depository. We filmed sequences of Holland and me talking on the underpass and then walking to the area behind the wooden fence. We also filmed an interview at the place behind the fence where Holland said at least one shot had originated. As the crew was setting up the equipment there, two Dallas deputy sheriffs drove into the area and parked. They observed the camera and slowly walked over to me. One inquired, "What are you doing back here? I've seen a hundred or more cameras around here, but they're always taking pictures of the building." He indicated the Book Depository with his hand.

I was about to offer some excuse about the lighting, hoping that he knew even less about cameras than did I, when Holland walked over. The deputy said, "Hi, skinny. What's going on?" Holland answered, "These people are not like the others. They're back here 'cause that's where a shot came from. They're making a picture about what happened, not about what the Government wants to believe happened." The deputies looked at each other and left. About ten minutes later, a truck backfired while passing through the underpass. I turned to ask the sound technician if the noise had affected his equipment, to find that he was stretched out on the ground. He explained that he thought someone had been shooting at us.

Perhaps the most extraordinary setting for any of the interviews was the one filmed in the United States Post Office building on Dealey Plaza. J. C. Price had been on the roof of that building when the shots were fired.[12] The Commission never questioned him, but I was anxious to.[13] I called him at the building and he invited us to join him, saying that he would "leave word with the guard" to admit us to the basement, where his office was located. The guard did lead us to Price, and when the interview there had been concluded, I asked if we might film from the roof of the building as well. Price and the guard arranged that also.

The most impressive of the witnesses was Lee E. Bowers, Jr.[14] His wry sense of humor and his excellent memory made him perhaps the finest witness I have ever questioned. He was behind the fence in a railroad tower when the shots were fired.[15] He saw two men in the area and something that attracted his attention to the fence when the shots were fired.[16] He was not sure as to what it was, but he believed it was a puff of smoke or a flash of light.[17] He added that just as he was about to give that information to Joseph Ball, a Commission lawyer, Ball interrupted him.[18] That filmed interview contains the only full record of what Bowers observed when the shots were fired. Less than five months later, Bowers was dead.

I was anxious to locate N. J. Daniels, a former Dallas police officer who apparently had seen Ruby enter the basement just before he killed Oswald.[19] His telephone was unlisted, and I did not even know if he still resided in Dallas. I called the Dallas Police Department and announced, "Hello. I'm Mark Lane and I would like to contact N. J. Daniels, who was with your department some time ago. Can you tell me where I can reach him?" The response was, "Just a minute, sir." Approximately a minute later, the voice returned with Daniels' address and telephone number. I called him at once, arranged for an immediate appointment and completed the interview in less than one hour.

We had filmed twenty interviews, and the film crew was of the very strong opinion that we had already outlasted our welcome in Dallas. I agreed that we had filmed far more than we could have reasonably hoped for, and when Dean Andrews, a New Orleans lawyer, said that he would talk with us, we packed our belongings and drove there. When we arrived in New Orleans, however, Andrews had changed his mind, saying that he had been warned by "Washington, D.C.," that he would "have a hole blown in his head if he talked" with us. Andrews was later indicted for perjury in New Orleans and convicted.[20] His appeal is presently pending.

In London, just before returning to the United States for the film, my wife and I met Paul McCartney at a cocktail party given by Benjamin Sonnenberg, Jr., who had edited my book, and his wife, Wendy. McCartney became deeply interested in the subject and asked if he could read the manuscript. A copy was sent to him, and several days later a chauffeur returned it. Later that day, McCartney called to say, "Well, he could not have done it, could he?"

We met for dinner twice during the next few nights, and McCartney agreed to write the musical score for the film after I had raised that possibility. I warned him that the subject was highly controversial and might have an adverse effect upon his career. He said that he was aware of that but unconcerned by it. I asked him why he might be willing to jeopardize his future, and he replied, "One day my children are going to ask me what I did with my life, and I cannot just answer that I was a Beatle." Eventually we decided that the film should be stark and didactic, and therefore without music.

When *Rush to Judgment* opened in America, it was well received by the critics. Far more important, it evidently influenced the judgments of some of them. Bosley Crowther, writing in the *New York Times*, said that the film "serves further to convince the viewer that there was evidence the Warren Commission failed to assemble or neglected to evaluate in preparing its report. . . .[21] If the purpose of this film is to rouse its viewers into having doubts about Oswald's total guilt," Crowther concluded, "then it eminently succeeds."[22]

The first statement to be published in the liberal New York *Post* in more than three and a half years that discussed but did not disparage my efforts appeared in Archer Winsten's film review.[23] *Rush to Judgment* will, he said,

> tend to destroy your peace of mind. This will surely happen because it raises a large number of compelling reasons why the Warren Commission's report is to be doubted. We listen to evidence from people who believed the first shot came from behind a fence, not from the Texas Book Depository building. We listen to people who knew that the Dallas police were very close to Jack Ruby, not remote as asserted by the Chief. We are made to feel that there were at least two marksmen, not one, and that Oswald couldn't have been a good shot. All this and a great deal more is brought to the screen in filmed interviews with lawyer Mark Lane doing the questioning and then drawing his own conclusions which undermine the Warren Commission.[24]

Winsten chose to conclude his review by quoting Penn Jones from the film: "I really believe that the only way you can believe the Warren Report is not to read it."[25]

Penelope Gilliatt, on leave from the London *Observer* and writing in *The New Yorker*, said that "most of the evidence is arrestingly independent."[26] She concluded:

> The pauses and puzzlement of some of the witnesses are as eloquent as their testimony. It is hard to get some of the shots out of one's mind: obdurate Western faces against lace antimacassars, old workingmen waiting to think before making an uncustomary judgment about the high-ups. "Well, I always found it peculiar," says one, "but I thought that was the way they did business."[27]

The New York *Daily News*, which had editorially referred to Oswald alternately as a "red," a "rat," a "Commie" and a "punk murderer," and on occasion as many as three such flattering appellations in one sentence, gave an excellent account of the film: " 'Rush to Judgment,' Mark Lane's 'brief for the defense' of Lee Harvey Oswald, should lend ammunition to the arguments of the Doubting Thomases who found the Warren Commission report a whitewash."[28] Kathleen Carroll added:

> Some of these witnesses were never called to testify before the Warren Commission, Lane almost gleefully points out. Much of the testimony of those who did talk to the Commission, Lane indicates, seems to have been misinterpreted or even ignored. Lane concludes that the "only way you can believe the report is not to have read it." The deliberately cold, unobtrusive style of the film adds further support to Lane's arguments. It is one thing to read written testimony, but quite something else to observe witnesses' facial reactions to questions and hear testimony from their own lips. The camera—as they say—never lies, so it is hard not to believe these sober-sounding, sober-faced eyewitness accounts. The selected interviews—just barely edited—make the arguments for the defense seem more and more reasonable. Lane may never officially win the case, but the film should win new skeptics of the Warren report over to his side.[29]

It seemed clear that the film review pages, as in the case of the book review sections, operate with an admirable independence of the forces that afflict so much of the rest of the media. Yet before the film opened in the United States, it appeared on the Government-owned television network in Great Britain.[30] It fared about as well there as it would have had it been premiered in America on the one television station in Austin, Texas, and for much the same reasons, I fear.

10 A WORLD PREMIERE

The film made its world premiere on British television.[1] De Antonio had arranged for its showing there, and I was requested by the British Broadcasting Company (BBC) to be present for the debut. I was also told that a debate with two Commission lawyers would follow the showing of the film.

If you were in England viewing BBC-2 for almost five hours on January 29, 1967, you should have been informed that the distortion was not caused by a faulty television set. It originated at BBC's Lime Grove studio. It was, in fact, planned that way.

On January 17 I drove to a college in Philadelphia in anticipation of a debate with Arlen Specter, one of the most inventive of the

Warren Commission's lawyers. Mr. Specter had been a young Democrat, given an assignment as an assistant district attorney by the Democratic District Attorney of Philadelphia. His employer permitted him to serve as a Commission lawyer, an extracurricular bit of activity that enhanced both his reputation and his finances. Specter returned from Washington, changed his political party, announced his candidacy for the office of District Attorney, and evidently the prestige that his work for the President's Commission brought enabled him to defeat his former friend and supporter. On the very afternoon of my arrival in Philadelphia, the leading newspaper announced that Specter would be the Republican candidate for Mayor.

You may well imagine my desire to meet so famous a person in public debate in his own city. But it was not to be. Specter's office announced that he must retire early that night (the debate was set for 7:30 P.M.), for he was required to catch an early plane for London the next day in order to debate with me—twelve days later. (In the interim before flying to London I flew to California, appeared on radio and television programs there and debated another Warren Commission lawyer at the University of California at Los Angeles.)

However, as the reader will discover, perhaps to his amusement, and, as I discovered, much to my regret, my absence from London was apparently an error, for I missed the BBC rehearsals for the extemporaneous-debate program. In retrospect, I must add that I am not now sure that my mere presence in London would have ensured my knowledge of the rehearsal schedule or an invitation to the preparations.

It seemed just a bit odd to me that Specter, an American politician, would refuse to debate with me in America—the major networks and leading universities had sought to arrange such debates on many occasions, but Specter was adamant in his rejection of every such invitation—and so quickly agree to cross the ocean for the encounter. One less naïve might have taken this as a clue that the BBC had somehow made the confrontation most attractive to the Commission's representatives. I confess to having speculated about the matter with myself for a moment or two. I concluded that the suites at the luxurious Connaught, the expense account, the trip to London for the lawyers—and presumably their wives or associates—and perhaps even the fee might have tipped the balance.

The program's format was soon to become the question of the day. This being so, let me trace my association with it from the outset. The film's director, Emile de Antonio, bore the burden of the original negotiation with the BBC officials. He told me that the BBC had agreed to show the film on January 29 and that it would be followed by a general discussion in which it was hoped that I would participate. I agreed at once. The BBC insisted that I sign a document in which I agreed not to appear on any other radio or television program to be broadcast in England prior to January 29. This effort at the creation of a very small monopoly hardly seemed appropriate, but as it was the condition for the showing of the film, and as I did not plan to be in London much before that date anyway, I executed the document and it was submitted to the BBC. Subsequently, the BBC officials signed the contract purchasing the film for one showing.

My first direct contact with a BBC representative took place when I was in Los Angeles. A call came from London and a very correct and polite English voice informed me that it was owned by one Peter Pagamenta, who was the assistant director of the program, which had been named "The Death of Kennedy." He called to find out when I would arrive and to be sure that I understood the approach that the director had taken to the program.

I would arrive on the twenty-eighth, I said, and I should like to hear the director's approach. He explained that the showing of the film would constitute the opening statement of "your case," as he put it. Then the Commission lawyers would be permitted to make comments. Didn't I think it fair that they should speak next? I did indeed. "And then you will rebut and the debate will proceed." It all sounded fine, I said, but weren't there to be two other participants? "Oh, yes. Lord Devlin—you know who he is?" I did. "Well, he and a Professor Bickel will speak later in the program."

"In other words," I said, "you will have four Commission supporters present the Commission's case and I alone will speak for the critics?"

"In a sense you might say that," he replied, "but Lord Devlin and Professor Bickel are not Commission personnel."

I said I would like to suggest that Professor Hugh Trevor-Roper be invited. Among his credentials to qualify as a participant was the fact that he had read the twenty-six volumes, and his writings on the subject seemed to demonstrate that he was almost the only person in England to have bothered to examine the evidence. Certainly Lord Devlin gave no sign of such an acquaintance with the facts. The answer was that Professor Trevor-Roper was not to be a participant. And now that that's out of the way, what hotel would you like to stay at? I said I did not care and that any would do. "Well, then," came the reply, "we'll make a reservation for you at the Grosvenor House, and if there is any change we'll have a message waiting for you when you arrive at the airport. Please cable Dick Francis the time of your arrival and contact Paul Fox after you're settled in your hotel in London."

The cable was sent: "ARRIVE JANUARY 28TH 7:00 A.M." And that was the first and last word regarding the format of the program before my several-thousand-mile journey from Los Angeles to London in reliance upon that conversation.

I arrived at 7:00 A.M. and it was raining. I was tired from the trip from New York to Los Angeles, a busy schedule on the West Coast, the flight to London from Los Angeles and the thought of flying back to New York in three days for two days there before flying back to Paris. But this was an important program and well worth the effort. By worth the effort, I did not mean that it would be financially rewarding, for since I was not paid a farthing for the program, and in fact was compelled to cancel speaking engagements for which I was to have been paid, the program was, in that sense, to be worse than a total loss.

But the chance to meet the imaginative creator of the single-bullet theory in an open, no-holds-barred encounter, before some seven million viewers, with the knowledge that it would be fully reported in my own country, was worth any sacrifice of time or money. Still, I was tired. I cleared immigration quickly with a greeting from the clerk. He said he'd be watching the program. Customs too was fast and pleasant. There was no message waiting.

I called the Grosvenor House to find that there was no reservation. Since de Antonio had told me that the Commission lawyers, Specter, who has already been introduced, and David Belin from Iowa, were to stay in rather luxurious quarters at the Connaught, I called there as well. No reservation for me. I called the BBC. A gentleman, obviously a nighttime receptionist hoping the early morning would pass without the kind of problem I was about to present, answered. He said he had no authority: "Of course Mr. Fox is not in, and he won't be for hours, and, sir, no one is in, except me, and I know nothing about hotels; perhaps you might call back in a couple of hours."

Two hours passed rather slowly in the drafty terminal building. It was almost nine and I had left New York the evening before and had not yet been to sleep. In due course, a responsible and concerned young lady at the BBC was located and a reservation made at a hotel. I was too tired to care that the hotel was undergoing noisy renovation and that the lobby resembled a bombed-out village or that the room was dark and musty.

Before I left the United States, de Antonio had told me that the BBC had constructed a most elaborate model of Dealey Plaza and that it was hoped, by the BBC, that instead of aerial photographs of the area which appeared in our film, live on-camera shots of the model might be substituted. De Antonio agreed to the substitution upon my agreement that the model was accurate.

I took a shower, shaved and called Paul Fox. The operator at the BBC cut me off. I called again. He was not in but would call back. He never did. I called Peter Pagamenta. He was at a meeting, and his office would switch me to the meeting room. We were cut off again. I called back. Mr. Pagamenta will call you in a minute. He didn't.

I called back in fifteen minutes and reached him. I said that I would like to see the model. He said, sorry about the renovation at the hotel; hope it hasn't disturbed you. I said that it was quite all right, thinking that if he knew about it he might have booked a room at some other hotel.

"I would like to see the model," I said.

He said, "How would tomorrow do?"

"Not too well," I said, "for if any changes have to be made you may need some time and tomorrow is the day of the program."

"Well, let's see what time might be convenient for us for you to arrive," he considered. He said he'd call back.

The phone rang and it was Per Hanghoj, a journalist for the Danish afternoon newspaper, *Ekstrabladet*. I asked him if he would like to see the BBC model and meet some BBC officials. He said he would like to, and we took a taxicab to the BBC Lime Grove studio. There we met Pagamenta, who permitted us to see the model. It was breath-taking in detail. And in each crucial respect it was inaccurate.

One of the participants, Bickel, in an effort to prove that no shots could have come from behind the wooden fence, the area from which some of the shots originated, had written in *Commentary* that "people were milling about this area and looking down on it from the railroad bridge over the underpass, and no one saw an armed man."[2] Bickel's argument obviously rests upon the allegation that one can observe the area behind the wooden fence from the railroad bridge, which is above it. His ignorance of the geography of the area can probably be explained by his failure to visit the location, but should not have formed the basis for his curious theory. The railroad bridge is on a level with the base of the five-foot fence, not above it, and the fence area is heavily landscaped with bushes and trees so dense that it is absolutely impossible to see anyone behind the fence from the bridge.

Yet the BBC model seemed almost designed to accommodate Bickel's false impression, although I felt quite certain that slovenly supervision, not mischievousness, was responsible for the model, which placed the bridge well above the fence and removed all the bushes and most of the trees from the area, thus giving the model witnesses a view which the real witnesses could never have secured.

In its Report the Commission had said that a most important witness, S. M. Holland, was living proof that no shots came from behind the fence, since he ran to the area behind the fence from the railroad bridge "immediately" after the shots were fired.[3] In the film Holland answered that incorrect conclusion by stating that it took him two or two and a half minutes to get to the fence, since the area between him and that destination was "a sea of cars." He said they were so tightly packed, bumper to bumper, that he had to climb over them.[4] Again the BBC model accommodated the Commission rather than the facts. There was no "sea of cars," just a few scattered models that would not have prevented Holland from speeding to the fence.

Pagamenta resisted my suggestions for changes in the model. I suggested that we compare the model to photographs. "We don't have any photographs here at the studio," was the reply. "How could you construct a detailed model without photographs?" I asked, but, interrupting myself, I said, "Never mind, I have some at the hotel and I'll fetch them now."

Before I left to get them, I observed the remainder of the set. On the far left, appearing almost as if it were in a hole, was a small table, at which I was told I would sit during the program. A larger table, raised as is a judge's bench, stood in the center, and it was this that created the impression that my table sat in a hole in the ground. To the right was another larger table for two, and still further along the set still another for the impartial moderator, Kenneth Harris.

"Why the elevated table?" I asked.

"For the two judges or assessors, as we call them," was the reply.

"And who might they be?"

"As I told you before, Lord Devlin and Professor Bickel," was the reply.

I observed, "I thought that they were participants in the debate."

"Well, they will participate as judges; that is, they will give their verdict at the end of the program, and as to debate, it will not really be a debate. That is, you will be given a chance to speak when you are personally attacked."

"When," not "if," I thought. He makes it sound as if it is already set.

"Surely," I said, "I didn't come all this way to defend myself. I came to discuss the facts surrounding the death of the President. Isn't that the name of your program?"

"Well, you had better talk with Mr. Fox about this," was the answer.

Hanghoj and I were ushered into a small downstairs room to await Fox. In time he appeared with Kenneth Harris. We were offered a drink, as is the custom at the BBC. I accepted. The whiskey arrived almost at once with ice and water, as all Americans presumably like it, although I had said I would prefer it straight. Harris' gin arrived just as we began to depart.

Fox seemed irritated. "I understand you have some problems," he said. I explained them all. The model was not accurate. How could two Warren Commission apologists be judges? Lord Devlin had served as the almost official salesman for the Warren Report in England for more than two years. He had endorsed the Report before the evidence was published, and since the publication of the twenty-six volumes he had betrayed no trace of having examined them. Bickel, on a smaller scale, had tried to serve the Establishment in his own country in much the same way. How could Fox suggest that they be judges?

Fox said, "After all, we are showing your two-hour film, so there is no need for everyone on the panel to agree with you." I submitted that he had not understood my point. If he desired, he could have a dozen Warren Commission spokesmen on the program and I would not object. What was unsatisfactory was the idea that the BBC sought to establish two such spokesmen as judges.

Fox, now aided by the moderator, said that they could hardly be expected to withdraw the invitation to Lord Devlin or Professor Bickel. I did not expect or hope that would be done. I merely suggested that they be stripped of their black robes and made mortals like the rest of us. "Cannot be done," said Fox.

I then suggested that they be introduced properly. That is, let the audience know that they had written in support of the Commission's central conclusion that Oswald was the lone assassin. "Surely," said Fox, "you don't doubt the integrity of two such important men in public life. Surely you believe that they can be swayed by the evidence if it proves that their previously held position was wrong." Their integrity was irrelevant to the discussion, their prejudice central, I offered. Harris resolved the problem by stating that he would introduce them as two men who had supported the Commission's view. He added that if I wanted to discuss my objections to them on the air, I would be given every opportunity to do so. I said that I would do so.

Then we approached the crux of the matter—my role in the debate. It was set, it could not be changed, I could only respond to personal attacks, said Harris and Fox in one voice and several times. "I doubt that the audience cares much for hearing personal attacks made or defended against," I said. I thought that perhaps they would like to hear about the death of the President, which might be why they would turn to the program called "The Death of Kennedy."

"If you want to do another program, called 'Mark Lane Attacked and Defended,' I will come back for it, but I do not suppose that anyone will care to watch it," I added.

"The format is set. It cannot be changed. The film will be presented in four segments. The Commission lawyers will attack each portion and if, in doing so, they make any personal attacks upon you, you will be permitted some time to respond. In addition, as we have agreed, you will be given ample time to point out what you consider to be weaknesses in the program's format and in its choice of assessors."

"In four segments?" I asked. "The film was the result of two years of investigatory endeavor. We sacrificed to make it. This is its world premiere. Why do you intend to chop it up into four pieces? Let it be seen as it was made, and then let your critics say what they will. The film has an integrity and an identity of its own. Do not destroy that."

Fox said that according to the contract that de Antonio signed "we have the right to show the film in segments and we intend to do it that way." I wrung but one concession from the BBC. Harris and Fox both agreed—both gave solemn commitments—that I would be given ample time at the outset of the program to dissent from the format, to explain my objection to the judges, to explain that the film could not encompass the entire case against the Report but only those portions which were filmic and that in my view the BBC formula defeated a genuine exchange of the facts. We shook hands and were about to depart when Hanghoj, as journalists will do, asked a few questions of Harris.

Q. Don't you write for *The Observer?*
A. Yes, I do.
Q. What is *The Observer's* position on the assassination?
A. We don't have one.
Q. You don't have one?
A. No.
Q. Don't you think that the subject is sufficiently important for you to think about it and take a position?

A. Well, we did do that when the Report came out.
Q. Yes?
A. Well, we supported the Commission.
Q. Have you taken another position since then?
A. No, we haven't.
Q. Then *The Observer*'s position is in support of the Warren Commission?
A. Well, you might say that.
Q. Wouldn't you say that?
A. Yes, I suppose so.
Q. You will be the moderator tonight?
A. Yes.

I arrived back at the studio one hour and a half before air time. The parties were well separated. I was placed in a small cubicle, lavishly furnished with food, liquor and excellent wine. Some doors away were Specter and Belin and the visiting BBC brass, all of whom, we were told in whispers, had arrived for the program—the longest live studio production in British history.

Just before air time, I asked what was to be done about makeup. A veteran of several hundred appearances in America, I had expected that matter to be disposed of in a dressing room long before then. "It will be taken care of in the studio." Makeup was applied to some, but not to me.

Of serious concern was the fact that there was but one set of the twenty-six volumes and these were given to Belin and Specter and placed far out of my reach. As the program began, it became clear that Harris was working from a script and that both Belin and Specter had copies of it. I had none; and, in fact, I had thought that the spontaneous program which had been described to us would preclude the use of one.

The London *Times* reported on its front page that the BBC switchboard had been jammed with viewers complaining that the program was unfair. The *Daily Mirror* said, "Chairman Kenneth Harris officiously and, for me, embarrassingly clumsily silenced Mr. Lane whenever he tried to cross verbal swords with the rival lawyers." The *Daily Sketch* said that Harris conducted the program "far too brusquely." The *Daily Express* headlined its story, "Viewers Protest 'Unfair' During TV Marathon," and added, "Harris *did* appear to behave pompously." In a story headed "Verdict on Harris," the "Londoner's Diary" in the *Evening Standard* evidently found Harris guilty of being "nervous," "too abrupt" and "fairly childish."

On the facts, the *Times* pointed out that many witnesses did insist that the shots came from behind a fence on a grassy knoll, and the *Guardian,* an early and strong supporter of the Commission, did a complete turnabout: "Mark Lane seems now to have won his case, or Oswald's case." And: "Now it seems clear to almost everyone but the Warren Commission that it was indeed a rush to judgment."

Could one bullet have hit both the President and Governor Connally? Said the *Daily Mirror,* "It just doesn't seem possible." If not, there were at least two assassins.

The next day the *Times* of London ran a fairly lengthy and scrupulously fair and accurate story presenting some of my objections and the BBC reply. By combining that reply with the Kenneth Harris statement to the *Standard* the day before, the definitive Establishment position can be ascertained.

After the witnesses in the film said that they heard shots come from behind the fence and saw a puff of smoke come from that location as well, Cliff Michelmore, not waiting for the Belin-Specter response, said for the BBC that the whole of Dealey Plaza is bowl-shaped and that the area behind the fence is crisscrossed with steam pipes thereby accounting for the "smoke." Ignorance, Bickel's only excuse, cannot be brought forward in defense of that false allegation, since the BBC had sent Michelmore to Dallas to look about. The area behind the fence is not crisscrossed with steam pipes. There is but one pipe anywhere in the entire area and it runs in a straight line from the overpass and not behind the fence. Did Michelmore believe that a man who had spent forty-one years working that section of the railroad yards, as in the case of Holland, would state that he saw smoke, that he knew that it came from a weapon and be totally unaware of the presence of steam pipes that the clever Michelmore found on his first trip there? I mention Michelmore's crisscrossed pipes because it was unfortunately typical of several false statements that he made—all of which conformed to the Commission's case if not to the facts.

While the film was playing, the debate in the studio flourished, only to die under Harris' heavy hand when the live broadcast, so to speak, commenced. An example: During an early segment of the program, Harris began questioning Belin, asking him in effect if he had been engaged in any correspondence with me regarding the making of the film. Belin, it seems, had film aspirations and felt that de Antonio should provide a camera, film, a crew and an opportunity for him to speak in the film for a minimum of thirty minutes. Belin was well prepared for the leading questions put to him. He had the correspondence in question spread out before him even before the first question was asked, which, I must confess, raised some question in my normally unsuspicious mind regarding the possibility that the area had been explored before the program began.

I quickly put that thought aside, but it recurred in a more persistent form shortly thereafter when, for a moment, Harris forgot what he was about and departed from the script. Harris, perhaps to establish his own identity, asked Specter about a glaring inconsistency that the BBC had tracked down in the Warren Report. The FBI agent, Robert Frazier, had testified that an examination of the President's shirt did not prove that a shot came from the rear but only that it was "possible" that a shot came from the rear. In the Report, the word "possible" was escalated into "probable." Despite Harris' sheepish grin at this discovery, it must be said that he appeared to have been fishing in shark water and to have hooked a baby minnow.

Specter, who had no answer at first for this deviation from the script, began to stutter and wander. Then Belin handed him the wrong page of the volume, after I had volunteered the correct one, and there the word "probable" did appear but in another context. Specter read "probable" with his booming district attorney voice, and thus the matter was settled. That is, almost settled. I asked if I might comment upon that for just a moment. The answer from Harris, who had now regained his composure and commitment, was a stern "no." The matter was settled. But it was not forgotten. Soon a portion of the film was shown.

This generally would herald an immediate period of relaxation, but this time when the cameras in the studio went off, the tension began to build. Specter scowled and raised his voice, registering in menacing tones. His anger was directed at a crumbling Harris. "Why did you ask that question? We never went over that. If you do that again—well, you'd better not. I'm not fooling now." And then the prosecuting attorney gestured toward me while still addressing Harris. "And you'd better shut that guy up too—I'm telling you now." I had spoken but a few words; mostly, they were, "May I say something now?"

Harris apologized. He promised to depart from the prearranged script no further. I left my little table and casually approached Harris. "Sir," I said, "I have the feeling that I have missed something by not arriving a week ago. Have you been having rehearsals in my absence?" Harris said that they had gone over the general area of the questions with the Commission lawyers. "Yes, we have." I suggested that it appeared that even some specifics had been agreed upon, based upon Specter's anger regarding one question and Harris' agreement to stray never again. Harris replied that "Mr. Specter only meant that if he was not prepared for a specific question then he would be placed in the embarrassing position of having to fumble for papers," and, added Harris, "Mr. Specter was certainly more than half right about that."

I observed that Harris had never even discussed general areas with me. I then asked Harris if I might have a copy of the script. He said that there were but three—his, Belin's and Specter's. Of course I could not doubt his word, but it seemed unusual that the BBC would mimeograph just three copies of a document, and it was that which prevented me from fully accepting his answer. During the next four hours I made fifteen requests to four different BBC representatives for a copy of the script.

At about 11:00 P.M. I found Fox and told him that he had made a solemn commitment to me the day before—that it had been agreed that at the outset of the program I might register a dissent from the program's format and choice of judges. Fox said that I would be able to have time at 11:30. While that did not meet my conception of the program's outset, I agreed. Closer to midnight than eleven, Harris said I could have a few minutes. I began by saying that the BBC had rendered a disservice to the truth when Harris stopped me and then picked up his phone to converse with the powers that be at the BBC.

On camera, silence. Then Harris spoke. I could almost have sympathized with him had he appeared torn between his commitment to his word of honor and the word from above. But that conflict evidently did not confront him. He said, "You may not discuss that subject at all." I then began to discuss the single-bullet theory. At this moment, Specter, who invented the whole thing, left his seat and charged over to Harris, telling him quite loudly, and now on camera, that I should not be allowed to trifle with his theory. I presume that since it had contributed to making him a district attorney and a candidate for the mayoralty, it was not to be fooled with. Harris supinely yielded once again, saying that I could only discuss subjects that came up in the second part of the program. I asked him to tell me what to talk about and I promised to discuss any subject he wished to hear, when he informed me that my time was up.

During a studio intermission, it had become plain that Bickel had a surprise in store. He was going to depart somewhat from his previously published position and say that he was not quite satisfied with the single-bullet theory and that if the single-bullet theory failed, there might be two assassins. Specter was livid. The fixed jury was no longer under control. Specter demanded an opportunity to answer Bickel, who had uttered hardly a word for almost five hours.

Harris indicated that Specter would be permitted to answer Bickel after he rendered his verdict. They must have wild court scenes in Philadelphia, I kept thinking. Bickel seemed a bit put out. Harris was insistent, at last showing the stern stuff he was made of, and Bickel evidently yielded.

After Bickel spoke briefly, Harris, as if the thought had just struck him, turned to Specter and said, sir, would you like to comment on that. Well, as long as he was asked, Specter was willing. It did occur to me during this exchange that this was the very subject that I was prevented from discussing because it was not in the "second part of the program"—whatever that meant. Surely, now that it had been introduced twice more, I would not be denied my first comment on the subject. Waiting until Specter concluded, I addressed a rather brief request to our chairman. "May I comment upon that?" The reply was "no."

The evening ended on an unmistakably light note. Lord Devlin summed up. He wanted us to let President Kennedy's soul rest in peace—anyway, suppose there was another assassin; no one had proved that he was a subversive, and if he wasn't subversive, what difference did it make? I was about to ask Lord Devlin for a definition of the word "subversive" that does not include one who kills his own President, but I decided not to.

The BBC officials invited me to wine and dine in my cubicle below. I was somehow neither hungry nor thirsty, just anxious to say a few words. Reporters from two London daily papers were there. They asked for an interview. I agreed. A young BBC official approached. He said no rooms were available for a press conference. It was not much before one in the morning, and I found it difficult to believe that the BBC could not scare up one empty room. "Oh, it's not that," the young man replied, "but we cannot permit you to talk with the press here." I said that the BBC had made a room available to me and that I wished to utilize it for a conference. He said that "it cannot be done."

The reporters were incredulous. We began to pack our belongings for a trip back to my hotel for the conference when the BBC relented and permitted it to take place there. I said, "The program had been rigged by the BBC to protect the Warren Commission lawyers from debate." I added that "we never ran into that sort of trouble in countries, France as one example, whose economies are not entirely dependent upon the United States. The Socialist government, indeed. Lenin must be twirling in his tomb."

I left BBC's Lime Grove studio to find a few citizens waiting outside. One offered his hand and his sympathy and said that "BBC does not speak for the English people, not this disgraceful night it doesn't." Others agreed.

At my hotel, a delegation of three, sent by twenty who had watched the program, expressed similar views but in stronger language. At Oxford University the next day, the students made their views known also. Hundreds of letters of support, sent by barristers, law students, the Royal Shakespeare Company and most often just by ordinary viewers, reached me in the next few days.

Harris told the *Evening Standard*, "I don't think Mark Lane has any grounds for complaint. He was here for one purpose, and one purpose only. As it was stated weeks ago, he was invited to attend so that if anybody made charges against him personally—for example, he was just interested in making money out of the whole business or that he was a Communist—he could answer the charges against him." Harris added that if he had permitted me to debate with Specter or Belin, "I should have had trouble with the two lawyers. They only came on the basis of this agreement." Harris added that if he had allowed me to enter the debate, the two Commission lawyers "would have walked off."

I have never refused a debate on equal grounds with Commission personnel. One must wonder what the two lawyers know about their own case which would cause them to walk away rather than debate.

The BBC told the *Evening Standard*, "We arranged a viewing session for a number of representatives from foreign TV networks, and they all made a point of saying how impressed they were by Mr. Harris' handling of the program." That statement appears to be untrue. I spoke with just one representative, Klaus Toksvig, of Danish TV. He told me that he was the only representative present from a foreign television network and that he believed the BBC program to have been extremely unfair.

The BBC spokesman concluded, "We arranged a press conference for Mr. Lane after the program ended."

As I prepared to leave London, a BBC program announced that Barrow and Southampton had tied, 2–2. I just knew that I couldn't be sure unless I read it in the London *Times* the next morning.

PART TWO: THE DEFENDERS

I · A CBS News Inquiry

11 TWO DOCUMENTARIES

CBS presented "The Warren Report" on four consecutive evenings beginning Sunday, June 25, 1967.[1] In a press release dated June 13, the network referred to its broadcasts as "unprecedented."[2] Very likely the four programs were dissimilar in length and expense from any that had gone before, but the conclusion offered was not unlike that submitted by CBS more than two and a half years earlier. On Sunday evening, September 27, 1964, the very day the Warren Report was issued, CBS presented its first Warren Report documentary.[3] That program was comprised of carefully edited interviews designed to provide support for the Commission's conclusions.

Emile de Antonio and I had agreed to make a film documentary to fill in many of the gaps created by the publicly available material. His previous film, *Point of Order*, which dealt with the Army-McCarthy hearings, had been constructed entirely out of film from the CBS kinescope archives, and the agreement that permitted the production made de Antonio and CBS partners in the venture.[4] In the spring of 1966, soon after he and I had returned to New York from interviewing witnesses in Dallas for the film, *Rush to Judgment*, de Antonio spoke with the CBS film librarian who offered to make the out-takes from the September 1964 CBS program available to us. Of course, we were quite pleased that material previously unavailable, including film sequences which we could not possibly duplicate (in at least one case the witness had died), might now be examined. The librarian explained that since the employees at CBS were unavailable for screening the footage for us during office hours, the viewing sessions would have to be held during the evening hours. We agreed, and an appointment was made for the late afternoon with the understanding that the session would last for several hours. When de Antonio and I arrived at CBS, we were ushered into a small workroom with a "Movieola."* The film was not projected onto a screen but run from one reel onto another through the machine, which permitted easy access to the film. This editing equipment allowed us to see and hear important sequences more than once without difficulty.

De Antonio has been in the film business for some time, and I had been in New York politics for a while. I think, however, that life had not adequately prepared us for that moment. The out-takes—the portion of the filmed interviews which were not shown to the public—revealed the technique that CBS had employed in making its first documentary. We saw footage for many hours that evening. Although the CBS charge per foot for the film (and film moves with great speed through a camera, as I had discovered) was by far the highest we had encountered, we agreed to purchase a great deal of it.

A contract is nothing more than an offer and acceptance. The CBS offer to sell the footage was initially made by its librarian by a telephone call. Thereafter we examined the subject of the proposed sale and immediately after doing so signed what is known in the industry as a "blue-sheet contract," the submission of which by a CBS employee constituted an affirmation of the original offer. In signing the contract we became liable for the cost of the film and CBS was thereby authorized to prepare copies of the film, assured that we had become financially responsible under the terms of the contract.

The next morning, de Antonio called the CBS library to arrange for another appointment to view additional footage. The first evening we had examined approximately five hours of what appeared to be some seventy hours of film. The librarian told de Antonio that a terrible mistake had been made. CBS would not sell any of the footage to us; in fact, CBS was soon going to destroy the film. The librarian then added that we could, of course, view no more film but that CBS had decided that we were not to be charged for the time spent by the CBS employee the evening before. Its decision was final and there was no appeal from it.†

* A "Movieola" is "a projection device for a motion-picture film allowing one person to see the film through a viewer and control its motion and speed, used in film editing, preparing titles, etc." [5]

† The general question of the exclusive control of all out-take material by the networks is an important one and requires serious study. Networks assert that they own the material and that they may do what they wish with it. They further assert that a breach of a confidential relationship between the electronic journalist and the person who is filmed might be occasioned by the release of the out-takes.

Yet there does exist a certain public interest in the material. The networks

Nevertheless, de Antonio wrote to the appropriate CBS executive, explaining that the obliteration of that film, some of it unique, would be the destruction of the raw material of history. Too much of the evidence had been destroyed by burning, too much was unavailable for examination and too many witnesses were no longer alive to be reinterviewed. CBS was in the truth-gathering business, and surely no news medium could eradicate the facts, could make them unavailable. The executive replied that he was sorry but that CBS could not make the film available.

What had de Antonio and I glimpsed that evening that evidently caused the network to reverse its policy within twenty-four hours? We had seen that which CBS, like the Warren Commission, has never made public—the working documents from which the final product was culled. The documentary was apparently constructed by experts in the entertainment business as if it were a fiction program. By way of contrast, in Sweden, when a filmed documentary was produced on the same subject, it was directed by a leading historian and professor of historical methods at the University of Stockholm.[6]

CBS evidently began with a script. Although the Report was published on the same day that the program was broadcast, the master script had been available for some time. The Report contained no surprises, the press reported when it was released. In addition, CBS apparently enjoyed excellent rapport with Commission personnel.* The script said that Oswald was the lone assassin. Many

---

share a monopoly that is government, therefore publicly created and regulated. Had an ordinary citizen equipped with a Brownie camera sought entrance into the basement of the Dallas Police and Courts Building to film the abortive transfer of Lee Harvey Oswald he might well have been denied admission. Yet the local officials welcomed the film crews of the networks due, no doubt, to their official capacity. Credentials, which grant access to historical moments, are given, by the public, to the networks, but are denied to the ordinary citizen. Do the networks then, having accepted that public trust, have the right to treat the resultant material as private property to be suppressed or destroyed at will?

* The CBS line into the Commission was almost too good. When the Report was initially written, it seems that little credence was placed in the bewildered testimony of Howard L. Brennan, who, although said to be an eyewitness to Oswald's firing of the weapon at the President, failed to pick Oswald out of a police line-up later that day. One report of an interview with a Commission lawyer stated that originally it had been decided to ignore Brennan as an important witness.[7] CBS had announced that it was to present its interviews with twenty-six of the important witnesses and apparently at that time Brennan was not included. However, it is reported, the Commission decided that Brennan was required as a witness, and the section of the Report which had dis-

hours of interviews were filmed, some with important witnesses. When a witness said something that challenged the script, that portion of the interview was snipped away and thus turned into an out-take. If the witness said, for example, that he heard the shots and at the time believed that they had come from the knoll, the interview might be halted and then begun again. What was said during the respite has not been recorded and remains as much an enigma as the Commission's all too frequent "off the record" discussions. When the filming resumed, the witness might say that, while at the time he thought the shots originated from the knoll area, he now believed that the evidence showed that the shots came from the Book Depository. When asked to repeat his conclusion as to where the shots originated, he might say, "Well, from the Book Depository." CBS would then present just that last fragment as the interviewee's answer.

The several hours of out-takes that we examined that spring evening in New York demonstrated the process employed first by the Commission itself and then later adopted by CBS. Professor Hugh Trevor-Roper, in writing of the Commission's effort, referred to it as the "quiet transformation" of evidence.[9] In the "Summary and Conclusions" of the Report, as in the final CBS document, "there is no hint" of a difference of opinion.[10] In the Report itself the statements and conclusions suggesting the central conclusion reached by the Commission are given prominence.[11] "It is only in the 'Hearings' that we see the process by which this conclusion was reached," observed Trevor-Roper.[12] But the electronic counterpart of the Commission's hearings, unlike much of the Commission's evidence, remains unpublished and unavailable. What we saw of it no doubt explains the reason for that determination. But for millions of Americans the program provided as reliable a view of the issues as would a glance at the visible portion of an iceberg reveal its true mass and shape to an inexperienced observer.

Not long before CBS's second effort, its much-heralded four-hour documentary, was aired, CBS contacted de Antonio. CBS decided to interview Malcolm Perry, who had seen the wound in the President's throat before he extended it by performing a tracheotomy.[13] The network was anxious to compare Perry's latest assertion with the much-publicized press conference at the Parkland Hospital where, immediately after the announcement of the President's death,

---

missed his importance was rewritten.[8] CBS, previously unprepared for the escalation of Brennan, flew him to New York and conducted an interview with him in time to meet the program's deadline.

Perry described the wound. Although that important interview was filmed and broadcast by CBS,[14] its representative said that, for some unexplained reason, CBS no longer possessed the film or tape. Then de Antonio inquired as to the reason for the telephone call and was informed that CBS thought that perhaps Judgment Films Corp. (the company that owned *Rush to Judgment*) had previously acquired a copy of that footage.

In the volume *Rush to Judgment*, I had suggested that the Commission should have secured a copy of the transcript of the Perry press conference and published it.[15] I added that the Commission failed to publish the transcript and that my efforts to locate the television and radio tapes of the broadcast had been fruitless, since the "networks and the local Dallas stations no longer possess them."[16] Defenders of the Report implied that such an allegation was "absurd."[17] Since the publication of *Rush to Judgment*, an interesting document bearing upon this question has come to my attention.[18] It is a letter to be found among the Commission's unpublished material in the National Archives from the director of the Secret Service, James J. Rowley, to the Warren Commission, dated March 25, 1964. This letter states:

> Reference is made to your letter of March 18, 1964, requesting certain documents for the examination of the Commission. The video tape and transcript of November 22, 1963, of the television interview of Doctor Malcolm Perry mentioned in your letter has not been located. After a review of the material and information available at the Dallas television and radio news stations, and the records of the NBC, ABC and CBS networks in New York City, no video tape or transcript could be found of a television interview with Doctor Malcolm Perry. CBS located in its New York office a television news clip on video tape of a broadcast by Walter Cronkite on November 22, 1963, in which he comments upon an interview with Doctor Perry by newsmen in Dallas. This, however, was not a television interview of the doctor. They also located a news clip covering an interview with Doctor Shaw at Parkland Hospital, in which Doctor Shaw comments upon the wounds received by Governor Connally, but in which no mention was made of the President's wounds.[19]

Since CBS was unable to secure a copy of its own film, it presented a recent interview with Perry and followed that with Cronkite's observation that "the neck wound, he told the press, looked like an entry wound, and he pointed to the front of his neck. In the transcript of that news conference there's no doubt that Dr. Perry made it sound as if he had a firm opinion."[20]

A number of the television and radio stations surrendered their films and tapes to Federal police officers. CBS said that it would destroy some of those that were left. Yet CBS was to say at the conclusion of its historic fourth hour that "it would be utterly impossible" for one to suspect that a "fierce and free press" might yield any of its prerogatives.[21]

For many months before the program was broadcast, those interested in the assassination and the Warren Report and those with insight into the media's activities were aware that CBS was planning something big. When it was all over, *TV Guide* said that program "took nine months, involved scores of people and cost just about $500,000."[22] *Newsweek*, in quoting CBS News President Richard S. Salant about the project, reported that a "staff of 25 spent six months and more than $250,000 on the effort."[23] In a press handout prepared by CBS, Salant said that the unit "worked for nine months" and that "more than 90,000 feet of film was shot for the broadcasts, with about 5,300 used on the air."[24]

I had been characterized as a Commission critic for some time, and I was therefore surprised that CBS had not contacted me. My publishers—Holt, Rinehart and Winston—had been acquired by CBS after the publication of *Rush to Judgment*, and through their good offices I inquired about the program. I was informed that the content was secret. I requested an opportunity to make a statement for the documentary, and several days later I received a telephone call from one of the associate producers, Robert Richter. He was in New York and I in Stanford, California. He said he could fly to the West Coast to interview me. I suggested that getting a film crew to my somewhat inaccessible location on the Stanford University campus might be too much trouble and that I planned to be in New York in the next few days anyway. He explained that CBS was not going to conduct a filmed interview with me but that he wanted to ask me a few questions.

I called Richter when I arrived in New York and we arranged to meet at my hotel. It was a warm and sunny day, and at my suggestion we walked through Central Park as we talked. He impressed me as having a good grasp of the evidence. He was familiar with the many weaknesses in the single-bullet theory and other aspects of the Commission's case. I made two requests to CBS through Richter. I asked for an opportunity to cross-examine one of the witnesses.*

Richter contacted me later with the news that CBS had agreed to

* The witness was Seymour Weitzman, who together with another officer located a rifle on the sixth floor of the Texas School Book Depository.[25] This question is more fully explored later in this book.[26]

film an interview with me, but he did not know whether it would be broadcast. He added that CBS had decided that I could not question any witness. The interview was to be shot in Stanford. Richter later said that CBS had also decided to interview William Turner, a former FBI agent, and he asked if that interview could be conducted in my home as well. I agreed and the film crew, Turner, Richter and Bill Stout, who conducted the interviews, arrived. In order to preserve a record of the interview, I tape-recorded it on my own portable machine.

I had expected that little of what I had to say would be broadcast, since the network's lack of enthusiasm for the interview was only too obvious. Then *TV Guide* carried a half-page "close-up" regarding the special and listed but four persons who were to appear: "Texas governor John Connally, writer Mark Lane, Oswald's mother, and DA Jim Garrison of New Orleans."[27] The editor of *TV Guide* informed me that the "close-up" was "based on information provided by the producer of the program."[28] The rumors that preceded the program implied that the documentary was to support the Warren Report, yet of the four persons listed as participants in the most important promotional device, three had rejected the Report's conclusions and one had quarreled with an essential aspect of the Commission's case. The programs were, of course, a defense of the Commission's lone-assassin theory.

Had CBS deliberately misled its audience as to the nature of its program in order to appeal to the vast majority who could not accept the official explanation, or had *TV Guide* made an error?

In either event, the stage was set for the CBS spectacular. Connally was used in an attempt to soften his original damaging statement that the bullet which hit him had not first hit the President.[29] I appeared in a fragment or two.[30] Mrs. Oswald, who had been ridiculed in the past, was heard to allege again that her son was innocent.[31] And Garrison was presented so that he could be refuted.[32]

Even before the first CBS broadcast, there were indications that CBS may have entered into the investigation with a preconception. Eleanor Roberts, writing in the Boston *Traveler* more than two months before the programs, said:

> A most unusual television experiment is taking place at CBS News—the preparation of a documentary on another look at the Warren Commission Report—which may never be telecast. Camera crews are fanning out all over the country—one was in Framingham last week—developing material for the news special. But unless it sheds new light on the report, weakening the argument of those who criticize it, it may never be aired, a CBS spokesman revealed. . . . "If we get some-

thing new and constructive, we hope to air the documentary by mid-June," the CBS News executive said, "but we're playing it by ear until all the films are in."[33]

While Miss Roberts has not, to my knowledge, revealed the source for her story, she has reaffirmed her belief in its accuracy.[34]*

Raymond J. Marcus was an early critic of the Commission's conclusions. He has thoroughly examined two areas: the single-bullet thesis, about which he has published an excellent monograph;[36] and the still and motion pictures taken on the scene. Richter visited him in Boston on May 22, 1967. Marcus urged CBS to broadcast the still photograph taken by Mary Moorman, who was standing to the left and rear of the Presidential limousine when the fatal shot was fired.[37] Her picture was taken at about the time of that shot and appears to correspond approximately to frame 313 of the motion picture taken by Abraham Zapruder.[38]

The Moorman photograph, when enlarged, reveals the presence of man-like images behind the wooden fence and the concrete wall on the knoll. Of course the figures are not of the quality that a portrait photographer might boast. In order that persons unfamiliar with photographic analysis might relate the figures to some other and similar experience, Marcus added to his portfolio of assassination photographs the picture showing James Meredith sprawled on a road in Mississippi which revealed his assailant in the background. Marcus said that he was struck by the similarity in appearance of the man who shot Meredith and a figure in the Moorman photograph: "I do not mean that I ever took them to be the same man, but only that the two faces, obviously photographed under somewhat similar lighting conditions, and both against mottled backgrounds, appeared so similar that I believed the image in the Meredith picture lent further (though unnecessary) credence to the validity of [the image in the Moorman photograph] as a human figure."[39]

On May 29 Marcus met in New York with Richter and Leslie Midgley, the producer of the CBS documentary. The various photographs had been shown to Midgley by Richter before the meeting, and they were again examined at the meeting. Midgley insisted that he saw nothing in the Moorman photograph that he would take to be a man. By way of contrast, he pointed to an enlarged portion of one photograph where he said he did see a man, explaining, "That's the man who shot Meredith."[40] He had, in fact, inadvertently selected an

* Subsequently the television reviewer for the *New York Times* reported that the program's producer planned the broadcasts as an answer to *Rush to Judgment*.[35]

enlargement of the Moorman photograph and had pointed to the figure behind the wall on the knoll.[41]

That reluctant but confident identification by Midgley tends to confirm the study by Marcus, Richard Sprague and others who have examined still and motion pictures taken from various angles which appear to show at least two men, both holding straight objects, in the area behind the wall on the knoll. This certainly would seem to have been a fruitful area for exploration by CBS. In producing a filmed documentary, that material which appears to be important but which is not filmic may have to be rejected, but here was evidence of potentially great importance which existed entirely on celluloid.

On June 19 Marcus wrote to Midgley and established a written record of Midgley's identification of the figure in the Moorman photograph.[42] Four days later, Midgley responded, stating that when Marcus had showed him the picture which "you [Marcus] believe to be a picture of a rifleman, I then said—having just been over it with Mr. Richter—that it was a picture of the man who shot Meredith."[43]

Under the circumstances, I looked forward to the CBS analysis of the images behind the fence and wall on the knoll. I had met two important CBS executives at a social affair not long before the broadcasts. They informed me that their program would offer no conclusions, would point out facts and would permit the viewer to reach his own conclusions. CBS had conducted a number of significant tests, one of them informed me. He added that CBS had resolved the question of the Dealey Plaza acoustics by conducting on-site tests with sound measuring devices. I told him how pleased I was, since I had been advocating that test for some years. I had, in fact, publicly urged the Commissioners to make such tests, but they had declined. I asked, "What have the tests shown?" The executive said, "That's a secret. You'll just have to wait for the program to find out."

Due to the statements of CBS officials, I anticipated broadcasts that might present a serious analysis of the images in the Moorman photograph and that would demonstrate the acoustics in Dealey Plaza. I certainly was entirely unprepared for the oversimplified conclusions, repeated catechetically by Walter Cronkite throughout the series. CBS concluded that there could have been no second assassin, for it was inconceivable that one would have vanished without leaving a trace behind. The network made no reference to the personal conclusion of the program's producer that he saw "a picture of the man" when he had examined the Moorman photograph, and no analysis of that picture was presented.

Midgley was later to state publicly, "Nothing would have pleased me more than to have found a second assassin. We looked for one and it isn't our fault that we didn't find one. But the evidence just isn't there. There's no physical evidence at all."[44]

The results of the acoustics test were not presented and CBS made no reference to their executive's claim that such a test had been conducted.

In paid advertisements preceding the four one-hour programs, CBS urged its potential audience thusly: "They could very well be the most valuable four hours you ever spent with television."[45] The network had gathered "new material on every vital question concerning the events surrounding the assassination," but that promise was kept no better than the commitment to reveal "new and enlightening tests."[46]* What had evidently been the original approach—to present the evidence and permit the viewer to draw his own conclusions—bore no resemblance to the final concept.

12 DID OSWALD SHOOT THE PRESIDENT?

The first of the four one-hour CBS programs was devoted primarily to answering the question, "Did Lee Harvey Oswald shoot President Kennedy?"[1] In order to answer that question, the network said, "we must resolve some lesser questions."[2] The first was: "Did Oswald own a rifle?"[3]

Before he had examined a single piece of evidence relating to that question, Walter Cronkite answered it for his viewers: "There is no reasonable doubt that Oswald owned a Mannlicher-Carcano rifle No. C2766."[4] Later he turned his attention to a photograph which purportedly showed Oswald posing with a rifle.[5] This photograph, Cronkite said, referring both to Oswald and the alleged assassination weapon, "shows him with an identical rifle."[6] Perhaps that assertion constituted part of the "new material" that had been promised. But it seems that there is no basis for the allegation, which, in fact, conflicts with the testimony of Lyndal L. Shaneyfelt, the FBI photography expert.[7] Shaneyfelt told the Warren Commission that he was unable to state that the rifle depicted in the photograph was the same weapon identified as Commission Exhibit 139, the alleged assassination rifle.[8]

In addition, Cronkite said, "a professional photographer and photo analyst [had] made an independent study, of the original picture and negative."[9] The "professional photographer" who had made the

* An analysis of the published tests is to be found in later chapters of this book. See pages 98–115.

"independent study" was Lawrence Schiller, former business agent for Jack Ruby, referred to in CBS's advance publicity blurbs only as a "photographic expert."[10] While the expertise and independence of the network's "professional" remain in doubt, there need be no withholding of judgment as to the authenticity of the "negative" which CBS claims he examined.[11] It does not exist.[12] Said the Warren Commission, "The negative was never recovered."[13] Surely, then, this constitutes the "new material."

If CBS sought the services of a professional photographer, it is to be hoped that one might have been located among its own employees. I have appeared on scores of programs broadcast by CBS stations and affiliates. In many instances, I have sought the advice of trained cameramen employed by the stations regarding the picture in question. In almost every instance those professional photographers have suggested that the picture appears to be an obviously doctored photograph. Certainly CBS was required to go beyond its own personnel for medical and ballistics opinions. Yet its need to seek outside assistance for photographic aid is less easily demonstrated. In the event that supplementary help was deemed a necessity, the special qualifications of its singular choice raise additional questions. Available to CBS and its substantial budget were the services of the country's finest photoanalysts in industry and at the leading universities. The only known special qualification possessed by Schiller, other than his relationship with Jack Ruby, was his insistence long before the CBS program that the photograph was authentic.[14]

It is interesting to fathom the CBS concept of the life of the average American if it imagined that watching Jack Ruby's business agent after he studied a nonexistent negative might constitute "the most valuable" time spent watching television.

The magic medium of television transported the audience rapidly from the ridiculous to the sublime. Before the series had been concluded, Cronkite asked, "Why did Ruby kill Oswald?"[15] In response, CBS produced four witnesses and a conclusion.[16] Barney Weinstein, a competitor of Ruby's in what the press has politely called the Dallas nightclub business, guessed that "he thought that would make him above everybody else"—including his competitors, was the impression conveyed.[17]

The next two CBS witnesses were identified as "two of Jack Ruby's girls."[18] While that anomalous description was less than adequate, further investigation has revealed that they were strippers who had at one time performed at Ruby's Dallas club.[19] The full name of neither was provided, but Dan Rather's question provided a clue as to the first name of one: "Diana, why do you think Jack shot Oswald?"[20] A CBS transcript, not generally available to the viewing public at the time of the broadcasts, referred to the other as "Alice."[21] But Dan didn't refer to Alice's first name in inquiring about why Jack shot Oswald.[22]

Next, George Senator, Ruby's former roommate, cryptically suggested that the answer resided in Ruby's own explanation of his act.[23] Not to be outdone, Cronkite, for CBS, offered his own suggestion.[24] "Ruby died six months ago of cancer," he remarked, "maintaining to the last that he was no conspirator, that he had killed Oswald out of anger and a desire to shield Jacqueline Kennedy from the ordeal of a trial at which she would have had to appear as a witness."[25]

Three months earlier, however, *Newsweek* magazine had presented the facts about that hoary myth concerning Ruby's motivation.[26] The magazine reported that the comment about Jacqueline Kennedy, "one of the reasons he [Ruby] frequently gave" as an excuse, now seems to have been a deliberate falsehood."[27] *Newsweek* continued:

> In 1964, Ruby, who feared that his cell was bugged, signaled lawyer Joe Tonahill for a sheet of notebook paper and a pencil. He scribbled a note that Tonahill only now has revealed. It read: "Joe, you should know this. Tom Howard told me to say that I shot Oswald so that Caroline and Mrs. Kennedy wouldn't have to come to Dallas to testify. OK?" Howard, now dead, was Ruby's lawyer for a short time. Ruby insisted to Tonahill that he didn't know why he shot Oswald.[28]

But based upon the decidedly old material, CBS concluded that "the Oswald murder today still appears to have been not a conspiracy, but an impulse—meaningless violence born of meaningless violence."[29]

CBS endorsed the Commission's conclusion that a package which Oswald carried to work from Irving, Texas, on the morning of the assassination contained the disassembled Mannlicher-Carcano rifle.[30] Only two witnesses—Wesley Frazier[31] and his sister, Mrs. Linnie Mae Randle[32]—saw Oswald carrying the package that morning.[33] Each testified that the disassembled weapon, which measured 34.8 inches,[34] could not possibly have been contained in the short package which Oswald carried.[35] In order to give a contrary impression of their statements, however, CBS was obliged to misrepresent their remarks.[36] Dan Rather, the CBS commentator, said:

> Within this package I have a disassembled Mannlicher-Carcano rifle identical to Oswald's. Before I tell you the dimensions, you might want to try to estimate them, as Mrs. Randle and Wesley Frazier did, from memory. Mrs. Randle variously estimated Oswald's package . . . as 27

or 28 inches long; her brother, Wesley Frazier, said about two feet, "give or take a few inches."[37]

Thus Rather created the impression that both Frazier and Mrs. Randle had merely taken a casual guess as to the length of the package.[38] There need be no imprecision on this point. On December 1, 1963, the FBI asked Frazier to mark the point on the back seat of his automobile where the bag reached when placed there with one end against the door.[39] The FBI agents noted that the "distance between the point on the seat and the door was 27 inches."[40] Similarly, Mrs. Randle was asked by FBI agents to indicate the size of the bag that Oswald carried.[41] She caused the sack to be folded over until it reached "the proper length of the sack as seen by her on November 22, 1963," the FBI reported, which, when measured by the agents, was "found to be 27 inches long."[42]

Not only were the estimates of the only two witnesses who had seen the package consistent, but the accuracy of these estimates is supported by the fact that they were asked to indicate the length involved in different ways.[43] Frazier testified that Oswald had walked ahead of him to the Book Depository Building, carrying the package tucked into his armpit with the bottom of it cupped in his palm.[44] "From what I seen walking behind he had it under his arm," Frazier told the Commission, "and you couldn't tell that he had a package from the back."[45] When Rather cupped the 34.8-inch package in his palm, the top of the bag protruded well above his shoulder.[46] "You can decide whether Frazier, walking some 50 feet behind [Oswald] and, in his own words, not paying much attention, might have missed the few inches of the narrow end of such a package sticking up past Oswald's shoulder," Rather remarked.[47]

But before you could decide—in the next breath, in fact—Cronkite saved the audience the trouble: "Despite the dispute about just how he carried his package, the reasonable answer to this question is that he did take a rifle to the Book Depository Building."[48] Of course there was no "dispute" about how Oswald carried the package.[49] Only one man saw him carry it into the Book Depository, and he was not doubtful about how it was carried or what was visible from the rear.[50] And "just how he carried the package" in the circumstances was determinative of the question: Could it have been the rifle? Furthermore, CBS did not inform its viewers of the testimony of Jack Dougherty, an employee of the Depository who saw Oswald enter the building that morning from the front and who said he did not see Oswald carrying a package.[51] If the package was tucked close to Oswald's side and under his arm, as Frazier testified it was, it is understandable why Dougherty did not see it.[52] His testimony would be incomprehensible, however, if Oswald had carried a package like Rather's which protruded well above his shoulder.[53]

In *Rush to Judgment* I pointed out that the Warren Report had quoted Mrs. Randle as stating that Oswald "carried a 'heavy brown bag.' "[54] This was misleading, I noted, since it can clearly be seen when read in context that Mrs. Randle applied the adjective "heavy" to the texture of the paper of which the package was made and not to the weight of the package itself.[55] This may well be crucial, since it is said that Oswald claimed to have carried lightweight curtain rods, not a heavy rifle.[56] In an excerpt from an interview shown on the CBS program, Mrs. Randle confirmed this: "It was made out of a heavy brown paper with heavy-looking tape on it."[57] Repeating the Commission's distortions as well as its conclusions, CBS said that Oswald carried "a heavy-looking package."[58]

"Our next question," Cronkite said, "concerns Oswald's whereabouts at the time of the murder: Where was Oswald when the shots were fired?"[59] CBS presented interviews with a number of Book Depository employees, who were heard to recount that they had observed Oswald at various times on November 22 prior to the assassination.[60]

But CBS did little to explore the question it had raised itself.[61] "The last man known to have seen Lee Harvey Oswald before the assassination," Dan Rather said, "was another co-worker, Charles Givens."[62] Givens said he saw Oswald on the sixth floor at about noon that day, half an hour before the shooting.[63] Although Givens may have been the last man known by CBS to have seen Oswald before 12:30 P.M., he was not of necessity the last person.[64] An employee of the Book Depository, Mrs. Carolyn Arnold, told the FBI on November 26, 1963, that she had left her office on the second floor of the building "to go downstairs and stand in front of the building to view the Presidential Motorcade. As she was standing in front of the building, she stated she thought she caught a fleeting glimpse of Lee Harvey Oswald standing in the hallway between the front door and the double doors leading to the warehouse, located on the first floor. She could not be sure that this was Oswald, but said she felt it was."[65] In a subsequent signed statement which she executed for the same agency, Mrs. Arnold said she "left the Texas School Book Depository Building at about 12:25 PM, November 22, 1963."[66]* If Mrs. Arnold saw Oswald on the first floor of the De-

* In the statement of November 26, which is not signed and which the witness did not have an opportunity to see in order to verify its accuracy, the FBI agent who conducted the interview said Mrs. Arnold "believed the time [when she saw Oswald] to be a few minutes before 12:15." [67]

pository, near the front entrance, only minutes before the assassination, then clearly he was not, as CBS stated, "on the sixth floor" at that time.[68] The significance of Mrs. Arnold's comment is appreciated when placed alongside the testimony of the Commission's witness who claimed that the man he saw fire from the sixth-floor window had been there for about seven minutes before he fired.[69]

A well-known photograph taken during the assassination, which shows the persons standing at the front entrance of the Book Depository Building, may provide corroboration for Mrs. Arnold's observation.[70] This picture depicts an individual who bears a striking resemblance to Lee Harvey Oswald.[71] The Commission alleged that this individual was another employee of the company, Billy Lovelady, but it failed to resolve substantial contradictions in the evidence relating to that question.[72]* CBS could have made a positive contribution to the fund of information now available regarding Oswald's whereabouts by interviewing Mrs. Arnold and Billy Lovelady, but neither witness appeared on the program.[74]

If Oswald could not have descended from the window at the southeast corner of the sixth floor rapidly enough to reach the second-floor lunchroom, where he was seen by the superintendent of the Depository, Roy S. Truly, and a police officer, Marrion L. Baker, slightly more than a minute after the shots were fired, then this would constitute persuasive evidence that Oswald may not have been "on the sixth floor" at 12:30, as CBS contended.[75] According to the Warren Report's account of the incident, Truly and Baker entered the building almost immediately after the shooting and ran up the rear staircase.[76] The Report continued:

> When they reached the second-floor landing on their way up to the top of the building, Patrolman Baker thought he caught a glimpse of someone through a small glass window in the door separating the hall area near the stairs from the small vestibule leading into the lunchroom. Gun in hand, he rushed to the door and saw a man about 20 feet away walking toward the other end of the lunchroom. The man was empty-handed. At Baker's command, the man turned and approached him.[77]

The individual in question was, of course, Lee Harvey Oswald.[78] The Commissioners conducted timed tests which indicated to their satisfaction that Oswald could have reached the lunchroom from the sixth-floor window just in time to have been observed by Baker at the location where the patrolman said he saw Oswald.[79] There were certain circumstances, however, which might have virtually pre-

* These contradictions are discussed in detail in *Rush to Judgment*.[73]

cluded the possibility that Oswald had run down from the sixth floor. If, for example, Oswald was not "emptyhanded" but, as the original reports had it, had been drinking a Coca-Cola—there was a vending machine in the lunchroom where the encounter occurred—then he almost certainly could not have left the sixth-floor window after firing the shots, hid the rifle on the sixth floor, run down to the second floor, entered the lunchroom, operated the machine, waited for the bottle to be dispensed, opened it and been "drinking a Coke" when stopped by Baker.[80] There is evidence that indicates that Oswald was "drinking a Coke" at that time.[81]

When Baker testified before the Commission on March 25, 1964, he claimed that Oswald "had nothing" in his hands at the time.[82] Subsequently, however, Baker was asked—for unexplained reasons—to submit a handwritten "voluntary signed statement" regarding certain aspects of his activities on November 22.[83] "On the second floor, where the lunch room is located," Baker wrote, "I saw a man standing in the lunch room, drinking a Coke."[84] The words "drinking a Coke" were subsequently scratched out and the change was initialed "MLB" by the patrolman.[85] If Oswald was "emptyhanded" when Baker saw him, then why should such a mistake occur in a handwritten statement so many months later?[86]

A reasonable answer seems to be that Oswald may have been "drinking a Coke" when stopped by Baker shortly after the shooting on November 22. CBS, however, which declared that its conclusions were undoubtedly the most "reasonable" that could be reached, declined to explore this sensitive area.[87]

"We now come to our fourth question for tonight," Cronkite continued.[88] "Was Oswald's rifle fired from the building?"[89] In answer to this, CBS cited the "physical evidence found within the building" upon which the Commission "placed major reliance," and the network concluded that "from the ballistic evidence it seems that the answer to the question . . . is yes."[90] Yet the program promoted as an answer to the critical questions failed to raise any of the basic points mentioned by the critics regarding the Mannlicher-Carcano rifle itself.[91] For example, in *Rush to Judgment* I pointed out that the FBI, after testing the C2766 rifle, stated that "a small amount of white smoke was visible" when the weapon was fired in broad daylight.[92] Yet none of the witnesses who testified that they had seen a rifle being fired from the sixth-floor window said he had seen any smoke emitted when the shot was fired.[93] CBS failed to explain, let alone mention, this discrepancy.[94]

The network dealt superficially with the issue of the identification of the rifle found on the sixth floor of the Depository less than an hour after the assassination.[95] Two officers—Seymour Weitzman[96] and Eugene Boone[97]—discovered the weapon, and each stated explicitly in a signed report on November 23 that the rifle was a 7.65 Mauser.[98] Weitzman's statement was a sworn one, and he gave a detailed description of the weapon both in that affidavit and in an interview with the FBI.[99] The Commission alleged that Weitzman had only a "glimpse" or a "glance" at the rifle, and that accounted for the so-called misidentification of the weapon.[100] But the Report never dealt with the other officers who also said it was a Mauser, and it never explained how Weitzman could swear to such a detailed statement about the rifle if he had only glanced at it.[101] CBS, which purported to be filling the gaps left by the Commission's less than thorough investigation, had had two years in which to elicit new information, yet here again it offered nothing more than a rerun of the Warren Commission's conclusions, which could have been presented, word for word, more than two years earlier.[102]

CBS presented Weitzman, who said again that he had seen the weapon at a glance, that at the time he had said "it's a German Mauser," that "it's an Italian-type gun," and that "it looked like a Mauser, which I said it was."[103] Rather summed up in this fashion: "So Mr. Weitzman now seems sure that the rifle was indeed Oswald's Mannlicher-Carcano."[104] Yet Weitzman had not said that.[105] He had neither mentioned Oswald nor a Mannlicher-Carcano, and there is no evidence to suggest that the circumstances have altered since Weitzman's testimony before the Commission, which had declined to allow him to examine the weapon for purposes of identification then.[106]

I had met with Robert Richter, an assistant producer of the CBS program, under circumstances that have been previously described. I told him that many of the Commission's defenders had agreed that the Report had been flawed by the decision to deny counsel to the accused. I suggested that CBS might make an important contribution to the evidence and create an exciting program if it arranged for an adversary procedure.

"Let me give you an example," I said. "Since you plan to have Weitzman on the program, if you were to give me approximately two minutes to cross-question him we might learn something new. The Commission was satisfied with his 'just a glance' answer, but logic demands that he be asked how he could give so many details about the weapon, why he swore to them in an affidavit and why his associates on the police force agreed with him at that time. Also, a trip to the Archives could be arranged, where he might see the alleged murder weapon. Then we could ask him, for the first time, if that was the weapon he found. I'm willing. I want no fee, I'll travel where necessary and at any time that's convenient for CBS and Weitzman."

When next I met him, Richter said that CBS had declined the offer. The failure to ask the relevant questions in this instance could not be explained by ignorance.

13 CBS IS CONTENTED

On the third night, June 27, 1967, CBS turned its attention to the circumstances surrounding the death of Officer J. D. Tippit, allegedly slain by Oswald forty-five minutes after the assassination.[1]* "Could Oswald have made his way to the scene of Officer Tippit's murder?" Cronkite asked.[3] And: "Did Oswald have time to get to Tenth and Patton in time for the fatal encounter with Tippit?"[4] I know of no responsible critic of the Commission who has raised this point, which CBS pretended was a vital argument of the critics.[5] Oswald had more than half an hour to cover the distance of approximately four miles.[6] A motor vehicle averaging less than ten miles per hour could have delivered Oswald there in sufficient time. The basic issue is whether or not Oswald appeared at all of the places en route to the Tippit killing site that the Commission alleged he did.[7] The CBS answer, undocumented and unexplained, to this essential question consumed only a few seconds: "A CBS newsman, following the Warren Commission blueprint, found that 45 minutes was ample time."[8]

The next question dealing with the Tippit murder was: "Why was Officer Tippit in Oak Cliff off his normal beat?"[9] CBS alleged that "a lot of critics," all unnamed, "have made quite a thing out of the fact that Officer Tippit was not in his district when he was killed."[10] The network presented Murray Jackson, the Dallas police radio dispatcher, who said that Tippit had not been sent to Oak Cliff alone. Tippit and another patrolman—R. C. Nelson, who was in another squad car in Oak Cliff—were instructed to "move into [the] Central Oak Cliff area."[11] No other patrol cars in the entire city of Dallas received such specific orders at that time.[12] But neither Jackson nor CBS revealed the full story.[13] Tippit alone went to Oak Cliff.[14] Nelson proceeded to the Texas School Book Depository.[15] Thus there is some doubt about the broadcast which allegedly directed both Nelson and Tippit to the central Oak Cliff area, where

* The second program in the CBS series was devoted to a discussion of the source of the shots and the medical evidence.[2] I have dealt with these issues in separate chapters in this text. See pages 185–250.

Tippit was killed shortly thereafter.[16] Moreover, CBS did not ask Dispatcher Jackson to explain why he had ignored two calls from Tippit at 1:08 P.M., a very short time before the officer was slain.[17]

Cronkite seemed content with a simple solution: "The answer to this question is that he had been sent to Oak Cliff by the police dispatcher."[18] Since we have known that answer for more than three and a half years, it seemed reasonable to assume that CBS would then probe the real question: "Why?" Instead: "Who shot Officer Tippit?"[19] Only two eyewitnesses were presented by CBS to answer this question.[20] One was Ted Callaway, who never mentioned Oswald on the broadcast.[21] The other was Domingo Benavides, who had testified three years earlier before the Warren Commission.[22] At that time the witness swore that he had told Dallas police officers on November 22 that he could not identify the dead patrolman's assailant and for that reason was not even taken to a police line-up to view Oswald.[23] When asked by the Commission attorney if he could add anything to that, "he testified that the picture of Oswald which he saw later on television bore a resemblance to the man who shot Officer Tippit," according to the Warren Report.[24] Even the Commission appeared to concede that Benavides could not make an identification of Oswald.[25]

Nevertheless Benavides contradicted his sworn statements for CBS.[26] His memory having apparently improved with the passage of time, it was fresher in June 1967 than it had been on November 22, 1963, and at the time of his appearance before Commission counsel in April 1964.[27] Benavides told CBS that there was "no doubt at all" in his mind that Oswald had killed Tippit.[28] "I could even tell you how he combed his hair and the clothes he wore and what have you, all the details. And if he had a scar on his face, I could probably have told you about it, but—you don't forget things like that."[29] But he had, of course, forgotten all of that, just after he had witnessed the shooting, when he informed the police that he could not identify the killer.[30] It had remained forgotten five months later when Benavides appeared before counsel for the Commission.[31] Only for CBS did Benavides recall that which he had previously forgotten.[32] A witness, of course, has the right to change his mind. Had the CBS program been an official inquiry, Benavides might have found himself facing a perjury indictment, so different were his statements there from what had gone before.[33] Concomitant with the witness' right to reverse his original recollection of his observation is the right of the assessing public to be informed as to the reason. Yet CBS asked not a single question of that nature.[34] Further, CBS refused to inform its audience that Benavides had ever previously taken a different position.[35] The only descriptive or background information afforded were Cronkite's words that Benavides "was at the wheel of a truck across the street from the scene" and that for unexplained reasons he did not go to the police station that night.[36]

A discussion of the murder of Officer Tippit brought out the best of neither the Warren Commission nor CBS.[37] The Commission, however, presented more of the relevant evidence.[38] In his appearance before the Commission, FBI firearms expert Cortlandt Cunningham testified that "it was not possible from an examination" of the bullets found in Tippit's body "to determine whether or not they had been fired—these bullets themselves—had . . . been fired from Oswald's revolver."[39] He added that he had examined test bullets that had been fired from the revolver and that even in a controlled test situation where maximum care was taken to preserve the individual microscopic characteristics that might be present "it was not possible . . . to determine whether or not consecutive test bullets obtained from this revolver had been fired in this weapon."[40]

An Illinois police expert, nevertheless, claimed that he could find sufficient markings on one bullet "to lead me to the conclusion that that projectile" was fired by the pistol in question, a conclusion characterized by the FBI expert as "not possible."[41] The Commission's Report presented both conflicting opinions.[42] CBS interviewed only the Illinois police expert and declined to disclose his police ties, identifying him only as an "Illinois ballistics identification expert."[43] Cronkite observed that one of the bullets "could be positively identified with that revolver."[44] The network failed to mention Cunningham or his conclusions.[45]

After having adduced the statements of two eyewitnesses, one who never mentioned Oswald in the televised interview and the other who had originally stated that he could not make any identification just following the crime, and having ignored the ballistics evidence of the FBI expert, CBS asserted that the answer to its question "is that Lee Harvey Oswald shot J. D. Tippit."[46]

As the third program drew to a close, CBS presented a fragment from a filmed interview with me.[47] I referred to a model of Dealey Plaza and then said:

> The first shot struck the President in the back of the right shoulder, according to the FBI report, and indicates therefore that it came from some place in the rear—which includes the possibility of it coming from the Book Depository Building. The second bullet struck the President in the throat from the front, came from behind this wooden fence, high up on a grassy knoll. Two more bullets were fired. One struck the Elm—the Main Street curb, and caused some concrete, or

> lead, to scatter up and strike a spectator named James Tague in the face. Another bullet, fired from the rear, struck Governor Connally in the back. As the limousine moved up to approximately this point, another bullet was fired from the right front, struck the President in the head, drove him—his body, to the left and to the rear, and drove a portion of his skull backward, to the left and to the rear. Five bullets, fired from at least two different directions, the result of a conspiracy.[48]

William Turner, for ten years an agent of the Federal Bureau of Investigation, commented next.[49] In addition to mentioning that he is "a former FBI agent," Cronkite introduced him as a man with "an even more elaborate account" and one who "has become a warm supporter of District Attorney Garrison."[50] Turner had conducted an independent investigation and his conclusions were similar to mine.[51] Cronkite summed up, "In the light of what we have exposed over the past three evenings, it's difficult to take such versions seriously."[52]

The program concluded on what was unmistakably intended as a light note. Cronkite, Rather and Eddie Barker, the news director from CBS's Dallas affiliate, had been presenting the Government's case for three hours. Cronkite observed that "this is a natural moment to pause."[53] He then interviewed Rather and Barker to find out how they felt about the Warren Report.[54] Rather said of the shot from the sixth-floor window not known to have been duplicated by any marksman since November 22, 1963, despite repeated efforts, "It was an easy shot."[55] The viewer might have had some doubts, since CBS cameras provided a shot of the motorcade route from the window. To those who prefer to make up their own minds, ostensibly the audience CBS sought, Rather added, "A much easier shot than even it looks in our pictures."[56]

Cronkite asked Rather, "Are you contented with the basic finding of the Warren Commission?"[57] Rather said he was "contented with the basic finding of the Warren Commission," indicating that he wasn't convinced about some evidence which he did not consider to be absolutely necessary to the final conclusion.[58] He added, "As to the basic conclusion, I agree."[59]

> CRONKITE: Eddie?
> BARKER: I agree with it, Walter.[60]

Barker then added that he "felt the night of November 22nd that he [Oswald] was the one who had shot the President, and nothing has come to light since then to change my opinion a bit."[61] Barker felt that Oswald was guilty even before Oswald had been charged with the crime by the Dallas authorities and before any evidence was available. One was constrained to agree with Cronkite at last. It is difficult to take some versions seriously, and CBS had indeed exposed much over the past three evenings.

14 AMERICANS ARE CONSPIRACY-MINDED

The fourth evening was perhaps the most revealing. CBS presented John McCloy, a member of the former Commission.[1] He too agreed with the Commission's conclusions, stating that "there was nothing fraudulent about it, there was nothing sinister about it—either conscious or subconscious, in my judgment."[2] He conceded that "we may have erred somewhere along the line," but that he was satisfied with the conclusions.[3] In his lengthy interview, McCloy was not asked a single question about the problems raised by the evidence.[4] Perhaps CBS felt that McCloy, who fortunately was able to make the show, might not be too knowledgeable regarding the facts since during the ten months he served as a Commissioner he had attended only sixteen of the Commission's fifty-one sessions.[5]

Cronkite introduced the final question, "Could America believe the Warren Report?" by asking "why, by a considerable margin, more people have bought copies of books attacking the Report than have bought the Report itself."[6] There was no direct answer forthcoming, for it appeared that CBS had erred again, this time in regard to book sales figures. Dr. Seymour Lipset, a Harvard sociologist, offered, "If the President is assassinated, not because of a rational plot, but because of just a nut who has a gun, then any—not only any President can be assassinated this way—which he can be—but anybody else can."[7] That having been established, Henry Steele Commager was introduced: "And we were—I think we have been persuaded very largely since the beginnings of the Cold War to be more receptive to conspiracy theories. I don't think we'd become paranoid. But we were on the road to a paranoid explanation of things."[8]

Eric Sevareid, another CBS commentator, was the next witness.[9] His credentials were less academic than his predecessors and seemed to consist almost entirely of his agreement to watch the CBS documentary.[10]

> CRONKITE: In Washington, Eric Sevareid has been watching these four programs with you, and we turn to him now for his thoughts on the Warren Commission and its work.[11]

Sevareid suggested that Americans are conspiracy-minded in general.[12] Present in his fellow citizens, he had discovered, was "this automatic reaction that there must be a conspiracy somewhere."[13] Disbelief in the official findings was equated with the belief that "obscure Reds in the State Department, teachers and writers here and there must have delivered vast China to Communist hands" or that "Roosevelt conspired with the Japanese to bring about the Pearl Harbor attack."[14] Referring gratuitously to Oswald as a "skinny, weak-chinned, little character," he observed, according to the CBS transcript, that those who do not accept his lone guilt are to be compared with "people who think Adolph [sic] Hitler is alive, people who think the so-called learned Elders of Zion are engaged in a Jewish plot to control the world."[15] He added that the "notion" that the Commission members "knowingly suppressed or distorted decisive evidence" is "idiotic."[16]

Since Sevareid is stationed in Washington, D.C., he might easily have journeyed to the National Archives and there have asked for the index of the basic source material relied upon by the Commission.[17] Many of the more than fifteen hundred files referred to by the index, including those containing some of the most important evidence in the case, have been suppressed—cannot be seen.[18] While the suppression may seem to some to be idiotic, the "notion" that the documents are suppressed is based on fact.[19] The Federal Government would not permit CBS to test the alleged assassination weapon.[20] In that sense that important piece of evidence remains "suppressed."[21] No CBS employee was permitted to examine the autopsy photographs and X-rays. That material as well remains "suppressed."

The CBS finding that Americans are conspiracy-minded signified that the media had come full circle. When evidence about the assassination was available in Europe, but by and large unpublished in America, the domestic press explained the disparity revealed by public opinion polls.[22] Americans were sound and reasonable folk. Europeans, quite used to palace intrigue, were by nature conspiracy-minded.[23] With the publication of the critical works in America and the beginning of a real debate, Americans, according to the Gallup and Harris polls, rejected the Warren Report by an overwhelming majority.[24] CBS then explained that Americans were uniquely conspiracy-minded.[25]

CBS was pleased with its program. It published a full-page advertisement in the *New York Times* congratulating itself.[26] Headlines set in letters one inch tall read, ". . . to restore a much-needed sense of balance . . ."[27] The advertising copy concluded with the assurance that CBS used the same judgment to bring America its four-hour special and the "same sense of balance" that CBS News exercises "not just on four nights in June but every day throughout the year."[28]

CBS News President, Richard S. Salant, distributed a press release in which he quoted himself on the subject: "The Warren Report," he said, is a "truly great achievement."[29] In the release Salant apologized to the program's producer for the fact that "I have neither the eloquence nor the vocabulary to say properly how proud and grateful I am."[30] He added, "There are two words which are badly overused—'professional' and 'genius.' They are entirely applicable here."[31] The press was a little less enthusiastic, but the television critics seemed to approve of the show. Jack Gould, writing in the *New York Times*, was impressed.[32] He said that the executive producer of the program had in mind as his "objective" to "make clear that the criticism of the Warren Report by such persons as Mark Lane, author of 'Rush to Judgment,' should not be left to stand by itself."[33] There was no need for CBS to go to all that trouble just on my account.

TV Guide thought the program "ranks as a major journalistic achievement."[34] It was "a masterful compilation of facts, interviews, experiments and opinions—a job of journalism that will be difficult to surpass."[35]

In his closing statement, Sevareid offered the opinion that an effort "to cover up something" would be "utterly impossible in the American arena of a fierce and free press."[36] For the first time it appeared that he had not been home watching the show with us.

15 THE SINGLE-BULLET TEST

The heart of the CBS program was a series of three tests which the network represented as being scientifically precise (and, in fact, superior to the similar endeavors undertaken by the Warren Commission), but which were at best pseudo-scientific and likely worse than that.[1] These three tests involved the trajectory of the single bullet which the Commission contended passed through President Kennedy's neck and then caused all Governor Connally's wounds;[2] the capability of the Italian Mannlicher-Carcano rifle alleged to have been used by Lee Harvey Oswald;[3] and the running speed of Abraham Zapruder's motion picture camera which filmed the assassination sequence.[4]

CBS published a full-page advertisement in the *New York Times* with a bigger-than-life-size photograph of Commission Exhibit 399 and headlines that shouted, "This is the bullet that hit both President Kennedy and Governor Connally. Or did it?"[5] The advertisement claimed that "CBS News, with a perspective sharpened by time, has spent more than six months investigating every aspect of the report."[6] CBS had conducted "new and enlightening tests," the advertisement continued, and was "substituting understanding for confusion and meaningful analysis for shrill debate."[7]

According to the Commission's hypothesis, a single bullet—Commission Exhibit 399—passed through the President's neck and then into the Governor's back, shattered his fifth rib, fractured his wrist and then entered his thigh.[8] While the Commission favored that theory, it understandably appeared reluctant to be wed to it. In *Rush to Judgment* I presented evidence which showed that the finding that Oswald was the lone assassin was in fact dependent upon that unlikely chain of events.[9] CBS agreed: "Despite its [the Commission's] own words, the single bullet theory is essential to its findings."[10]

Two questions then require answers. Could one bullet actually make such a journey? If it did, could it resemble the almost pristine and undeformed Commission Exhibit 399 pictured in the CBS advertisement?[11] CBS implied that it had conducted "new and enlightening tests" which might provide answers to both questions.[12]

In *Rush to Judgment* I criticized the test conducted by the Commission.[13] Instead of attempting to fire one bullet through substances representing the President's neck, the Governor's torso and wrist and into a substance representing his thigh, the Commission chose an almost meaningless test.[14] Under the supervision of Dr. Alfred G. Olivier, separate bullets were fired, each into a substance representing one of the areas of impact.[15] No effort was made to fire a bullet even through two of the four human tissue simulants.[16] Yet each test bullet described in testimony before the Commission suffered more deformation than Commission Exhibit 399.[17]

"It seemed to us," Cronkite stated, "that the only completely valid test would be a single shot directly through a series of objects with the same thickness and density as the two bodies. We decided to make that shot."[18] Accordingly, a test was conducted in which bullets were to be fired through four objects.[19] CBS asked Dr. Olivier to supervise its tests as well.[20] In order to simulate the President's neck, a block composed of gelatin in a 20 percent solution was used, since the Commission alleged that the bullet which it said passed through President Kennedy's neck struck no bone tissue in its flight.[21] In order to simulate Governor Connally's chest, however, the network merely used another gelatin block.[22] This clearly failed to simulate the

Governor's fifth rib, which was struck with sufficient force to shatter it, according to the Governor's physicians, and cause the rib fragments to become secondary missiles, several of which punctured his lung.[23]*

During the CBS broadcast, Dr. Olivier said, "In his [Governor Connally's] case, the bullet passed along the rib, fractured the rib, throwing fragments into the lung."[25] As to the CBS simulation, Olivier sheepishly admitted, "Of course we have no rib here, but this still simulates passing through the flesh."[26] Yet Cronkite had previously promised that the bullet would be fired through "a series of objects with the same thickness and density as the two bodies."[27] The test was thus invalidated from the outset. But that omission did not represent the network's only failure to conduct the experiment properly.

In order to simulate the Governor's wrist, CBS used a third gelatin block which contained a piece of masonite, said to represent the correct thickness and density of the wrist bone.[28] CBS presented no scientific evidence indicating that masonite is an appropriate substitute for bone.[29]† The fourth and final object used in the CBS test was another gelatin block, which represented Governor Connally's thigh.[31]

According to Dr. Olivier, an undisclosed number of bullets were fired during the CBS test, but not all of them were able even to pass entirely through the masonite representing the wrist bone.[32] "In some cases, it passed through the wrist," Dr. Olivier explained.[33] "In other cases, it lodged in the wrist."[34] Furthermore, he added, "In none of the cases did this thing [the bullet] actually penetrate that [the fourth gelatin block]."[35]

CBS then contended that it had conducted a "valid test" and that "our tests confirm that a single bullet could indeed have wounded both men."[36] Neither assertion is supported by the facts.[37] Even Professor Alexander M. Bickel, a defender of the Warren Commission's conclusions, felt constrained to write:

> And what he [Olivier] reported on the air was that in none of his tests did the bullet "actually penetrate" as far as it was required to in order to support the theory, although "it would have taken very little more velocity to have caused a similar wound." In other words, the only significance of the tests was that they disproved the theory. But

* When the Commission fired a test bullet through a goat carcass and produced an injury to the goat rib which Dr. Olivier testified was "very similar" to the Governor's wound, the bullet was flattened at the nose, a characteristic not possessed by Commission Exhibit 399.[24]

† The Commission's test utilized wrists from human cadavers, and there seems to be no reasonable explanation why CBS could not have done likewise.[30]

CBS had Walter Cronkite conclude, right in the next breath, that "our tests confirm that a single bullet could, indeed, have wounded both men." The non-sequitur of the year![38]

CBS did not inform its viewers of the speed with which the bullet entered the first gelatin block, although that factor is of the essence when one hopes for just "a little more velocity" at the last simulator.[39] According to the Commission's hypothesis which was under examination, Commission Exhibit 399 was fired from a distance of between 176.9 and 190.8 feet.[40] How close to the first gelatin block was the rifle used by CBS? Did the bullet enter that block at the correct speed? CBS failed to divulge that information to the public.[41]

I initially became suspicious of the CBS presentation of this test when the network showed only filmed bits of various aspects of the test but not a single "long shot" which revealed the rifle's position. I had produced a documentary film of the subject myself, and, although a novice in that field, it was obvious even to me that such an establishing view was the natural way to open the sequence. Cronkite had implied, but never stated, that the rifle was the correct distance, referring to the need for a "completely valid test," then adding that "we decided to make that shot."[42]

Although CBS had officially suppressed the data regarding its program (with the exception of that portion which was actually aired), I have learned that Walter Lister, a CBS field producer who arranged the test, later claimed that the rifle was fifty feet from the first block. However, later CBS told *True* magazine that the rifle was but twenty feet from the first target and that some powder had been removed from the cartridges to compensate for that inaccuracy.[43] In the Warren Commission test, which CBS condemned for being invalid, the rifle was fired at the correct distance of 180 feet from the target.[44]

Midgley also told *True*, "We didn't try to be super-scientific. We simply didn't have the time or the money to run tests that would be a thousand percent accurate."[45] Yet the validity of the test would have been entirely undermined if the bullet entered the first target at the incorrect velocity.

The significance of this factor may be appreciated when one discovers that, according to the Commission, the bullets it tested lost more velocity traveling the 180 feet to the first target (the animal meat and gelatin blocks which simulated the President's neck) than they lost in striking the target, penetrating it and exiting from it.[46] In fact, the bullets suffered a greater loss of velocity just traveling the proper distance through the air than the combined loss occasioned by penetrating the first target and severely fracturing the wrist of a cadaver.[47] Yet despite every assistance from the network, evidently including considerably greater velocity and targets of considerably less density, the bullets just could not perform as wished.[48]

The second relevant question that CBS implied it would answer related to the shape of the tested bullets.[49] Could they weather collisions with various gelatin simulators and a piece of masonite and retain the almost pristine form of Commission Exhibit 399? While the Commission published pictures of its spent test bullets, all revealing substantial distortion, CBS, its perspective sharpened by time, refused to share its results with the public.[50]

"Could a single bullet have wounded both President Kennedy and Governor Connally?" Cronkite asked.[51] The CBS test proved that it could not. What would a bullet, spent in that effort, look like? CBS has the answer—it has the bullets—but we may not see them.

Evidently CBS concedes that its failure to display the bullets was an error. Later Lister said that it was a serious mistake. He added, "It didn't strike us as very important then."[52] Salant agreed: "I was watching the show at home with my family and my 14-year-old son picked that up immediately. 'Yeah, but what did the bullet look like?' he wanted to know. And he was right."[53]

At the conclusion of the test, CBS asked Dr. Olivier one last question: "Did someone outline these experiments for you?" Olivier replied, "No, I'm afraid I'm guilty of the whole business."[54] Come now, Dr. Olivier, surely you are too modest. Didn't CBS have a hand in it?

16 THE RIFLE TEST

The rifle test conducted by CBS was probably the most ambitious single project undertaken by the network during the course of its investigation.[1] "The rate of fire for this bolt action rifle and its accuracy against a moving target were critical to the Commission's case against Oswald," Walter Cronkite declared.[2] "And yet, incredibly, all tests for the Commission were fired at stationary targets."[3] He explained that CBS had decided to conduct a rifle test in order "to explore glaring omissions in the tests fired for the Commission."[4] Cronkite claimed that "to simulate Oswald's problem of hitting a moving target from a sixty foot high perch, the FBI conducted its firing tests on a fixed target, from a 30-foot height. Certainly, if CBS News could duplicate the conditions of the actual assassination for a firing test, the feat's not beyond the capability of the FBI."[5]* CBS

* Certainly, if anyone reading the evidence could discover that the U.S. Army—and not the FBI—conducted the rifle test in question, that feat is not beyond the capability of CBS.[6]

did possess the resources to "duplicate the conditions of the actual assassination"—meaning by that phrase the prevailing conditions according to the Commission's reconstruction of the slaying.[7] Yet in almost every essential respect it failed to do so.

The CBS rifle test was held "at the range of the H. P. White Ballistics Laboratory, in rolling farmland, north of Belaire, Maryland."[8] The riflemen fired from a tower said to be the same height as the sixth-floor window of the Book Depository Building at a target moving away from the tower at a speed of eleven miles per hour, which CBS said was "approximately the speed of the Presidential limousine."[9] William Greer, the Secret Service agent who drove the President's car, in testimony before the Commission estimated the speed of the limousine at twelve to fifteen miles per hour, according to the Warren Report.[10] The Commission, however, was satisfied that an examination of the Zapruder film disclosed that the vehicle moved at an average speed of 11.2 miles per hour during the shooting.[11] Thus CBS selected for its moving target a speed slightly slower than the slowest figure cited by the Commission.[12] While that disparity may be of little or no consequence, CBS did ignore significant evidence in arriving at the determination that its target should travel at a uniform speed of eleven miles per hour to approximate the "average" speed of 11.2 miles per hour.[13] A considerable body of testimony before the Commission indicated that the limousine slowed abruptly and then accelerated rapidly when the shots were fired.[14] CBS could have ascertained the precise movements of the vehicle by viewing the Zapruder film, which can be seen at the National Archives in Washington. It is unquestionably easier to fire at a target moving at a predictably uniform rate of speed than at one which suddenly decelerates and then speeds up without warning.*

According to the network, the heights and distances involved "match[ed] exactly the heights and distances in Dealey Plaza" and the "target track was angled to match precisely the angle of Elm Street."[15] It was not difficult to discover that the heights, distances and angles in the Warren Commission's rifle test did not match the Dealey Plaza statistics, since details to that effect were provided in the twenty-six volumes of evidence.[16] CBS, however, provided no statistics, making it impossible for its viewers to know whether or not

* An analysis of the figures accepted by the Warren Commission and adopted by CBS regarding the speed of the President's limousine reveals that it traveled at a speed of under two and a half miles per hour at one point while on Elm Street and in excess of seventeen miles per hour moments later. The maximum speed was attained well before the final shot. This analysis appears as Appendix IV.

the heights, distances and angles did, in fact, "match" the actual measurements involved.

In fact, after the broadcasts were concluded, I learned that although the manager of H. P. White had known that Elm Street was curved, he did not conform the test area to the curve. He said, "The actual road, of course, was slightly curved and our track had to be straight. It was made of angle irons."[17]

The target used in the CBS test, described as a "standard FBI silhouette," represented the upper portion of a man's body.[18]

CBS reporter Dan Rather described the credentials of the riflemen who participated in the experiment as follows:

> Eleven volunteer marksmen took turns firing clips of three bullets each at the moving target. None of the men had much familiarity with the Italian Mannlicher-Carcano, although each was given time to practice at a nearby indoor range; and most of the volunteers were experienced with bolt action rifles.[19]

Rather subsequently revealed the identities of three of the eleven marksmen—two were Maryland state troopers and the third was a "technician" at the H. P. White Ballistics Laboratory.[20] But he offered no standard rating or evaluation, nor any indication of previous performances, for any of the firers.[21]

During the time that Lee Harvey Oswald was in the United States Marine Corps, he was tested on two occasions to determine his proficiency with a rifle.[22] In December of 1956 he obtained a score of 212.[23] In May of 1959 Oswald scored 191, which was a single point over the minimum for ranking in the lowest Marine Corps category.[24] The head of the Records Branch of the Marine Corps Personnel Department, who testified before Commission counsel, evaluated the lower rating as a "rather poor shot."[25] Between October 1959 and June 1962, Oswald resided in the Soviet Union.[26] According to the Warren Report, he went hunting "about six times" during this period, but he used a shotgun and not a rifle.[27] In June of 1962 Oswald returned to the United States, and soon thereafter, according to his brother's testimony, he went hunting on one occasion in Texas, using a borrowed .22 caliber bolt-action rifle.[28] The Commission's investigation, however, disclosed no evidence that Oswald had practiced firing a rifle or had gone hunting on any occasion during the year preceding the assassination.[29] Thus it seems doubtful that the degree of proficiency of the CBS marksmen was at all comparable to Oswald's capability with a rifle on November 22, 1963.

The U.S. Army experts who conducted the test for the Warren Commission used the same weapon purportedly fired by Oswald—

Commission Exhibit 139, the C2766 Italian Mannlicher-Carcano rifle.[30] But CBS used a different Mannlicher-Carcano, which, according to Rather, was "of the same make and age as Oswald's" and, according to Cronkite, was "like Oswald's."[31] Although Rather's assertion may well have been accurate, it seems certain that Cronkite's was not. Robert Frazier, an FBI firearms expert who fired the C2766 rifle itself for the Commission, testified that three shots in "4.6 seconds is firing this weapon as fast as the bolt will operate" and that this speed could be achieved only in a situation in which stationary targets were employed.[32] If the target was moving, Frazier told the Commission, a longer interval would be required in order to fire three shots with that rifle.[33] Yet the results of the CBS test showed that one marksman using the substitute weapon fired three shots at a moving target in only 4.1 seconds—evidently an impossible feat with the original one.[34] Thus the rifle used by CBS may have looked "like Oswald's" to a television commentator, but clearly it was a superior weapon.[35]

A further complication which CBS apparently avoided was the defective telescopic sight mounted on the C2766 rifle.[36] When the FBI tested that weapon, according to Director J. Edgar Hoover, the "telescopic sight could not be properly aligned with the target, since the sight reached the limit of its adjustment before reaching accurate alignment."[37] In order to utilize the rifle for its test on behalf of the Commission, the Army had to have gunsmiths stabilize and adjust the sight by adding metal shims.[38] Although CBS alleged that its Mannlicher-Carcano "was fitted with the same four-power telescopic sight found on his [Oswald's alleged] rifle," that was not true since the "same" sight remains affixed to the C2766 rifle, which CBS did not secure for reasons which it failed to disclose.[39]

In one respect the CBS test was identical with the Commission's test: both used oversized targets.[40] The thesis under examination was predicated upon the assumption that Oswald's goal was to kill President Kennedy. From the sixth-floor window the President's head, neck and shoulders could be seen, the remainder of his body being shielded by the automobile.[41] It appears unlikely that the possibility of inflicting a flesh wound in the shoulder would have interested the prospective assassin—presumably the President's head would have been his target. In any event, of the shots fired on November 22, at least one—the fatal one—struck the President's head, and at least one, according to the Report, hit his neck.[42] The Commission's test employed targets that represented a human head and neck as part of a larger silhouette target.[43] The entire target was, in fact, more than three times as large as the head.[44] The Commission's riflemen fired eighteen shots, but not one struck the head or neck portion of the targets.[45] CBS used similarly oversized targets, but, unlike the Commission, declined to display the targets or photographs of them. Thus the network's viewers were unable to learn whether its marksmen were as unsuccessful as the Commission's experts.

Moreover, CBS failed to inform its viewers that on January 31, 1967, it conducted a rifle test with a rifle expert, Colonel Edward B. Crossman. Crossman writes for gun magazines under the name "Col. Jim Crossman." The technicians and workmen at H. P. White completed their work, and Lister arranged for Crossman to be tested with an Italian Mannlicher-Carcano which CBS had purchased for $150. Oswald had allegedly paid under $13 for his rifle. Crossman tested the weapon six times, each time firing three shots. He was unable to fire as quickly or as accurately as Oswald allegedly had.[46] Subsequently CBS discounted that test and tested eleven other riflemen.

CBS declined to reveal to its viewers that Crossman had ever fired and that his time average had been excluded from the final CBS tabulation. He was not one of the "eleven volunteer marksmen" to whom CBS referred.

Thus the CBS test in fact bore little relation to the known facts. Oswald was a "rather poor shot" and apparently had not practiced for a year preceding the assassination, but CBS selected marksmen with undisclosed, albeit evidently superior, qualifications.[47] Tests demonstrated that the CBS rifle was capable of being fired more rapidly than the C2766 Mannlicher-Carcano allegedly used by Oswald.[48] The CBS rifle presumably had an accurate telescopic sight, whereas the C2766 possessed a defective sight.[49] The target moved at a speed slower than the slowest figure suggested by the Commission.[50] The target moved at a predictably uniform speed, although the Presidential car evidently changed speed radically—and without warning—during the assassination interval.[51] The target was slightly more than three times as large as it should have been.[52]*

Yet even under these more favorable circumstances, the CBS riflemen evidently experienced some difficulty in matching the feat attributed to Oswald by the Warren Report.[53] "Altogether the eleven volunteer marksmen made 37 attempts to fire three shots at the moving target," CBS reported.[54] "Seventeen of those attempts had to be called no time, because of trouble with the rifle."[55] CBS offered no further information as to the basis for its "no time" rule. I have learned that CBS later explained that the "no time" rule was

* In addition, CBS failed to take into account the fact that the President's head was a moving target within a moving target, since President Kennedy slumped downward to his left between the first and last shots.

invoked if the rifleman failed to fire all three shots "before the target reached the end of the track and stopped moving."[56] Thus, when CBS later announced the "average" time consumed by the riflemen, it did so after having mechanically removed the possibility that the "average" might be anything more than an average of the fastest efforts.

In addition, the network declined to disclose how many of the shots hit its oversized target or even if any of the shots considered to have "hit" the silhouette targets actually struck the head or neck area, where the Commission said the President's wounds were inflicted.[57]

While CBS was less willing than the Commission to expose its working documents, it was not at all reluctant to share its conclusions with the public.[58] Walter Cronkite summed up the network's evaluation of the rifle test in these words: "From our own tests we were convinced that a rifle like Oswald's could be fired in 5.6 seconds or less, and with reasonable accuracy, at a target moving much the same as the Presidential limousine was travelling away from the Book Depository's sixth-floor window."[59] It is difficult to determine on what logical basis that conclusion was reached, for it does not seem at all reasonable, based upon the evidence of the CBS test (uncomplicated as it was by the intricacies that the facts would have imposed), to conclude that even an expert marksman could fire three shots, with two hits (one in the head and one in the neck), in 5.6 seconds or less.

If that can be said of an expert, what may one reasonably conclude regarding the capability of Lee Harvey Oswald, a "rather poor shot" who evidently had not practiced on a single occasion during the year prior to the assassination?[60] "It seems equally reasonable to say that Oswald, under normal circumstances, would take longer," Cronkite conceded.[61] "But the circumstances were not normal. He was shooting at a President. So our answer is: probably fast enough."[62] One might have hoped that the usually acquiescent Walter Cronkite might at last have resisted that portion of the script, since he is known on occasion to exercise some editorial discretion. But very likely at CBS when the documentary was prepared, the circumstances were not normal.

What was "probably fast enough" at 10:40 P.M. became "fast enough" without any qualifying word fifteen minutes later:

CRONKITE: How fast could Oswald's rifle be fired? Fast enough.[63]

And the next evening:

CRONKITE: How fast could Oswald's rifle be fired? Fast enough.[64]

And the next evening:

CRONKITE: How fast could Oswald's rifle be fired? Fast enough.[65]

17 THE CAMERA TEST

On June 25, 1967, CBS suggested that it was possible to determine from an examination of the film taken by Abraham Zapruder the precise number of shots fired during the assassination and to pinpoint the moment at which each of them occurred.[1] The network said its historic conclusion was based upon work done by Luis Alvarez, a physicist at the University of California, and Charles Wyckoff, described as "an expert photo analyst . . . of the Massachusetts firm of Edgerton, Germeshausen and Grier."[2]

Wyckoff said that the Zapruder film was blurred at several points.[3] He hypothesized that a loud report—in this case presumably rifle fire—may have startled Zapruder and made his hand jerk involuntarily, thus causing the film to blur for an instant.[4] According to Wyckoff, this blurring effect on the film was apparent in three frames—190, 227 and 318.[5] Since the film unmistakably depicted a bullet shattering the President's skull at frame 313, Wyckoff reasoned that the blurring in frame 318 marked Zapruder's initial reaction to the sound of that shot—an interval of 5/18.3 of a second.[6]* Presuming that the other two blurred frames, 190 and 227, each followed by a similar interval a shot which had startled Zapruder, Wyckoff concluded that this constituted impressive evidence that three shots were fired—the fatal one at frame 313 and the earlier shots at frame 185 or 186 and frame 222 or 223.[8]

A re-enactment of the assassination conducted in Dealey Plaza on May 24, 1964, by the FBI and the Secret Service had established that an oak tree partially blocked the President from the view of an assassin at the sixth-floor window between Zapruder frames 166 and 209 inclusive—except for a single frame, 186, when the foliage parted and the President was fully visible for an instant.[9]†

This detail seemed to CBS to coincide with Wyckoff's findings regarding the blurring of the film. Accordingly, the network reasoned that the first shot was probably fired through the gap in the

* Examination of the Zapruder camera established that it ran at a speed of 18.3 frames per second.[7]

† After the President emerged from beneath the tree at frame 210, no other obstruction impeded the view of him from the window while the shots were being fired.[10]

tree at frame 186, missing the Presidential limousine and its occupants.[11] This shot caused Zapruder's hand to jerk, blurring frame 190 of his film.[12] A second shot was fired at frame 222 or 223, after the President had emerged from behind the tree, CBS explained.[13] This bullet, which caused Zapruder's film to blur at frame 227, passed through President Kennedy's body, according to CBS, and went on to inflict all Governor Connally's wounds.[14] The final shot, fired at frame 313, killed the President and caused the film to blur a third time, at frame 318.[15]

This explanation, ostensibly resolving the discrepancies in the Warren Report while supporting the Commission's conclusion that Oswald acted alone, raised more problems than it resolved. Indeed, if the blurs on the film do represent shots, as CBS implied, then the inescapable consequence of that presumption, as I shall demonstrate shortly, is that Lee Harvey Oswald, using the C2766 Mannlicher-Carcano rifle, could not possibly have committed the murder without assistance.*

CBS failed to inform its viewers of even one of the several factors which tend to preclude the possibility that a sixth-floor assassin would have fired at frame 186.[22] In the first place, the President came into view only for a single frame at that point in the film—i.e., for approximately one-eighteenth of a second.[23] If the first shot was fired at frame 186, the assassin would of necessity have made the mental decision to fire—and must have translated that mental decision into the necessary physical action—at some previous frame, a fraction of a second earlier, when the tree obscured his view of the President.[24] The Warren Report rejected the possibility of such an early shot from the sixth-floor window on the ground that it was "unlikely that the assassin would deliberately have shot at him [President Ken-

* It appears that this issue is academic, since the evidence is overwhelming that the CBS hypothesis is seriously flawed. In the first place, the Zapruder film is blurred in many other frames besides those mentioned by the network.[16] Such an effect is visible, for example, in frames 195, 203, 290 and 331, and in several other frames as well.[17] Evidently because this would not have suited the CBS hypothesis, it declined to share that information with its viewers.[18] Secondly, CBS did not take into account the fact that Zapruder was forced to turn his body to the right in order to keep the moving limousine in his line of sight.[19] CBS conducted an experiment in which two persons filmed a stationary automobile with movie cameras while a rifle was fired nearby.[20] But since that limousine was not in motion, the cameramen were not required to turn or pan in order to keep it in view.[21] For the purposes of this discussion, however, in order to examine the CBS hypothesis within the context suggested by the network, I shall accept the CBS hypothesis that the three blurs it selected may represent reactions to rifle shots.

nedy] with a view obstructed by the oak tree when he was about to have a clear opportunity" when the car emerged from behind the tree at frame 210.[25]

Moreover, the Commission remarked, the "greatest cause for doubt that the first shot missed is the improbability that the same marksman who twice hit a moving target would be so inaccurate on the first and closest of his shots as to miss completely, not only the target, but the large automobile."[26]*

CBS had posed the question, "What was the time span of the shots?"[28] It concluded that the answer—with the first shot being fired through the gap in the tree at frame 186—was "seven or eight seconds" and not "5.6 seconds, which is the time the Commission reported Oswald probably had to take."[29] The Commission never concluded that 5.6 seconds was the time span of the shots.[30] Indeed, the final sentence of Chapter III of the Warren Report states that the Commission concluded "that the three shots were fired in a time period ranging from approximately 4.8 to in excess of 7 seconds."[31] Moreover, the Report stated, "If either the first or third shots missed, then . . . [there would have been] a minimum time of 7.1 to 7.9 seconds for the three shots."[32] Thus the representation by CBS that the Commission had concluded the second shot missed and the time span of the shots was 5.6 seconds, and that the network's investigation had disproven those contentions, was inaccurate.[33] No doubt to suggest an image of objectivity, at the same time that CBS endorsed the Warren Commission's major conclusions, it stoutly denied that it was doing so.

If CBS was accurate that "our analysis of the Zapruder film suggests strongly that the first shot was fired at frame 186" and the second shot at frame 222 or 223, then the network inadvertently proved beyond doubt that Oswald was not the lone assassin.[34] It will be recalled that earlier in this chapter I cited the testimony of Robert Frazier, the FBI firearms expert, to the effect that the alleged assassination weapon required an absolute minimum of 2.3 seconds between shots and that this time period represented the fastest the bolt can be operated.[35] In the Warren Report the Commission said that "tests of the [C2766] rifle disclosed that at least 2.3 seconds were required between shots."[36] Since the Zapruder camera ran at 18.3 frames per second, a minimum of 42 frames must have elapsed between consecutive shots fired by the C2766 Mannlicher-Carcano

* An examination of the interior of the Presidential limousine by the FBI, according to that agency, revealed that no damage that could have been caused by a bullet striking the car was found.[27]

rifle.[37] But if, as CBS implied, shots were fired at frames 186 and 222 or 223, then not more than 37 frames elapsed between those shots, and the rifle allegedly used by Oswald is incapable of such a performance.[38]*

Thus CBS was faced with a serious dilemma. Through a most selective presentation CBS was able to enhance one essential aspect of its lone-assassin hypothesis, but in doing so it entirely enervated another. As Walter Cronkite and his staff loaded the scale with weighty improbabilities, the hoped-for result was at last achieved—one part of the scale was grounded. But since the underlying hypothesis required that both portions be grounded, an impossibility, the viewer might observe that the scale seemed less inclined to that posture than before. That credibility which the Warren Report enjoys lies in its refusal to foreclose all of its options. CBS was less astute. Although its desire had been otherwise, it had proved that Oswald was not the lone assassin. It was now obliged to disprove what it had just established.

The network attempted to salvage the conclusion that there was a lone assassin by suggesting that Zapruder's camera actually ran slower than the speed of 18.3 frames per second which the Commission believed to be correct.[40] As CBS quite correctly noted, nearly all that is known about the timing of the shots has been based upon the running speed of the Zapruder camera, which literally served as the "clock" for the assassination.[41] The Warren Report stated that "examination of the Zapruder motion picture camera by the FBI established that 18.3 pictures or frames were taken each second, and therefore, the timing of certain events could be calculated by allowing 1/18.3 seconds for the action depicted from one frame to the next."[42] Although I had no way of verifying the accuracy of that statistic, I accepted it in *Rush to Judgment* for the purpose of analyzing the Commission's case against Oswald within the framework established by the Warren Report.[43] I have done so in this book as well, since, in my opinion, no evidence has been produced which would tend to invalidate the correctness of that figure.

If the film did, in fact, run slower, as CBS suggested it "probably" did, then the interval in which the shots were fired—whatever that interval may have been—would be lengthened proportionately and an assassin would have had more time to fire the shots than is generally believed to have been the case.[44]

How did CBS go about proving that Zapruder's camera "proba-

* CBS determined, of course, that other rifles may be fired more rapidly, but that in no way relates to the capability of the C2766 rifle.[39]

bly" ran slower than 18.3 frames per second?[45] By examining other cameras.[46] According to Wyckoff, who also conducted this experiment for the network, five "similar" cameras were run against an electric clock to determine the rate at which motion picture film passed through them.[47] Three of them actually ran faster than the Commission's figure for the Zapruder camera, and only two ran slower.[48] In the face of this test, CBS concluded that Zapruder's camera probably ran slower.[49]

CBS did not test the camera which filmed the assassination, and it did not explain why it did not.[50] The FBI had tested Zapruder's Bell & Howell camera in December 1963.[51] Lyndal L. Shaneyfelt, the FBI photography expert, testified before the Commission that the running speed of the Zapruder camera was determined by "focusing the camera on a clock with a large sweep-second hand."[52] CBS implied that it had employed a superior technique to test its five cameras.[53] Without sharing Shaneyfelt's testimony regarding the mechanics of the FBI test with its audience, CBS duplicated that test.[54] But the FBI had tested the authentic camera; CBS did not.[55] Shaneyfelt concluded, "The Zapruder camera was found to run at an average speed of 18.3 frames per second."[56]

Three years later, on December 7, 1966, according to the *New York Times*, Peter G. Peterson, the president of the Bell & Howell Company, stated, "We recently tested the [Zapruder] camera in our engineering laboratories. Our results would appear to corroborate the FBI testimony before the Warren commission that the average speed at which film passed through the camera was at 18.3 frames per second. In fact, our test showed the camera speed to be within less than one-tenth of a frame per second from the figure reported by the FBI."[57] Thus, after two independent examinations of the Zapruder camera had confirmed that it ran at 18.3 frames per second and after three of the five other "similar" cameras tested by CBS ran faster, CBS concluded that it considered the evidence persuasive that Zapruder's camera "probably" ran slower than 18.3 frames per second on November 22, 1963.[58]

Putting together its own conclusions regarding the rifle and camera tests it had conducted, the network concluded that the Warren Report was wrong about the time interval of the assassination and that the killer had had more time than the Commission believed.[59] A different rifle had been tested; it had been tested under very different conditions; different cameras had been tested; and the Commission's conclusions had been distorted beyond recognition.[60] But CBS, unperturbed by these details, remained implacable and serene. It had made its contribution to history. It evidently mattered little to CBS that its contribution had been a disservice to truth.

18 THE ELECTRIC BULB TEST

In addition to the three tests, CBS presented a question raised by some critics, caused a bullet to be fired through a bulb and concluded that the criticism had thus been rendered invalid.[1] Cronkite posed the question properly: "In Abraham Zapruder's film of the assassination, the fatal shot appears to move the President's head back. The critics contend this can only mean the shot came not from the Book Depository, but from somewhere in front."[2]

I had raised that question and made that point in *Rush to Judgment*.[3]* Other critics had probed that question more intensively.[5] Tracings of frame 313, at which point the effect of the bullet upon the President's head can be observed for the first time, had been superimposed upon a subsequent frame by Vincent Salandria, a Philadelphia attorney.[6] This demonstrated a sudden and violent movement to the left and rear immediately following frame 313.[7]

Cronkite observed, however, "Not for the first time, nor for the last in these reports, we find equally qualified experts in disagreement. We put the question of the President's head movement to an experienced photo analyst and two expert pathologists."[8] If CBS had indeed put that question to the three men Cronkite described, it declined to share their answers with the audience.[9] One physicist, presumably the photoanalyst, and one pathologist, not two, were presented.[10] The physicist discussed a different question.[11] He said:

> Well, the—in frame 313, the—there was an apparent explosion at this point, which would be on the front side of—of the head. Now, characteristically, this would indicate to me that the bullet came from behind, and this is what's called spalling. It's a minor explosion where pieces of material have—have left and go generally in the direction of the bullet.[12]

* I had written: "By the time the fatal shot was fired, the limousine had reached a point on Elm Street alongside the knoll, which was to the right. When the bullet struck the President's head, as one can see from the photographs, he was thrown to his left and toward the rear of the limousine. How could the Commission explain the sudden violent move of the President's body to the left and to the rear? So long as the Commission maintained that the bullet came almost directly from the rear, it implied that the laws of physics vacated in this instance, for the President did not fall forward."[4]

At this point the screen showed the result of a bullet fired through a fixed object, a secured bulb.[13] Quite naturally some of the bulb material flew in the same direction as the bullet.[14] The President, however, was not a fixed object, and he did not remain stationary after the bullet struck him, as did the bulb.[15] The question that CBS said it was contemplating was the "question of the President's head movement"; what force drove him backward and to the left?[16] Yet that question was abandoned despite the assurance that it was about to be answered.[17]

Although Cronkite had posed the matter with admirable clarity, Rather confused the matter still further, asking, "But now, the explosion, this minor explosion, occurs forward of the President. Now, wouldn't that indicate the bullet coming from the front?"[18]

WYCKOFF: No, quite contrary. It does indicate that the bullet was coming from behind.

RATHER: Well, you're aware that some critics say that by the very fact that in the picture you can clearly see the explosion of the bullet on the front side of the President, that that certainly indicates the bullet came from the front.

WYCKOFF: Well, I don't believe any physicist has ever said that.[19]

Quite right, Mr. Wyckoff. He might have added that despite Rather's untrue assertion, no critic, to my knowledge, has ever said that either.

Wyckoff continued to discuss the light bulb experiment in response to Rather's irrelevant inquiry.[20] Never having been asked, he never commented upon the President's head movement.[21] Thus, despite the fact that the question that Cronkite had commented upon had never been asked, much less answered, Cronkite observed at that point, "That is one explanation from a physicist as to how a head could move backward after being struck from behind, which seems to many laymen not possible."[22]

There is no evidence to indicate that it seems possible to Wyckoff either. Wyckoff's statements are not without value, however, for they have application when placed in the context of the events in Dallas. What appeared to a witness to be a portion of the President's skull was observed flying over the left and rear of the limousine just as the bullet struck his head.[23] The motorcycle officers to the left and rear of the limousine said that they were struck by flesh and blood driven in their direction.[24] If Wyckoff was accurate when he asserted that the fragment of the struck object should move in the same direction as the bullet, he lent additional scientific support to the conclusions of the witnesses to the assassination.[25] At least one shot had been fired from the right front.

The one pathologist interviewed on the question said that the head movement was consistent with the bullet having originated from in front of the President—from the direction of the knoll.[26] As to the likelihood that the bullet came from the Book Depository, he said, "I say that it is quite unlikely."[27] He added that the hypothesis that the bullet which drove the President backward and to the left hit him in the back of the head "is difficult for me to accept."[28]

Although the published segments of the filmed interviews upon analysis show no inconsistency, CBS insisted that the "experts [were] in disagreement" and that "even film analysts often produce as many problems as they solve."[29] The scientific analysis of the undeniable evidence which indicated that there was a second rifleman thus was dissipated in a miasma of commentary by two CBS correspondents after both had revealed an inability to distinguish between the two separate questions that had been answered:[30] What is the meaning of the movement of the President following the fatal shot? What is the meaning of the movement of the fragments from the President's skull? Not content with intertwining the answers to different questions as if they were identical, CBS declined to make available to its audience at that time the evidence regarding the direction in which some skull and flesh portions were driven.[31]

19 A LOSS OF MORALE

CBS said that "certainly all objections that go to the heart of the Report vanish when they are exposed to the light of honest inquiry."[1] One is tempted to inquire, under the circumstances, how CBS might know. The network's documentary was a plea for acceptance of the Report, for it "is the best account we are ever likely to have of what happened that day in Dallas."[2] Unfortunately the full facts may never be disclosed. The Government has determined that indispensable evidence may not now be seen and the media are biddable. Cronkite asked whether we would "be more comfortable believing that a shot was fired by a second assassin" who vanished leaving no evidence behind.[3] Perhaps not, yet if the evidence compels the conclusion that he was there and that he did fire at least one shot, is our comfort, or fear of losing it, grounds to turn away? I think not.

I think that the CBS plea to leave bad enough alone cannot be heeded. For even in what was surely a presentation of just one side of the case, major discrepancies were uncovered. CBS stated without qualification that "the single bullet theory is essential" to the finding that Oswald was the lone assassin.[4] Rather, who appeared inclined to accept most of what the Government offered, balked at accepting that theory: "I'm not totally convinced about the single bullet theory."[5] How can we consider the case closed when CBS was unable to convince its own correspondent about the viability of a theory which it considers to be indispensable to the case against Oswald as the lone assassin?[6]

As the last of the programs ended, it found Cronkite stating that CBS had found

> that there has been a loss of morale, a loss of confidence among the American people toward their own government and the men who serve it. And that is perhaps more wounding than the assassination itself. The damage that Lee Harvey Oswald did the United States of America, the country he first denounced and then appeared to re-embrace, did not end when the shots were fired from the Texas School Book Depository. The most grievous wounds persist and there is little reason to believe that they will soon be healed.[7]

It was absurd to argue that the death of President Kennedy may be less "wounding" than the refusal of the American people to accept the Commission's findings. Equally absurd was the suggestion that Oswald continues to be the lone assassin, of morale in this instance, after his death. The uncritical devotion of CBS to the basic conclusions of the Report, in the face of contrary facts, is a symptom of the illness that continues to prevail.

The day following the last program a CBS press release carried the subheadline, "[CBS] Says Question of Oswald Connection to CIA, FBI Not Frivolous."[8] Earlier, Rather had said, "I am not content with the findings on Oswald's possible connections with government agencies, particularly with the CIA."[9] He added that Oswald "may have had more connections than we've been told about, or that have been shown."[10] Cronkite appeared to agree, adding that "the Commission's handling of that question is scarcely justifiable."[11] He said that "there remain disturbing indications" that there may have been "some kind of link between Oswald and various intelligence agencies of the United States."[12]

By what standard of logic could CBS state unequivocally that Oswald had "denounced" his country, that he was anti-American and then concede that he may have been working for the Government during the entire period? How could CBS concede that Oswald may have been involved in covert activity with secret intelligence agencies—in official conspiracies, if you please—and then state unequivocally that "Oswald was the sole assassin"?[13]

20 UNEQUAL TIME

During the last of the four programs, CBS aired a portion of an interview with me.[1] Immediately following my comments, Cronkite, Barker and Charles Brehm were heard:

CRONKITE: But Mr. Lane, who accuses the Commission of play-fast and loose with the evidence, does not always allow facts to get in the way of his own theories. In "Rush to Judgment," for example, he writes: "The statements of eyewitnesses close to the President tended to confirm the likelihood that the shot came from the right and not from the rear." Lane then quotes Associated Press photographer James Altgens, and another eyewitness, Charles Brehm, as giving testimony that would support the idea of a killer on the grassy knoll. Yet Mr. Altgens, as we saw Monday night, is entirely certain that all of the shots came from behind, a fact that Mr. Lane does not mention. As for Mr. Brehm, Eddie Barker discovered that he holds no brief either for the grassy knoll theory or for the use of his words by Mark Lane.

BARKER: Well now, some critics of the Warren Report have taken your testimony, or interviews with you, to indicate that you thought the shots came from behind the fence over there. What about that?

BREHM: Well, as I say, it was not a number of critics. It was one critic, Mark Lane, who takes very great liberties with adding to my quotation. I never said that the—any shot came from here like I was quoted by Mr. Lane. Mr. Lane would like me to have positively identified the—what I saw fly over here—his skull—although I told him I could not—I did not—I thought it was but I could not. So, he has added his interpretations to what I said, and consequently that's where the story comes from that—that I said that the shots come from up there. No shot came from up there at any time during the whole fiasco that afternoon.

CRONKITE: Nor are these the only examples of Mr. Lane lifting remarks out of context to support his theories. Perhaps the most charitable explanation is that Mark Lane still considers himself a defense attorney for Lee Harvey Oswald—and a defense attorney's primary duty is not to abstract truth, but to his client.[2]

Cronkite claimed to have discovered errors in *Rush to Judgment*.[3] In carefully guarded language he vaguely alluded to alleged errors, but the reader may notice that while he created the impression that there were mistakes, he never pointed to a single one.[4] He indicated that I quoted Altgens and Brehm as "giving testimony that would support the idea of a killer on the grassy knoll."[5] The word "testimony" is Cronkite's, not mine.[6] Brehm never testified before the Commission or before counsel for the Commission, and I never had said that he had.[7] Cronkite could have discovered that by reading *Rush to Judgment*, for that in fact was my complaint: "The Commission took the testimony of 552 persons during an investigation which its Report characterized as 'prolonged and thorough', but it declined to call Brehm as a witness and his name was not mentioned in the Report."[8]

Regardless of what Altgens told CBS years after the event (and when he was not under oath), he had testified before counsel for the Commission.[9] There he swore, "There was flesh particles that flew out of the side of his head in my direction from where I was standing, so much so that it indicated to me that the shot came out of the left side of his head."[10] The knoll was to the right of the President at the time of the fatal shot.[11] The Commission contends that the bullet was fired from almost directly behind the President and that it damaged just the right side of his head.[12] The actual testimony of Altgens was not mentioned by Cronkite.[13]

Only through the most skillful manipulation of language, not to say distortion, was it possible for CBS to leave the distinct impression that I had misquoted Brehm.[14] An angry Brehm denied that he had told me that the shots originated at the knoll.[15] He was correct.[16] He had never made that statement to me.[17] He also denied that he had "positively identified" that which he saw fly to the left and rear as a portion of the President's skull.[18] He insisted that he thought it was but that he could not be positive.[19] He is quite correct.[20] He never told me that he was positive that it was skull material—merely that it appeared to be a portion of the skull.[21]

There is but one page in *Rush to Judgment* in which Brehm's name appears.[22] Other than material in a footnote regarding the failure of the Commission to call him, which has been referred to above, Brehm's name is mentioned in but one paragraph:

> Another eyewitness, Charles Brehm, standing with his young son at the south curb of Elm, was approximately 20 feet from the limousine when the bullet shattered the President's head. 'I very definitely saw the effect of the second bullet that struck the President,' Brehm told me in an interview in Dallas. 'That which appeared to be a portion of

the President's skull went flying slightly to the rear of the President's car and directly to its left. It did fly over toward the curb to the left and to the rear,' he said.[23]

While Brehm is correct in denying that he told me that the shots came from the knoll and that he was certain that he observed a skull particle, it is also true that I did not quote him as making either statement.[24] Brehm told CBS exactly what he told me and what I had reported in *Rush to Judgment* almost a year before.[25] The reason for Cronkite's careful language now seems clear. Although CBS charged that I had demonstrated no duty to the truth and that I did not "always allow facts to get in the way" of my "theories," the network was unable to substantiate that allegation with a single example.[26] The network chose to demonstrate the validity of its assertions by presenting a false impression draped in innuendo.

Within the hour, I sent a telegram to CBS requesting equal time to respond to "an entirely untruthful and personal attack" in the broadcast that evening. Ten days later I received a letter from Leon R. Brooks, who serves CBS as vice president and general counsel.* Ignoring the single question that I raised regarding the last program, he went on to present a brief history of the relationship between the four CBS programs and Mark Lane.[27] For example, he stated, "Thus, in Part I, reference was made to your challenge of the photograph of Lee Harvey Oswald which showed him with a Mannlicker-Carcano rifle."[28] Brooks seemed certain enough that it was Oswald with the assassination weapon, even if he was unable to spell the name of the rifle correctly and even if the FBI expert was not sure.[29]

Unfortunately, he never did respond to the specific question that I had raised; but while his reasoning was enigmatic, his conclusion was clear enough: "Accordingly we will not grant your request for time to respond."[30]

Subsequently I wrote to CBS asking for an opportunity to examine the many hours of film which they had declined to show to the public.[31] All statements not presented in their entirety are taken out of context. I asked for permission to examine the out-takes so that I might determine whether the portions which were televised were representative of the witnesses' statements.[32] "We are not," Kenneth R. Frankl, senior attorney for CBS, wrote, "persuaded that this is a case in which we should depart from our policy—with which you are familiar, I believe—of not making non-broadcast material available for outside use. Your request for permission to examine unedited filmed interviews is, therefore, also denied."[33]

* The letter is reproduced as Appendix V.

Prior to these four programs, NBC-TV had presented a one-hour documentary clearly designed as an attack upon the New Orleans District Attorney.[34] He was subsequently given thirty minutes to reply.[35] At the conclusion of the original NBC program, an announcer read this statement: "The filmed testimony you have seen was edited. The unedited film is available to any authorized investigator with a legitimate reason to see it."[36] Accordingly, I wrote to NBC asking to examine the unedited film.[37] I offered my credentials in the matter to demonstrate that I had "a legitimate reason," and I referred to the fact that NBC had interviewed me on scores of occasions as an expert on the case.[38] William R. McAndrew, the president of NBC News, replied:

> NBC News does not generally release to the public material obtained in the course of preparing news programs if such material is not actually broadcast. In this instance, in light of the legitimate interest which official agencies might have in the portion of the interviews not broadcast, we concluded we would provide authorized investigators an opportunity to view the unedited interviews. This offer was made solely for the use of investigators acting on behalf of such agencies and while we can understand your concern and interest, we believe we should continue to confine our offer to official investigations.[39]*

If NBC meant that the filmed interviews would be made available to the FBI and CIA only, there appears to have been no real need for broadcasting the closing statement. A couple of letters would have sufficed.

* This letter is reproduced as Appendix VI.

II · The Advocates

21 THE PRESIDENT AND THE COMMISSIONERS

FOLLOWING the release of the Warren Report, the official response to questions about the Report was silence. Warren made it plain that he himself would not discuss the document, and it was equally clear that he expected his former colleagues and assistants to follow his example. Complicating the quest for additional information was the nonexistence of any governmental body to consider the various importunate demands. The Commission had disbanded on September 24, 1964, when the Chief Justice submitted the one-volume work to President Johnson, who had established the Commission by an Executive Order.[1] The only remaining official spokesman was the President.

On November 4, 1966, more than two years after the Report was presented to him, the President made a public comment about it.[2] At a press conference he was asked about the "alleged mysterious disappearance of [the autopsy] photos [and] X-rays."[3] The reporter inquired, "I wonder why that was not disclosed before and also why this material is still not available to competent nongovernment investigators."[4] Johnson replied, "I think that every American can understand the reasons why we wouldn't want to have the garments and the records and everything paraded out in every sewing circle in the country to be exploited and used without serving any good or official purpose."[5] I know of no one who had even considered such a grisly suggestion regarding the use of the evidence other than President Johnson at that press conference.

The President also said that the evidence had been "available to the Warren Commission any time it wanted to see it," but neglected to deal with the question of why the Commission had not examined the vital documents.[6] He added that the evidence now is available to "the Government, the Justice Department [and] the FBI."[7] He never responded to the question regarding the refusal of the Government to allow "competent nongovernment investigators" to examine the evidence, nor did he address himself to the failure of the Government to disclose the facts surrounding the autopsy photographs and X-rays until after, as the reporter put it, "two or three books . . . were written."[8] The polls had just revealed that two-thirds of the population had doubts about the Commission's conclusions.[9] The President commented, "I know of no evidence that would in any way cause any reasonable person to have a doubt about the Warren Commission, but if there is any evidence that's brought forth, I'm sure that the Commission and the appropriate authorities will take action that may be justified."[10] Any knowledgeable person knew that the Commission, having been disbanded, could not take any action.

The President's simplified, not to say puerile, rejoinders made it clear that those seeking a serious official response must look elsewhere. As *Rush to Judgment* reached the top of the best-seller lists, two Commission members offered their first public defense of the Report.[11] Congressman Gerald R. Ford said that there had been no "new evidence," although there had been "speculation about the Commission's report in recent months."[12] Ford considered that comment to be dispositive of an analysis of the Commission's work.[13] He said that the speculation was "triggered by a student's thesis and by the writings of an attorney whose services were rejected by the mother of Lee Harvey Oswald at the time of the Warren Commission hearings."[14] The former reference, although obscure, is to Edward Jay Epstein's book, *Inquest*.[15] The latter reference, although false, is evidently to me.[16] I was retained by Marguerite Oswald to represent her son's interests before the Commission.[17] The Commission refused to permit me to do so.[18] Ford concluded that criticism of the Warren Report is "a disservice to all of the American people and to the memory of the late President Kennedy."[19] As to the former, it may be said that the majority of the American people evidently do not agree, and to the latter, it seems doubtful that that for which President Kennedy lived can best be served by the issuance of a mendacious account of his death.

Allen Dulles spoke more softly, stating, "I am in complete agreement with Congressman Gerald Ford that no new information has been produced by any of the critics of the Warren Commission report which could reasonably cast any doubts upon the findings or conclusions of that report."[20]

During March 1967 the Chief Justice himself spoke out in defense of the Report.[21] At various press conferences in Latin America he repeated that he was "personally satisfied with the conclusions of the Warren Report."[22] Yet nowhere present in the comments of the

President, the Commission's chairman and the two other Commission members were there any facts.[23] Nowhere was an effort to grapple with the countless important and unanswered questions that were troubling thinking people. And there is evidence that at least one of the important officials sought to prevent a public discussion of the facts.

I had been invited to discuss the Warren Report on a telephone-format television program broadcast by the ABC affiliate in Denver. The host and hostess of the program, Jack Wilson and Barbara Story, became very interested in the subject and asked if I might return for a special open-ended late night broadcast. I agreed, and the response to the subsequent program was such that I was asked to return once more for a full-scale debate on November 22, 1966. In the interim, Congressman Ford arrived in Denver to campaign for a local Republican candidate. When he appeared on the same program, many of the questions that were directed to him related to the Warren Report, not to the specific political purpose of his visit. The station invited him to debate with me, but he declined. He was informed that I would appear without an adversary unless the Commission was able to provide one.

At about that time, a group of housewives in Denver initiated a supermarket boycott to protest high prices. The boycott quickly spread to many other states and became a matter of national significance. Wilson warned Ford that interest in the Warren Report was very high in Denver and that a movement for a new investigation, started there, might be as successful as the supermarket protest. Ford asked Wilson to call him later in Washington. When he did, Ford said that he could not debate with me and implied that the station should not permit me to speak, for Ford had investigated me. The results of the investigation, Ford said, were startling. He had discovered that I had a serious criminal record—that I had been convicted of heinous crimes. Wilson was incredulous. He immediately contacted the various district attorneys' offices in New York to confirm the accuracy of the charges. When he discovered that Ford's accusation was false—that I had never even been charged with a crime—he gave me the details and agreed to testify in any defamation action against Ford that might ensue.

22 JOSEPH A. BALL, ESQ.— ON SCURRILOUS JOURNALISTS

It was soon apparent that neither the Commission members nor the Executive who appointed them were disposed to discuss the facts, nor in all likelihood were they capable of doing so. Fortunately for those who desired further disclosure, some of the former Commission lawyers, the men who had questioned most of the witnesses who were questioned and who wrote the Report, became inclined to speak out. After completing their assignments, they returned to their communities to await the publication of the Report. They basked in the favorable attention the press gave the Report. Some lectured before local bar associations; others discussed the development of the historical document at the universities at which they taught. America accepted the document, and the attorneys who had played a part in making it what it was had assured for themselves a secure, albeit a small, niche in history. They were ill-prepared for criticism directed not alone toward the conclusions reached but at the very methods they had employed.

Despite the wishes of the Chief Justice that silence be maintained, some of the lawyers were motivated to speak. Unlike the majority of Commission members, who were engaged in active politics and therefore quite used to having their integrity called into question, some of the lawyers became enraged, for a number of the attorneys equated an assault upon the Commission's work with an onslaught upon their virtue. Thus they desired to respond. Their position was dissimilar from most of the Commission members in another respect as well. They were in possession of specific information regarding the Commission's case against Oswald.

Among the first to accept an invitation to confront a critic was Joseph A. Ball of Long Beach, California. We were both invited to debate by a local civic organization in Los Angeles. I accepted, but Ball declined. The organization then asked him if he would consent to any format which might include the two of us in a discussion. Ball said that he would agree if I spoke and then he was permitted to cross-examine me. Ball specifically precluded the possibility that I might ask him any questions. I agreed. Ball then insisted that he have the right to bring two other lawyers with him who might also question me. I agreed. The meeting was held in the very large auditorium of the Beverly Hills High School.[1] When I arrived that evening, the moderator told me that Ball and his two colleagues had insisted that they speak as well as cross-examine me. I replied that I had no objection to that change in the format, provided that I be permitted to question Ball after he spoke. Ball was adamant. He would not submit to questioning, and if I did not accept the unilateral modification in the program he and his colleagues would leave. I accepted the new terms.

Just before the formal proceedings began, a reporter for radio station KPFK-FM asked each of the speakers if he would consent to his taping and broadcasting the entire event. Every speaker agreed. However, when the session ended, Ball approached the radio reporter and told him that he did not want the program broadcast. The reporter reminded Ball that he had already given his consent. Ball became irate and shouted that he would sue the station if the tape was played. That exchange was tape-recorded as well, and subsequently the station did broadcast the evening's proceedings with the statement that Ball had tried to prevent it from doing so. Since that occasion, Ball has consistently declined each of the numerous invitations to debate that have been extended to him.

Although he refuses to defend the Report in a debate format with any of the critics, he has given many interviews to the press and has addressed various groups on the subject. In a published address delivered in January 1967, entitled "Scurrilous Journalists Lie, Cheat, and Draw Conclusions Unfounded by Evidence," Ball said that "we [of the legal profession] attempt to solve our problems with honesty and dignity."[2] He said that the Commission was made up of "men of integrity and proven worth" while the staff was made up of men of "integrity."[3]

"I'd like to compare the integrity of the men of the Commission and staff with the integrity of the men that are now writing: Mark Lane; Epstein; Weisburg [*sic*], the chicken farmer from Maryland; Leo Sauvage, the Frenchman."[4] He added, "It seems to me that we start out with a presumption in our favor because the integrity of the men of the Commission must count for something."[5] He said that "some of these people who cast doubts are beneath contempt."[6] He did not mean Harold Weisberg, he said: "Weisburg [*sic*], the chicken farmer, isn't really dishonest; he reasons within the limits of his very limited ability. A few years ago, he suffered a misfortune in which all of his chickens were killed by a sonic boom."[7] Thus far Ball had sought to establish but two points: Weisberg was a chicken farmer and the Commission members and staff were men of integrity.[8] Weisberg raised geese. Low-flying helicopters disturbed them, but it is unlikely that they, the helicopters, ever got up enough speed to break the sound barrier.

The entire attack upon Sauvage, other than upon his place of birth, consisted of three sentences: "Sauvage has no scruples, and he reasons from a record which he himself considers adequate—I don't. Sauvage says, 'I see nothing to indicate that Oswald was the assassin of President Kennedy.' Need I say more?"[9]

Regarding Epstein, Ball said, "*Epstein quotes me as saying we did all the work; the Commission did nothing. This is a gross libel.*"[10]

Yet in a radio broadcast, another Commission lawyer, Wesley Liebeler, subsequently said that the young lawyers had "almost unlimited power" both "in directing the FBI, for example, and conducting the investigation."[11]

In November 1966, in a speech delivered to the Associated Press Managing Editors convention, Ball addressed himself to the witnesses who said they had seen a puff of smoke rise from the wooden fence on the knoll: "What does a puff of smoke mean? Does it mean that there's a rifle? Of course not. Since when did rifles give off a puff of smoke? They don't do it."[12] This matter will be explored more fully in the portion of the work dealing with evidence relating to the grassy knoll.[13] It may be sufficient to state here that an FBI test of the alleged assassination weapon revealed that it issued a small amount of white smoke when fired.[14] Evidently the document containing that information, which was published by the Commission in November 1964, had escaped the attention of Ball for some two years.[15] Immediately after Ball's remarks, however, he was informed of the document and its contents. Nevertheless, during his January 1967 address, Ball said, "Do rifles give off puffs of smoke which can be seen rising in the air? No, not with modern smokeless powder. This is impossible."[16] Ball had still refused to share the FBI test report with his audience.[17]

He did speak about the alleged assassination weapon in another context.[18] He said that it was a Mannlicher-Carcano and that Seymour Weitzman and Deputy Sheriff Eugene Boone discovered it.[19] "And later on that day they both said it was a Mauser—a German Mauser," Ball said.[20] He added, "Weitzman made the mistake."[21] Weitzman's affidavit identifying the weapon was actually made the next day.[22]

One of Ball's former colleagues on the Commission staff, Wesley J. Liebeler, offered an imaginative explanation on behalf of Weitzman.[23] The Commission concluded that an Italian Mannlicher-Carcano carbine had actually been uncovered by the officer and that Weitzman had made an error since he had only glanced at it.[24] Said Liebeler, "And, of course, Mr. Weitzman is Jewish."[25] While the relevance of the officer's religion may not seem apparent at the outset, Liebeler's presentation of Weitzman's motive places it in context.[26] Since "the Germans have been picking" on the Jewish people "for the last 50 years," Weitzman reasoned, according to Liebeler, that he "got one back at them."[27] Ball, who continues to assert that Weitzman made an innocent error, evidently is unaware of Liebeler's discovery that Weitzman may have actually been striking a blow against anti-Semitism.

Toward the conclusion of his address, Ball said, "Never in my life have I been so scurrilously attacked as by Mr. Lane in his 'Rush to Judgment.' When Mr. Lane says I am a fraud, a cheat, I say Mr. Lane is my enemy; and I say, Mr. Lane, you're the biggest fraud of all."[28] Ball's name does not appear in *Rush to Judgment*.[29]

23 ALBERT E. JENNER, JR., ESQ.—ON IRRESPONSIBLE AUTHORS

One senior lawyer did consent to an open discussion of the case. Albert E. Jenner, Jr., of Chicago agreed to meet with me on the Jerry Williams radio program, which is produced in that city. We were to spend the entire evening discussing the case, but before the program ended Jenner said that he remembered that he "had to catch an airplane," and he left the studio. He also said that he would never debate with me again.*

It should be noted here that I do not claim to be an impressive public speaker or more than a pedestrian conversationalist. I am prepared to discuss the Warren Report. Indeed, it would be surprising if I were not able to do so after having spent some years studying it. The inability of the Commission attorneys to create a favorable climate in which the Report might be accepted when confronted by a critic is due not at all to the critic's skill but to the difficulties imposed upon Commission counsel by the Commission's case and by their own past conduct in developing that case.

Jenner has stated, "These people who write these articles postulate all the time, isn't it possible there was somebody else? And that was one of my assignments—my assignment was conspiracy, motive, and the complete life and background of Oswald."[1] According to the Commission, on May 24, 1962, the American Embassy in Moscow "renewed Oswald's passport for 30 days, stamped it valid for direct return to the United States only and handed it to him."[2] Under the procedures in effect at that time, a "lookout card" should have been prepared and filed in the "lookout file" in the Passport Office.[3] Whenever anyone applied for an American passport in any city in the world, the application was forwarded to the Department of State

* However, he did meet with me on one subsequent occasion. At that time he appeared with another Commission lawyer to assist Louis Nizer, who discussed the matter with me in a television broadcast. Jenner, however, declined to answer questions which I put to him, stating merely that he refused to answer such evidentiary questions as: Did the FBI firearms expert state that he could trace the bullets taken from Tippit's body to "Oswald's" pistol?

Passport Office and the name of the applicant and date of birth checked against the "lookout file."[4] In ordinary circumstances, several reasons should have caused Oswald's name to appear in the file. He had attempted to renounce his American citizenship, he had informed an American Embassy official in Moscow that he was about to give classified information to the Russians and he had been granted a loan by the State Department so that he might return to the United States.[5] Yet his name never appeared in the file.[6] Mine did, evidently for asking why his did not. When Oswald applied for a new passport at the New Orleans office on June 24, 1963, it was issued to him the next day.[7]

Commission Exhibit 917 was a document that had long intrigued me.[8] It is the photostatic copy of a cablegram from the United States naval attaché in the American Embassy in Moscow to the Department of the Navy, the Department of State, the Immigration and Naturalization Service as well as to the FBI, CIA and Marine Corps.[9]* The relevant portion of the document states, "Concerning the renunciation of US citizenship and request for Soviet citizenship by Lee Harvey Oswald former Marine and—," at which point approximately forty-one letters were deleted before publication by the Commission.[10] The document concludes: "Oswald stated he was radar operator in Marcorps and has offered to furnish Soviets info he possesses on US radar."[11]

Normally Oswald would have been denied a passport and very likely arrested upon his return. From the then available evidence it appeared possible that the deleted material offered a further description of Oswald, and in view of questions regarding Oswald's possible Government affiliation, insight into how a naval attaché at the Embassy described him on November 3, 1959, seemed a likely area for further inquiry. Accordingly, I asked Jenner, into whose assigned category the matter fell, what words had been deleted. Jenner answered, "I don't know what those words are. The only way I ever saw that cable was after those letters had been deleted. I never saw the deleted words." I then asked him who had deleted the words. He said, "No, I don't know who deleted them. And I have faith that whoever did it had a good reason."

Four months later during a television interview, in the absence of a Commission critic, Jenner was asked, "If you were going to start the Commission all over again, if you were really going to start from scratch, what would you do differently in a new investigation?"[12]

* The cablegram is reproduced as Appendix VII.

Jenner answered, "You know, I can't think of a single thing I can do. I had a responsibility for three major segments of this investigation, and I had a fine staff of very able lawyers. I had available to me any FBI agent in the entire United States, the CIA, the intelligence services of the Army, Air Corps, Marines, and the Navy, and I used them, the State Department, the Secret Service, the Immigration and Naturalization Service—any request we made, never did we have a single demurrer."[13]

During that program, Jenner made a number of statements about the evidence that are without foundation.[14] When opposed by a critic or questioned by a knowledgeable interviewer, the Commission lawyers generally remained fairly close to the evidence, sometimes revealing valuable and previously undisclosed information. On their own, however, they tended merely to present a digest of the Commission's conclusions and when pressed to defend some particularly untoward conduct might even invent a detail or two. Jenner's interview two days before Christmas 1966 provides a good example.[15] The three reporters who asked the questions were in an expansive mood, possibly due to the holiday spirit.[16] The station was WNYC, the station of the City of New York, which placed it within the jurisdiction of the attorney for the City of New York, J. Lee Rankin, former general counsel to the Warren Commission, who in that capacity had served as Jenner's superior counsel.[17]

A reporter asked Jenner to discuss the autopsy photographs and X-rays, and Jenner said, "They were never—I'll put it this way: some members of the Commission saw both the film and the colored pictures, and the X-rays. We did not, as staff members, introduce those before the Commission at any formal hearing. We of the staff saw them ourselves."[18] Jenner's allegations about the photographs and X-rays appear to be untrue. Other Commission lawyers have said that neither the attorneys nor the Commission members ever saw the documents, and the three Commission members to comment upon the question have made it quite clear that the Commissioners did not see those exhibits.[19] John J. McCloy said that his only regret as a former member of the Commission is that the Commission did not look at the photographs and X-rays.[20] During a subsequent television broadcast, I confronted Jenner with the contradiction and asked him if he had in fact ever seen the photographs and X-rays. He said that he refused to answer the question.*

* Immediately following that broadcast a young lady unknown to me but said by some members of the studio audience to be Jenner's daughter rushed to him and asked him if he had ever seen the photographs and X-rays. Jenner

Jenner began to summarize the proof that all the shots had originated from a sixth-floor window of the Texas School Book Depository.[21] A motorcycle officer heard the shots and raced to the building, Jenner said.[22]

> And the policeman took him by the arm and they rushed into that building to go where? The policeman wanted to get up to the sixth floor, to that corner, where he had—had reached the conclusion, as a trained man, that these shots, at least, had come from that window. Oswald, as we subsequently find, had jimmied the elevator door on the sixth floor by sticking a stick in it, to hold it back so as to disengage the electrical impulses, and that held the elevator up there on the sixth floor. Roy Truly and the policeman with his gun drawn rushed up, they were going to go all, right up those six floors, and they reached the second floor, who was the first man this policeman saw, was Oswald with a bottle of Coke. And he rushed over to him with his pistol. And held him. Roy Truly said that's one of our men, Mr. Oswald, there's nothing wrong with him. But these men, intent on getting to the sixth floor, where they thought the person—whoever he was—who had discharged this rifle.[23]

Just a few minutes earlier, in an effort to discount the testimony of witnesses who thought the shots originated at the knoll, Jenner had said that due to "reverberations from a rifle shot" it was "very difficult to determine the place from which it comes."[24] In any event, Truly did not believe that the shots came from the building.[25] He testified, "I thought the shots came from the vicinity of the railroad or the WPA project [the pergola on top of the knoll]."[26] He said that he thought the officer, Marrion L. Baker, wanted to enter the building so that he might go to the roof and overlook the area behind the knoll—the railroad yards.[27] In fact, Truly and the officer did rush to the roof and, according to Truly, "the officer looked down over the boxcars and the railroad tracks."[28] There is nothing in the officer's testimony to indicate that this "trained man" thought that any shots "had come from that window."[29] After the fact the officer said that he believed at the time that some shots had been fired from one of two buildings behind the limousine, but he was unable to determine which building, much less which window in the building, the shots came from.[30]

Each of Jenner's claims about the officer and Truly is untrue.[31]

---

urged her to be quiet, but she repeated the question. Jenner replied that he had not seen them but that he did not wish to discuss it then and there. The young lady then asked him why he had said that he had seen them. Jenner's answer was not audible.

The statements that they rushed "right up those six floors" and that "these men [were] intent on getting to the sixth floor, where they thought the person [was]—whoever he was—who had discharged this rifle" are contrary to the known facts.[32] Baker testified that they went to the roof and remained there for between five and ten minutes.[33] He then walked to the elevator, stopped at either the third or fourth floor to talk to another officer, then went to the first floor and left the building.[34]

Jenner's claim that Oswald "had jimmied the elevator door on the sixth floor by sticking a stick in it" is unique.[35] There were two elevators.[36] The Warren Report indicated that the east one was on the fifth floor.[37] As to the other, the Report states, "Jack Dougherty, an employee working on the fifth floor, testified that he took the west elevator to the first floor after hearing a noise which sounded like a backfire."[38] Nowhere in the Report or in the volumes of evidence is there any support for Jenner's illusion regarding Oswald and the elevator.[39]

If Jenner is correct in stating that Baker saw "Oswald with a bottle of Coke," this would, as we have seen, virtually preclude the possibility that Oswald had fired the shots from the sixth floor for he would not have had time to arrive on the second floor and purchase the Coca-Cola before the arrival of the officer.[40] Jenner also said, "We found that on the Mannlicher-Carcano rifle were threads from the jacket that he [Oswald] wore that particular day."[41] The Hair and Fiber Unit of the FBI Laboratory had tested several cotton fibers allegedly found in a crevice between the butt plate of the rifle and the wooden stock.[42] The Commission made no reference to Oswald's jacket.[43] As to his shirt, the expert testified that the fibers "could have come from this shirt," but he was unable to state that they did come from the shirt.[44] Jenner continued, stating that the pistol allegedly used in the Tippit murder "had his [Oswald's] fingerprints on it in generous proportions."[45] Yet the Warren Commission was unaware of that discovery.[46]

In a matter of minutes and in the course of a few sentences, Jenner had made eight untrue assertions: they "wanted to get up to the sixth floor"; Baker "had reached the conclusion" that shots "had come from that window"; Oswald "had jimmied the elevator door"; the elevator was on "the sixth floor"; they were going "up those six floors"; the men were "intent on getting to the sixth floor"; threads were traced to Oswald, they were traced to a jacket; the pistol had Oswald's fingerprints.[47] Jenner concluded his presentation of the evidence with an accurate statement. He complained that "none of these affirmative things are called to the attention of the public when they read these books."[48] Therefore, he reasoned, the authors of the critical books are "irresponsible."[49]

24 WESLEY J. LIEBELER, ESQ.— A VOCAL SPOKESMAN

No less plangent than Jenner but perhaps less discreet was a junior attorney—Wesley J. Liebeler. It may be said that he had the most to make amends for, since he had provided most of the material that Epstein had used in his book.[1] Liebeler subsequently referred to the Warren Report as "a good second draft," implying that an additional work was required.[2] At the same time he was not unwilling to fill the vacuum with his own book, which he was then preparing for publication. While all the Commissioners and the majority of the attorneys have declined to debate with the critics, Liebeler has stated that he is always available for debate. That statement has proven to be partially true, for he has been more willing to debate than most of his former colleagues but nevertheless not universally available. The Denver television station referred to above invited Liebeler to debate with me during November 1966. I agreed to appear and I stated that I would not charge the station for traveling or other expenses that might be incurred. I, of course, asked for no fee. Liebeler said he would appear only if his plane ticket and hotel accommodations were paid for by the station and if he were paid an additional sum of $500. The station's budget could not permit such an expenditure and the debate was reluctantly abandoned. At one point Liebeler was asked if he might be willing to place a collect telephone call to the program and debate with me in that fashion. He refused, stating that he would be placed at a disadvantage if the public could not see him.

Students at UCLA, where Liebeler teaches, invited me to debate with him before his own student body. I accepted the invitation and a tentative date was chosen, pending Liebeler's approval.* Liebeler

* A front-page story in the student newspaper stated that I had agreed to debate there and that the student organization was awaiting Liebeler's reply. Subsequently, when Liebeler was interviewed by the *New York Times,* he asserted that I was afraid to debate with him for he could prove that my book was inaccurate. The *Times* departed from its usual procedure of checking out such allegations with the person who is accused and ran the untrue allegation in a news story. I wrote to the *Times,* enclosing the student newspaper which predated the *Times* story and asked that my letter be published. The *Times* declined to publish the letter but did have a reporter call me. No story, however, was published. I traveled to Europe, and upon my return I called Clifton

subsequently agreed, and the much heralded debate at UCLA was set for January 25, 1967. Liebeler had repeatedly asserted that less than 10 percent of the statements in *Rush to Judgment* are factual. That unsubstantiated charge has since been adopted by a number of less than cautious defenders, evidently on the basis that Liebeler would not have made such a charge without any basis.[3] Consequently, at least one book and one law review article have relied upon that accusation.[4] Under the circumstances, I was delighted with the opportunity to confront Liebeler with his own charge. At the press conference that preceded the debate, I challenged Liebeler to document his assertion, to "list just a few of the several thousand errors" he claimed to have discovered in his "massive analysis" of my work.*

But Liebeler was already in retreat. He had told the Los Angeles *Times* that he "and his fellows on the commission staff are particularly incensed" with me since they had uncovered "at least 15" errors in my book.[6] From more than four thousand to "at least 15" marked a substantial reduction, but I was still interested in those fifteen. I asked Liebeler if he might mention two or three as an example. Liebeler was not unprepared. He passed out six-page brochures—a two-page press statement together with four pages of documentary material. The release found Liebeler stating, "I have previously referred to his book as a 'tissue of distortion' and I welcome the opportunity today to confront Mr. Lane personally and

---

Daniel, the Managing Editor, at the *Times* and again requested that the matter be attended to. I told him that I had been abroad and therefore unable to read the *Times* daily, but that I had been assured by my publisher that the promised story had not been published. Daniel said, "You are doing exactly what you charged the Commission with doing." I asked him if the story had in fact been published, and he replied that the matter was of little consequence to him and that he did not know. I asked him if he would be good enough to find out. Later an assistant called, said the correction had not been published but that the matter would be taken care of. I subsequently discovered that the reporter who had originally called had written a story but that it had been "killed," in the newspaper parlance, by someone in authority. Finally, a note was published stating that I would debate with Liebeler, but not stating that the *New York Times* was in possession of information which demonstrated that Liebeler's original statement was erroneous.

* Liebeler was directing a project at UCLA in which twenty law students, most of them in their third year, were participating. Liebeler told the Los Angeles *Times* that he "frankly admits the study was spawned by two books critical of the Warren report—'Rush to Judgment,' by attorney Mark Lane, and 'Inquest,' by Edward Jay Epstein."[5] Liebeler assigned various chapters of *Rush to Judgment* to students so that each of the more than 4,500 citations would be checked out.

demonstrate this fact." The demonstration consisted of photostatic copies of parts of three pages of *Playboy* magazine with the assertion that Liebeler did not accept the statements in the interview and one mimeographed sheet which found Charles Brehm stating that he could not positively identify the fragment he observed flying from the President's head as a skull particle, an allegation not attributed to him in *Rush to Judgment*.[7] Surely there was more. Liebeler had not yet pointed to a single alleged inaccuracy in the book.

His written statement concluded:

> I have spent considerable time over the last few months studying and researching the various criticisms leveled at the conclusions of the report. With the help of other members of the law school and university community, I have developed certain physical evidence which we think conclusively demonstrates the validity of the Warren Commission's conclusions. Furthermore, we think that this evidence proves that the President could not have been shot from the side or the front —Lane's grassy knoll area. I hope to go into this evidence in some detail in today's debate.

The reporters asked what the new evidence was. Liebeler replied that they would have to wait for the debate; he could not reveal it at that time. That answer was given fifteen minutes before the debate was scheduled to begin. "What errors have you found in Lane's book?" another reporter asked. Liebeler waved the six-page document, which made not a single specific allegation about the book. After months of study with a staff of twenty, Liebeler was apparently unable to find a single error. The reporters, pens poised for a story, seemed somewhat disappointed.

The debate took place. After Liebeler spoke, I pointed out that the press had been less than accurate when it reported upon the activities of the critics and defenders in the past. I suggested that in order to acquaint the press with the facts in this instance, it might be helpful if the students who accepted the Warren Report's conclusions signified so by raising their hands. Less than one-fifth of the students did so. I then asked those who could not believe it to raise their hands and approximately three-quarters of the students then did so. A few others said that they wished to abstain.

When the debate concluded, the press corps was more discouraged than before. Liebeler, despite his promise, offered no new physical evidence, no new evidence of any nature, which even suggested that the shots could not have originated "from the side or the front."*

* Liebeler produced but one item of evidence—a picture which he said showed that the evidently disparate shadow formation from the face and from the body of the picture which allegedly showed Oswald with a rifle could be

Liebeler also spoke at Stanford University after I had addressed the student body. There he placed the blame for the rejection of the Warren Report upon the populace: "There is still the madness of crowds and popular delusion today that there was at the time of the crusades, alchemists, and witchcraft."[8] Later Liebeler gave a radio interview.[9] He was asked about a photograph taken by Mary Moorman that may have shown the sixth-floor window of the Depository at about the time that the shots were fired.[10] The photograph had not been published by the Commission, an oversight of which I had complained.[11] Liebeler replied that I had seen the photograph and that I knew that the photograph was not relevant.[12] He also implied that I might not have questioned Mrs. Moorman properly: "And Mr. Lane also knows that, because he was down in Dallas and interviewed Mrs. Moorman about this. And, she said that all he was interested in was the possibility that she had been detained or—or kept—uh—under wraps by some secret—uh—mysterious agency of the government that's—uh—going around thwarting this investigation. Well, the photograph, the reason, the reason the photograph isn't—isn't in the Report or the 26 volumes is that it doesn't even show the sixth floor of the School Book Depository Building. It shows about the bottom two floors."[13]

Since I have never spoken with Mrs. Moorman in person or by telephone and since to my knowledge there is no document, however erroneous, that might suggest that I did, Liebeler's fanciful and detailed description of a conversation, replete with allusions to a "secret mysterious agency," must raise questions regarding his credibility. This is all the more unfortunate since it is his description of the photograph that constitutes the only quasi-official response to questions about its suppression. The photograph was described quite differently in the Supplementary Investigation Report of the Dallas Sheriff's Department, dated November 23, 1963.[14] There the officer who took possession of the picture wrote:

> I got all these pictures and looked at them and in one picture Mrs. Moorman had taken a picture of the lead motorcycle officer, in the background of this picture was a picture of the Sexton Building [Book

---

duplicated. This photograph was presented in the form of a huge blow-up, after the debate had been concluded and during the question period. It was offered in answer to a question which Liebeler had planted through one of his students. There was no time to look at the photograph then, but subsequent examination of it by Raymond J. Marcus revealed that it was inadequate in several respects, the direction of the shadow, the angle of the head, etc. Subsequently, Liebeler has admitted that the photograph may not have duplicated the conditions it purported to. In any event, it was not evidence related to proof "that the President could not have been shot from the side or the front."

> Depository Building] and the window where the gunman sat when doing the shooting. I took this picture to Chief Criminal Deputy Sheriff, Allan Sweatt, who later turned it over to Secret Service Officer Patterson.[15]

As we have previously observed, CBS clearly posed the important question of the President's head movement immediately following the impact of the fatal bullet.[16] "In Abraham Zapruder's film of the assassination, the fatal shot appears to move the President's head back. The critics contend this can only mean the shot came not from the Book Depository, but from somewhere in front."[17] When asked about that physical evidence of a shot from the right front, Liebeler said, "Frankly, the Commission didn't really examine this question. I think it's safe to say that we didn't really pay any attention to the President's head movement."[18] He explained that the Commission was "quite satisfied" with the testimony of the military physicians.[19]

However, Liebeler also appeared to call into question the skill of those physicians by stating that a bullet had passed through the President's neck but that "it's quite clear that the autopsy surgeons did not conclude that night [November 22, 1963] that the bullet had in fact passed through the President's body."[20] That determination was not arrived at until after the body and the other evidence had been made unavailable to the surgeons, he explained.[21]

Liebeler was asked if it was true, as the critics have stated, that almost two-thirds of the witnesses who were questioned and who stated that they could offer an opinion as to the origin of the shots said that at least one shot was fired from the knoll.[22] He replied, "I don't know whether two-thirds of the witnesses said that they thought that the shots came from that area. I know Mr. Lane says that, but I haven't taken the trouble to check that out."[23] He added that "the value of that evidence to me and I think to any lawyer—uh—in view of the fact that there was such an echo chamber effect there, is worth almost nothing."[24] Yet some of the witnesses saw smoke, and since the Commission declined to conduct an acoustics test of the plaza, allegations as to "an echo chamber effect" are speculative.[25] As to the tests, Liebeler explained, "we just didn't think it was worth our time to do it."[26]

The most serious evidence suggesting a shot from the right front includes the testimony of the majority of the questioned witnesses who had an opinion regarding what they saw and heard and the evidence of the head snap in the Zapruder film.[27] Yet the Commission lawyer who has become its most outspoken defender has stated that he does not know what the majority of the witnesses said since he hasn't "taken the trouble to check that out."[28] Yet he discounted the evidence with which he is not fully familiar because of a purported "echo chamber effect."[29] Yet he does not know if there is such an effect since the Commission conducted no test to determine whether it existed because "we just didn't think it was worth our time."[30] Regarding film of the head snap, perhaps the most important recorded document on the question of the origin of the fatal bullet, the Commission just "didn't really pay any attention" to that matter.[31]

25 WESLEY J. LIEBELER, ESQ.— A SILENT WITNESS

On July 21, 1964, Wesley J. Liebeler took the testimony of a New Orleans lawyer, Dean Andrews, who previously had told agents of the FBI that a man calling himself "Clay Bertrand" had called to enlist him as Oswald's attorney shortly after the assassination.[1] The Commission was sufficiently disinterested in "Clay Bertrand" to refrain from making reference to him in its Report.[2] Yet the potential significance of the Andrews testimony can be ascertained by the fact that the first man indicted for conspiracy to assassinate President Kennedy was Clay Shaw, a man charged by the New Orleans District Attorney with being "Clay Bertrand."[3]* Liebeler had before him perhaps the most important witness he had questioned, yet he seemed rather unconcerned about going into the heart of the matter.

In response to Liebeler's questions, Andrews testified that Lee Harvey Oswald had visited him at his New Orleans law office to discuss his desire to secure an honorable discharge from the Marine Corps and for advice regarding the institution of citizenship proceedings for his wife.[5] Andrews said that Oswald had been accompanied by some young Mexican men, apparently homosexuals.[6] Liebeler asked, "Where did you see these gay kids after the first time?"[7] Andrews replied that he saw them in the police station after they had been arrested.[8] Liebeler asked, "You do represent from time to time some of these gay kids, is that correct?"[9] Andrews answered in the affirmative.[10]

After Andrews said that he had subsequently seen Oswald distributing leaflets, which he described as "these kooky Castro things,"

* This criticism of the Commission's indifference to potentially important testimony is not offered here solely with the benefit of hindsight. The name "Clay Bertrand" does appear in *Rush to Judgment,* and the New Orleans District Attorney has stated that his interest in the case was stimulated in large part by reading that book.[4]

Liebeler launched an inquiry as to the color of the leaflets.[11] A discussion of the possibility that the leaflets were either white or yellow ensued, but just as the attorney was narrowing the choice, Andrews stated, "I am totally colorblind."[12]

Andrews subsequently made this voluntary statement: "There's three people I am going to find: One of them is the real guy that killed the President; the Mexican [whom he had said was with Oswald when he visited Andrews' office]; and Clay Bertrand."[13] Liebeler pointed out that the witness was basing his conclusions upon newspaper stories.[14] Andrews replied that he had been "an ordnanceman in the Navy" and that "this civilian" could not possess the requisite skill for the assassination.[15] Liebeler replied, "You are making certain assumptions as to what actually happened, or you have a certain notion in your mind as to what happened based on material you read in the newspaper."[16]*

After concluding the discussion of Andrews' law practice, his expertise with a weapon, his inability to distinguish the color of the leaflets and the presumed sexual proclivities of his clients, Liebeler moved obliquely toward Clay Bertrand.[18] He asked, "Did there come a time after the assassination when you had some further involvement with Oswald, or at least an apparent involvement with Oswald; as I understand it?"[19] Andrews answered, "No; nothing at all with Oswald."[20] Then he continued, "I was in Hotel Dieu, and the phone rang and a voice I recognized as Clay Bertrand asked me if I would go to Dallas and Houston—I think—Dallas, I guess, wherever it was that this boy was being held—and defend him. I told him I was sick in the hospital. If I couldn't go, I would find somebody that could go."[21]

Liebeler told Andrews that he had been in New Orleans in April 1964 and that he "was going to take your deposition at that time, but we didn't make arrangements."[22] In the interim—Liebeler questioned Andrews on July 21, 1964—agents of the FBI questioned Andrews repeatedly.[23] Liebeler summarized those meetings: "In your continuing discussions with the FBI, you finally came to the conclusion that Clay Bertrand was a figment of your imagination?"[24] Andrews said that while the agents may have written that, he had not given that information to them.[25] In fact, he said, he had seen Bertrand again "about 6 weeks ago."[26] Liebeler asked a number of addi-

* Although Liebeler clearly appeared to be arguing with, rather than questioning, the witness during this exchange—he later charged, "However, as we have indicated, it is your opinion"—the Commission evidently sought to correct the impression retroactively by placing a question mark after the statement.[17]

tional questions, including, "Is this fellow [Bertrand] a homosexual, do you say?" and, "And mostly he refers, I think you said, these gay kids, is that right?" but he did not ask the most obvious question to test Andrews' credibility.[27] Andrews had said that he told Bertrand that if he did not represent Oswald he would "find somebody that could go."[28] The FBI, unable to locate Bertrand, was willing to conclude that he did not exist and that therefore the telephone call was a figment of Andrews' imagination.[29] The Commission was content to adopt that hypothesis.[30] Liebeler had failed to ask Andrews what he did to meet his obligation to Bertrand regarding securing other counsel for Oswald.[31] Liebeler said, "I don't think I have any more questions. Do you have anything else that you would like to add?"[32] Andrews said that after Bertrand had called him he called an attorney, Monk Zelden.[33] Zelden, he said, has since confirmed the fact that he talked with Andrews: "Only thing I do remember about it, while I was talking with Monk, he said, 'Don't worry about it. Your client just got shot.' That was the end of the case. Even if he was a bona fide client, I never did get to him; somebody else got to him before I did. Other than that, that's the whole thing, but this boy Bertrand has been bugging me ever since. I will find him sooner or later."[34] Liebeler then asked, "Does Bertrand owe you money?"[35]

Later Andrews was called before an Orleans Parish Grand Jury, and as a consequence of his testimony there he was subsequently indicted for perjury.[36] The New Orleans District Attorney, Jim Garrison, requested that Liebeler appear at the trial so that the jury might secure all the facts regarding the testimony of Andrews.[37] Liebeler, although willing to travel great distances for some radio and television programs, refused that request.[38] The District Attorney's office then filed a request for attendance by Liebeler with Criminal District Judge Frank J. Shea.[39] Shea signed an order directing Liebeler to appear in New Orleans,[40] and he ordered that Liebeler be supplied with funds to meet his travel expenses.[41] The District Attorney's office, in requesting Liebeler's return to New Orleans, said that he was a material witness in the state's case against Andrews.[42] Speaking for the office, Assistant District Attorney James L. Alcock said that testimony by Liebeler was necessary to show the materiality and relevance of the grand jury's questioning of Andrews and to show prior inconsistent statements.[43]

Apparently the only valid defense available to Liebeler for his refusal to cooperate with the lawful prosecuting authority might be the assertion that the published record in Volume XI of the Commission's twenty-six volumes contained and revealed all that he knew about the matter.[44] Yet there are two reasons that cast some doubt upon the efficacy of that defense. The published record of the Andrews testimony may not be identical with the actual stenographic transcript of that session. The Commission had stated that it was not bound to publish precisely that which the witness had sworn to, but that it had indulged in "editing of the transcript prior to printing in these volumes."[45] The Commission reported that the changes it made were "designed to improve the clarity and accuracy of the testimony."[46] The original transcripts are sealed in the National Archives and are presently unavailable.* It may be that the New Orleans District Attorney was anxious to determine, from the attorney who took the testimony, how much the Commission had improved the transcript prior to publication.

Toward the end of the Andrews testimony, Liebeler said, "Off the record."[48] A parenthetical note indicated that there was "discussion off the record" between Andrews and Liebeler.[49] Following that secret exchange, Liebeler returned to the record with this question: "Did you just indicate that you would like to find Mr. Bertrand and he did run off? Did you see him run off?"[50] There is no other clue as to what transpired in the exchange.[51] I have learned that the District Attorney was anxious to explore that area at the Andrews trial.†

* The Commission stated that "all the original transcripts prepared by the court reporters, of course, have been preserved and will be available for inspection under the same rules and regulations which will apply to all records of this Commission."[47] Despite the Commission's implied promise, the records remain unavailable.

† An earlier encounter with Liebeler regarding his recollection of another "off the record" exchange did not encourage the belief that his memory was infallible. While speaking at UCLA, I referred to Commission Exhibit 5, a photograph of the back of a house occupied by Major General Edwin A. Walker.[52] In the foreground an automobile was clearly visible. It was said to have been found by the Dallas police among Oswald's belongings.[53] The police transferred it to the FBI, who in turn gave it to the Commission.[54] The picture was utilized by the Commission as proof that Oswald planned to shoot Walker, although why, since he was allegedly acting alone and had to be there to take the picture anyway, it might be thought that the photograph could be useful to him has not been explained.[55] Marina Oswald was shown the photograph by FBI agents and later by Commission personnel.[56] When Liebeler showed her the photograph she complained that someone had torn a hole in it, thereby obliterating the automobile's license plate which had been visible when the FBI and Commission personnel had displayed the picture earlier.[57] She said she was positive there had been no hole when she had previously seen the photograph and asked why the Commission did not explore the mutilation of the evidence.[58] At that point, another "off the record" conference began.[59] I said that it was unfortunate that the picture suffered such defacement

and that the Commission did nothing to rebut the disturbing charge that the picture had been altered after coming into its possession.[60] At UCLA, in Liebeler's presence, I said in reference to the "off the record conference" that "we do not know what happened."[61] Liebeler interrupted me to indicate that he had the answer.[62] I responded, "Oh, fine, then maybe you'll tell us about it; how it happened, if you would?"[63] Liebeler said, "If I get a chance I will."[64] I then yielded the floor. A tape recorder was present to record Liebeler's response. The unedited transcript of Liebeler's response to questions from students at his own university, prepared by a director of the UCLA radio station, follows:

LIEBELER: This whole discussion—uh—where we focus on the—uh—on the license plate is a discussion of why some material appears—or why off-the-record conversations appear—or why the notation off the record appears in the—in the printed version. Marina Oswald did ask why—uh—as I recall it, why somebody wasn't—uh—trying to find out what—how this hole got in the picture. And that's exactly what I was trying to do. The first thing I was trying to establish is whether or not that hole—uh—that black spot appeared in that picture when the Commission first showed that document to Marina. I had no way of knowing whether it had or not because I wasn't present at the time and there was no records to it or mention of it in the [unintelligible word] testimony that Marina first gave to the Commission. So obviously the first thing that had to be done was to find out whether or not the hole was—was poked in the picture at the time Marina was first shown the picture. Now, Marina testified—and that's all that Marina could testify about is presumably—particularly in view of the fact that she testified that the hole wasn't there. So how do you say she couldn't tell us anything about how it got there because it wasn't there when she turned it over to the—to the FBI? It apparently got there at some time later or it was a different picture or in fact it was a photograph. The thing that I had before her at that time was a photograph of the picture that apparently she'd been shown because the hole wasn't actually in the photograph. It was just a black mark there which showed that the—that the picture had been gouged at some point along the line so that the license plate was obliterated. Now, isn't that right, Mr. Lane? That's right. Now, what I was trying to find out was how it got there—how the hole got in the photograph—why or how the license plate was obliterated. And this was the preliminary basis of the—of the—of trying to do it. Find out from Marina whether it was there at the time she testified before the Commission, that it wasn't and we went on from there trying to find out how the hole got there. I'm very sorry to have to say that I was not able to find out how the hole did get there.

(Laughter)

ANONYMOUS VOICES FROM THE AUDIENCE: Why off the record? Why off the record?

LIEBELER: I don't recall what the off-the-record conversation was at the time, but it had nothing to do with any—

ANONYMOUS VOICE: You just stated that that was off the record. Now I'm asking you why was it off the record.

LIEBELER: What—her—I don't—I don't recall why it was off the record

Liebeler, however, fought against the efforts to return him to New Orleans where he might testify.[66] According to assistant District Attorney Alcock, Liebeler expressed his reluctance to testify in a telephone conversation with him but he was, at that time, unable to conjure up a valid legal excuse. According to a two-sentence note subsequently published in the New Orleans *States-Item,* "A district court judge at Brattleboro, Vt., denied the DA's request after Liebeler said he had personal business conflicting with the trial dates. Liebeler had declined to come to New Orleans voluntarily."[67] The "personal business" appears to have arisen somewhat suddenly and while Liebeler was on vacation. Although the *New York Times* was willing to run, but unwilling to retract, a false charge by Liebeler that I had refused to debate with him, it was reluctant to feature the refusal of that Commission attorney to testify in an important trial. I do not doubt that some American newspaper in addition to the one published in New Orleans found some room for the story of Liebeler's refusal to testify, yet I have not read it elsewhere and I have regularly read several major daily newspapers, as well as *Time, Newsweek* and *U.S. News & World Report.*

Despite Liebeler's absence, a jury convicted Andrews of three counts of perjury early in the morning on August 14, 1967.[68] The jury brought in a unanimous verdict after deliberating for less than three hours.[69] Andrews was then incarcerated, as is required by law in New Orleans in the case of a convict awaiting sentence.[70] Nowhere was the media's commitment to the Commission's conclusions and its antipathy to those who challenged them more nakedly in evidence than in the treatment of Garrison's investigation. During the trial Hugh Aynesworth, *Newsweek's* reporter assigned to the Garrison investigation and formerly a reporter for the Dallas *Morning*

---

because—I'll tell you that it was not off the—uh—uh—I'll tell you it was not off the record out of any—uh—there are all—all kinds of reasons why —uh—lawyers were off the record. Her lawyer interrupted and wanted to make some remarks and—and—and—and—and talked about it and I don't recall if it was I who asked us to go off the record or Marina or him or any of the kind. But I can tell you this, that the reason it went off the record—I don't remember what it was—it had nothing whatever to do with—

(Shouting from the audience, including, "If you don't remember why you went off the record, how do you know why you didn't go off the record?")

LIEBELER: It had nothing whatever to do with any attempt to suppress any evidence of anything. Now—now—now—you—you—at this point you —you—at this point there are two ways in which that—well, at this point there is no way in fact in which that—in which that question could be answered.[65]

News, flew to New Orleans in an effort to intercede on behalf of Andrews.[71] The court ruled that his proffered testimony was valueless.[72]

The evening of the conviction, ABC-TV presented an interview with Andrews' attorney.[73] The network reporter asked, "How come Dean had to go to jail like a criminal?"[74] The reporter, not the attorney, suggested that Garrison, not Andrews, was really guilty of untoward conduct.[75] Back in the studio the television commentator said that Andrews had "allegedly" lied to a grand jury.[76] Possibly for the first time that qualifying term had been applied to a man who had been convicted of a crime. No interview with a representative of the District Attorney's office was presented.[77]

The "Huntley-Brinkley Report" on NBC contented itself with a terse, two-short-sentence report of the conviction.[78]

Three weeks before the conviction, Walter Cronkite had stated that Garrison had made many statements, "but until the trial Mr. Garrison's promises remain just that, and cannot be tested."[79] He added that "so far, he [Garrison] has shown us nothing to link the events he alleges to have taken place in New Orleans, and the events we know to have taken place in Dallas."[80] The conviction of Andrews for committing perjury in denying that he knew the real identity of Clay Bertrand certainly did not prove that a conspiracy took the life of the President. Yet it was the first step that Garrison had promised. Of the "many statements" to which Cronkite referred, one was Garrison's statement that Andrews had committed perjury and would be convicted.[81] That statement had just been tested. Cronkite was spared the embarrassment of commenting upon the Andrews conviction since CBS News refused to report that Andrews had been convicted.[82] There was time in the thirty-minute network broadcast to reveal that forest rangers had killed two bears in Montana and to present a film showing a class of Chinese students chanting the words of Mao as an illustration of brainwashing far from our shore.[83] Eric Sevareid commented, "This country is insanely out of balance."[84] He was making reference to the fact that too many people live in the large cities and too few in the Western lands.[85]

26 THE VOLUNTEERS

In addition to the President, the Director of the FBI and the Commission members and staff who comprise the official defenders of the Report, there was an auxiliary army of volunteers. The volunteers seemed inclined to rely upon faith that the Report would not have been written had it not been accurate. Since our subject is not theology, while we note their presence in passing, we shall not stop to dwell upon the varying circumstances that created their need to believe.

Typical of their approach was the lead editorial in the International Edition of the New York *Herald Tribune* published two and a half months after the publication of *Rush to Judgment*.[1] It was entitled "The Ghouls" and charged that "the merchants of morbidity keep setting new highs in output and new lows in taste by refusing to let go of the horror of Nov. 22, 1963—and refusing to let the memory of John F. Kennedy rest decently in peace."[2] It said that many of the critics "seem motivated by a hunger for a buck, a thirst for publicity, a drive for circulation at all costs."[3] It might be noted here that later the parent *World Journal Tribune*, following the *Tribune's* merger with two other papers, very widely advertised that an article dealing with the subject would appear in its weekend supplement, no doubt as part of its drive for circulation.

The editorial concluded with this request: "We think it is time to ask the ghouls, the buckchasers, the sensation-mongers and the character assassins to desist—to shut up until or unless they can put up, as so far they have notoriously failed to do."[4] One suspects that the *Tribune*, generally more reserved in its language, might have been more moderate had it been more secure in its facts.

Yet at least as extravagant in defense of the Report and in open hostility toward those who could not accept it were Drew Pearson, Walter Winchell, I. F. Stone and Bob Considine. Merriman Smith, the United Press International White House reporter, was quoted in a lead editorial published by the Dallas *Times Herald* regarding his advice to those who were critical of the President.[5] He suggested that decent folk should tell "the dirty-mouths to shut the hell up."[6]

Smith had been awarded the Pulitzer Prize for his eyewitness reporting of the assassination. If ever one wishes to develop an argument against such awards, one need merely reread the Smith dispatches from Dallas in the light of the facts now known, making allowance for the fact that standards which an historian might be expected to adhere to cannot be applied to a reporter.

In the past years quite literally hundreds of people have told me exactly where they were when they heard that the President had been shot. Yet Merriman Smith is the only person about whom I can state that three years after the event which he witnessed he still was totally confused as to his whereabouts at the time of the shooting. During November 1966, Smith wrote a special dispatch for UPI as an answer to the critics.[7] In it he claimed that "I have been a hunter and target marksman for many years."[8] He conceded, "There are some professional experts who regard me as being competently familiar with many weapons and their behavior."[9] Having established himself as an expert of sorts, he reported:

> I was only a few hundred feet from Kennedy when he was shot. I would swear there were three shots and only three shots fired at his motorcade. The car in which I rode was not far from the presidential vehicle and in clear view of it. We were coming out of an underpass when the first shot was fired. The sound for a split second resembled a big firecracker. As we cleared the underpass, then came the second and third shots. The shots were fired smoothly and evenly. There was not the slightest doubt on the front seat of our car that the shots came from a rifle to our rear.[10]

Smith was in the press pool car, four cars behind the Presidential limousine.[11] There is but one underpass in Dealey Plaza and the President's car was proceeding toward it and was 348 feet from it when the first shot was fired and the underpass was still 260 feet ahead when the last shot was fired.[12] Smith's automobile, far behind, could not possibly have been "coming out of an underpass when the first shot was fired."[13] There just were no underpasses within miles except for those ahead of the President's car. Smith's car actually was on Houston Street when the shots were fired, as the still and motion pictures of the event demonstrate conclusively.[14] His car was moving toward the Book Depository Building, which was directly ahead, not "directly to our rear," when the shots were fired.[15] If Smith is correct and he states that he is certain that "the shots came from a rifle to our rear," he has proven that there was no lone assassin.[16]

Not to be outdone by a rival news service, the Associated Press entered the lists on behalf of the Commission. During the middle of 1967 it authorized and distributed an attack upon the critics which it described as "more than 20,000 words long" and "the longest single story ever moved over the AP wires."[17] An indication of the objectivity that the AP brought to its task may be ascertained by determining that the AP reporters interviewed the Commission lawyers, published selections from their views—"As long as people can make a quarter or a half-million dollars, we're going to have these books" —but refused to interview the critics.[18] The only person known to have made that sum of money from a book about the assassination is William Manchester, but he supported the Commission's conclusions.

Much of the AP story concentrates upon the evidence related to the origin of the shots, and it is discussed in detail at a subsequent point in this volume, together with the similar allegations of others.[19]

The leader of the volunteer forces, although as the author of a commercially published foreword to the Report his amateur status may be in doubt, is the prominent and respected attorney Louis Nizer.

To paraphrase Edmund Wilson in another context, there are moments when one is tempted to feel that the cruelest thing that has happened to the Warren Report was Doubleday's decision to publish it along with Louis Nizer's foreword. Professor Hugh Trevor-Roper has referred to it as a "panegyrical preface."[20] Nizer calls it his "analysis and commentary" of the Commission's work, yet he has subsequently admitted that at the time he wrote it he had neither examined the evidence of a single witness nor read any of the other material contained in the twenty-six volumes of testimony and exhibits. As if to demonstrate that fact, Nizer has made repeated references to the "20 volumes."

In one brief radio broadcast, for example, Nizer said, "Now, I could go on, and anyone who has really read these 20 volumes of testimony could go on for hours, to demonstrate the authenticity of this Report."[21] A few minutes later, he was critical of those who had not rejected my work: "And I am astonished at some of the distinguished people who read this book, and without reading the 20 volumes and finding out how incorrect many of these assertions are."[22] He offered some advice to book reviewers: ". . . if they'll just take the trouble, as a critic should, who is going to review a book, to read the 20 volumes of testimony."[23] He had a word of advice about the evidence for a member of Congress also: "And Congressman [Theodore] Kupferman is an able man. Let him read the 20 volumes and the Report itself and then tell me whether he wants to put in this resolution, because some people have written some books on this."[24] The interviewer, in thanking Nizer, said that "unfortunately, I am not qualified to quote from the 20 volumes—very few people are."[25]

It would be unfair to criticize Nizer for not having read the evidence when he wrote his preface to the Report. His preface was published in September 1964 and the evidence was not released until November of that year.[26] The question is not why he had not read the evidence when he wrote the preface but rather why he wrote the preface when he could not read the evidence. The unavailability of the evidence at that time did not prevent Nizer from making reference to it: "The evidence gathered by the Warren Commission shows . . ."[27] As if in command of the facts, rather than the Commission's conclusions, he offered each conclusion as a fact for which he was able, indeed eager, to vouch. Of those who wish to read the evidence, Nizer states, "There will be some who will resist persuasion."[28] In his following sentence he explains why: "The word *prejudice* derives from the Latin *pre judicare*—to judge before one has the facts."[29]

But it would be uncharitable to analyze Nizer's credulous defense brief for the Report written before he could have ascertained the presently known evidence contained in the volumes. Indeed, it may even be considered less than benevolent to examine his public utterances since. Given the choice, however, I choose the latter.

When *Rush to Judgment* was published in August 1966, I was invited to appear on the NBC morning program "Today." Nizer was also invited. He refused. Subsequently, I was interviewed by Barry Gray in New York. Gray told me that Nizer was very much a Warren Commission defender. On the air, I offered to make a $500 donation to the John F. Kennedy Memorial Library if Nizer would meet me in open debate on Gray's show. Nizer declined.

Nizer agreed, however, to appear on the program in my absence. On that occasion he said he was reluctant to debate "because I felt it was giving credence to a very irresponsible series of attacks upon the Warren Commission Report. And I think that debate is just perhaps what these irresponsible people would like. I call them irresponsible deliberately, and I think with some justification. I, as you know, have studied the Warren Commission Report and wrote the commentary for the Warren Commission Report."[30] Since two-thirds of the American people had been represented by the polls as disbelieving the Report, it was a little difficult to understand Nizer's argument that by debating with the critics it would be "giving credence" to his opponents.

Later, at a conference in Bridgeport, Connecticut, Nizer charged that the Commission critics were "an outrage."[31] The critical books were "false" and "inaccurate."[32] Nizer's own book was almost ready for publication. He added that he was "considering" answering the critics.[33] Fortunately, Nizer's decision that the time had come to answer the critics coincided with the publication of his own book and his promotional efforts on its behalf. Thus the two efforts might be merged. Nizer then agreed to appear with me on a television broadcast, but when it concluded he declined to debate again.

The two officers—a deputy constable and a deputy sheriff—who discovered the alleged assassination weapon on the sixth floor of the Texas School Book Depository described it as a German Mauser.[34] Later it was said that the rifle discovered there had been a Mannlicher-Carcano.[35] As part of Nizer's preliminary "reply to the entire nation," he explained this discrepancy:

> There was a story that the gun was a certain kind of a make—a Carbonari [*sic*] or a Howzer [*sic*] or something. The captain at the time, who went on television with the world's spotlight upon them—they all were dizzy with the vanity involved, nobody knew how to say I don't know, everybody knew everything—there was no marking on it, so at the first moment flush on the television, he said, yes, what kind of a make is it, Captain? It's a Carbonari something, I forget which it was. It turned out not to be that. Now, the accusation—how is it that they have changed the make of the gun to fit Oswald?[36]

The Carbonari were members of a secret political society in the early part of the nineteenth century active in France, Spain and Italy. There is no indication that they were involved in the assassination. The weapon Nizer evidently sought to refer to is a Mannlicher-Carcano. There is no "Howzer." A howitzer is a cannon with a short barrel used primarily for firing shells at a high angle of elevation. Perhaps Nizer meant to refer to a German Mauser rifle. The first public announcement about the weapon described it not as "a Carbonari something" but as a German Mauser, 7.65 mm. It is true, as Nizer observed, that "it turned out not to be that," but his explanation as to how that happened—the question that he was apparently addressing—does little to clarify. The only contribution to that question in his comment is the reference that "there was no marking on it," which he meant, it seems, to apply to the discovered weapon. There he is wrong. The weapon is clearly marked "MADE ITALY" and "CAL. 6.5."[37] Not only captains evidently are susceptible to the malady Nizer described.

Nizer also addressed himself to the questions related to the rifle's capability: "There was a theory that this gun could not have been fired within the time—the number of bullets."[38] He explained:

> The evidence of outstanding experts in military forces, experts in these guns, took that very same gun up to the sixth floor of that Trade Mart building, had an automobile at the same place that the President was hit at, with a skull of the President's size and of the same strength, and bullets were fired from that same gun, from that same distance, within the time specified, and struck that skull and split it open in precisely the same way as had occurred on that tragic day, the day that will never end.[39]

The test thus described makes interesting and almost impressive reading. However, no such test was ever conducted.[40] The Commission caused no rifle to be fired from the Texas School Book Depository or from the "Trade Mart," which was miles away from Dealey Plaza.[41] The timed tests with the rifle were conducted at a U.S. Army range.[42] There bullets were fired at cardboard silhouette targets, not a "skull of the President's size and of the same strength."[43] No "automobile" was utilized for the test, since the targets were stationary.[44] Two of the three experts did not fire "within the time specified."[45] Not one of the bullets fired struck the head or neck portion of the target; thus even if there had been "a skull of the President's size" on the cardboard target, since no bullets struck that portion of the target they would not have "struck that skull and split it open precisely the same way."[46]

Following an explanation of the test and the identification of the weapon, Nizer said, "Now, I could go on, and anyone who has really read these 20 volumes of testimony could go on for hours, to demonstrate the authenticity of this Report."[47] That demonstration included the allegation that "there was some of the silver plate from the bullet—or whatever it was" on the windshield of the Presidential limousine[48] (the Commission said lead[49]); that "a thread was found on the gun [and] it was traced to the shirt he [Oswald] was wearing on that day by outstanding experts"[50] (there was but one expert; he said he was unable to say with certainty that the thread on the weapon came from Oswald's shirt[51]); "he kept it [the rifle] in a crib and it was covered with a quilt"[52] (the Commission said that it was in a garage[53]); that "the FBI arrived, I think only 40 minutes later" and found the rifle missing[54] (the Dallas police, not the FBI, arrived, and it was approximately two hours later[55]); Oswald had used "a microscopic sight—that's what made his aim so good"[56] (the Commission said telescopic, and the experts said it was defective[57]); "he was able to place his back against a support"[58] (the Commission conceded there was no back support[59]).

Louis Nizer surely is one of America's most prominent lawyers. Lawyers are supposed to deal with facts. The radio broadcast we have just discussed constituted Nizer's first public comment on the matter after the evidence had been published almost two years before. He offered himself as a student of the evidence and as one who had agonized for some time before reaching the conclusion that the very "irresponsible" people who could not accept the Commission's findings must be answered for the good of the country. He embarked upon his abortive mission with obvious sincerity and with the desire to set the record straight. Yet it is difficult to find any substantial allegation that he made about the evidence that is true. "It is bad enough," he said, "that he was assassinated, but to suggest that there was some conspiracy, in or out of government, or some other strange forces to do so, raises some even more troublesome questions."[60]

Are we afraid of troublesome questions? Are the implications that flow from the conspiracy to assassinate President Kennedy better ignored? What is it that paralyzes the thought processes of men who are charged with public responsibility or those, as in the case of Nizer, who volunteer their services? If Nizer prepared one of his important law cases as he prepared his defense of the Commission Report, his prominence at the bar would be illusory. Yet if he had properly prepared for his defense, he could not have made it. This much is clear: only by choosing to remain ignorant of the evidence may one insist that the Commission's Report is entirely adequate.

Yet one question remains without answer. What compulsion drives men to defend that which the Government has decreed when it is, in rational terms, clearly indefensible? Does not that compulsion unknowingly betray our concept of democracy? And does it not as well reveal its defenders to be fools? The press and electronic media, it is true, have been inordinately generous in overlooking the errors of the Commission supporters, but in open debate, despite the assuaging encouragement of the Establishment, they have been ridiculed. Why have men, otherwise reputable, offered their dignity and their reputations for such a lost and unworthy cause?

If one can determine the strength of the force by the distance from logic and the facts that the defenders have been driven, it needs be a most powerful one. How comforting it would be to believe that a telephone call from Washington is responsible for the entire effort. Thus the virus could be isolated and the disease susceptible of treatment. Yet it is perhaps far more complicated. The virus exists within us, and little is required to activate it. I speak not in theological or metaphysical terms but of what man has become in the steady march toward 1984 in a complicated society. Unless thinking people can distinguish false governmental edicts from proper ones and unless they are prepared to act against the invalid ones, hopes for a democratic society cannot be realized.

III · The Academicians

27 ON PROCEDURE AND PRECEDENT

The Report of the President's Commission on the Assassination of President Kennedy by shattering old precedents established new ones. Serious questions were raised by the conduct of the Commission, by the identity of the Commission members and by the fact of the Commission and the task which it undertook. On the face of it, a political body, the majority of the Commission, being members of the Congress, was asked to investigate as a police force might, hold hearings as an administrative agency might and render a verdict as to the guilt or innocence of the accused in the same fashion that a court or jury would be required to act. The Chief Justice of the United States served as the Commission's chairman although one of the matters pending before the Commission, Ruby's murder of Oswald, might well have been subsequently passed upon by the Supreme Court.

In the United States it is not customary for an official inquiry to pass upon the guilt or innocence of the accused after his death. Nor is it usual to deny counsel to the accused. The Commission provided ample material for academicians to ponder, but they showed marked reticence to do so. The *New York University Law Review* was among the first to comment upon the questions.[1] But that distinguished publication's effort had an aura of special pleading about it. Norman Redlich, assistant to J. Lee Rankin, the Commission's general counsel, was at that time on the law school's faculty.[2] The same university had previously sought to prevent a meeting from taking place at Town Hall, which it owned, because it charged that Marguerite Oswald might "proclaim her son's innocence."[3] Mrs. Oswald did state that she believed that Lee Oswald should be presumed "innocent until proven guilty." The *Law Review* articles appearing in the May 1965 issue were more a defense of the Commission than an analysis of its work.[4]

Arthur Goodhart, one of the Commission's most vocal defenders, writing in that issue, pointed out that "comparatively little attention has been paid to [the procedural problems] even by the legal profession itself."[5] Two years later the circumstances were little altered, as Richard M. Mosk, a former member of the Commission's staff, indicated in the legal journal *Case & Comment:* "Hopefully, those in the academic and legal communities will examine the Commission's efforts, not only to appraise its conclusions but also to gather information on the suitability and effectiveness of current institutions, doctrines and procedures in coping with routine as well as abnormal events."[6]

Almost four years after the assassination the academic world remained timid regarding an assessment of the propriety of the appointments to the Commission and the methods of the Commission. Those few who did comment often came to their task with what appeared to be a fixed opinion. Goodhart, for example, had stated that Earl Warren is a good friend and that he feels constrained to defend him. Mosk, as we have noted, was employed by the Commission.[7] Their work, as might be expected, appears flawed by a preconception. I do not, could not, disparage the role of the advocate. I favor the adversary system, which system the Commission decided to avoid and in which decision both Mosk and Goodhart concur.*

It seems that the academic and legal worlds have had two responsibilities—to comment impartially and to permit a genuine adversary dialogue to take place in their publications. Yet they have done neither. That the result would be less than satisfactory might be assumed. It may be demonstrated as well. Among the most manifest of the Commission's curious procedures was its determination to take testimony adduced before it under conditions of utmost secrecy. The press was excluded, as were all spectators. The transcripts were then classified, in at least some cases marked "Top Secret." On occasion the Chief Justice would then reveal selected portions of the testimony (always, it seemed, testimony which was inclined to show Oswald's guilt, and often testimony taken out of its proper context) at an impromptu press conference.

It would seem unlikely that an effort might be made to demonstrate the probity of such conduct. Yet Mosk stated that "it should

* Both Goodhart and Mosk were asked to participate as adversaries in public debates on the subject. Although neither is reluctant to write or lecture on the subject, both declined the opportunity to debate, Goodhart explaining that he could not debate with me since Earl Warren had previously expressed his disapproval of my conduct in dissenting.

be noted that the proceedings were not secret,"[8]* while Goodhart defended the secret proceedings: "Now whatever may be said for our open trial system, it is not one to encourage people to give evidence voluntarily or freely."[14] A closed hearing, called by a Presidential Commission and presided over by the Chief Justice at which leading questions are asked and from which counsel for the defense has been excluded, hardly seems to be the best way to secure truthful testimony. Might not a witness, who had already been informed of his Government's conclusion regarding Oswald's lone guilt, seek to cooperate in that effort? Might he not be influenced by the import of the questions and the importance of the Commissioners? Indeed, Goodhart has detected a perceptible change in the witnesses' conduct brought about, he says, through the use of the private hearing. Oddly enough, he seems to approve of this: "A study of the fifteen volumes in which the evidence collected by the Commission has been published, shows that those witnesses, who at first seemed to be hesitant and nervous, seemed to gain confidence in the quiet atmosphere of a private hearing."[15]

The title of the Mosk article—"The Warren Commission and the Legal Process"—certainly appeared to encompass a wide scope and permitted, indeed almost required, intensive analysis of the Commission's unprecedented departures from the norm.[16] One might have expected particular attention to those innovations that had been widely criticized. Mosk's restraint in assessing the Commission's

* As proof that the witnesses were not compelled to testify in secrecy, Mosk states, "The witness could demand an open hearing," and cites page xiii of the Warren Report.[9] The relevant portion of the Report states: "Commission hearings were closed to the public unless the witness appearing before the Commission requested an open hearing. Under these procedures, testimony of one witness was taken in a public hearing on two occasions. No other witness requested a public hearing."[10] Both Mosk and the Report clearly seek to convey the impression that at the outset the Commission had established standards which encompassed both types of hearings.[11] But such is not the case. Since I am the "one witness" the Commission referred to who testified in public I am fully familiar with its procedure in that area. Witnesses were not informed that they had the option of secret or public testimony. They were informed that they could secure counsel and that they might purchase a transcript (although sometimes an edited one) of their testimony. Since I abhor secrecy in public matters, I informed the Commission that I did not wish to follow its ordinary procedure and testify behind closed doors.[12] After some consultation among the Commission members (no record of that off-the-record conference appearing in the published transcript), it was determined that my request should be granted.[13]

work was noteworthy.[17] He responded to charges that to my knowledge had not been made.[18] For example, he defended the Commission against the "critics [who] have commented adversely on the plethora of attorneys on the staff."[19] Of course, the Commission should have chosen as many attorneys as it wished. I cannot think of anyone who has suggested otherwise. Some questions have been raised as to the qualifications of the attorneys, who for the most part either were inexperienced, as in the case of Wesley J. Liebeler,* or had served previously as well as prosecutors for the Government, as in the case of Francis W. H. Adams, Burt W. Griffin, Leon D. Hubert and Albert E. Jenner, Jr., or both, as in the case of Arlen Specter.[22]† Mosk's failure to grapple with or perhaps understand the essential criticism regarding the odd procedures does little to resolve the doubts as to the competence of the staff.[25]

28 ARTHUR GOODHART AND THE BAR ASSOCIATION

Arthur Goodhart, after having complained of the paucity of attention directed to the procedural problems posed by the Commission and its work "even by the legal profession," was published in the journal of the Bar Association of New York City more than two years later.[1] However, there he abjured an analysis of those questions in favor of retaliation against those who had questioned the findings of the Chief Justice.[2] The article was curiously entitled, "Three Famous Legal Hoaxes: The Tichborne Case; The Dreyfus Affair; The Alleged Conspiracy to Assassinate President Kennedy."[3] Five pages are devoted by Goodhart to an analysis of *Rush to Judgment*.[4] That analysis contains thirty-six errors.[5] The relatively minor errors include incorrect names for witnesses, attributing to witnesses statements which they never made, entire quotations purportedly from

* Liebeler himself has observed, "The men who did the bulk of the work in drafting the Report and in conducting the investigation were fellows who were five or six years out of law school, like myself."[20] He added, "You take a group of young lawyers like this, and put them in a situation of—uh—where they at that point really have almost unlimited power in—in—in directing the FBI, for example, and conducting the investigation that they want to conduct —it would have been an incredible thing for any of us to have shown that the FBI had made a mistake, or a series of mistakes."[21]

† Most of Specter's professional life had been spent as an assistant district attorney.[23] He evidently came to that work not unprepared, having been a deputy sheriff at the age of three.[24]

Rush to Judgment but which do not appear in the book and incorrectly summarizing portions which do appear.[6] Even Goodhart's allegation as to the number of pages in *Rush to Judgment* was incorrect, although close.[7]

He alleged that "Lane must have felt safe in assuming that hardly any of his American readers and none of his European ones would check his stories against the evidence that can be found in the 26 supplementary volumes published by the Commission."[8] Of course, quite the contrary was true. I knew that my English and American publishers would have the work closely studied before deciding whether it was to be published. Historians and leading lawyers in both countries examined the work and made written reports of their findings. The book was then published by the firms. I also expected that the book would be subjected to hostile scrutiny by those who kneel before the Establishment and cavil at its request, and my expectations were realized. It is Goodhart who can rest assured that his citations will not be checked, since he offers none.[9]

Goodhart said that he would deal with the facts relating to the evidence of six witnesses who were discussed in *Rush to Judgment*.[10] His work bears the badge of consistency—he made serious errors about each.[11] First, as to Julia Ann Mercer, he wrote: "A green truck which 'looked like it had 1 or 2 wheels on the curb' of Elm Street blocked her way. She saw one of the two men in the truck 'take out from the truck what appeared to be a gun-case,' and then walk 'up the grassy slope.' "[12] Goodhart claimed to quote three fragments from an affidavit that Miss Mercer signed for the Dallas Sheriff's Department on November 22, 1963.[13] All three fragments are incorrectly quoted: a word left out here, a tense changed there, a word changed here.[14] More important is Goodhart's claim that this all occurred "nearly four hours before the assassination took place."[15] That statement is unsupported by any known information.[16] The only mention of Miss Mercer in the twenty-six volumes (she is not referred to at all in the Commission's Report, and she was never questioned by the Commission or by its counsel[17]) is in the affidavit just referred to, and there is no reference to the time of the occurrence that she witnessed there.[18] Evidently Goodhart manufactured the time in order to dismiss Miss Mercer's evidence.[19] There is a reference to a truck believed to be stalled in that general location in the Dallas police radio log, but that was just eighty-one minutes before the assassination.[20]

Goodhart then examined the statements of Lee Bowers.[21] According to Goodhart, Bowers was "able to note that three cars which entered the area bore Goldwater campaign stickers, but the relevance of this is not apparent as it is not suggested that Senator Goldwater was involved in the assassination."[22] Bowers had testified that two cars, not three, carried Goldwater stickers.[23] They probed the sensitive area behind the wall and fence on the knoll that had otherwise been sealed off by the police.[24] In another car the driver had what appeared to be a microphone in his hand.[25] The relevance should be apparent to Goodhart, a long-time student of the case. I had commented upon it in the one page in *Rush to Judgment* in which the Bowers comment was discussed: "It bore a Goldwater-for-President sticker and, therefore, presumably was not a local or federal police car."[26]

Goodhart first charged that Bowers did not see anyone "doing anything suspicious."[27] But Bowers had stated that when the shots were fired his attention was attracted to the area just behind the fence because of something that caught his eye there: "Now, what this was, I could not state at that time and at this time I could not identify it, other than there was some unusual occurrence—a flash of light or smoke or something which caused me to feel like something out of the ordinary had occurred there."[28] Goodhart, his original statement notwithstanding, ruled, "This is nonsense because a puff of smoke and a flash of light cannot be confused."[29]

If Bowers was unworthy of belief because he had not been precise enough, then J. C. Price, who saw a man flee from the area of the knoll just after the shots were fired, "illustrates the legal maxim that an over-precise witness is usually telling an untruth."[30] Goodhart charged Price with "meticulous precision."[31] On the record thus far established, Price could scarcely be justified had he returned the accusation.

S. M. Holland, referred to by Goodhart as "G. M. Holland," was disposed of next.[32] "The fourth witness was G. M. Holland [sic], who was accompanied by a lawyer when he gave his evidence, and then had to retire to bed."[33] One can hardly come away from that sentence without understanding Goodhart to have said that Holland retired to bed after testifying.[34] No doubt, Holland went to sleep sometime that night, but that should not be taken as an indication that Holland was not an astute and truthful witness. The confusion arises from Goodhart's misreading of the evidence. Holland testified that after he had seen the President killed he had difficulty sleeping that night.[35] He made no reference to going to bed after "he gave his evidence" some four and a half months after the assassination.[36]

The fifth witness referred to is Deputy Constable Seymour Weitzman, whose rank is stated incorrectly by Goodhart and whose name Goodhart spells differently twice, both times incorrectly.[37] Goodhart summarized Weitzman's testimony in this fashion: "He met a railroad employee who said he thought that 'he had seen somebody throw something through a bush.' Weizmann [*sic*] himself was not impressed by this, and rushed over to the Book Building where he helped to find the assassination rifle."[38] While Goodhart's effort to quote Weitzman accurately almost succeeded, he was completely off regarding Weitzman's movements immediately following the receipt of the information from the railroad worker.[39] Weitzman testified, "I asked a yardman if he had seen or heard anything during the passing of the President. He said he thought he saw somebody throw something through a bush and that's when I went back over the fence and that's when I found the portion of the skull."[40] Weitzman explained that as soon as the shots were fired he ran to the grassy knoll, scaled the wall and subsequently encountered the yardman.[41] He then saw the skull particle in Elm Street, climbed back over the fence and went down the hill to Elm Street.[42] He crossed the street until he approached the skull particle, which was located, he testified, approximately eight to twelve inches from the curb on the south side of the street.[43]

Goodhart concludes this section stating, "Finally the reference to James L. Simmons is of special interest. He saw a motorcycle policeman drive up the grassy slope, jump off his motorcycle and then run up the rest of the hill. Simmons thought that he saw exhaust fumes of smoke. He advised that in his opinion the shots came from the direction of the Texas Building [*sic*]."[44] Of course Goodhart is entitled to state his view of what Simmons thought when the shots were fired.[45] Simmons also has a statement regarding the question.[46] In a filmed and tape-recorded interview, Simmons said, "As the Presidential limousine was rounding the curve on Elm Street there was a loud explosion. At the time I didn't know what it was, but it sounded like a loud firecracker or a gunshot, and it sounded like it came from the left and in front of us toward the wooden fence, and there was a puff of smoke that came underneath the trees on the embankment."[47] Simmons was asked where the puff of smoke was, and he replied, "It was right directly in front of the wooden fence."[48] He added, "I was talking with Patrolman Foster at the time, and as soon as we heard the shots, we ran around to the wooden fence, and when we got there, there was no one there, but there was footprints in the mud around the fence and there was footprints on the wooden two-by-four railing on the fence."[49]

While Goodhart, as has been observed, offers no citations for his allegations, the source of his misinformation about Simmons is not difficult to locate.[50] Goodhart has adopted not only the conclusions of the FBI hearsay report, repudiated by Simmons, but the special language of the Federal police reports as well: "He advised that . . ."[51] Simmons said that he had made the same statement to the FBI agents that he had later made in the filmed interview. Thus Simmons joined the alarmingly large number of witnesses who questioned the accuracy of the FBI hearsay reports.[52] And Goodhart joined those other defenders who preferred repudiated hearsay reports to first-hand evidence.[53]

After incorrectly presenting the statements of six witnesses, Goodhart concluded, "This is the whole of Lane's so-called direct evidence that there was another assassin shooting from the knoll."[54] On what basis Goodhart decided to ignore Austin L. Miller, Richard C. Dodd, Walter Winborn, Thomas Murphy and Clemon E. Johnson, all of whom were on the overpass with Holland and Simmons, and on the same page of *Rush to Judgment* with them as well, is not clear.[55] Five more witnesses with evidence to support that finding appear on the next page, four more on the following page, and so on.[56] The medical evidence and the photographic evidence corroborate the eyewitness evidence and are also presented in detail in *Rush to Judgment*.[57] Yet none of this may be included in Goodhart's category of "Lane's so-called direct evidence."[58]

But after assuring the reader that there was no more, Goodhart evidently reconsidered and decided to write some more:

> Lane's final point would seem to be a conclusive one. It is that as the wound in the front of the President's neck was an entrance wound, the bullet must have been fired either from the knoll or from the overpass. He says that: "Every doctor at Dallas' Parkland Hospital who examined the wound in President Kennedy's throat and made a statement to the press on the day of the assassination said the throat wound was an entrance wound. That means the bullet entered from the front." You can judge Lane's book by this because it is deliberately misleading.[59]

And one can judge Goodhart's imaginative review by the quotation which he attributes to my book—for it does not appear there at all.[60]

To prove that the quotation was wrong, Goodhart next wrote of Dr. Malcolm Perry: "It is, of course, impossible to prove what the exact words were that Dr. Perry used when he was hurriedly interviewed by the press after he left the operating room, but he has repeated again and again that all he could have said was that the wound *might* have been an entrance wound."[61] (Emphasis in the original.) If Dr. Perry was in a hurry after the President's death had been announced, it was because, as Walter Cronkite observed, "Dr. Perry was rushed from the emergency room to a news conference."[62] Cronkite continued, "In the transcript of that news conference there's no doubt that Dr. Perry made it sound as if he had a firm opinion."[63] Cronkite explained that "the neck wound, he told the press, looked like an entry wound, and he pointed to the front of his neck."[64] At the conference Perry said, "There was an entrance wound below his Adam's apple."[65] Other physicians agreed, including Kemp Clark and Charles Carrico.[66]

Goodhart seeks to dispose quickly of Edward Jay Epstein's book, *Inquest*.[67] He charges that "most of his more important notes are misleading, and his quotations are untrue."[68] Epstein interviewed a number of Commission members and Commission lawyers.[69] Goodhart declares that he "made enquiries and I found that" various quotations were "repudiated as being false."[70] Goodhart does not disclose the nature of his private investigation or who it was that said he had been misquoted.[71] Nor does he explain on what basis he can determine whether Epstein or the quoted party was telling the truth.[72] Goodhart's record thus far, however, does little to inspire confidence either in his ability to quote accurately or in his judgment.

Goodhart said that "it struck me as odd" that the lawyers should have told Epstein that the Commission members were not really involved in the investigation and that the attorneys did the work.[73] Each of Epstein's quotations, Goodhart states, "was repudiated as being false."[74] At about the time that Goodhart's article was being published, a former Commission lawyer, Wesley Liebeler, on a radio program broadcast at Stanford University, repeated that which Goodhart had stated was untrue.[75] Liebeler said that most of the work was done by "fellows who were five or six years out of law school" and who had "almost unlimited power."[76]

In the section entitled "Conclusion," Goodhart offers a few oddities.[77] He claims that "in Lane's book and articles the number [of "important witnesses" that have been murdered] has steadily risen to over 23. It includes Miss Dorothy Kilgallen."[78] Both statements are absurd. I have never said that twenty-three witnesses, important or otherwise, have been murdered, and I have neither said nor written that I believe that Miss Kilgallen was murdered or that she was an "important witness."[79]

Goodhart's misdirected passion can perhaps be excused, but it appears at last that it has completely fogged his mind. Going back to his analogy with the Dreyfus case, he writes, "In the Dreyfus Affair every officer in the army was threatened with ruin if he expressed the view that Dreyfus was innocent."[80] "Lane has now," Goodhart concludes, "threatened President Johnson with political ruin."[81] Where was this done? Says Goodhart, "In *Playboy*."[82]

29 A LAW JOURNAL'S BONAR

A recent and valuable addition to the sparse contribution of the academic community was made in the *Yale Law Journal.*[1] It has become fashionable, once persuaded by the logic of the critics, to dissociate oneself from them. This perhaps is to permit the impression that one is above the fray and therefore able to offer a disinterested, therefore more valuable, view. It may also tend to exempt one from the not inconsiderable hostility of the defenders. The *New York Times*, for example, took great pains to point out when it editorially reversed gears that its new position was reached "not because of any of the specific charges brought by the dozens of books, TV shows and articles about President Kennedy's assassination."[2]

Marcus Raskin reviewed *Rush to Judgment* in the *Yale Law Journal.*[3] While he endorsed many of the points made in that work, he said near the outset, "There are flaws in Mark Lane's book, some of them disturbing because they cast doubt on Lane's entire effort."[4] That charge was documented with a footnote which read as follows: "For example, Lane refers to a Dr. Howard Bonar, who allegedly was the eye doctor for an alleged eyewitness to the man in the sixth-floor depository window. No Dr. Bonar is listed among Dallas doctors and optometrists or in the AMA Directory."[5] The only reference in *Rush to Judgment* to Dr. Bonar appears on page 90, where I repeated the assertion of a Commission witness, Howard L. Brennan, that he had been examined by Dr. Bonar.[6] If there was no Dr. Bonar, the initial error was made by the Commission witness and not by the author who presented that allegation.[7] If Brennan, who was one of the Commission's most important witnesses, had invented an eye doctor, then Raskin's research had uncovered a disturbing flaw, but not in my book. Yet he chose to assess the fruits of his work as an indication that my entire book must be doubted, not that Brennan must be cautiously re-examined. It was somehow reassuring that so persistent a reviewer who ingeniously went beyond the millions of words published by the Commission in preparation for his review was unable to locate a single other alleged error in a work that contained more than 4,500 citations.[8]

It would be unfair to leave the reader with the impression that Brennan was in error, for there is a Dr. Bonar.[9] Raskin's research was faulty.[10] I do not know why he chose to examine the list of "Dallas doctors and optometrists," since nowhere in *Rush to Judgment* or in Brennan's testimony may one find the assertion that Dr. Bonar was a

Dallas optometrist.[11] Indeed, had he checked the citation on page 90 of *Rush to Judgment* he would have been referred to Volume III, page 157, of the Commission's evidence, and there have learned that Brennan stated that Dr. Howard Bonar "is in Port Lavaca. He is the only leading optometrist there."[12] Or if Raskin, in his effort to bypass the basic material, had consulted the *Blue Book of Optometry* for the year 1964, the date of the witness's testimony, he would have discovered therein the name of Dr. Howard Bonar, an optometrist in Port Lavaca, Texas.

In a letter to Raskin I suggested that at that point he might have communicated directly with the American Medical Association regarding any complaints against its directory rather than permit them to intrude into a book review.[13] A most encouraging demonstration of integrity was contained in Raskin's prompt reply.[14] He wrote, "I am appalled at my error and beg your pardon. Needless to say, I will communicate this to the *Yale Law Journal* and ask for space to correct my unforgivable mistake."[15]

We all err, of course. Sometimes in detail and sometimes in judgment, and no mistake, if honestly made, is unforgivable. Unfortunately this standard may not so easily be applied to the work of John Kaplan, then assistant professor at the Stanford University Law School.[16]

30 AN AMERICAN SCHOLAR

John Kaplan's analysis of five works critical of the Warren Commission bore the imprimatur of *The American Scholar*, the journal published by the United Chapters of Phi Beta Kappa.[1] McGeorge Bundy, president of the Ford Foundation and sometimes assistant to President Lyndon B. Johnson, lauded the article at a meeting of the American Society of Newspaper Publishers. Bundy regretted the fact that the article, written by a scholar, had not been afforded more publicity. He urged the publishers to correct that injustice.

The article is entitled "The Assassins."[2] The title does not refer to those who killed President Kennedy, for Kaplan makes it quite clear that only one man was involved in that act as far as he is concerned.[3] "The Assassins" are those who doubt the findings of the Warren Commission, for in the words of the professor, "Even the most baleful excesses of the McCarthy era were not as unfair, irresponsible and reckless" as the Commission's critics.[4] Indicating some political confusion, he also alleges that it is obvious that "the great body of complaint about the Commission has come from the left" and then adds that "a leftist conspiracy—if there was a political conspiracy at all—is far more likely than a rightist one."[5] Evidently Oswald acted alone, but if not, Kaplan knows the probable politics of those who assisted him.

One of the early books on the subject was originally self-published.[6] Of it, Kaplan wrote: "We may pass over *Whitewash* by Harold Weisberg, in just a sentence. It is the most strident, bitter and generally irrationally biased of all the attacks on the Commission. Out of charity, we shall mention it no further."[7] It is true that one may hardly read Weisberg's work and escape his rather unique style. Yet he did uncover evidence of importance, and so long as Kaplan's credentials as a critic of belles-lettres are in doubt, and so long as he pretended to examine the evidence referred to by the critics, his summary dismissal of *Whitewash* was irresponsible.[8]* The writings of both men reveal that while of the two Weisberg was alone knowledgeable, both men seemed inspired by a passion they found difficult to contain. Indeed, if Kaplan's sharp words—"most strident, bitter and generally irrationally biased of all"—were turned about toward the Commission's defenders, his contribution might not be considered ineligible.

Many of Kaplan's transgressions regarding the books that he did review fall into the area of his misunderstanding of the evidence relating to the origin of the shots and the meaning of the medical evidence. Here he is not original among other Commission defenders, and his position is analyzed, together with those of his colleagues, at a later point in this book.[11]†

He charges that less than a tenth of the assertions in *Rush to Judgment* "stand up to careful scrutiny."[16] Three examples that he adduces in support of that conclusion are, first: "Thus, Lane does not

* Curiously, Weisberg later was to indulge in that same form of criticism.[9] In a subsequent work he charged that a document was written in a "nasty" style and therefore, "if for no other reason, from its language alone not worthy of credence."[10] Surely Weisberg would be the first to agree that what is sauce for the goose is sauce for the gander.

† Kaplan did make one unique assertion that other defenders of the Commission, including the members of the Commission and its counsel, have not made.[12] He speculated that "there may well be no evidence that the Commission failed to consider."[13] It had been known for some time that among the important evidence the Commission never examined were the photographs and X-rays taken of the President's body.[14] One of the Commission members, John J. McCloy, appeared to agree with those who stated that the Commission had been negligent in failing to examine that evidence: "I think that if there's one thing that I would do over again, I would insist on those photographs and the X-rays having been produced before us."[15]

mention one word about the circumstances of Oswald's arrest—the reader of *Rush to Judgment* might well conclude that Oswald had turned himself in."[17] Yet at page 81 of *Rush to Judgment* I stated that "Oswald was arrested in the Texas Theatre at approximately 1:50 P.M."[18] When I asked Kaplan about that at a public meeting, he said that he had made an error.[19]* Second, Kaplan condemned me for not having mentioned the fact that James Simmons, an eyewitness, had "testified before the Warren Commission."[21] When I asked Kaplan about that, he said that he had made an error.[22]†

Kaplan wrote that

> Lane's third basic technique is to set himself up as his own expert witness—although not of course under oath. He states that a picture taken at the time of the assassination shows Jack Ruby in the crowd, not in the offices of the Dallas *Morning News*, where the Commission placed him. To this type of assertion one can only say that as close an examination of the picture as I could make did not reveal to me that this was Jack Ruby (indeed, I would say quite the contrary) and I am certain that I am as familiar with Jack Ruby's picture as is Mr. Lane.[24]

The only mention of the photograph in *Rush to Judgment* appears on page 349.[25] On that page the photographer is quoted as saying that the man in the picture appeared to him to be Jack Ruby.[26] The photographer is also quoted as stating that FBI agents told him that the man in the photograph was Ruby.[27] I have never offered my

* At a public meeting at Stanford University, the following colloquy took place:

> LANE: Did you state in your article, at page 285, "Thus, Lane does not mention one word about the circumstances of Oswald's arrest—the reader of *Rush to Judgment* might well conclude that Oswald had turned himself in"?
>
> KAPLAN: Yes, I did, and that's wrong.
>
> LANE: That's wrong?
>
> KAPLAN: Yes. There is a phrase about Oswald's arrest on page 81.
>
> LANE: And therefore, after reading that phrase one could hardly conclude that Oswald turned himself in?
>
> KAPLAN: You're quite right. I don't deny that. It is tucked fairly innocently into a sentence and I did miss it. I won't deny it.[20]

Rush to Judgment is comprised almost entirely of sentences.

† LANE: Did Simmons testify before the Warren Commission?
KAPLAN: No.
LANE: Did he testify before counsel for the Warren Commission?
KAPLAN: No. . . . I was wrong.[23]

opinion on that question. I have invited the readers of *Rush to Judgment* to examine the photograph and to make their own decision.[28] At my request my publisher sent copies of the picture to newspapers throughout the country along with a picture of Jack Ruby and a request that the newspapers permit their readers to decide. In the film *Rush to Judgment*, the photographs are presented with the request that the members of the audience make their own determination. In Dallas I asked a radio correspondent, who had known Ruby for some time and who had been a witness at the Ruby trial, if he could identify the man in the picture. On the air he said he thought it was Ruby.

As in the other cited instances, Kaplan's charge was false. When confronted with it at a public meeting, he admitted that he was wrong.[29]* Since Kaplan had offered himself as a witness, stating that his personal examination of the picture "did not reveal to me that this was Jack Ruby," he was guilty of the very transgression that he had incautiously charged.[31]†

Rush to Judgment contains more than 4,500 references.[36] Kaplan's blunderbuss assault presumed that he had located more than 4,000 errors.[37] Yet he was unable to cite one that remained standing when examined, despite what he referred to as his "careful scrutiny."[38] Indeed, it appears that Kaplan admitted that he had made more errors in his brief undocumented article than he even purported to cite in my entire book.[39]‡ That a law professor ill-armed with the

* LANE: Where in my book . . . have I established myself as my own witness and stated that the picture is a picture of Jack Ruby?

KAPLAN: Well, I will look and I will read, but I think I can tell you already that you did not state so flatly.

LANE: Well, where did I state it not flatly—roundly? Where did I state it at all? . . . Is there anything in my book which indicates that I state that the man is Ruby?

KAPLAN: No, but I think that it is fair to state that you do imply that the man is Ruby.[30]

† I read Kaplan's statement to him and asked him if, although I had not offered myself as a witness, he had in fact done so.[32]

KAPLAN: Yes. I did exactly the same thing that I accused you of doing.

LANE: Which I didn't do, but which you did.

KAPLAN: Precisely, and I made no bones about it.[33]

Kaplan was then asked if he had ever seen Jack Ruby, whom he identified as not being depicted in the photograph.[34] He replied that he had not but that he had seen "over 5,000 pictures of him."[35]

‡ At a public meeting after Kaplan had been apprised of the flaws in his work, he stated, "In fact, there are fewer sloppy errors in his [Lane's] long book than there are in my article in *The American Scholar*. I won't deny I've

facts published an article is neither unique nor significant. The importance that attaches to "The Assassins" is that *The American Scholar* agreed to publish the extreme document but did not offer an opportunity to answer.* The uncritical endorsement by McGeorge Bundy of the uncorrected article, it can be said in retrospect, reflected more upon him than upon the article, yet it afforded to an article already draped in academese an air of official approval. When the article, rewritten, appeared in the *Stanford Law Review*, it was described as a "corrected" version of the original.[42] But it was the original, admittedly erroneous, document that had been certified as correct by scholarly and governmental circles.

"The Assassins" at stage two of its development remains seriously error-ridden but somewhat less reckless than before.[43] This improvement, it may be said, resulted from the tardy application of the adversary system. Had Oswald lived, that system would have required the submission of each charge against him to the rigors of cross-examination. The hearsay evidence that the Commission accepted would have been excluded. His guilt would have been established beyond a reasonable doubt to the satisfaction of the members of an unbiased jury or there could have been no conviction. Yet Kaplan wrote: "The fact is that the death of Oswald made the work of the Commission vastly more difficult. If Oswald had been alive, his failure to point out any possible theories of innocence would have been taken as an admission that there were no valid ones, and his refusal to testify or provide any evidence—the highly artificial command of the fifth amendment notwithstanding—would have been taken as an effort to cover up guilt."[44]

If Oswald had lived, and had he been tried, presumably there would have been no Commission. In that sense, but only in that sense, Kaplan is correct in stating that his death made the Commission's task more difficult. Any other interpretation renders the sentence unintelligible, while this explanation merely reveals it to be inane. In the closing paragraphs of my first work on this subject, I observed that the readiness with which the Commission's findings were accepted was symptomatic of disease; that when law is suspended and traduced, the illness may not be arrested.[45] From the Warren Commission's lack of concern for the rights of an individual

---

made some errors. I didn't even know about them until the *Stanford Law Review*, which is republishing the book [*sic*], sent its citation checkers looking through and going over every word and I heard from them. There's no doubt there are errors in *The American Scholar* article."[40]

* The publication placed the article in a section labeled "Controversy."[41] That word is defined as "a discussion in which opinions clash; debate."

flows the Kaplan analysis, which suggests—perhaps approvingly, certainly without protest—that a portion of the United States Constitution is highly artificial and that a man charged with the commission of a crime no longer may be presumed innocent. Yet it is that presumption that is the cornerstone of our system of justice. It is that presumption that specifically protects the defendant from the allusion that his failure, not refusal, to testify or provide any evidence may not be considered by the jury and certainly may not be "taken as an effort to cover up guilt."[46]

Kaplan had been an assistant prosecutor. I doubt that there is a jurisdiction within the United States where he might have uttered those words in a courtroom and not provided the defendant with an excellent opportunity to move for a new trial and the judge with the responsibility to admonish him for improper conduct. It is not the obligation of a defendant to prove his innocence—"to point out any possible theories of innocence"—nor is it the function of our courts to see to it that "his failure" to do so is "an admission that there were no valid ones." That concept of law is as foreign to our present jurisprudence as are its antecedents—trial by fire and trial by ordeal.

This thinking, this recklessness, is the heritage of the Commission's abuses—from Goodhart's advocacy of secret hearings in important cases and his evident contempt for facts to Kaplan's abrogation of the presumption of innocence. In quite another context, one commentator has observed that the damage that was done to our country did not end when the shots were fired in Dealey Plaza. As that day, and the days that followed, have shown, violence begets violence, and perfidy, perfidy.

IV · The Books

31 WILLIAM MANCHESTER

The Death of a President by William Manchester represents a triumph for anti-intellectualism. Walter Lippmann called the book "*petite histoire*"—an accumulation of little stories incidental to history.[1] In view of the fact that Manchester had exclusive access to many persons who played a major role in Dallas on November 22, 1963, it is unfortunate that serious defects—his inability to distinguish trivia from substance; his insistence upon projecting himself into the thread of his narrative; his servility to the crucial conclusions of the Warren Commission; his highly emotional style; and his unashamedly hysterical treatment of Lee Harvey Oswald—flaw whatever literary or historical merit his work might possess.

Nevertheless, the book might rank as a valuable reference work were citations or some other form of documentation afforded the reader in support of Manchester's many contentions.[2] No such documentation is offered, however.[3] In these circumstances the reader is required to rely entirely upon Manchester's memory, accuracy and judgment. But a careful examination of those areas in which his assertions may be compared with known facts and which are therefore susceptible to informed analysis indicates that Manchester is too often grievously in error.

Aside from this shortcoming, the reader is often frustrated by an inability to determine just where that which Manchester alleges to be fact ends and where that which he concedes to be opinion begins. For example, he cited the statement that Marina Oswald observed her husband watching television after dinner on the evening of November 21.[4] "Apparently," Manchester wrote, Oswald "was intent upon the flickering Zenith screen. In fact, he was going mad. . . . [And] it seems clear that the total eclipse of his reason occurred shortly before 9 P.M. that evening."[5] In the foreword to his book, Manchester claimed that although he offered no documentation at all, "every statement, every fact, every quotation in my manuscript could be followed by a citation."[6] I believe it is fair to assume that the citation for the "fact" that Oswald "was going mad" while watching television "shortly before 9 P.M. that evening" would constitute a contribution of no little consequence to the literature of psychophysics, and I cannot deny that I should be very interested to learn what information that citation would contain.

Manchester describes himself as a "contemporary historian," but the manner in which he approaches Oswald is sufficient to question his credentials as an historian, however that word may be qualified.[7] "He shot the President of the United States in the back to attract attention," Manchester declared.[8] "Noticing him, and even printing his name in history books, therefore seems obscene. It is an outrage. He is an outrage. We want him Out [*sic*]."[9]

According to Manchester, "the barbarous obbligato" that Oswald "played that Friday" demonstrated "the potentialities of human depravity."[10] Oswald had "the physique of a ferret"; Manchester characterizes his cadaver as "chaff"; and, as if this too were Oswald's own fault, the author even disparages Oswald's coffin as a "cheap, moleskin-covered pine box."[11]

Errors of fact simply abound in Manchester's volume. In describing the ceremony in which Lyndon Johnson was sworn in as President, Manchester claimed that every male Kennedy aide, except Dr. George Burkley, had declined to be present for this event.[12] He cited pictures taken by Major Cecil Stoughton in support of his contention, but Stoughton's photographs show conclusively that Manchester was wrong.[13] Nineteen of these pictures, published in *Time* magazine on February 24, 1967, record the presence of five male Kennedy aides at the swearing-in.[14] This error is far less disturbing than Manchester's published assertion that Kenneth O'Donnell, one of the aides photographed as he stood quietly alongside Jacqueline Kennedy, was "pacing the corridor like a caged tiger, his hands clapped over his ears as though to block the oath."[15]

O'Donnell said that Manchester, who interviewed him, never asked about the subject, and Mary Gallagher, who Manchester later said was the source of the quote, denied that she ever said it.[16] When he was questioned by newsmen during a television interview, Manchester admitted that he may have been in error and casually suggested that it would be "presumptuous for a contemporary historian . . . to claim that he bats one thousand."[17]

The allegation regarding the presence of Kennedy aides at the swearing-in appeared in the serialization of Manchester's book in *Look* magazine.[18] The comments by Kenneth O'Donnell and Mary

Gallagher, and Manchester's comment on television, all were made after the *Look* article appeared but before Manchester's book was published.[19] Yet in the book no correction of this point was made.[20] On page 321 of *The Death of a President*, the following statement appears: "Despite the width of the Hasselblad lens, the photographer did not record the presence of a single major Kennedy aide."[21] And four pages later, Manchester wrote: "Mary Gallagher and Marty Underwood were watching Ken O'Donnell, who was pacing the corridor outside the bedroom like a caged tiger, his hands clapped over his ears as though to block the oath."[22]

Charles Brehm was one of the closest witnesses to the Presidential limousine during the latter stages of the assassination interval.[23] Brehm told me in a filmed and tape-recorded interview that he saw something which may have been a portion of President Kennedy's skull fly to the left and rear of the limousine when the fatal bullet shattered the President's head.[24] This would suggest that the shot came from the right front, the direction of the grassy knoll. Yet Manchester never reveals any of Brehm's crucial observations to his readers.[25] Indeed, he never even discloses his name, referring to him incorrectly as "Brend" on each occasion.[26] Manchester might have entitled his version of Brehm's conduct on the scene *the anatomy of a wave*: on page 150, "Charles Brend, a young Dallas father, kept repeating to his five-year-old son, 'Be sure and wave at the President, and maybe he'll wave back' "; on page 154, "Charles Brend held his son aloft: now was a good time to wave at the President"; on page 155, "Brend's five-year-old boy timidly raised his hand. The President smiled warmly. He raised his hand to wave back"; and on page 159, "Charles Brend has thrown his son to the ground and is shielding him with his body."[27] No other reference to Brehm appears in the book.[28]

After the assassination, Manchester alleged, a roll call of the Depository employees was held, and Oswald was "the only Depository employee to have been missing."[29] This statement is untrue.[30] In *Rush to Judgment* I noted that out of a total of seventy-five persons employed in the building, forty-eight were outside at 12:30 and five had not reported for work that day.[31] Others left the building immediately after hearing the shots.[32] Many employees were not allowed to enter the building after the assassination and thus were absent when the police search began.[33] In fact, even among the eight employees known to have been on the sixth floor that day, Oswald was not the only one who could not be accounted for after the assassination.[34] In addition, there was no such comprehensive roll call as contended by Manchester.[35]

Moving on to the Tippit killing, Manchester claimed that the patrolman was slain "beside a drugstore."[36] Photographs of the vicinity of the killing published by the Commission show clearly that there was no drugstore on that block on November 22.[37] This is confirmed by eyewitness statements;[38] and I have visited the location several times but have never noticed a drugstore there.

According to his testimony, Marrion L. Baker, a motorcycle policeman, was riding behind the last press car in the motorcade on November 22.[39] When Baker rounded the corner from Main Street onto Houston Street, he proceeded only a few feet north on that street before he heard the first shot.[40] The Commission determined that Baker was two hundred feet from the front entrance of the Depository Building.[41] Manchester, however, placed Baker in two different locations at the same moment, neither of which was the correct one.[42] He initially said the officer was riding "right beside" the Presidential car; later in the book, he said that at the same moment Baker was "directly under the gun."[43]

Manchester evidently felt compelled to produce more evidence than the Commission uncovered. Whether that evidence is without basis is apparently unimportant to Manchester. For example, although the Commission conceded it could not ascertain the source responsible for the description matching Oswald's description which was broadcast on the police radio less than fifteen minutes after the shooting, Manchester was able to make that determination.[44] The Commission suggested it might have been Howard L. Brennan.[45] In *Rush to Judgment* I explained at length the contradictory evidence which disabled that suggestion.[46] Manchester, however, stated flatly that Brennan was the source of the description.[47]

The Commission concluded that Oswald shot Officer Tippit and then ran to the Texas Theater, a cinema about half a mile away from the murder scene.[48] But the Commission was admittedly unable to produce any eyewitness testimony to establish the route allegedly taken by Oswald.[49] Manchester, who said he had "darted over the last lap of Oswald's flight to the Texas Theater," decided to fill that gap in the evidence.[50] At 1:35 P.M. on November 22, ten minutes before the police alert to surround the Texas Theater was dispatched, according to Manchester, Oswald ran "past the Bethel Temple and the accompanying signs—'PREPARE TO MEET THY GOD' and 'JESUS SAVES.' "[51] The Bethel Temple is located along one of the possible routes from the Tippit killing site to the Texas Theater.[52] Apparently intrigued by the thought of Oswald having seen the two signs, Manchester arbitrarily selected that escape route for the alleged killer of the patrolman.[53]

Manchester displays a peculiar sensitivity in discussing conservative political elements, both in Dallas and in general. For example, he noted that "five thousand cheap handbills" bearing two photographs of the President and the headline "Wanted for Treason" were distributed in Dallas the day before the President's arrival.[54] He was willing to offer his own opinion as to its effect: "Any hater, left or right, could find fuel in it."[55] In fact, the handbill charged President Kennedy with "turning the sovereignty of the U.S. over to the Communist controlled United Nations," being "lax in enforcing Communist Registration laws" and giving "support and encouragement to the Communist inspired racial riots."[56] It is hard to conceive how Oswald, ostensibly of the left, could have gained encouragement from the contents of that handbill.

Manchester also contended that "in Europe anti-American journalists seized upon the obvious readiness of the soldiers who were to parade in Monday's funeral [for President Kennedy] to charge that [Defense] Secretary [Robert S.] McNamara had been rehearsing troops for the funeral before the assassination."[57] Although it is not stated therein, Manchester's allegation suggests that the "anti-American" newsmen were left-wing and not conservative.[58] The Commission, however, had investigated the allegation and traced it to "an interview with U.S. Army Capt. Richard C. Cloy that appeared in the Jackson, Miss., *Clarion-Ledger* of February 21, 1964."[59] Thus it appears that the rumor was domestic, not foreign, and from the right, not the left.

Manchester also discussed an anti-Kennedy advertisement which had appeared in the Dallas *Morning News* on November 22, 1963.[60] The ad was signed by Bernard Weissman, and the sponsor was represented as "The American Fact-Finding Committee," which the ad described as "an unaffiliated and non-partisan group of citizens who wish truth."[61] But the Warren Report stated, "A fictitious sponsoring organization was invented out of whole cloth. The name chosen for the supposed organization was The American Fact-Finding Committee. This was 'Solely a name,' Weissman testified."[62] Yet Manchester, apparently unfamiliar with that portion of the Warren Report, referred to certain persons in Dallas as "the committee's most prominent members."[63]

Manchester devotes little space to the facts of the assassination itself, and his indifference to the intricacies of the testimony is little short of monumental. One of the few eyewitnesses to whom he does make reference is Arnold Rowland.[64] Rowland's account of his observations just before the shooting was found to be so challenging to the Commission's conclusion that Oswald acted alone that nearly two pages of the Warren Report were utilized in an attempt to discredit his damaging testimony.[65] Yet Manchester innocently, almost merrily, adduced Rowland's testimony in support of Oswald's lone guilt: "He [Rowland] saw Oswald silhouetted in the window, holding what appeared to be a high-powered rifle mounted with a telescopic sight."[66]

Rowland did not testify that he saw Oswald.[67] He said he saw two men on the sixth floor of the Texas School Book Depository.[68] In the window from which the shots allegedly originated, Rowland said he saw an unarmed Negro man.[69] In a window far removed from that one, Rowland testified, he saw a man with a rifle.[70] If Rowland's evidence is to be credited, then the Commission's conclusions—and Manchester's—must fall. If Rowland is disbelieved, then those conclusions can be temporarily salvaged. But only through the most blatant misrepresentation, such as Manchester indulges, can Rowland be brought forth as a Commission witness.

Thus, in lieu of documentation, Manchester's book demands a deep investment of faith, generally reserved for matters less empirical and more theological. In the face of Manchester's less than perfect batting average, as he himself has put it, this faith appears to be unwarranted.

32 CHARLES ROBERTS

In the modestly titled little book *The Truth about the Assassination*, Charles Roberts evinces little interest in either the assassination or the truth. For example, in a nine-page chapter called "The Grassy Knoll" Roberts makes reference to me or to my work sixty-seven times.[1] He refers to President Kennedy three times and to the President's automobile four times.[2] Thus the Roberts book was among the first of the reaction books and served as a prototype for others.

Most of the points Roberts makes are related to the portion of the evidence that is reviewed later in this book.[3] There his work is analyzed along with the other Commission defenders who have made the same or similar allegations.[4] Here we will discuss his original contributions, although they relate to peripheral questions.

Perhaps the most significant technical deficiency in Roberts' ethereal book—118 pages of text—is the lack of documentation for nearly all of his variegated allegations. Since many of them are demonstrably incorrect, one best be a trifle cautious in assessing the others, which may or may not be accurate but for which, in any event, no sources have been cited. A few examples will serve to illustrate this shortcoming.

The Warren Commission published 160 frames of the Zapruder film of the assassination.[5] This display, a portion of Commission Exhibit 885, comprised all of the frames numbered 171 to 334 inclusive—with the exception of 208, 209, 210 and 211.[6]* Since it is almost certain that those frames depicted an interval extremely close to the point at which the first shot was fired, it is conceivable that they could be of considerable assistance in determining the exact timing and sequence of the shots, and the omission of four such crucial frames was a most regrettable failure on the part of the Commission.[10] On February 6, 1967, *Newsweek* magazine quoted a former Commission attorney as having explained that the frames in question "were destroyed accidentally by Life magazine photo lab technicians working on the original film which Life bought from . . . Zapruder."[11] The lawyer said that frames 208 through 211 existed on the copies of the film which Zapruder had had made before the sale to *Life* was consummated.[12]

"To the conspiracy buffs," Roberts wrote, this explanation "must have been a disappointment."[13] He added:

> "Thus," said *Life*, "there never have been any missing frames." And to prove it they released for publication, from their copy [of the original], frames 207 through 212. The so-called "missing" frames showed nothing but a smiling Kennedy, waving at the crowd, before he was shot. Another conspiracy theory, rooted in human error rather than evil design, hit the cutting room floor.[14]

One need not have seen "frames 207 through 212" to know that they most certainly do not show "nothing but a smiling Kennedy, waving at the crowd."[15] At about this point in the film, the President disappeared from Zapruder's view behind an intervening road sign for about one second as the limousine moved down Elm Street.[16] Lyndal L. Shaneyfelt, the FBI photography expert who scrutinized the Zapruder film on behalf of the Warren Commission, testified that after frame 206 "the frames are too blurry as his [the President's] head disappears [behind the sign and] you can't really see

* Actually, that which the Commission identified as frame "212" was a composite of the upper portion of frame 208 and lower portion of frame 212 crudely spliced together.[7] Thus the lower portion of frame 208, the upper portion of frame 212 and all of frames 209, 210 and 211 are omitted.[8] In another exhibit the Commission reproduced what it represented as frame 210, but this frame has been cropped, removing a substantial, and valuable, section of the photograph.[9]

any expression on his face."[17] As for the claim that the frames showed the President "waving at the crowd," Shaneyfelt testified that "205 and 206 are the last frames where we see any of his, where we see the cuff of his coat showing above the signboard indicating his hand is still up generally in a wave."[18] In the light of this information, there would seem to be a limited number of explanations for Roberts' false assertion. Either he had seen "the so-called 'missing' frames" and deliberately misrepresented their content or he had not seen them but nevertheless offered what purported to be an authoritative opinion about them.

In his chapter dealing with the murder of Dallas Police Officer J. D. Tippit, Roberts discussed the statements of eyewitnesses to the flight of the patrolman's assailant.[19] "In the next block," Roberts wrote, "four men saw a white man running with a pistol in his right hand."[20] Yet it was Roberts, not the witnesses, who said the pistol was in the assailant's "right hand."[21] The observations of these four witnesses are recorded in five FBI reports and four affidavits published by the Commission.[22] In addition, one of the men testified before Commission counsel and the transcript of his hearing was subsequently published.[23] There is no indication that the murderer was carrying the pistol in his right hand, and the taxi driver whom Roberts considered "perhaps the best witness" at the scene of the crime testified before the Commission that the police officer's assailant was, in fact, carrying the gun in his left hand.[24] A left-handed gunman could not have worked the Mannlicher-Carcano rifle bolt quickly enough. If the man who killed Tippit also had shot the President, then he too must be right-handed. Thus it is Roberts' desire for consistency, not the evidence, that prevailed.

Roberts offered another detail regarding the Tippit killing for which the testimony of eyewitnesses provides no corroboration. Although this detail may be considered minor, its implications are indeed portentous. The Warren Report made the flat assertion that "Tippit stopped the man [his slayer] and called him to his car."[25] If that were true, the rumors that the killer knew Tippit and approached him might be dismissed, but the conclusion is without basis.[26] Undeterred by its conflict with the evidence, Roberts repeated the Report's claim ("the policeman's killer . . . was . . . stopped by Tippit") while, like the Commission, failing to furnish an iota of documentation in support of it.[27] Thus what was advertised as "the answer to the Warren Report critics" began more and more to resemble a *Reader's Digest* condensation of the original work.

On June 27, 1964, Mrs. Helen Markham, an eyewitness to the

Tippit killing, was visited at her home in Dallas by Mrs. Marguerite Oswald and two independent investigators.[28] Apparently because a document published by the Commission notes that Mrs. Markham's son later told the FBI that one of the investigators "claimed to be an attorney," Roberts believes that I was the attorney who visited Mrs. Markham.[29] This is untrue. On June 27, 1964, I was in London, a fact which Roberts could have learned had he read the evidence. The attorney who visited Mrs. Markham on that day was Vincent Salandria, a leading critic of the Commission.

Roberts works for a magazine. Even reporters who do not write books or read evidence do ask questions. A telephone call to me or to Mrs. Oswald would have resolved the matter. Since Salandria's visit to Mrs. Markham, I have been interviewed by other reporters for *Newsweek*, where Roberts works. Yet Roberts was content to violate the basic tenet of his profession, to provide implications instead of facts. One is not a scholar merely because a university pays his salary, and one requires more than a regular paycheck from a newspaper or magazine to qualify as a reporter.

Another and more serious example of Roberts' casual approach to facts can be found in his treatment of the allegation that Lee Harvey Oswald had been an employee of the Federal Bureau of Investigation.[30] One of the persons who had raised this possibility was Alonzo Hudkins, a reporter, who had written a story in the Houston *Post* on January 1, 1964, bearing the headline "Oswald Rumored as Informant for U.S."[31] At an "emergency session" on the afternoon of January 22, 1964, the Commissioners decided unanimously "that the only way to proceed was to conduct extensive and thorough hearings of as many witnesses as was necessary to exhaust . . . this rumor."[32]

Roberts implied that the Commission's investigation of the allegation—which the Report concluded was unfounded—was as "extensive and thorough" as it should have been.[33] "Through three Texas officials who had heard it," Roberts claimed, "they [the Commissioners] traced it to a Houston *Post* reporter, Alonzo Hudkins, and determined that its original source was probably none other than Marguerite Oswald."[34] The story, once traced back to Mrs. Oswald, was thoroughly discredited by Roberts.[35]

Yet since there is compelling evidence that the "original source" was not Marguerite Oswald, one wonders on what information Roberts based his assertion.[36] That must remain a mystery, for he offered no documentation in support of it.[37] In view of the fact that he "talked with Hudkins . . . about it" in February 1967, Roberts' failure to discover the source is even more surprising.[38] In any event, there is no need to speculate on the identity of the individual in question. In the National Archives there is a report submitted by Secret Service Agent Lane Bertram summarizing an interview with Hudkins on December 17, 1963.[39] This report, which was not published or mentioned by the Commission either in the Warren Report or in the twenty-six volumes of evidence, states:

> On December 17, Mr. Hudkins advised that he had just returned from a weekend in Dallas, during which time he talked to Allan Sweatt, Chief Criminal Division, Sheriff's Office, Dallas; Chief Sweatt mentioned that it was his opinion that Lee Harvey Oswald was being paid $200 a month by the FBI as an informant in connection with their subversive investigations. He furnished the alleged informant number assigned to Oswald by the FBI as "S172."[40]*

Thus it appears that the "original source" for Hudkins' information was the chief criminal deputy sheriff of Dallas County.[41]† Astonishingly enough, neither Hudkins nor Sweatt testified before the Commission or before Commission counsel.[49] Neither was asked to submit an affidavit or a statement.[50] It is clear that the Commission's investigation of the allegation that Oswald had worked for the FBI was neither as extensive nor as thorough as Roberts would have his readers believe.[51]

Roberts was not the progenitor of the *ad hominem* approach to the Warren Commission critics, but he advanced the movement considerably, and was the one person working for a respectable

* This report is reproduced as Appendix VIII.

† On July 12, 1966, in *Look* magazine, Fletcher Knebel alleged that "Hudkins, now a Baltimore newspaperman, says he was never interviewed on this matter by the Secret Service, that he never heard the rumor from Sweatt, that he heard a similar rumor elsewhere and that later, because of his own work on the case, he became convinced that Oswald had not worked for the FBI."[42] Hudkins' "own work on the case" is entirely irrelevant, since the information disclosed in Secret Service Agent Bertram's report indicates that if either party possessed firsthand information regarding Oswald's FBI ties it was Sweatt and not Hudkins.[43] The statement by Hudkins that "he was never interviewed on this matter by the Secret Service" constitutes a serious charge.[44] Had Hudkins been called as a witness by the Commission, both he and Lane Bertram could have been confronted with the Secret Service document and questioned closely about its contents.[45] Knebel himself might have done that if he had secured a copy of the interview report. Not only did he fail to do this; he even went so far as to imply that no such report existed.[46] Knebel alleged further that Sweatt "says he never made any such statement to Hudkins or to anyone else, and that he had no knowledge of Oswald's connections with any Government agency."[47] This conflict too could have been resolved by a confrontation under oath before the Warren Commission.[48]

publication who became a spokesman for it and at the same time appeared to be sensitive to the implications of appealing to prejudice rather than to intellect. In a chapter called "The Critics—Scholars or Scavengers?" Roberts asks, "Are they bone fide [*sic*] scholars" or are they "journalistic scavengers"?[52] He then asks, "Are they interested in abstract justice—or profits even at the expense of truth?"[53] Of course the integrity of the critics is not necessarily related to the integrity of the critical works. *Rush to Judgment* contains thousands of citations and references to the Commission's own evidence, and its integrity is to be found or challenged between its two hard covers. Roberts, evidently aware that this is so, writes of his own questions, "To ask these questions a year ago would have been impertinent. Books are—or were—judged on their contents, not by McCarthy-like inquiries into the credentials, methods and motives of their authors. But these tenets must be reconsidered in the light of what Lane, Epstein, and others have wrought."[54] What we have wrought is the reconsideration of a governmental edict. Why must "these tenets"—judging books by their content, arguments by their validity—be dismissed in favor of what is acknowledged in advance to be a "McCarthy-like" inquiry?[55]

After indulging for several pages in a highly personal and biased attack, as he had just promised that he would (including unkind remarks directed toward those who had not been unkind in reviewing *Rush to Judgment*—e.g., "Alistair Cooke, revealing an appalling ignorance of the events in Dallas, wrote that Lane 'destroyed beyond a reasonable doubt the whole theory of a single assassin' "), Roberts concluded, "With royalties from his book, his 'documentary' film, and lecture fees rolling in, he can chuckle all the way to the bank."[56] I have received no royalties from the film, having established a corporation which required that each investor be entirely repaid before any funds be distributed elsewhere. For more than two years I lectured at scores of universities and churches throughout the country. I accepted no fees. I have lectured in Denmark, before the country's major forum, paid my own air fare to and from that country, and donated the proceeds to the John F. Kennedy fund for retarded children there. My book, which required more than two and a half years of work and, in paperback, has 399 pages and sells for seventy-five cents. Roberts' 128-page paperback book, written in a few weeks, sells for one dollar. McCarthyism is defined as an accusation "in many instances unsupported by proof"—the persistent use of "unfairness in investigative technique."

Roberts' final charge against the critics is that they fail to name the guilty and that therefore they are "unlike Emile Zola and

Lincoln Steffens, who rocked national and local governments by *naming* the guilty."[57] (Emphasis in the original.) That has been an oversight. I concluded *Rush to Judgment* with these words: "As long as we rely for information upon men blinded by the fear of what they might see, the precedent of the Warren Commission Report will continue to imperil the life of the law and dishonor those who wrote it little more than those who praise it." I accuse Charles Roberts.

33 THE SCAVENGERS

The Scavengers and Critics of the Warren Report by Richard Warren Lewis and Lawrence Schiller is probably the least important of the defense books that became a minor industry following the success of the critical works. Written primarily by Lewis, a Hollywood gossip writer, it was a bit livelier than the others and was the first to employ the word "scavenger" in its title, although its author and "investigator" appear to be among the most vulnerable to that charge. Unlike most of the other defense works by officials, Commission employees, media representatives or prominent persons, this work was written by two obscure persons who were therefore able to mask their objective until the publication of their product. The book itself requires little serious examination, but the story behind it is of interest for it involves a giant record company and an important New York newspaper.

Toward the end of 1966 I was in New York City for a brief stay to video-tape a one-hour program with William F. Buckley. A telephone call apprised me of the fact that two representatives of Capitol Records were anxious to interview me for a documentary record that they were preparing on the assassination. A date was set and the men, Schiller and Lewis, subsequently arrived at my hotel room with a tape recorder. They told me that the record was to be an objective document which would not take sides but which would permit the critics and the defenders to present their views. They both assured me that they personally could not accept the Commission's Report but that the record would be entirely impartial. They asked if I would be willing to donate my royalties for the record to the John F. Kennedy Memorial Library. I said that I would be happy to do so but that I wanted some assurance that the Library would accept the offer. Paul Fay, the Under Secretary of the Navy in the Kennedy Administration, had publicly offered three thousand dollars to the Library, but Mrs. Kennedy rejected the sum, saying that it would be hypocritical of her to accept it. I explained that I wanted my gift to be unpublicized and that I wanted an indication in advance that it would be accepted. Schiller told me that Capitol had already secured such assurances from Robert Kennedy and from Stephen Smith. He then produced a letter on Capitol Records letterhead, signed by the president of the company, asking me to donate "an amount equal to the standard artists' royalty of 5%." On the back of the letter was a release. I signed the form and thereby donated my prospective income from the record to the Library.

The two interviewers seemed innocent of the facts, despite their statement that they sympathized with the critics. Schiller was very proud of his association with Capitol, which he referred to repeatedly as the largest record company in the country. The interview was rather pedestrian, since the interviewers were less than knowledgeable. At one point, Lewis asked me if I would care to answer the charge that I had begun to wear "mod" clothing since the publication of my book. I said that the question was silly since, as he could see, I was wearing a gray worsted double-breasted suit and because it had no relevance to the subject matter of the record. At the conclusion of the interview I told them that I did not wish to hear and answer the statements made to them by the defenders as that would be unfair, but that I presumed that my interview would not be given to a defender to answer unless I could respond. They both said that they alone would hear the interviews and that the record would be fairly edited.

The record, called "The Controversy," was released during January 1967. It was a defense brief for the Warren Report. Where I had offered a conclusion and then presented the evidence to support it, the Capitol record presented a fragment of my conclusion, no supporting evidence for it, and a long rebuttal by a former Commission lawyer. Although it was advertised as an album that "presents the views of both sides," that claim was untrue. The other critics were ridiculed and denied an opportunity to present a case. I contacted Capitol at once and urged them to cease their misleading advertising of the record and to refrain from stating specifically that my view was contained in the record. They refused to modify their campaign. The largest picture on the back of the album jacket was a picture of me. The advertising presented my name first among the critics and defenders. I told Capitol that it seemed apparent that they hoped to trap those who might wish to hear my view into purchasing a record which did not contain it.

Capitol was adamant, despite my telephone calls and my visit to their Hollywood offices, possibly due to the fact that the record was selling well. By the end of February, gross sales were 37,683.[1] Then, on several radio and television programs, I urged listeners not to purchase the record. During the next three months there were less than a thousand sales and more than ten thousand records were returned.[2] Although Schiller and Lewis had assured me that the Library had agreed to accept royalties, I was no longer convinced that that was so. A Capitol executive had supported the Schiller-Lewis allegation, and the signed letter from Alan W. Livingston, Capitol's president, also seemed to offer support for that belief. On June 29, 1967, I wrote to Charles H. Tillinghast, the record company's attorney, and asked if the Library had consented to accept royalties earned from the record "The Controversy."[3] On that same day I made the same request of the John F. Kennedy Memorial Library.[4] Within a week, Miss Helen Keyes, the Library's administrator, replied:

> On January 3, 1967, Stephen E. Smith, Treasurer of the John Fitzgerald Kennedy Library Corporation gave the following press release to the wire services at 2 P.M. "Capitol Records, Inc. did offer as a donation to the John Fitzgerald Kennedy Library Corporation a portion of the royalties payable in connection with the Ruby Album (The Controversy). The Directors of the Library Corporation do not accept contributions from commercial enterprises such as this." There has not been any change in library policy since that time.[5]

More than two weeks later, Capitol's attorney answered the same question in a different fashion: "The John F. Kennedy Memorial Library has not given Capitol a final answer as to whether it would accept royalties from the album."[6] He added that the record was doing very poorly and that there might be no royalties, but insisted that "in the unlikely event that there are royalties, Capitol will seek to give them to the Library."[7]

Shortly after the release of the record, the *World Journal Tribune* began advertising that an article called "The Scavengers," written by Lewis, would appear in its magazine section. It promised the inside story about those "obsessed by the assassination." The obsession seemed to be elsewhere, however. Lewis revealed that when interviewed I was wearing a "stylish English Mod jacket."[8] (My double-breasted suit had been purchased in Stockholm.) To acquaint readers with my background, Lewis charged that "Lane was arrested and convicted of breaching the peace in Jackson, Mississippi," without filling in all the facts.[9] I was then a member of the New York State Legislature. Together with a prominent New York attorney, Percy Sutton, then president of the New York branch of the National Association for the Advancement of Colored People and now Borough President of Manhattan, I traveled through several Southern states. We were arrested at the Jackson airport for spending five minutes in the previously segregated waiting room. Before the actual trial took place (there had been a hearing), the district attorney of Jackson moved for a dismissal of the charges and the court granted that motion. As a result of these and other similar efforts, the Jackson facilities were desegregated for the first time since Reconstruction.

Not content with questioning the motives of those who dissented from the Commission's findings, Lewis charged that "the success of the book in England convinced Holt, Rinehart and Winston," the publishers of *Rush to Judgment*, "to print *Judgment* in the United States."[10] The first place that the book was printed was in the United States and by Holt, Rinehart and Winston. The success of the book in the United States may have affected its success abroad, but the facts would not have suited the argument. The only demonstration of impartiality in the long article was the egalitarian abandon with which Lewis misspelled the names of witnesses and Commission counsel alike.[11]

Less than three months after the article appeared, Dell published a somewhat enlarged version of it as a book. By the time it came out the New Orleans investigation was under way. The book was then advertised as "The Truth About: The New Orleans Conspiracy," although only two pages of the book make reference to that subject.

The travels of Schiller and Lewis, presumably financed by Capitol Records, are reminiscent of nothing so much as the ill-fated journey of Senator Joseph McCarthy's helpers, Roy Cohn and David Schine. The wayfaring authors visited various critics throughout the country, posing as objective journalists. Unlike Cohn and Schine, who proudly displayed their credentials, Schiller never disclosed the fact that he was Jack Ruby's business agent and that he had kept a substantial portion of the income derived from the sale of Ruby's final story to the press. Under the circumstances, one might have thought that the word "scavenger" might have been more sparingly employed by Schiller and Lewis.

The authors' most traumatic confrontation came when they met Brondo, a German Shepherd of impeccable taste. He lives with Mr. and Mrs. Joseph Field in Beverly Hills, California. Mrs. Field has been a diligent and important researcher, who was completing a study of the case when Schiller and Lewis arrived. Brondo, less naïve than the critics, who had been most hospitable, and evidently relying upon a superior instinct, bit Lewis in the buttocks. His failure to take similar action with Schiller remains a mystery but one which I believe the two journalists will not wish to pursue.

The authors then visited Shirley Martin in Owasso, Oklahoma. Her home they refer to as "her command post."[12] A few pages later the authors refer to Mrs. Field's living room as "a command post."[13] The defensive and decidedly hostile attitude toward Mrs. Martin and Mrs. Field is difficult to understand. The authors describe the very beautiful Mrs. Martin as "the graying woman," and if nothing previously had done so, that comment alone would constitute reason for questioning their judgment.[14] When the two men arrived at the airport in Oklahoma, Mrs. Martin was there to meet them. Lewis, sitting in a markedly peculiar fashion in the automobile on the way to the Martin home, asked if Mrs. Martin had any pets. Taking Lewis for an animal lover, she replied that she was so pleased with the question as she had twelve dogs and two cats. Lewis refused to leave the car and it appeared that the interview might never take place.

Lewis wrote, "She [Mrs. Martin] spent up to $200 a month telephoning buffs like Mrs. Joseph A. Field Jr."[15] That statement appears to be without any foundation. Mrs. Martin had never spoken to Mrs. Field by telephone until after that comment was printed and then primarily for the purpose of discussing the various false charges, that one included, that comprise *The Scavengers*. Lewis continued, "The wife of a stock broker, Mrs. Field employs a thinly-disguised pseudonym" in order to "conceal her activities."[16] Mr. Field is a stockbroker in much the same fashion that the president of General Motors is a mechanic, and his wife is sufficiently unconcerned about her identity that her name, not a pseudonym, has appeared twice in articles about the case in *Esquire* as well as in articles in *The New Yorker* and *West* magazine. She has also written innumerable letters about the case to Congressmen and Senators. Lewis, somewhat subjectively, charged, "A vicious German Shepherd intimidates unwanted guests at her $250,000 home, where Lane likes to float around the swimming pool between engagements."[17] Brondo's activities have been previously discussed, and while my wife and I have visited the Fields' home, neither of us has been for a swim.

Continuing with this line, Lewis stated that with my "encouragement, Mrs. Field first compiled 30 bulging scrapbooks and numerous 50-pound file boxes of clippings."[18] In fact, I had no idea that Mrs. Field was compiling material for a book until after she had submitted it to a publisher, who accepted it. She assures me that she has no fifty-pound file boxes about the house and is quite certain that she would have noticed them if they were there. Lewis speaks of Mrs. Field's "generous support of Lane," to which Mrs. Field replies,

"My support has always consisted of moral support, something Schiller and Lewis would not understand." And, she adds kindly, "It will continue."

Mrs. Martin, who had neither met nor spoken to Mrs. Field, was nonetheless described as "the Midwestern axis of the underground," while Mrs. Field was "the leader of the Western underground," and Sylvia Meagher, who had compiled the *Subject Index to the Warren Report and Hearings & Exhibits*, was described as a "widow" (that being her cover) who in reality has been unmasked "as the Eastern delegate of the housewives' alliance."[19] Further investigation revealed that Mrs. Meagher was not just a delegate but "the Housewives Supersleuth."[20] After weeks of digging, the two journalists had finally uncovered evidence of conspiracy.

The book is dotted with little errors which crop up with marvelous regularity. Schiller is wrong about the speed of the motorcade, unable even to accurately present the Commission's view on that subject.[21] Lewis asserts that Brooklyn College is my alma mater, a school that I never attended.[22] He states that I met Thayer Waldo, a Fort Worth journalist, "at the Dallas Press Club on December 7, 1963."[23] I had never been to Texas before the last day of 1963, and I met Waldo during 1964 in Fort Worth.

The authors are particularly concerned with the allegation that Jack Ruby, Officer J. D. Tippit and Bernard Weissman met at Ruby's Carousel Club on November 14, 1963, eight days before the assassination.[24] They seek to dispose of the question in this fashion: "During the introductions at the Carousel Club on December 14, Tippit's first name was never mentioned."[25] They add: "More thorough investigations reveal that there were actually three Tippits listed on the Dallas police-force roster at the time, Gayle M. Tippit, W. W. (Woody) Tippit and the deceased J. D. Tippit. The similarity of their names often caused confusion at the Dallas Police Department."[26] And not only there. W. W. spells his name "Tippett."[27] The authors continue: "The FBI investigated the whereabouts of Weissman and all three Tippits on December 14 and could find no evidence that they were at the Carousel Club."[28] That statement is undocumented, very likely due to the fact that the authors could find no evidence that the FBI ever investigated the whereabouts of J. D. Tippit for the night of the meeting.[29] Although the authors insist that the meeting is said to have taken place on December 14, that appears unlikely as Tippit was dead and Ruby in jail long before that.[30] Nothing in the Commission's Report reveals that the FBI sought to discover where J. D. Tippit, Bernard Weissman or Jack Ruby spent the late evening hours on November 14.[31]

Accuracy regarding dates and names did not constitute the

strength of the book—it incorrectly states the release date of the Warren Report* and alleges that "for weeks" the Commission "scrutinized" the man-in-the-doorway photograph "long before critics brought it to their attention."[33] Among the early critical questions asked about that photograph, which many persons thought revealed Lee Harvey Oswald as a spectator while the shots were being fired, were those raised by the San Francisco *Chronicle* on December 3, 1963, before the Commission had a staff and long before the Commission met to examine any evidence.[34]

When the authors attempt to analyze the more complicated aspects of the case, they become even more bemused. In examining a bullet's trajectory, they again begin with the incorrect speed for the limousine and state that "a bullet traveling approximately 1,979 miles per second, the speed of the fatal bullet fired by Oswald, theoretically could cover almost ninety miles in that 1/18th of a second."[35] The mathematics is sound enough so that one could state that the bullet theoretically could have traveled from Dallas to London and part way back before the bolt on the rifle could be worked again. It is the premise that is falsely stated. Schiller and Lewis have overcalculated the speed of the bullet by 500,000 percent, which even in *The Scavengers* stands out as extravagant.

The book carries an introduction by Bob Considine, who states, as we can see not without some justification, that the authors "do not merely repeat the evidence" but "instead, they develop new evidence to support the truth of the Commission Report."[36] Considine refers to the critics as "grave robbers" and "opportunists and crackpots" and laments the fact that "book critics were generally awed" by *Rush to Judgment*.[37] He observes that "like a malignancy, *Rush to Judgment* is still with us, spreading to the healthy tissue of that portion of the body politic that George Gallup clinically calls 'undecided.' "[38] Considine adds that "to date, he [Lane] appears indestructible" for "he has survived" hosts "of open confrontations at his lectures, and a televised bout with the formidable Louis Nizer."[39] Hopefully, the accuracy of the Schiller and Lewis book will return us to a sense of reality, Considine states; that is, if it "gets airborne."[40] If not, "we can count on the same cumulative and progressively irrational 'exposés' that have appeared since John Wilkes Booth killed Abraham Lincoln on April 13, 1865."[41] Lincoln died on April 15, having been shot on April 14.[42]

* On page 50 the correct year but the wrong day of the month is given; while on page 200 the correct day but the wrong year is offered.[32]

PART THREE: THE ISSUES

I · The Grassy Knoll

34 PHYSICAL TRACES

JEAN HILL, a Dallas schoolteacher, was the first eyewitness to the assassination whom I interviewed.[1]* She told me that she had been standing on the south side of Elm Street, directly across from a small rise, when President Kennedy was killed.[5] Mrs. Hill said she had heard four to six shots and thought they had come from behind a fence atop the slope opposite her.[6] She referred to this spot as "the grassy knoll."[7] That evening I played a tape recording of Mrs. Hill's comments at a public meeting in New York City,[8] and two weeks later I testified before the Warren Commission that Mrs. Hill had told me she believed the shots "came from the grassy knoll" west of the Book Depository Building.[9]

When the Warren Commission Report was published in 1964, researchers of the document noted that not one of the several maps of the Dealey Plaza area included in the Report depicted either the grassy knoll itself or any of its distinctive landmarks—for example, the concrete pergola, the wooden fence or the parking lot behind the fence.[10] In its issue dated October 5, 1964, as part of its coverage of the Report, *Newsweek* magazine printed a wide-angle aerial photograph of the area on which a number of locations—such as the sixth-floor window of the Depository—were pinpointed, ostensibly in order to assist the readers.[11] The grassy knoll, however, was not among the places thus identified.[12]

On the last day of 1963 I had wandered through Dealey Plaza, inspecting the knoll, the railroad overpass and other areas that had been occasionally mentioned but generally ignored by a press which

* I was not formally asked by Mrs. Marguerite Oswald to commence an independent inquiry into the events of November 22–24, 1963, until January 1964.[2] Although the Commission had been created on November 29,[3] it still had not questioned a single eyewitness to the slaying by the time I talked with Mrs. Hill on February 18, 1964.[4]

had begun to accept and publish little but the official story of the assassination. It was New Year's Eve, and I had watched groups of tourists make pilgrimages to the plaza, their attention riveted exclusively upon the sixth-floor window of the Book Depository looming in the twilight. I resolved at that time that I would endeavor to direct the attention of the American people to the area from which it appeared, even from the meager information then available, that shots had also been fired.

In part that aspiration has now been realized. On a recent visit to Dallas, I saw any number of amateur sleuths, armed with cameras, roaming through the parking lot and the railroad yards on the knoll. Three and a half years after the shots were fired in Dealey Plaza, *Time* magazine described "the small knob above Elm Street" as possibly "the most trampled patch of greenery in America."[13] And in his book published early in 1967, Charles Roberts, *Newsweek's* White House correspondent, used the identical photograph of the assassination scene which his magazine had printed in 1964.[14] This time, however, the grassy knoll was clearly identified by a title superimposed on the picture.[15]

Unable to wish the grassy knoll out of existence and unwilling to cope with the realities of the problem, the Commission's defenders have offered tenuous explanations replete with every variety of inaccuracy. Their purported explanations serve to illustrate rather vividly both the paucity of information possessed by the Commission's champions and an emotional rather than intellectual commitment to upholding the Report's findings.

One of the most popular, and to the uninitiated perhaps the most telling, argument designed by the anti-knollists is the assertion that since a sniper on the hill "would have been firing in full view of a crowded plaza," to borrow Walter Cronkite's phrasing, he could hardly have escaped notice.[16] Arlen Specter was more selective and therefore more specific—he said that the witnesses "on the [railroad] overpass . . . had a good view of the grassy knoll, and they saw no shooting from the knoll."[17] Yet the fact is that the wooden fence on the knoll, and the foliage from the bushes and trees immediately in front of it, provided more than adequate cover for anyone behind the fence. It is quite impossible to see the area just behind the fence from the overpass. I have walked all over Dealey Plaza in my many visits to Dallas. On one occasion an entire film crew was busily at work behind the fence while I stood on the railroad overpass, yet they could not be seen from my location.

S. M. Holland, who knows the area well, having worked for

railroad companies for some forty-one years,[18] said that it was "possible there could have been three or four people around there [behind the wooden fence on November 22] that wasn't observed, because that particular spot was just a sea of cars, and it would have been very easy for anyone to sit down over there or stand up without being observed, because there was a picket fence in front of them, there was cars all around behind them, and it's possible that there could have been maybe half a dozen people standing over there without being observed because everybody was watching the parade."[19]

Specter alleged that "there were officers on the overpass who had a good view of the grassy knoll, and they saw no shooting from the knoll."[20] Both parts of that statement are misleading. There were two policemen on the railroad bridge during the assassination[21]—J. C. White[22] and J. W. Foster.[23] White testified before Commission counsel that he could offer no firsthand account of what transpired when the assassination occurred because a "noisy train" which was passing between him and the scene of the murder at that moment prevented him even from hearing the shots.[24] Foster was standing near the railroad workers watching the motorcade from the overpass,[25] none of whom could see the area behind the wooden fence, although they could, of course, see the knoll itself immediately to their left. After the shooting, Foster and a number of the railroad employees ran behind the wooden fence and searched the parking lot for possible traces of an assassin or a weapon.[26] If Foster "had a good view of the grassy knoll" and "saw no shooting from the knoll,"[27] it would be interesting to learn why he ran there directly and searched the area after hearing the shots.[28]

Of course, it is true that the landscaping and the fence could not provide absolute secrecy from every conceivable angle. A man positioned in the railroad tower directly behind the fence would have been able to discern the presence of a man or men in that general area at about the time the shots were fired. A man was in the tower—Lee Bowers, Jr.[29] He did testify that he saw two men in that area at that time.[30] One who viewed the events transpiring below from the vantage point of the roof of the Terminal Annex Building just across the plaza could not have seen the area immediately behind the fence but could have observed anyone fleeing from that area after the shots were fired. A man was on the roof—J. C. Price.[31] He did state that he saw a man who carried something in his hand run from that area just after the shots were fired.[32] Since the Commission declined to call him as a witness,[33] one would expect that some of the defenders' animosity, arising no doubt partially from a sense of frustration, might better be directed toward the Commission for its manifold failures.

Specter, who was the Warren Commission attorney invested with the responsibility of writing the chapter of the Report dealing with the source of the shots,[34] said that "the witnesses in the vortex of the assassination event thought the contrary to what those farther away thought. They testified in terms of shots coming overhead and to the right and rear, as the witnesses in the presidential caravan itself said."[35] There appears to be little logical basis for establishing a new class of earwitnesses: those "in the vortex," as opposed to those in other locations in the plaza. There appears to be no logical basis for investing the former with greater credibility than the latter; indeed, perhaps just the reverse should prove to be true. Witnesses who have been fired at often are able to provide the least useful information as to the source of the shots. In the instant matter it would seem that witnesses just in front of the wooden fence or those in front of or inside of the Book Depository might have at least equally valuable observations to offer as to the source of the shots.

In any event, Specter was in error. Many witnesses "in the vortex of the assassination event" specifically pinpointed the grassy knoll as the source of the shots.[36] These included Jean Hill[37] and William Newman,[38] whose presence in close proximity to the President's car during the shooting is amply documented by motion picture and still photographs which have been published;[39] Mary Woodward,[40] whose first-person account of the assassination was printed on November 23, 1963, in the Dallas *Morning News;*[41] Mr. and Mrs. John A. Chism;[42] and others.[43]

One of the arguments often advanced by the defenders is that "not a single item of hard evidence" comparable to that discovered on the sixth floor of the Texas School Book Depository—a rifle with a palm print, for example[44]—was discovered on the grassy knoll after the assassination.[45] Indeed, a degree of carelessness not commensurate with the precision with which the murder was accomplished would have been required for such incriminating evidence to remain on the scene when the officers arrived. In the midst of Presidential security arrangements that had been heralded in advance as unprecedented with Dealey Plaza alive with armed Federal and local police, the President was assassinated and his murderers escaped from the scene. Even should one accept the Commission's hypothesis, one need merely transpose that assertion into singular form. If Oswald was the lone culprit, then the formidable expertise which he brought to the planning and escape stages was humbled by his as yet unduplicated feat with the weapon. Inasmuch as the total body of known fact points to another solution, are the defenders logical in asking us to abandon the direction dictated by the evidence primarily because too much efficiency would have been required of the assassins—to refrain from leaving their weapons, handily endorsed with their prints, about for the gendarmes?

The defenders insist upon hard evidence replete with fingerprints—for every moviegoer and television mystery fan knows that they are almost prerequisite indicia of criminal activity. Yet despite this widespread belief, that kind of evidence is rarely present. For more than fifteen years I have tried criminal cases with some degree of regularity. I cannot think of a single such instance where fingerprint evidence was required or even utilized. Perhaps the busiest and among the most efficient of prosecutors is Frank S. Hogan of New York. His bureau chief recently reported that "evidence other than the testimony of witnesses, or a confession, is unusual."[46] As to fingerprints in a criminal case, he added, "A real rarity—maybe once in a thousand times."[47]

That the fiction world's concept of criminal jurisprudence has dominated the televised defenses of the Report is perhaps understandable. Cronkite exclaimed on CBS-TV: "No bullets. No cartridge cases. Nothing tangible."[48] Thus he dismissed the admittedly impressive other evidence. Less explicable, however, was Roberts' similar assertion that "50 or more" police officers "rushed to the top of the knoll immediately after the shots were fired and found no weapon or trace of a weapon having been fired there,"[49] for *Newsweek* purports to be in the fact rather than the entertainment business. And impermissible was the assertion of Joseph Ball, a Warren Commission attorney, that "a good many people ran up there and they found nothing. They found no man with a gun. They found no gun. They found no shells. They found nothing."[50] If assassins with a modicum of efficiency or even a highly developed animal instinct for survival chose the fence for shelter while firing, it would have been surprising to discover that they left hard evidence behind. That which would surprise us by its presence may not also be held to surprise us by its absence. So long as there are reasonable possibilities which might account for the absence of any "hard evidence" behind the wooden fence, the other evidence that indicates the knoll as a point of origin cannot be dismissed.

For example, William W. Turner, a former FBI agent who served with the Bureau for more than ten years, suggested that a pistol or revolver could have been used by an assassin firing from the grassy knoll.[51] If that was the case, Turner said, "the escape was very simple. Number one, using a revolver or a pistol, the shells do not eject. They don't even have to bother to pick up their discharged shells. Number two, they can slip—put the gun under their coat."[52] If a revolver was, in fact, fired from the knoll during the assassination, it would not be surprising that no empty shells were found in the police search of the area conducted immediately afterward. Some corroboration for Turner's hypothesis can be found in the account of S. M. Holland, who observed the shooting from the railroad bridge over Elm Street.[53] Holland said he heard four shots, three of which were loud reports.[54] The penultimate shot, he observed, "wasn't nearly as loud as the two previous reports or the fourth report."[55] According to Holland, that shot, which he swore had been fired from the grassy knoll,[56] sounded "I would say about like a .38 target pistol."[57]

Under the circumstances which prevailed behind the wooden fence on the knoll on November 22, perhaps even a rifle would not have presented insurmountable difficulties to an assassin attempting to conceal his weapon after the shots were fired. According to Holland, the parking lot behind the fence was a "sea of cars" on the day of the assassination, and he suggested that it would have been an easy matter for a rifleman to have thrown his weapon into the trunk of a vehicle parked there.[58] Holland said the police did not open car trunks during their search of the knoll area.[59] Then, Holland continued, "anyone that was there could have melted into the crowd because he didn't have over thirty feet to walk to get back with the crowd in front of that fence. . . . [There] was so much excitement and everybody was running to and fro that it's possible they could have walked over there unobserved and been one of the bystanders."[60]

The investigation being conducted by Jim Garrison is not related only to events that transpired in New Orleans. That investigation has turned up facts about the physical environs of the assassination site not previously known. The area beneath Dealey Plaza, Garrison discovered, is honey-combed with sewer pipes. A very large pipe leads up to, and ends, just behind the fence on the knoll. It is covered with a removable metal plate approximately three feet wide and three feet long. It provides adequate space for a man and quite obviously much more than adequate space for weapons. Yet there is no indication that this area was searched either before or after the shots were fired.

There are many ways of being invisible, not all of them as metaphysical as the defenders imply. Bowers said that within minutes a hundred men, some spectators, and many dressed in ordinary clothing, presumably plain-clothes detectives or officers, were running about the knoll behind the fence.[61] "Presumably" is of course the operative word in that sentence. An assassin or two in the crowd of frantically searching men might not have been detected. Three officers did testify that in the search of the vicinity following the shots they encountered some "Secret Service" officers.[62] One police sergeant testified that the men "told me they were Secret Service" agents.[63] Immediately following the shots, J. M. Smith, a Dallas police officer, ran to the knoll area.[64] "I pulled my pistol from my holster, and I thought, this is silly, I don't know who I am looking for, and I put it back. Just as I did, he showed me that he was a Secret Service agent."[65]

COUNSEL: Did you accost this man?
SMITH: Well, he saw me coming with my pistol and right away he showed me who he was.[66]

There would, of course, be nothing suspicious about the presence of Secret Service agents on the scene minutes after the shots were fired. However, there were no Secret Service agents there, as the Commission conceded.[67]

In *Rush to Judgment* I observed that the Commission had erred in refusing to grant Abraham Bolden's request to testify. He had been a Special Agent of the Secret Service assigned to the White House detail and had stated that he possessed relevant and important information. On December 4, 1967, I was able to interview him for the first time and he told me then that it had been widely known in the Secret Service that an unauthorized person had used Secret Service credentials in Dallas on November 22. Evidently it was for that reason that all Special Agents were required to surrender their Commission Books, or identification documents, for an unprecedented service-wide check on November 27, 1963.

The Commission's lack of curiosity about those men who falsely identified themselves as federal police officers, in at least one case evidently to escape closer scrutiny, has left a less than complete record. Yet the defenders ignore the laxity of the investigatory work, pretend that it was excellent and then wonder how the assassins might have escaped in the face of so thorough an investigation.

There are reasonable explanations to account for the decision of the assassins to take their hardware with them, to scatter no fingerprints around and to decline to announce their true purpose or identity when confronted by the police. Yet it had been raining earlier that morning and the area between the parked vehicles and the fence was somewhat muddy.[68] Surely they could not have as easily obliterated all evidence of their presence. It is in the examination of this evidence that we discover that the Commission's defenders were not entirely accurate when they stated that the searchers "found nothing" on the knoll.[69] Holland testified that he had seen a station wagon "backed up toward the fence" with "mud up on the bumper" as if a person had "stood up on the bumper to see over the fence."[70] On CBS-TV, Holland noted that the footprints "were fresh. It had been raining that morning."[71] He added that "if you could have counted the footsteps there'd have been 200 or more on the muddy spots . . . and they was only two sets of footprints that I could find that left this station wagon and they went behind a white Chevrolet car."[72] Moreover, Holland told me in a filmed and tape-recorded interview, "That's about the spot where I saw the [puff of] smoke and heard the shot."[73]

Holland was not the only witness who offered such evidence.[74] James L. Simmons, another railroad employee, who had been standing with Holland on the overpass during the assassination, ran behind the wooden fence after the shots were fired and saw "footprints in the mud around the fence, and there was footprints on the wooden two-by-four railing on the fence."[75] Richard C. Dodd, a third railroad employee, saw "tracks and cigarette butts" in the same place.[76]

Professor John Kaplan of Stanford University contended that "there is no physical trace of any other would-be assassin."[77] This, too, is not accurate, even if one were to discount testimony regarding the footprints.[78] A bullet, or a bullet fragment, which apparently struck the curbing on Main Street during the assassination, made a mark on the stone which was examined by the FBI laboratory.[79] In a letter to the Warren Commission, Director J. Edgar Hoover stated that "metal smears" on the curb "were spectographically determined to be essentially lead with a trace of antimony. No copper was found."[80] The Commission concluded that the bullets allegedly fired by Oswald were copper-jacketed missiles.[81] It seems likely that the traces of lead on the curbing originated from a bullet that was not copper-jacketed.[82] To an impartial and objective investigator, the mark on the curb might certainly be considered to constitute a "physical trace of . . . [another] assassin."[83]

Kaplan also wrote that "attempting to assassinate from the knoll would be so dangerous that it is hard to believe that any assassin with even minimum rationality would have chosen such a spot."[84] An assessment of the physical environs ordinarily should follow, not precede, an examination of the area. Those, apparently unlike Kaplan, who have seen the spot have reached an entirely different conclusion. Former FBI Agent Turner expressed the opinion that the "Dealey Plaza site was ideal" for "a paramilitary operation."[85] There were "tall buildings at one end," Turner wrote, "at the other a grassy knoll projecting to within a stone's throw of the roadway and covered by foliage . . . [and] the slowly-rolling Presidential limousine was trapped in a classic guerrilla ambush—with simultaneous fire converging from the knoll and from a multi-storied building."[86]

In any event, the grassy knoll unquestionably provided a better vantage point for a sniper than did the sixth-floor window of the Texas School Book Depository from which Kaplan believes that Lee Harvey Oswald fired.[87] No foliage and no picket fence screened a man in the window from the view of spectators in the street below.[88] Furthermore, a sniper at that location would be required to descend six stories in order to escape from the building, which is isolated from nearby structures and can be surrounded by alert policemen in a matter of seconds.

35 THE WITNESSES

Arlen Specter has argued that "auditory response on the origin of shots is totally unreliable in so many situations, especially where you have the acoustical situation present at Dealey Plaza in Dallas."[1] For this reason, he explained, the Commission had rejected the consensus of earwitness evidence that shots fired during the assassination had come from the knoll.[2] Specter's conjecture about "the acoustical situation present at Dealey Plaza" is highly speculative, for the Commission declined to test the acoustics of the area.[3]

Similar arguments have frequently been raised by other defenders of the Commission's findings.[4] Joseph Ball, another Commission lawyer, suggested that "earshot testimony is something we could not rely upon and neither can Mr. Lane"; "but," Ball conceded, "it's true there's a good many people thought that the sound of the shot came from the grassy knoll area."[5] In their book Richard Warren Lewis and Lawrence Schiller quote at length from "an internal memorandum" of March 7, 1964, attributed to "Assistant Commission Council [*sic*] Melvin Eisenberg," which concludes that "very little weight can be assigned" to "the aural observation of bystanders."[6] In this cavalier fashion the conclusions of almost two-thirds of the witnesses were dismissed.[7]

In *Rush to Judgment* I stated that out of ninety witnesses present at the scene of the assassination who were asked about the source of the shots and could offer an opinion, "58 said that shots came from the direction of the grassy knoll."[8] Charles Roberts called this "an interesting statistic" and said it "deserves close scrutiny."[9] "For one thing," Roberts added, "many witnesses were ambivalent or self-contradictory on the point of origin of the shots."[10] In support of this contention, Roberts mentioned only one witness, S. M. Holland,[11] and reproduced the following exchange from the record of his testimony:

> Q. You had no idea, I take it, that the shots were coming from your area?
> A. No.[12]

This colloquy, Roberts implied, constitutes evidence that Holland did not hear any shots come from the grassy knoll: "It is important to observe that this exchange is *not* included in Lane's book, wherein Holland is undoubtedly counted as one of the 58 who 'said that shots came from the direction of the grassy knoll. . . .' "[13] (Emphasis in the original.) This allegation is misleading and inaccurate in a number of respects. Holland is "counted as one of the 58" in my compilation in *Rush to Judgment*.[14] That category—as Roberts could have ascertained by reading with care—comprises those witnesses who "said that shots" came from the direction of the knoll.[15] They need not have said that all of the shots came from there—the phrasing of the language which defined that classification makes it perfectly clear that if a witness believed that one or more shots came from the direction of the knoll that fact would suffice to include him among the fifty-eight.[16] No serious reader of *Rush to Judgment* can leave that volume with the impression that the author believes that all of the shots originated from the knoll.[17] Clearly some shots came from the rear of the limousine—the wounds inflicted upon the President and Governor are irrefutable evidence of that fact.[18] The question that required exploration was whether all the shots came from the general direction of the Depository or whether evidence revealed that the fence on the knoll was the source of one or more shots. Holland was, of course, anything but "ambivalent" when he stated that at least one shot came from there.[19] "There was definitely a shot fired from behind that picket fence," he said.[20] "One of those shots came from behind that picket fence, and there's no doubt in my mind, and never will be, because I was on the spot, I saw the smoke—heard the report and saw the smoke from behind that fence."[21] The fact that he also heard shots come from the general direction of the Book Depository, which

Roberts mentioned,[22] serves to corroborate the not inconsiderable evidence that shots were fired from the rear of the Presidential limousine but in no way disqualifies or discredits Holland's statement that an additional shot was fired from the grassy knoll.[23]

More insight into Roberts' methods is given by scrutinizing the conversation from the Commission hearings which he represented as an indication that Holland did not think shots came from the knoll.[24] When Holland replied in the negative to the question of whether he believed "the shots were coming from your area," he understood his "area" to be the railroad overpass and not the grassy knoll, a distinction which can be readily appreciated when the exchange is not wrenched out of context.[25]

Roberts, evidently having rejected the Specter "vortex" syndrome, claimed that "the Commission found that witnesses who were near the Book Depository thought the shots came from that building."[26] In fact, the Commission found precisely the opposite to be true.[27] The Report stated, "When the shots were fired, many people near the Depository believed that the shots came from the railroad bridge over the Triple Underpass or from the area to the west of the Depository."[28] This statement is not buried in an obscure paragraph of the 888-page Report.[29] It appears in a small section of the third chapter which the Commission devoted to assessing the evidence that shots may have been fired from an area in front of the Presidential limousine.[30] Since Roberts spent an entire chapter of his brief book discussing this matter,[31] his lack of familiarity with even the Commission's abbreviated mention of the subject is noteworthy.[32]

Roberts opened his chapter (entitled "The Grassy Knoll—Gunman or Chimera?") by alleging that "the idea that President Kennedy was shot by an assassin firing from the grassy knoll" is supported by "evidence that is based entirely on the testimony of eyewitnesses."[33] That statement appears to be erroneous. However many bullets may have been fired in Dealey Plaza on November 22, 1963, only one of them—a missile that shattered President Kennedy's head—took a human life.[34] The evidence is compelling that this bullet was fired from the grassy knoll, and the most significant portion of that evidence is not the statement of any eyewitness but the Zapruder film of the assassination.[35] This film shows dramatically that when the bullet struck the President's head it drove him instantly and forcefully to the left and to the rear,[36] indicating that—unless Newton's Law of Motion vacated—it came from the right and the front, the direction of the grassy knoll. Roberts did not devote a word to discussing the question of the "head snap" depicted in the Zapruder film.[37] Rather, he relied upon a general disclaimer which misrepresented the strength of the evidence pinpointing the grassy knoll as a source of shots.[38]

Roberts insisted that the "theory" that shots were fired from the grassy knoll was "hatched" out of "a deposition—and later the testimony—of one man who witnessed the tragedy from the overpass."[39] Roberts identified this "man who unwittingly came to the aid of the theoreticians" as S. M. Holland, who testified he saw a "puff of smoke" on the knoll when the shots were fired.[40] According to Roberts, "Holland's 'puff of smoke' story . . . is at the heart of Lane's grassy knoll theory."[41] These various allegations are all false. I first learned of Holland's testimony on September 25, 1964, when I read the Warren Report for the first time. At no time prior to the publication of the Report did I refer to Holland, either in my public lectures on the case or in my two appearances before the Commission.[42]

I did mention the "grassy knoll" long before September 25, 1964, however.[43] The first time I heard the phrase used, the reader will recall, was when I talked with Jean Hill more than half a year earlier.[44] In fact, on March 4, 1964, in my testimony before the Warren Commission in Washington, I presented Mrs. Hill's belief that the shots "came from the grassy knoll";[45] and between March and September 1964 (when I learned of Holland's "deposition" and "testimony" for the first time) I referred to the grassy knoll on innumerable occasions in lectures in the United States and in Europe. Thus, quite contrary to Roberts' misinformed conjecture, the "idea that President Kennedy was shot . . . from the grassy knoll" was not at all "hatched" by Holland's "deposition—and later . . . testimony."[46] Holland's assessment, made public in September 1964, did, however, offer corroboration for the other known evidence.[47]

Roberts next declared that none of the eyewitnesses mentioned in the first two chapters of *Rush to Judgment*—wherein I analyzed the testimony and evidence indicating that the grassy knoll was the source of some of the shots[48]—"claimed to have seen a gun or gunman there."[49] These witnesses included Julia Ann Mercer, who deposed that she had seen a man walk up the knoll on November 22 prior to the assassination carrying "what appeared to be a gun case";[50] Lee Bowers, who said he saw two men behind the wooden fence at the time of the shooting and observed what was possibly "a flash of light" there when the assassination occurred;[51] and J. C. Price, who stated that immediately after the shots were fired he saw a man run from the grassy knoll carrying something which "could have been a gun."[52] This is some of the evidence which Roberts purported to have summarized fairly when he contended that "none [of the eyewitnesses] claimed to have seen a gun or gunman there."[53]

On page 29 of *The Truth about the Assassination,* Roberts did turn his attention to Miss Mercer.[54] Hopefully, this page and the half-page that follow do not typify Roberts' dependability. For in approximately five hundred words Roberts made thirteen errors.[55] Three were minor, merely an inaccurate citation,[56] a misspelled word[57] and a technically incorrect quotation.[58] Ten were more substantial and ran the scale from misrepresentations to apparently outright falsehoods.[59]

After citing a sentence from *Rush to Judgment* in which I alluded to Miss Mercer's mention of "what appeared to be" a gun case, Roberts charged that "thereafter he [Lane] slyly refers to the object that 'appeared to be a gun case' to Miss Mercer simply as 'the gun case,' without qualification."[60] The charge is just untrue. The unqualified phrase "the gun case" does not appear anywhere in the analysis of Miss Mercer's testimony in *Rush to Judgment.*[61] I guardedly referred to the object in question as "the so-called gun case" or placed the phrase in quotation marks.[62]

Secondly, said Roberts, "He [Lane] also neglects to mention a couple of other things in her affidavit: First, Miss Mercer originally described the objects in the rear of the truck as 'what appeared to be tool boxes.' "[63] That allegation is also false. On page 29 of *Rush to Judgment* the following statement appeared: "Along the back of the truck were 'what appeared to be tool boxes.' "[64]

Roberts said that "in her deposition Miss Mercer told the Sheriff's Office" that the incident she observed occurred "on the morning of the assassination."[65] There is no basis for that allegation, for there is no mention of the time of day anywhere in the "deposition."[66] He also alleged that I failed to place the Mercer affidavit, which he dismissed as "insignificant," in its proper context.[67] "The truth," Roberts declared, "is that Miss Mercer's affidavit was one of some 60-odd similar statements volunteered to the Sheriff's Office after the assassination, each putting a different gunman or 'suspicious' person at a different location somewhere near the scene of the murder."[68] The series of affidavits to which Roberts made reference, identified by the Warren Commission as Decker Exhibit No. 5323,[69] contains exactly thirty—not "60-odd"—"similar statements."[70] Of these, only a small fraction—not "each"—allude to "a different gunman or 'suspicious' person."[71] Moreover, Miss Mercer's evidence placed the individual in question at the scene of the murder and not "somewhere near" it.[72]

Roberts alleged that "Miss Mercer's statement . . . follows a statement by another Dallas citizen" who said he saw a man "carrying a rifle near Elm Street just minutes before the assassination."[73] This contention is inadequate in several respects. The deponent of the affidavit preceding Miss Mercer's was not "another Dallas citizen."[74] The affidavit from which Roberts quoted reveals that he lived in Richardson, Texas.[75] In addition, he stated flatly that, although his "friend" told him a man walking in the street was carrying a rifle, "I did not see the rifle."[76] More important is the fact that Roberts' curious vagueness about the precise location at which the man was seen—"near Elm Street"[77]—becomes understandable when the affidavit of the deponent's friend is scrutinized.[78] This latter document discloses that the man was observed at least half a mile from the scene of the assassination and was walking in a direction away from Dealey Plaza at the time.[79] Yet to Roberts the Mercer affidavit, which placed a man with "what appeared to be a gun case" on the grassy knoll[80]—the vantage point from which fifty-eight witnesses thought shots were fired during the assassination[81]—"was no more startling" than the affidavit mentioned just above.[82] Some reporters evidently are not easily startled.

Not content with this one imperfect analogy, Roberts offered still another.[83] This "similar" statement revealed that the deponent saw a man with a rifle at a location far removed from the assassination site at a time which Roberts described as "shortly after the shooting."[84] In this instance, Roberts' "shortly after" is in fact more than four hours.[85] Concluding his breath-taking examination of Miss Mercer's evidence, Roberts contended that the man she described "is no more suspect than dozens of others" because "Dallas was a city crawling with rifleman [*sic*]."[86]

Next, Roberts dealt with the testimony of Lee Bowers regarding the two men whom he saw standing behind the wooden fence when the shots were fired.[87] According to Roberts, "Lane says on his own that in appearance they were 'not unlike' the two men Miss Mercer saw with the Ford pickup truck."[88] My statement in *Rush to Judgment* was not exactly Roberts' version of it: "His [Bowers'] description of the two men behind the fence was not unlike Miss Mercer's description of the two men she observed."[89] I based this statement exclusively upon the evidence of the two witnesses involved.[90] One of the men observed by Bowers was described by him as "middle-aged" and "fairly heavy-set";[91] Miss Mercer said one of the two men she saw was in "his 40's" and "heavy-set."[92] The other individual whom Bowers noted was said by him to be "about midtwenties, in either a plaid shirt or plaid coat or jacket";[93] Miss Mercer testified that the second man she saw was in his "late

20's or early 30's" and wearing a "plaid shirt."[94] Roberts apparently felt that to characterize these descriptions as being "not unlike" one another is to summarize unfairly the evidence of Bowers and Miss Mercer.[95]

Roberts took exception to my mention of another portion of Bowers' testimony: "He [Lane] notes that to Bowers they [the two men behind the wooden fence] were 'the only two strangers in the area.' "[96] According to Roberts, "What is really remarkable, rather than portentous, about the scene Lane depicts is that with the President of the United States about to pass by, and hundreds of people milling into the area, there were only two men in the parking lot Bowers did not recognize."[97] Contrary to the impression Roberts sought to create, there were not "hundreds of people milling into the area" behind the wooden fence—the "area" to which Bowers referred.[98] In a filmed and tape-recorded interview in 1966, Bowers told me that "other than these two [men behind the fence] and the people who were over on the top of the underpass who, for the most part, were railroad employees or were employees of a Fort Worth welding firm who were working on the railroad, there were no strangers out on this area."[99]

Bowers' statement was corroborated by Patrolman J. W. Foster,[100] one of the two officers stationed on the railroad overpass at the time of the assassination.[101] Foster was asked by Commission counsel, "Had you seen anybody over at the railroad yard north and west of the bookstore [Book Depository Building] before you heard the shots fired?"[102] He replied, "No; other than people that had come up there and I sent them back down the roadway."[103]*

Professor Alexander M. Bickel of Yale University has also written that "people were milling about this area [behind the fence], and looking down on it from the railroad bridge over the underpass, and no one saw an armed man."[104] The record of testimony before the Commission, some of which has been cited above, makes it quite plain that no one was "milling about this area."[105] It is worth noting that neither Roberts nor Bickel mentioned any testimony or evidence in support of their contention.[106]

Furthermore, it seems clear that Bickel's belief that a person standing on the overpass can look "down" on the area behind the fence flowed solely from his abysmal ignorance of the topography of Dealey Plaza. The railroad bridge is not above the base of the

* Foster could not see the area immediately behind the wooden fence from his post on the overpass. Thus the two unidentified men described by Bowers would not have been visible to him.

wooden fence on the knoll but quite level with it. In addition, there are a number of trees and bushes in the immediate vicinity of the fence, and even in winter, when the foliage is not at its densest, it is impossible to see anyone behind the fence from the overpass, a fact which I have personally verified numerous times by on-the-spot observations.

In my examination of Lee Bowers' testimony in *Rush to Judgment,* I noted that at a key point in his interrogation by Commission counsel, when the witness appeared to be on the verge of disclosing some vital information related to his observations of November 22, he was abruptly interrupted by the attorney and moments later the hearing was concluded.[107] When I talked with Bowers in Arlington, Texas, in 1966, he told me that he had construed this interruption by counsel to be a suggestion that no further information from him on that particular point was desired:

> Well, I was there only to tell them what they asked and—so that when they seemed to want to cut off the conversation, I felt like that was the—as far as I was concerned, that was the end of it. After all, I'd been invited either to testify there or, if I refused, which was within my rights, to be flown to Washington. And since I didn't have time for a vacation at that time, I just answered their questions. . . . I mean I was simply trying to answer his questions, and he seemed to be satisfied with the answer to that one and did not care for me to elaborate. . . . I was cooperating by telling them what I knew and not attempting to be difficult in any manner, but simply to go along with the questions that they were asking. When he changed the subject, well, I had no choice but to answer his questions.[108]

Bowers' evident reluctance to "be difficult in any manner"—which apparently included volunteering previously undisclosed information when the interrogator tacitly hinted that he "seemed to be satisfied with the answer" and "did not care for me to elaborate"—is understandable in view of his previous experiences with investigators of the assassination.[109] On the afternoon of November 22, Bowers was "taken in a squad car to police headquarters," where he was placed alone in a small interrogation room.[110] "Someone must have gotten slightly excited over it [his account]," Bowers told me in a filmed and tape-recorded interview in 1966, "at least for a moment, because, after talking to others, I find that I was the only one accorded this treatment. Why at that time they thought it was important and decided later it wasn't . . . [or] decided it was better not to talk about it, I just really wouldn't know."[111] Bowers told his questioners that the second and third shots he had heard when the assassination occurred were "almost on top of each other."[112] "And," said Bowers, "they made no comment other than the fact that when I stated that I thought the second and the third shots could not have been fired from the same rifle, they reminded me that I wasn't an expert, and I had to agree."[113]

A number of the Commission's defenders have accused me of misrepresenting the evidence bearing upon Bowers' interruption by Commission counsel at his hearing in Dallas.[114] For example, Roberts charged that the Commission lawyer "had asked Bowers twice before to describe the 'commotion' [that he said he saw on the knoll when the shots were fired] and twice at the end of his testimony asked him if he recalled anything further. Bowers replied he could remember 'nothing else.' "[115] Kaplan made the same point, accusing me of "rank distortion."[116]

But, of course, all these criticisms circumvent the real issue involved here. Bowers explicitly stated to me in our filmed and tape-recorded interview* that he understood the interruption to constitute a sign that the subject was to be dropped.[119] I merely reported Bowers' own opinion in *Rush to Judgment*.[120] The opinion of the witness himself is certainly more relevant than the speculations of Roberts, Kaplan and others as to whether or not the witness had ample opportunity to disclose all of his evidence.[121] He expressly stated that he withheld knowledge he possessed after counsel interrupted him and changed the topic.[122] That, in my mind, is the only pertinent consideration.

Roberts formulated an imaginative hypothesis to account for the fact that so many eyewitnesses believed that "something had occurred" on the grassy knoll at the time of the assassination.[123] He theorized that "they formed their opinion or *assumed* that the shots came from the knoll because they saw policemen, including the motorcycle cop who rode up the bank with drawn pistol, converging on the knoll."[124] (Emphasis in the original.) This conjecture has several significant defects. In the first place, it does not explain why the police officers themselves "converg[ed] on the knoll" imme-

* Roberts also disparaged the authenticity of the remarks made to me by Bowers in our interview.[117] He stated, "Lane produces [in *Rush to Judgment*] a bit of what he says is a later filmed interview with Bowers" in which Bowers said he saw what might have been "a flash of light" behind the picket fence when the shots were fired.[118] This assertion by Bowers was originally mentioned in my book and was subsequently incorporated into a film which was seen by millions of British viewers on BBC television on January 29, 1967, and later in cinemas in several major American cities. Unfortunately it is no longer possible to elicit further information or clarification from Bowers—on August 9, 1966, he was killed in an automobile crash near Midlothian, Texas.

diately after the shooting.[125] Secondly—and perhaps more important—the figure of fifty-eight witnesses cited in *Rush to Judgment* included only those who stated explicitly that they heard shots coming from the direction of the grassy knoll.[126] I also established another category: "34 others are known to have run toward the knoll or directed their attention there at the moment the shots rang out."[127] While it is possible, it can hardly be stated as an irrefutable fact that these thirty-four witnesses reacted in that manner because they saw the police officers converging on the knoll. It is clear that the evidence of the other fifty-eight persons is not related to that factor.

Roberts also said that Bowers (who testified before Commission counsel that "something occurred in this particular spot [behind the wooden fence] . . . which I could not identify" and which he later told me may have been ("a flash of light") "probably" saw nothing more than the "out-of-the-ordinary sight of a motorcycle policeman, pistol in hand, pursuing a gunman who, if real, had just committed the crime of the century."[128] When read in context, however, Bowers' testimony establishes a clear distinction between the moment when "something occurred in this particular spot" and when, in the witness' own words, "immediately following [this] there was a motorcycle policeman" who came up the knoll.[129] In my filmed and tape-recorded interview of Bowers, the distinction between his observation of these two occurrences is equally obvious.[130]

Richard Warren Lewis and Lawrence Schiller, in their book *The Scavengers and Critics of the Warren Report*, made an unworthy effort to belittle the evidence of S. M. Holland.[131] "Lane places great faith," they contended, "in the recollections of S. M. Holland, a man in his early sixties who wears corrective eyeglasses."[132] Holland was fifty-seven years old on November 22, 1963.[133] The pejorative implication regarding Holland's eyeglasses is meaningless, since persons who wear glasses often can see better with them on than those who do not wear glasses at all. Holland wore his on November 22. In any event, nothing that Holland observed on November 22 has not been corroborated by independent eyewitness accounts.[134] This is not the case, however, with Howard L. Brennan, the man who alleged he saw Lee Harvey Oswald firing a rifle from the Book Depository window 107 feet away from Brennan's position and six stories up.[135] Brennan also "wears corrective eyeglasses," and his so-called identification of Oswald received no independent eyewitness corroboration whatsoever, but Lewis and Schiller preferred not to mention that fact.[136]

Nor did they reveal that Brennan admitted when he testified before the Commission that he was not wearing glasses when he made his crucial observation.[137]

The two authors also found fault with Holland's general credibility as an observer, citing the fact that he purportedly saw "curious phenomena in the motorcade."[138] For example, they noted, he said that when the shots were fired a Secret Service agent "in the President's car" stood up with a machine gun in his hands and pointed it "right towards that grassy knoll behind that picket fence."[139] "Actually," said Schiller and Lewis, "a Secret Service agent did draw an automatic rifle in the car more than thirty feet behind the Kennedy limousine. Holland's inability to pinpoint exactly where the event took place therefore casts considerable doubt on his capacity to observe where and when the puff of smoke [which he testified he saw on the knoll] originated."[140] It is true that the automatic rifle was drawn by an agent in the car behind the Presidential vehicle, but that car was only five—not "more than thirty"—feet behind the Kennedy limousine.[141] Holland was five feet off in his observation as the events occurred.[142] With the leisure afforded by more than three years to examine the record, Lewis and Schiller were more than twenty-five feet off in theirs.[143]

36 A PUFF OF SMOKE

Evidently uncertain whether or not they had succeeded in discrediting S. M. Holland's testimony, the authors of *The Scavengers* fell back upon their second line of defense.[1] They published a photograph taken from the railroad overpass looking toward the grassy knoll and the Book Depository Building beyond.[2] Suggesting that the puff of smoke Holland said he saw at the wooden fence was in fact emitted by a rifle being fired from the sixth-floor window of the Depository—since the two points, according to Lewis and Schiller, are nearly, although not precisely, in a straight line—they wrote: "From his [Holland's] vantage point on the railroad bridge spanning the Triple Underpass, the sixth-floor window of the Texas School Book Depository lies behind the arcade, the grassy knoll and distinctly above a clump of trees."[3] There are a number of obvious flaws in this line of reasoning. First, the photograph in question does not depict correctly the spot at which Holland said he saw the puff of smoke.[4] It is significant to note that Schiller and Lewis—rather than Holland himself—incorrectly marked the photograph published in *The Scavengers*.[5] I am in a position to speak with some authority on this matter because Holland personally conducted me on a walk from the overpass to the spot at the picket fence where he saw the puff of smoke.[6] This walk was filmed on location and was subsequently seen by British television viewers as well as moviegoers in major cities in the United States.[7]

Secondly, at least six other persons standing on the overpass also stated that they saw smoke on the knoll when the shots were fired,[8] so a photograph taken from Holland's position at the overpass railing could not begin to dispose of this question.[9] Finally, a number of persons (of whom Holland was not one) not located near the triple underpass told the Commission that they saw a rifle being fired from the sixth-floor window,[10] but none of them said he saw smoke emitted when the weapon was discharged.[11]

The evidence relating to the puff of smoke has come under close and critical examination by the Commission's defenders, who have offered ill-informed and often bizarre hypotheses which purport to explain it away. Lewis and Schiller, as we have seen, sought to elevate it six stories and move it approximately three hundred feet laterally.[12] Others who have sought to dissipate the smoke are Joseph Ball, a Warren Commission lawyer;[13] Professor Kaplan of Stanford;[14] and the Associated Press.[15] Ball's explanation, which seems to be the one favored by his former colleagues on the Commission's legal staff, was given at the Associated Press Managing Editors convention in San Diego on November 17, 1966:

> And, again, he [Lane] says, "Well, there are some witnesses that saw a puff of smoke." What does a puff of smoke mean? Does it mean that there's a rifle? Of course not. Since when did rifles give off a puff of smoke? They don't do it. In addition to that, Mr. Lane doesn't tell you there's a steam line over there and . . . the railroad uses steam between its cars and you can see steam coming up there at any time of the day.[16]

Ball made two points in that excerpt from his speech—and both are contradicted by the facts. The first argument he used was that "rifles [don't] give off a puff of smoke."[17] It should be noted here that Ball was the senior lawyer who handled the evidence relating to the identification of President Kennedy's assassin and who, in that capacity, wrote the first draft of Chapter IV of the Warren Report,[18] a vital portion of which deals with the Mannlicher-Carcano rifle allegedly used by Oswald.[19] In these circumstances, it is not unreasonable to expect that Ball should possess more than average familiarity with the evidence relating to that weapon. Therefore it seems rather surprising that he is apparently unaware of Commission Exhibit 3133, a letter from J. Edgar Hoover to the Warren Commission, which stated that when the Mannlicher-Carcano rifle was fired in daylight, "a small amount of white smoke was visible."[20] Thus, contrary to Ball's uninformed and generalized speculation, a rifle can indeed emit smoke.[21] If the Commission could accept the fact that a rifle which gives off smoke could be the assassination weapon,[22] how could it dismiss summarily the evidence of the puff seen on the knoll on the ground that it could not have originated from a rifle?

The second argument upon which Ball relied was that there was a railroad "steam line" located "over there" and that "you can see steam coming up there at any time of the day."[23] The Associated Press has also charged that I ignored in *Rush to Judgment* the fact that "there was a steam pipe in the area."[24] I have spent many hours in the railroad yards behind the wooden fence and have never seen smoke, steam or vapor of any kind "coming up" from the "steam line over there." In any event, that is less important than the fact that the "steam line" mentioned by Ball is so far removed from the spot at which the smoke described by the railroad employees was seen that it is inconceivable that the puff of smoke seen near the corner of the picket fence could have come from that pipe.*

Kaplan's allegation was quite similar to Ball's.[25] "Actually, it was not disputed that there was a puff above the knoll," Kaplan conceded,[26] completely ignoring the allegations of his colleagues, Lewis and Schiller.[27] But he claimed that my "sleight of hand is going from the smoke to the assumption that the puff came from a gun fired at the President."[28] I do believe that when at least seven witnesses stated that they saw a puff of smoke on the knoll at the instant

* I first learned of the steam pipe alternative when I appeared for a televised panel discussion with Wesley Liebeler and others during 1966. Before the program began, Liebeler said that he then had the answer to the evidence of smoke on the knoll. Since the Report had long since been written, I observed that the explanation was a trifle tardy but that I was very interested in hearing it anyway. "It wasn't smoke," he said. "It was steam from the steam pipe back there." I had brought with me a large aerial photograph of the area and asked Liebeler to point out the steam pipe on the photograph. He said, "Well, I don't know exactly where it is." I asked him to approximate its location and he replied that he could not. When he asked me if I would point it out for him, I did so. He learned, evidently for the first time, that the pipe runs directly from the overpass and is not within one hundred feet of the area at which the smoke was seen. I presumed, since he quickly abandoned his argument that the smoke was caused by a steam pipe, that the matter was closed. But, as we have seen, it recurs on occasion.

the shots were fired and fifty-eight persons state they heard shots coming from that direction[29] it is reasonable to infer that the puff may have come "from a gun fired at the President."[30] Kaplan, however, considered this all but impossible—"unless the assassin fired a fifteenth-century harquebus* it is hard to see how a shot fired at the President could have made as much smoke as Lane implies was visible."[33]

(As initially published, this last phrase read, ". . . as much smoke as Lane convinces us was visible."[34] At a public meeting shortly thereafter, I challenged Kaplan to support his statement by indicating any portion of *Rush to Judgment*, or the statement of any witness cited therein, which alluded to a quantity of smoke other than a single "puff."[35] Kaplan was, of course, unable to produce any corroboration for his allegation; and his ultimate response evidently was to soften somewhat, but not correct, the wording of the charge in the redrafted version of the article.[36])

The characteristics of the harquebus and the year of its manufacture are of academic interest, but of greater relevance is the fact that the Mannlicher-Carcano, which was manufactured in the twentieth century, when fired emits "a small amount of white smoke" visible even in daylight.[37]

The Associated Press also obfuscated the issue regarding the quantity of smoke seen on the grassy knoll at the time of the shooting.[38] The AP implied that the smoke did not come from a rifle because "FBI tests showed the alleged assassination rifle produced only a 'small amount' of smoke when fired."[39] Yet no witness referred to any quantity of smoke other than a single "puff,"[40] which would appear to qualify as a "small amount."[41] Is it possible that both Kaplan and the Associated Press believed that if each of seven witnesses stated that he saw a puff of smoke on the knoll there must have been seven puffs there?

While the presence of one puff of smoke constituted a mystery of sufficient magnitude for most, for the two AP reporters the absence of three other puffs was even more intriguing.[42] In a dazzling display of logic, they reasoned that three missing puffs

* In the original version of his article, published in *The American Scholar*, Kaplan referred in this context to a "sixteenth-century arquebus [*sic*]."[31] The change was incorporated into his rewritten version of the article, which appeared in the *Stanford Law Review*, after I pointed out at a public meeting at Stanford University that the preferred spelling of the word is "harquebus."[32] I made no comment about the century, however. Perhaps Kaplan's original—and evidently mistaken—identification of the weapon was due to the fact that he had taken only a glimpse or a glance at first.

were proof that one puff that was observed was thereby dispelled.[43] The two reporters alleged that the Commission's critics "have not . . . stressed everything that people . . . did not hear or see" on the knoll.[44] They then cite a statement made by S. M. Holland on November 22:

> "I looked toward the arcade and trees and saw a puff of smoke come from the trees." That is what Holland told sheriff's deputies right after the assassination, and that is how Mark Lane quotes him in "Rush to Judgment." But there is more to the sentence, although Lane does not include it. It reads: ". . . And I heard three more shots after the first shot, but that was the only puff of smoke I saw." If one puff of smoke suggests someone shot a gun from the knoll, what does the absence of three subsequent puffs suggest? The jury, the reading public, was not asked to decide. Mark Lane did it for them. He decided not to raise the question.[45]

Had the AP reporters taken the trouble to interview Holland and put the question to him, they would have learned—as I did in my two interviews with the witness in 1966—that there is no conflict in Holland's statement on this matter, and, despite the implication of the AP story, three puffs of smoke are not missing.[46] Holland believes that, as I noted earlier, only one of the four shots he heard on November 22 was fired from the grassy knoll,[47] and it was at the time of that shot that he saw the single puff of smoke he observed.[48]

The AP reporters also criticized my comment in *Rush to Judgment* regarding Austin Miller,[49] a railroad employee who had stated in an affidavit on November 22, "I saw something which I thought was smoke or steam coming from a group of trees north of Elm."[50] They stated:

> When Miller was later questioned by commission counsel, Lane writes, Miller was "dismissed before he could mention the crucial observation contained in his affidavit." Actually, at the end of his interrogation, during which he indeed did not mention any smoke, Miller was asked if he could add anything "that might be of any help to the commission or to the investigation of the assassination." *Miller:* "Offhand, no sir, I don't recall anything else." Maybe he forgot the smoke, maybe not. But it is hardly accurate to convey the impression that the commission had turned Miller off before he could give testimony against the depository theory by "dismissing" him.[51]

If one were searching for the most glaring example of distortion via omission in the lengthy AP story, it would be very hard to find a better example than the excerpt I have just quoted.[52] The wire service reporters disingenuously omitted the most relevant portions of the statements made by both Miller and myself.[53] The unedited sentence from *Rush to Judgment* reads, "Counsel did not ask about the smoke, and Miller was dismissed before he could mention the crucial observation contained in his affidavit."[54] The fact that the witness was asked toward the end of the hearing whether he could recall anything else of relevance does not absolve David Belin, the Commission lawyer, from blame for his delinquency in not having elicited from Miller all the evidence he could have offered.[55] It was the responsibility of Belin to prepare for the interrogation session by reading any statements the witness had previously made to the Federal or local police and then to question the witness in detail about any point which was not entirely clear or fully explained in those earlier statements. We have just seen how Bowers, after an unpleasant experience with police interrogators immediately after the assassination, subsequently was reluctant to volunteer any information at his hearing before Commission counsel, preferring merely to respond to the questions put to him by the attorney.[56]

It is not unlikely that the same considerations obtained in Miller's case, since his evidence—like Bowers'—was damaging to the police case against Lee Harvey Oswald.[57] Consequently, Belin should have questioned Miller closely about the statement in his affidavit that he had seen "smoke or steam" on the knoll when the shots were fired.[58] Unfortunately no such questions were asked of the witness, and the haste with which the hearing was concluded was rather extraordinary.[59] Considering the importance of the evidence Miller could have offered[60] and the disproportionate amount of time spent by counsel taking the testimony of persons who could in no way assist the Warren Commission to fulfill its mandate to ascertain the full story of President Kennedy's assassination,[61] Miller's hearing was inordinately brief.[62]

Perhaps Belin's most brilliant omission (and the AP's) in regard to Miller's testimony is that immediately after he uttered the words quoted in the Associated Press story, that he couldn't "recall anything else," he quickly added, "My statement at the time may have some more."[63] Even after Miller's suggestion that his memory could be refreshed by referring to his "statement at the time"—the affidavit of November 22 in which he had mentioned having seen "smoke or steam" on the knoll[64]—Belin made no effort to secure that statement and read it to Miller.[65] Instead, he brought the hearing to a close.[66] While Miller did not have a subsequent opportunity to amplify his comments of November 22,[67] the AP reporters had the opportunity to place the entire matter in context. This they did not do.[68]

Kaplan charged that *Rush to Judgment* accepts the "statement" of railroad employee Clemon E. Johnson "that he saw white smoke" but does not accept "Johnson's statement that he 'felt that this smoke came from a motorcycle abandoned near the spot by a Dallas policeman.'"[69] The Associated Press made the identical charge, albeit somewhat more cautiously, referring to "Johnson's full statement as paraphrased by the FBI."[70] This crucial distinction is the key to the issue involved here. Although Kaplan's readers would not suspect it, Johnson's "statement" was a hearsay report drawn up by FBI Agents Thomas T. Trettis and E. J. Robertson, who interviewed Johnson in Dallas on March 17, 1964.[71] The report was subsequently submitted to and published by the Warren Commission.[72] There is no other statement or affidavit from Johnson in the twenty-six volumes, and his testimony was not taken by the Commission or by Commission counsel.[73] It is therefore important to consider the single document—the report of Agents Trettis and Robertson—which purportedly records Johnson's account of the events in Dealey Plaza.[74] Johnson was not under oath when interviewed by the agents, did not affix his signature to the FBI report and almost certainly was not asked to check the accuracy of the statement before it was submitted by the agents to their superiors.[75] Thus the report of Trettis and Robertson is nothing more than a hearsay account of the interview in the language of the two agents.[76]

In the circumstances, I accepted Johnson's reported statement regarding the smoke, which was corroborated by other similar statements, but rejected the solitary explanation that the agents said the witness offered[77] because of a recognized juridical principle known as "admission against interest." It should be remembered that on December 8, 1963, FBI Director J. Edgar Hoover dispatched to the Commission a report summarizing the Bureau's two-week investigation of the assassination.[78] In that summary report the Director concluded that Lee Harvey Oswald, the lone assassin, had fired all the shots from the sixth-floor window of the Book Depository Building.[79] As William Turner, the former FBI agent mentioned earlier in this chapter, has noted, after the Bureau—and J. Edgar Hoover—had publicly taken that stance so early in the investigation, no agent was likely to be enthusiastic about uncovering evidence which suggested that the Director was wrong in his hasty and unequivocal assessment of the facts.

In testimony before the Commission or before counsel, many witnesses protested that inaccurate statements had been attributed to them by FBI agents who had interviewed them and later had submitted reports of the interview.[80] Many witnesses said that statements they made to the agents had been omitted entirely from the reports.[81] It is not surprising that in almost every such instance the inaccurate statement supported the Commission's conclusion of Oswald's sole guilt while the actual statement of the witness had contradicted or conflicted with that hypothesis.[82] It was clearly against the interests of the FBI agents to report that a witness had observed smoke on the knoll at the time of the assassination; but in the report of Agents Trettis and Robertson the effect of that statement was counteracted by the qualification that the witness allegedly "felt that this smoke came from a motorcycle abandoned near the spot by a Dallas policeman."[83] The Commission should have called Johnson as a witness and questioned him closely about the smoke he observed when the shots were fired.[84] Unfortunately it did not, and the rhetoric of Kaplan[85] and the Associated Press[86] can neither alter nor conceal that fact.

The AP invested similarly unwarranted faith in the FBI on a related point. "The other four [besides Holland, Miller and Johnson] who Lane says saw smoke," said the wire service, listing Richard C. Dodd, Walter L. Winborn (whose name was misspelled as "Windborn" the only two times it was mentioned), James L. Simmons and Thomas J. Murphy, "were interviewed by him in 1966.* Whatever they told Lane then, only one—Simmons—mentioned smoke to the FBI when questioned during the assassination investigation."[90] How do the two AP reporters know what the four witnesses "mentioned . . . to the FBI when questioned during the assassination investigation"?[91] They have not seen a transcript or stenographic record of any of the interviews. And the derogatory connotation implicit in the wording of their phrase, "Whatever they told Lane then," is entirely undeserved.[92]

Contrary to the innuendo of the AP reporters, there is no necessity whatsoever to rely upon my own word in this matter. On the evening of January 29, 1967, millions of television viewers in Great Britain, and subsequently theatergoers and television viewers in many other countries, have seen Simmons and Dodd tell, in their own words, about the puff of smoke they saw on the grassy knoll on November 22. A copy of those interviews has been offered to the National Archives. In addition, the tape-recorded statements of Winborn and Murphy are available and can be examined upon

* That statement is untrue. While I did meet with Dodd and Simmons (and have recorded their impressions on film and tape),[87] I have never interviewed —or claimed to have interviewed—either Winborn or Murphy.[88] References given in *Rush to Judgment* clearly indicate that Stewart Galanor, an independent investigator, secured tape-recorded statements from Winborn and Murphy on May 5 and May 6, 1966, respectively.[89]

request. In any event, had the two wire service newsmen exercised even a little initiative and questioned any or all of the four railroad employees, the need to speculate on the authenticity of the films or tapes would have been obviated. But instead they preferred to rely upon the most unreliable evidence available and that which was farthest removed from the original source of the intelligence—the FBI agents' hearsay reports published by the Commission.[93]

Continuing to misrepresent the information offered by Simmons—whom they evidently never bothered to interview—the Associated Press writers stated:

> Simmons said he thought he saw "exhaust fumes" of smoke near the embankment in front of the Texas School Book Depository. He ran toward that building with a policeman, first looking over the knoll fence. Two years later [i.e., as quoted in *Rush to Judgment*] the "exhaust fumes" by the depository have become "a puff of smoke" near the fence.[94]

Each of those assertions is untrue. Simmons said he saw a puff of smoke on the grassy knoll when the shots were fired, thought the shots came from behind the fence on the knoll and ran to that area—not to the Book Depository Building—and searched there immediately after the assassination.[95]

Kaplan also had something to say about Simmons.[96] In his original article in *The American Scholar*, Kaplan wrote:

> . . . although there were certainly many witnesses who thought that the shots came from the grassy knoll area, Lane is not content merely with them. He quotes his own interview with witness James L. Simmons in which Simmons says that the sound of shots came from "the left and in front of us toward the wooden fence," without mentioning the fact that some eighteen months earlier Simmons had testified before the Warren Commission that he had the impression the shots came from the Book Depository.[97]

At a public meeting after the publication of that article, I pointed out that Simmons had not testified before the Commission or before counsel and that there was no sworn statement—and therefore no testimony—of any kind from him in the Commission's published evidence.[98] The statement regarding the Book Depository Building was nothing more than an unverified and uncorroborated hearsay remark by two FBI agents.[99] Kaplan acknowledged his error and then rewrote that portion of the article, among others, and when it was published in the admittedly "corrected" form in the *Stanford Law Review*[100] it read as follows:

> . . . although there were certainly many witnesses before the Commission who thought that the shots came from the grassy knoll area, Lane is not content merely with their recorded testimony. He quotes his own interview with witness James L. Simmons in which Simmons said that the sound of shots "came from the left and in front of us, toward the wooden fence." But Lane does not mention that some two years earlier Simmons had stated to the FBI that he had the impression the shots came from the book depository.[101]

Thus, although modifications were made, Kaplan persisted in equating the hearsay remark of a pair of Federal police agents[102] with the filmed and tape-recorded statement of the witness himself.[103]

I should be reluctant to leave the impression that the Commission's champions misused the statements of only the railroad employees among the many knoll witnesses. The defenders of the Warren Report displayed no such selectivity. For example, Charles Roberts wrote:

> . . . [In Chapter 2 of *Rush to Judgment*] Lane moves on to another point, namely that Dallas Police Chief Jesse E. Curry "just after the shots were fired . . . said into the microphone of his radio transmitter, 'Get a man on top of that triple underpass and see what happened up there.' ". This is not surprising since Curry, leading the President's car to Parkland Hospital, was at that moment heading through the underpass. As he did, he saw the railroad men overhead scrambling for cover. . . . Actually, as Curry sped away from the scene, radio reports from other officers in Dealey Plaza focused immediate attention on the Book Depository.[104]

Since that version of Curry's observations is not documented by Roberts, it is difficult to ascertain the basis for his misinformation.[105] Certainly there is no mention in the police chief's testimony of his having seen "the railroad men overhead scrambling for cover,"[106] nor is any corroboration for that notion to be found in the testimony of any of the men on the overpass.[107]

The other point mentioned by Roberts, while it bears a grain of truth, is deceptive. Although the Dallas police radio log does contain reports mentioning the Book Depository as soon as four minutes after the shooting,[108] it is incorrect to imply, as Roberts did—and as the Warren Report did[109]—that the attention of the police centered exclusively upon that building.[110] Captain J. Will Fritz, the police official in charge of the investigation at the scene of the crime,[111] testified before the Commission that "after" he arrived at the Book Depository at 12:58 P.M.—nearly half an hour after the shooting—"one of the officers asked me if I would like to have the building sealed and I told him I would."[112] In the aftermath of the shooting, scores of policemen converged on the knoll and conducted a prolonged search there.[113] Deputy Sheriff Charles P. Player, who drove his car into the railroad yards on the grassy knoll soon after the assassination, stated in a contemporaneous report to his superior, Sheriff Bill Decker, that he had "acted as a West command post for about 2 hours. No one was permitted to leave any of the parking lots until cleared and then a Dallas Police Officer took their names. Officers were directed to search all of the cars in the area, search the railroad cars and to bring anyone in that knew, saw or heard anything."[114] At the bottom of his report, Deputy Sheriff Player drew a map of the area and located "Command Post 'B' " near the railroad tracks behind the knoll area.[115]

In my filmed and tape-recorded interview with Lee Bowers, a similar story was recounted by the witness:

> During this period there were some trains moving through the railroad yards and these trains had been stopped for some reason or another just a little south of my area [Bowers' signal tower]. Since there was the possibility that someone could . . . have climbed aboard these, this freight train primarily, I pulled the train up immediately opposite the tower after alerting the police that I intended to do so, and I stopped the train and I gave them a chance to examine it and to be sure that there was no one on it.[116*]

Bowers said that the police "requested that I talk to them after three o'clock, which was when my relief came on," but that he "wondered for a while if I was going to get relieved because by this time they had sealed it [the area] off so effectively that the relief couldn't get in" and was delayed in reaching the signal tower.[118]

The Associated Press alleged that the Warren Report fairly presented the statements of witnesses who said the shots came from the knoll as well as those who said they came from the Depository.[119] To support its contention, the wire service cited two persons who were standing in front of the building when the shots were fired[120] —O. V. Campbell[121] and Mrs. Robert Reid.[122] Campbell said he heard shots being fired from the direction of the knoll.[123] He was not called as a witness by the Commission.[124] Mrs. Reid said the shots sounded as if they had come "from our building."[125] She was

* "As a matter of fact," Bowers told me, "there were three people on it [the freight train] who appeared to be winos, and were perhaps the most frightened winos I've ever seen in my life since there were possibly fifty policemen with shotguns and tommy guns and various other weapons shaking them out of these box cars. . . . And this was perhaps their rudest shakedown off of a freight train in their lives. Perhaps their last. It might have cured them."[117]

called by the Commission.[126] The AP reporters wrote: "Two witnesses. Two versions. Both appear in the Warren report."[127] The allegation that "both appear in the Warren report" is untrue.[128] Mrs. Reid's testimony is mentioned on page 154 of the Report,[129] but Campbell's statement is nowhere to be found in the 888-page document.[130]

37 THE PHOTOGRAPHS

A favorite technique of the Commission's defenders for upholding the Report's conclusions has been to select what purportedly represents a major criticism of the Report, demonstrate that the point is in fact invalid and then announce triumphantly that the demonstration proved the correctness of the Commission's findings and discredited the arguments of the critics. The fact that no responsible critic of the Warren Report had raised the point in question is not considered to be relevant, nor is the fact that the demonstration in no way affected the validity of the very substantial questions that had actually been raised by the Commission's critics.

An example of this technique was the announcement made by United Press International in a copyrighted story from Lexington, Massachusetts, on May 18, 1967.[1] The UPI story began:

> An analysis by one of the nation's top photographic laboratories has demolished a widely circulated theory that a second gunman was involved in the assassination of President Kennedy. The Itek Corporation disclosed today that a months-long study of an amateur movie of the shooting had disproved the existence of a rifleman pointing a weapon from the grassy knoll at the Kennedy car in Dallas on Nov. 22, 1963. Itek made the study as a public service.[2]

The film in question was taken in Dealey Plaza on November 22 by Orville Nix.[3] Several frames from the film had been published by the Commission.[4] On November 14, 1966, *Esquire* magazine released a previously unpublished frame of the Nix film.[5] This frame had "interested" an individual described by *Esquire* as "a New York hobbyist" because "it showed an object behind the wall on the grassy knoll."[6] The magazine explained that "it became clear that the object was in fact a vehicle. On the roof of the vehicle, he discerned a man aiming what appeared to be a rifle at the President's car."[7] On November 14 the magazine also disseminated a press release which, according to the *New York Times*, said the picture "appears to confirm the existence of an assassin now at large."[8]

Aside from the so-called "hobbyist,"[9] who should not be confused with any of the responsible critics, and the magazine itself in its press release,[10] no Commission critic, to my knowledge, ever stated that the Nix frame depicted a man with a rifle on the "vehicle." In its fifty-five-page report, the Itek Corporation referred only vaguely to the persons it alleged to be rebutting: "Some of those who have viewed the Nix film have claimed to see a man on an elevated object aiming a rifle. 'The man with the rifle,' however, was found to be nothing more than tree shadows on the wall of Shelter 3 of Pergola 2 on Dealey Plaza."[11] Thus, according to UPI, which had requested the analysis by the Massachusetts corporation as an answer to the irresponsible speculations of unnamed persons "who have viewed the Nix film,"[12] the Itek Corporation's study conclusively "demolished" the "theory that a second gunman was involved in the assassination."[13]

Itek had also stated in its report that "the area known as the 'grassy knoll,' which is bordered by the picket fence, the concrete wall, and Shelter 3, was carefully examined. No person was visible in the Nix film in this area."[14] In view of that assertion and Itek's statement that its study had been conducted "on a public service basis,"[15] it is interesting to note a sequel to the public announcement of Itek's conclusions which strongly suggests that the basic purpose of the entire undertaking by the Government-oriented firm was to erect a straw man, tear it down and then proclaim that the "theory [of] a second gunman" had been thoroughly discredited once and for all by a scientific endeavor.[16]

On May 19, 1967, the day after the announcement had been made, Ray Marcus, a responsible critic of the Commission who had made a detailed study of the numerous still and motion picture photographs taken in Dealey Plaza at the time of the assassination, contacted a representative of the Itek Corporation by telephone.[17] Marcus said he had photographs in his possession, including the Nix frame and a well-known Polaroid snapshot taken by Mary Moorman, an eyewitness to the shooting, which "contained far more credible images than the one [Itek] had so diligently analyzed" and that "at least one of these images was so clear that I felt confident [that] upon examining it he [the Itek representative] would quickly agree" that it was a "human figure."[18] Marcus explained that he was "only thirty minutes away from their offices" and "would be happy to show the pictures to them."[19] The Itek representative "voiced considerable interest" and said he would consult with some associates and "call back shortly."[20] Itek, however, has not accepted Marcus' invitation.[21]

This incident certainly lends credence to the suspicion that the Itek study was less of a "public service" than a major public relations effort made on behalf of those who seek to foreclose public discussion of the subject. If that was in fact the case, the effort was a failure. Despite the attempts of the Commission's committed defenders to end the debate over the grassy knoll, that once-obscure park slope in western downtown Dallas, a most unlikely candidate for the title of "most trampled patch of greenery in America," persists as one of the most enigmatic aspects of the assassination of John Fitzgerald Kennedy.

II · The New Evidence and the Wounds

38 THE UNDISPUTED FACTS

THE AUTHORS of the critical analyses of the Warren Report hoped to focus attention upon the still-unanswered questions which were in some cases caused by the incomplete state of the public record. Following—and very likely as a result of—the publication of *Rush to Judgment* and other books, there were a number of major developments, some designed specifically as a response to the critics. For reasons perhaps best understood, but never satisfactorily explained, by President Johnson, however, the photographs and X-rays of President Kennedy's body taken at the autopsy remained unavailable.[1] The suppression of the best evidence as to the number and nature of the wounds inflicted upon the President continues despite the complaints of the critics and even the pleas of the most important Commission defenders, including the Columbia Broadcasting System[2] and the most vocal, if not articulate, members of the Commission's legal staff.[3] But there were also developments which appeared to be a more positive reaction to the widespread criticism. These included the publication of a hitherto classified FBI report concerning the autopsy;[4] the initial official disclosure of the whereabouts of the autopsy X-rays and photographs;[5] and the first comments on the discrepancies in the medical evidence from the principal figures involved, including the autopsy surgeons themselves.[6]

In order to clarify the important issues involved, it is useful to summarize the essential facts about the wounds suffered by President Kennedy and Governor Connally and to mention the basic criticisms of the Warren Commission's analysis of the medical evidence.[7]

It is generally agreed that President Kennedy was struck by at least two bullets.[8] One of these hit the President's head and caused the fatal injury.[9] The President also had a wound at the Adam's apple and a wound in the back.[10]* According to the published conclusions of the autopsy surgeons, with which the Warren Commission agreed, the first bullet to strike the President "entered at the back of his neck and exited through the lower front portion of his neck, causing a wound which would not necessarily have been lethal. The President was struck a second time by a bullet which entered the right-rear portion of his head, causing a massive and fatal wound."[14]

The Commission's critics have disputed the accuracy of three major points in the Warren Report's summary.† First, they contend that the bullet which entered the President's back may not have passed through his body.[19] Secondly, they believe that the wound in the throat was very likely an entrance wound.[20] Thirdly, they believe that the bullet which caused the fatal head wound came from the right front, rather than the right rear.[21]

There is, of course, no controversy over the location of Governor Connally's wounds. His X-rays, evidently devoid of entanglement with national security and apparently no affront to good taste, have been published by the Commission.[22] He was struck "by a bullet which entered on the right side of his back and traveled downward through the right side of his chest."[23] He also incurred bullet wounds in his right wrist, which was fractured, and in his left thigh.[24] According to the Report, all the Governor's wounds were inflicted by the bullet which struck him in the back: "a single bullet had passed through his chest; tumbled through his wrist with very little exit velocity, leaving small metallic fragments from the rear portion of the bullet; punctured his left thigh after the bullet had lost virtually all of its velocity; and had fallen out of the thigh wound."[25]

* The precise location of the posterior wound has been perhaps the single most disputed aspect of the medical evidence. The critics believed that the most credible evidence revealed the wound to be in the President's back, somewhat below the neck.[11] While the Commission and its defenders contended that the wound was in the base of the back of the neck,[12] the Warren Commission Report was inconsistent in its terminology, referring to the wound both as a wound in the neck and one in the back.[13] To avoid semantic complication, I refer in this text to the posterior wound as a wound in the back.

† These three points represent the consensus of the responsible Commission critics.[15] Several critics vary in their interpretation of the individual points,[16] but the majority accept the three conclusions listed here.[17] I believe that these three conclusions are fully substantiated by the most credible evidence available.[18]

The key question in the controversy over Governor Connally's wounds, however, is whether he was struck in the back by a pristine bullet or by the bullet which the Warren Report alleged had passed through President Kennedy's neck.[26] The thesis that one bullet passed through the President's neck and then caused all of Governor Connally's wounds—the "single-bullet theory"—is indispensable to the Commission's conclusion that Lee Harvey Oswald fired all the bullets in Dealey Plaza on November 22, 1963.[27]* The most significant reason for this is that a motion picture film of the assassination showed that President Kennedy and Governor Connally were wounded within a shorter period of time than the interval in which the rifle allegedly used by Oswald could fire two shots.[35] Therefore, either both men were wounded by the same bullet or Oswald could not have fired both of the shots.[36]

This film of the assassination, which proved to be the most valuable evidence in reconstructing the sequence and timing of the shots,[37] was taken by Abraham Zapruder, a Dallas businessman, who stood on the grassy knoll to the right and front of the position occupied by the Presidential limousine while the shots were being fired.[38] The FBI laboratory[39] and the Bell & Howell Company[40] established in separate tests that the film ran through Zapruder's camera at the speed of approximately 18.3 frames per second.[41] Since the Mannlicher-Carcano rifle required at least 2.3 seconds between shots,[42] a minimum of forty-two frames of Zapruder's film must have separated any two bullets fired during the assassination if Oswald, using the Italian rifle, was the lone assassin.[43]

The frames of the Zapruder film were numbered, as the Report noted, "with the number '1' given to the first frame where the motorcycles leading the motorcade came into view on Houston Street."[44] An analysis of the film established several important facts:

1. President Kennedy was hidden from Zapruder's camera by a traffic sign alongside the Elm Street roadway between about

* A number of the Commission's defenders, perhaps sensing the very inadequate support which the evidence provides for the single-bullet theory, have suggested that this hypothesis is, in fact, not essential in order to sustain the Commission's central finding that Oswald acted alone.[28] The most notable advocate of this position is Arlen Specter,[29] considered to be the author of the single-bullet theory.[30] The explanation which Specter has offered in advancing this view is discussed later in this section.[31] However, it should be noted that almost all of those who have now undertaken the task of upholding the Commission's conclusions, including CBS[32] and the Associated Press,[33] concede that the single-bullet theory is indispensable.[34]

frame 207 and frame 224 inclusive.[45] When the President emerged from behind the sign at frame 225 he was apparently reacting to a bullet wound by moving his hands toward his throat.[46]

2. With the exception of a single frame—186[47]—the President was hidden from the sixth-floor window of the Texas School Book Depository Building, from which Oswald allegedly fired, between frames 166 and 209 inclusive by an oak tree on the north side of Elm Street.[48]
3. Governor Connally turned sharply to his right between frames 235 and 240 so that by the latter frame he was no longer in a position to have been struck by a shot fired from the sixth-floor window.[49] (The Governor has stated that he believes he was hit at frame 234.[50])
4. At frame 313 the bullet which caused the fatal wound struck President Kennedy in the head.[51]

39 THE UNDENIABLE EVIDENCE

The viability of the Commission's proposition that the same bullet which passed through President Kennedy's body wounded Governor Connally is inevitably dependent, of course, upon the validity of the assumption that the bullet which entered the President's back did, in fact, pass through his body and exit at the Adam's apple.[1] One must also make the complementary assumption that the wound in the President's back was higher than the wound at his Adam's apple, since, according to the Commission's findings, the bullet entered at a downward angle of approximately 17° and was not deflected in its passage through his body.[2] That these two assumptions are valid has yet to be demonstrated by the Commission's defenders; certainly the weight of the available evidence tends to preclude the possibility that either of them is correct.[3]

This evidence can be divided into four main subdivisions: (1) the testimony of the autopsy surgeons[4] and the published report of their findings;[5]* (2) the statements of FBI[6] and Secret Service[7] agents present at the autopsy; (3) a diagram illustrating the location of President Kennedy's wounds[8] and marked by one of the autopsy surgeons;[9]† and (4) the shirt[10]‡ and jacket[11] worn by the President

* See Appendix IX.

† This diagram is reproduced as Appendix X.

‡ See Appendix XI.

at the time of the assassination. All but the first of these is sharply at variance with the Commission's conclusions.[12]

After the assassination, President Kennedy was taken to Parkland Memorial Hospital in Dallas, where a team of physicians labored unsuccessfully to save his life.[13] A tracheotomy was performed in order to facilitate the President's respiration.[14] Since the incision for the tracheotomy was made around the wound in President Kennedy's throat,[15] it was possible for the autopsy doctors to state later that no visible trace of that wound remained after the operation at Parkland had been completed.[16]* The Dallas authorities tried to retain custody of the President's body so that they could conduct an autopsy at Parkland Hospital, as required by Texas law.[22] Presidential aides and Secret Service agents, however, disregarded the requests of the local officials and insisted on returning to Washington immediately with the body.[23]

When the Presidential plane reached Washington early in the evening of November 22, the body was taken to the National Naval Medical Center at Bethesda, Maryland, where the autopsy was performed[24] by three military physicians: Commander James J. Humes,

* Leading forensic pathologists have taken exception to this assertion by the autopsy surgeons.[17] Dr. Milton Helpern, the Chief Medical Examiner of New York City, noted in a published interview that the throat wound was not "obliterated by the tracheotomy" as the Warren Report claimed.[18] "No, you see, the staff members who wrote that portion of the report," Dr. Helpern said, "simply did not understand their medical procedures; and they did not know enough to seek medical guidance. Here's what the autopsy protocol says about the throat wound: '. . . it was extended as a tracheotomy incision and thus its character is distorted at the time of autopsy.' The key word here is *extended*. That bullet wound was not 'eliminated' or 'obliterated' at all. What Dr. [Malcolm] Perry [of Parkland Hospital] did was to take his scalpel and cut a clean slit away from the wound. He didn't excise it or cut away any huge amount of tissue, as the report writer would have you believe. . . . Certainly, its character is distorted in the sense that the original wound was *extended* in length by Dr. Perry's scalpel; but this throat wound could still have been evaluated. Its edges should have been carefully put back together and restored to their original relationships as nearly as possible. It should have then been studied and finally photographed."[19] (Emphasis in the original.) Dr. Helpern surmised that the autopsy surgeons had not done this because "their lack of experience deprived them of the knowledge of what should have been done."[20]

Dr. John Nichols, Associate Professor of Pathology at the University of Kansas Medical Center, said that "it is usually quite easy to identify wounds of entry and exit . . . by microscopic observation of the tissue after partial mutilation as was [the case with] the wound in the neck . . . when they [the Parkland doctors] extended it to a tracheotomy."[21]

the chief surgeon;[25] Commander J. Thornton Boswell;[26] and Lieutenant Colonel Pierre A. Finck.[27] Before the pathological examination commenced, a medical technician and a photographer took a series of X-rays and color and black and white photographs of the body.[28] The autopsy then began at approximately 8:00 P.M. and lasted about three hours.[29] In addition to the medical personnel present, the autopsy was attended by two Secret Service agents—Roy Kellerman[30] and William Greer[31]—and two agents of the Federal Bureau of Investigation.[32]*

The latter pair, James W. Sibert and Francis X. O'Neill, Jr., subsequently filed a five-page account of their observations which became a focal point in the controversy over the President's wounds.[35] The Commission did not mention or publish the Sibert-O'Neill report of November 26, 1963.[36] Neither Sibert[37] nor O'Neill[38] was called to testify before the Commission or before counsel for the Commission. Neither was asked to submit an affidavit.[39] And there is no evidence now available to indicate that the seven members of the Commission even considered the grave implications of the FBI agents' report.[40]

"During the latter stages of this autopsy," Sibert and O'Neill wrote in their report,

> Dr. Humes located an opening which appeared to be a bullet hole which was below the shoulders and two inches to the right of the middle line of the spinal column. This opening was probed by Dr. Humes with the finger, at which time it was determined that the trajectory of the missile entering at this point had entered at a downward position of 45 to 60 degrees. Further probing determined that the distance travelled by this missile was a short distance inasmuch as the end of the opening could be felt with the finger. Inasmuch as . . . inspection reveal[ed] there was no point of exit, the individuals performing the autopsy were at a loss to explain why they could find no bullets.[41]

At this point, Agent Sibert called the FBI laboratory in Washington and learned that a bullet had been found on a stretcher in Parkland Hospital.[42] "Immediately following receipt of this information," the FBI report continued, "this was made available to Dr. Humes who advised that in his opinion this accounted for no bullet being located which had entered the back region and that since external cardiac massage had been performed at Parkland Hospital, it was entirely possible that through such movement the bullet had

* At least two other Secret Service agents—William O'Leary[33] and Clint Hill[34]—were in the autopsy room for a brief time.

worked its way back out of the point of entry and had fallen on the stretcher."[43] On the basis of this intelligence, according to Sibert and O'Neill, Dr. Humes "stated that the pattern was clear" that a bullet "had entered the President's back and had worked its way out of the body during external cardiac massage."[44]

Thus the Sibert-O'Neill report provides impressive corroboration for the belief that the bullet which entered President Kennedy's back did not pass through his body and indicates that Dr. Humes himself apparently believed this to have been the case on the night the autopsy was performed.[45] The Warren Commission, however, felt otherwise.[46] Indeed, the Commission even claimed that the surgeons concluded on the evening of November 22 that the bullet had passed through the President's body.[47] Seeking to refute "speculation that the bullet might have penetrated a short distance into the back of the neck and then dropped out onto the stretcher as a result of the external heart massage,"[48] the Report alleged that "further exploration during the autopsy disproved that theory."[49] Then, according to the Commission, when Commander Humes talked by telephone with Dr. Malcolm Perry of Parkland Hospital on the morning of November 23 and learned for the first time of the existence of the throat wound, which had been extended by the tracheotomy in Dallas, his "conclusion that the bullet had exited from the front part of the neck" was thereby "confirmed."[50]

That sequence of events, asserted so unequivocally in the Warren Report in 1964,[51] has now been demonstrated to be inaccurate.[52] The Sibert-O'Neill eyewitness account of the autopsy indicates in unqualified terms that Dr. Humes did not believe on the night of November 22 that the bullet had gone through President Kennedy's body.[53] Some of the Commission's defenders have sought to explain that the Sibert-O'Neill document does not actually reflect the thinking of the physicians as the autopsy progressed.[54] For example, Arlen Specter, the Commission attorney who drafted the chapter of the Warren Report dealing with the medical evidence,[55] reportedly said that when the doctors were unable to find a path through the body, "both FBI agents" left the room to telephone this information to their headquarters.[56] While the agents were out of the room, according to Specter, the doctors were able to trace the bullet's path.[57]

The evidence on these two points is quite clear.[58] Specter was entirely in error in both instances.[59] One of the Secret Service agents present at the autopsy, William Greer, told the Commission that at least one of the FBI agents was present in the autopsy room at all times during the examination: "Those two agents were in during the autopsy; those two agents were in the autopsy room, with Mr. Kellerman and I, all night. Mr. Sibert and O'Neill were both in the autopsy room with us during that time, and the only time that any of us, either Mr. Kellerman or I, we never left the room, one or the other. We went and got some coffee and came right back, something like that, and the FBI did the same thing. One of them left; the other stayed."[60]

Specter should not have been ignorant of the fact that the call was made by Sibert alone,[61] since that is reported in a memorandum which Specter himself wrote after interviewing both Sibert and O'Neill on March 12, 1964.[62] Secondly, Sibert and O'Neill stated in their report that it was not until after the telephone call was completed and the information relayed to Dr. Humes that the physician "stated that the pattern was clear"—the bullet did not pass through the President.[63] One wonders what prompted Specter to make two important—and inaccurate—assertions when apparently there is no evidence whatsoever to support either of them.[64]

Charles Roberts has also attempted to perpetuate the myth that the two FBI agents missed a vital portion of the surgeons' discussion because they were absent from the autopsy room.[65] "They left the room at intervals for coffee, to relieve themselves, and to make phone calls," Roberts alleged without citing a source for his apparently exclusive information and without explaining, or even mentioning, Greer's unequivocal sworn statement that one of the FBI men was always present.[66] "Apparently they had tuned out as eavesdroppers early in the examination," Roberts continued, referring to Sibert and O'Neill.[67] "In any case, they had left the Bethesda morgue unaware that the doctors had discovered a bullet path through Kennedy's neck."[68] In addition, Roberts might have noted, Dr. Humes himself left the examination room unaware that he "had discovered" a bullet path through the President's body.[69]

It now appears to be well documented that, contrary to the Report's allegations,[70] the military physicians did not arrive at their conclusion that the bullet exited from the front of President Kennedy's neck until Saturday morning, November 23, after the autopsy had been completed.[71] Dr. Humes indicated that fact in his testimony before the Commission when he explained that the conclusion that a bullet traversed the President's body "represents our thinking within the 24–48 hours of the death of the President, all facts taken into account of the situation."[72] In July 1966, Fletcher Knebel, writing in defense of the Commission in *Look* magazine, provided further documentation for the fact that the doctors reversed themselves the day after the autopsy.[73] Citing "three Commission lawyers and one of the autopsy doctors" as his source, Knebel explained that when the existence of the throat wound was revealed to the autopsy surgeons by Dr. Perry on Saturday morning, "the Bethesda physicians then reconstructed and reanalyzed their autopsy work and came to the conclusion that the bullet passed through Kennedy, exiting at his neck."[74] And three months later, in an interview in *U.S. News & World Report,* Arlen Specter contradicted the Warren Report's account of the autopsy, which he had written,[75] by acknowledging that the comments attributed by Sibert and O'Neill to Dr. Humes "were based on factors which were originally thought to be true on the night of the autopsy."[76] According to Specter, "Dr. Humes had formulated a different conclusion . . . the very next day when he had a chance to talk to Dr. Perry."[77]

The significance of these admissions—that the autopsy conclusions accepted by the Warren Commission and then used to support the indispensable single-bullet theory were not formulated until Saturday morning[78]—is that they establish that after the body of the President, and the photographs and X-rays of it, were no longer available to the autopsy surgeons, the doctors developed an entirely new hypothesis to explain the President's wounds.[79] The doctors did not discover or trace a path for the bullet;[80] they inferred it—at a time when they were unable to authenticate their new theory because the evidence itself was no longer available to them.[81] As *Life* magazine noted, "In its most crucial conclusions, the autopsy report is not an on-the-spot record but a remembrance and reinterpretation of things irrevocably past."[82]

It might be possible to ascertain what Dr. Humes' original thoughts actually were had he not "destroyed by burning certain preliminary draft notes" relating to the autopsy.[83] "That draft I personally burned in the fireplace of my recreation room" on Sunday, November 24, Dr. Humes testified.[84] The surgeon was later to state that he had conducted approximately one thousand autopsies,[85] but he was not asked if as a general rule he burned his original documents pertaining to them.[86] Specter sought to explain this rather odd occurrence by offering Dr. Humes as an inexperienced Executive pathologist.[87] For Dr. Humes, he stated in a published interview, "had never performed an autopsy on a President."[88] Perhaps, as one critic has dryly observed, the doctor was out on a house call when President McKinley was shot. When subsequently pressed for a better answer, Specter offered another one: "He simply thought the papers weren't important, which, I have to admit, is hard to believe now."[89]

In the absence of the autopsy photographs and X-rays, one must seek to resolve the conflict between the published autopsy conclusions[90] and the information contained in the Sibert-O'Neill report[91] by examining the other relevant and available documents. These include the Autopsy Descriptive Sheet[92] and the photographs of President Kennedy's shirt and jacket.[93]

The Autopsy Descriptive Sheet contains front and rear outline drawings of the figure of a man upon which Commander Boswell, one of the autopsy surgeons, placed a series of marks to signify the location of the President's wounds.[94] On this document, Dr. Boswell located the wound in President Kennedy's back below the level of the tracheotomy incision (which had been made at the throat wound[95]), thus suggesting he did not believe that the bullet had entered the President's neck.[96]

The autopsy physicians and the Commission's defenders have alleged that the dot denoting the back wound on the Autopsy Descriptive Sheet was located incorrectly by Dr. Boswell and that measurement figures alongside the diagram correctly place the back wound higher than the throat wound.[97] Dr. Boswell himself told the Associated Press that "the dot was just meant to imply where the point of entry was [but] the notes describing the point of entry are near this mark and give precise measurements giving the exact location of the wound."[98] This explanation is less than satisfactory, since the weight of the published evidence—including the Sibert-O'Neill report,[99] the testimony of Secret Service agents present at the autopsy[100]* and the bullet holes in the President's shirt and jacket[104]—indicates that the dot is correct and the written measurements may be incorrect.†

* Roy Kellerman said the President had a wound in the "right shoulder."[101] William Greer referred in his testimony to "this hole in the right shoulder."[102] Clint Hill told the Commission, "I saw an opening in the back, about 6 inches below the neckline to the right-hand side of the spinal column."[103]

† Referring to my mention of the Autopsy Descriptive Sheet in *Rush to Judgment*, the Associated Press alleged that "to Mark Lane that errant dot is proof of a below the shoulder back wound."[105] No such statement, of course, appears in my book.[106] I merely noted that the weight of the other published evidence "lends credence" to the suspicion that Commander Boswell's dot is correctly placed on the diagram.[107]

The AP reporters also contended that "the [Warren Commission] report says" that the President had a wound in the back of his neck and not in the back and that a back wound "was never there—except to such scrutinizers as Lane."[108] Had the two AP reporters undertaken a little scrutiny themselves, they would have discovered that, quite contrary to their claim, the Warren Report itself contains numerous references to a wound in the President's

Dr. Boswell told the *New York Times* that he had made a "diagram error" on the document.[113] "If I had known at the time that this sketch would become public record," the surgeon said, "I would have been more careful."[114] This manifestation of so casual an attitude suggests that the Commission placed far too much confidence in Dr. Boswell and his colleagues. Dr. Milton Helpern, perhaps the outstanding expert on gunshot wounds in the United States,* appears to agree with this assessment.[117] In a published interview, Dr. Helpern stated that the Commission did not attempt to establish the qualifications of Commander Boswell in evaluating gunshot wounds because "he had absolutely none worthy of mention."[118]

In an interview broadcast on CBS-TV on June 26, 1967, Commander Humes came to the defense of Dr. Boswell.[119] Referring to his colleague's markings on the Autopsy Descriptive Sheet, Humes delivered the *coup de grâce*, stating that they were "never meant to be accurate."[120] The decision to permit Dr. Humes to perform the autopsy on the President of the United States also seems highly questionable. Dr. Helpern characterized the decision as "tragic"[121] and likened the participation of Dr. Humes in the autopsy to "sending a seven-year-old boy who has taken three lessons on the violin over to the New York Philharmonic and expecting him to perform a Tchaikovsky symphony."[122]†

During the CBS interview, Humes was asked by Dan Rather to "reconcile" the discrepancy between two Commission documents which depicted the back wound[124]—the Autopsy Descriptive Sheet[125] and Commission Exhibit 385 (a drawing of President Kennedy's upper body).[126] Humes explained that whereas the mark made by Boswell was incorrectly placed on the original autopsy sheet, in preparing Commission Exhibit 385 the doctors "were try-

---

back.[109] On one page of the Report, for example, mention is made of "the point of impact on the President's back" and "the point where the bullet entered the President's back,"[110] and on another page the Commission discussed "the bullet that hit President Kennedy in the back,"[111] and on another page the Commission refers to the fact that "the President had been hit in the back."[112]

* According to the *New York Times*, Dr. Helpern "knows more about violent death than anyone else in the world."[115] He has either performed or supervised approximately sixty thousand autopsies, and ten thousand of these have involved gunshot wounds in the body.[116]

† Dr. John Nichols, a forensic pathologist at the University of Kansas Medical Center, told me in a letter that "there are many things wrong with the [Kennedy] autopsy" and that the performance of the autopsy surgeons "would be considered mediocre for a medical student of this university."[123]

ing to be precise" and had marked the location of the back wound "as accurately as we possibly could."[127] Thus Dr. Humes claimed that a marking made in the autopsy room by Dr. Boswell, while the President's body was present, was inaccurate;[128] but a drawing made months later by an artist who worked without visual aids of any kind—the photographs and X-rays were unavailable to him[129]—and who depended exclusively upon the doctors' verbal description of where they recalled the wounds to be was accurate and precise.[130]

Oddly enough, Dr. Humes himself had testified three years earlier regarding the inherent inaccuracy of Commission Exhibit 385.[131] He told the Commission that "without the photographs" it was "virtually impossible" for the medical illustrator to depict the wounds with any degree of precision.[132] "I think that it is most difficult," Humes said, "to transmit into physical measurements the . . . exact situation as it was seen to the naked eye. . . . I cannot transmit completely to the illustrator where they [the wounds] were situated."[133]

In June 1967 the Associated Press announced that its reporters had learned from Dr. Boswell of "one corroborating piece of evidence which was inexplicably left out of the autopsy report."[134] According to the AP story, Boswell said that the surgeons had "conducted microscopic examination of tissue removed from the neck wound area and found foreign substances such as fiber particles."[135] Asked to account for the fact that this information had been omitted from the published findings of the physicians, Boswell said, "It was an unfortunate oversight. It was not intentional. I would say that three years ago we didn't presume that it would have been necessary to substantiate our findings."[136]*

Boswell's explanation seems inadequate, since at the time that the autopsy was conducted Lee Harvey Oswald was alive and was presumably to face trial.[140] The report of the autopsy surgeons would have been valuable evidence at that trial. It appears that even before the autopsy commenced Boswell was aware of this possible ultimate use of the material relating to the pathological examination of the President, for, according to the *New York Times*, "Dr. Boswell said the main purpose for the [autopsy] pictures having been

* In *The Death of a President*, William Manchester wrote, without offering any documentation, that at the time of the autopsy "Bethesda's physicians anticipated that their findings would later be subjected to the most searching scrutiny."[137] In view of Dr. Boswell's remark[138] and Commander Humes' belief that his preliminary draft notes "weren't important,"[139] one wonders on what information Manchester based this comment.

taken had been to have them as evidence against Lee Harvey Oswald . . . who had then been captured and was still alive."[141] Thus it seems difficult to ascribe the curious behavior of the doctors to mere carelessness or inadvertence. Informed and probing interrogation of the physicians by the Commission might have improved considerably the present state of the record. But such questioning would no doubt have left the Commission's findings with even less support than they presently enjoy, for, as Dr. Helpern has observed, "a rigorous cross-examination of the three autopsy surgeons would have ripped their testimony to shreds."[142]

An FBI report dated January 13, 1964, and submitted by that agency to the Warren Commission contained a photograph of the shirt worn by President Kennedy during the assassination.[143] The picture, not published by the Commission either in the Report or in the twenty-six volumes of evidence,[144] shows a hole in the back of the garment which was found to be 5¾ inches below the top of the collar.[145] This location is consistent with the position of the dot drawn by Commander Boswell on the Autopsy Descriptive Sheet[146] and with the position of the back wound as described in the Sibert-O'Neill report.[147] It could not be described as being at "the base of the back of [the] neck," where the Report alleged the bullet struck the President.[148]

The Commission did not discuss the likelihood of the top portion of a shirt "riding" up several inches (which would be the case if the shirt hole is to coincide with the Report's location for the posterior wound), and apparently no attempt was made to determine by experimentation whether or not this is possible.[149] The Commission's defenders have argued that such a considerable upward shifting of the shirt did occur and is not unusual.[150] "Put a jacket and shirt on any grown man with reasonably well-developed shoulders," the Associated Press suggested, "measure 5⅜ inches below the top of the collar and a bit to the right of the seam,* have him raise his right arm slightly as the president's was and mark the spot with a pencil point or chalk. Where does this touch the body? The base of the neck."[153]

President Kennedy, according to measurements taken at the autopsy examination, was 72½ inches tall and weighed 170 pounds.[154] I am 72½ inches tall and weigh 172 pounds. I have conducted such an experiment on numerous occasions, and, although the jacket does shift slightly, the shirt does not "ride" up even an inch.

* The AP referred here to the hole in the President's jacket, which was 5⅜ inches below the top of the collar.[151] The corresponding hole in the shirt was 5¾ inches below the top of the collar.[152]

Responding to the assertion that the Warren Commission failed to publish the pictures of President Kennedy's shirt and jacket contained in the FBI report of January 13, 1964, Charles Roberts declared, "A perusal of Volume XVII of the Warren Commission's Hearings, however, discloses two pictures each of the President's bloody shirt and jacket."[155] Roberts failed to inform his readers that the photographs selected by the Commission for publication are useless, since the hole in the back of each of the garments cannot be seen, while the holes in the FBI photographs—which were not published by the Commission—are clearly visible.[156] Faced with the choice of publishing either a set of pictures which did show the holes or one which did not, the Commission took the latter option.[157] Although the choice may not have been prompted by a desire to release only that evidence which was not damaging to the Report's conclusions, it did have that effect.

40 THE BEST EVIDENCE

Not the least remarkable aspect of the controversy over the President's back wound is the fact that the documents which in and of themselves would quite likely be dispositive of this question are in existence today. They are sixty-five X-rays, color slides and black and white negatives taken during the autopsy which were turned over to the National Archives by the Kennedy family on October 31, 1966.[1] Under an agreement between the President's executors and the Government, only Federal investigative agents will have the right to see the material without the permission of Burke Marshall, a lawyer designated by the Kennedy family to handle requests to see the items, for at least five years.[2] On November 3, 1966, the *New York Times* reported that "Mr. Marshall said he would grant no requests from journalists, historians, biographers and researchers for at least five years. . . . After the five-year period, selected scholars and researchers will be given access to the pictures and X-rays, he said, but the news media will probably still be excluded. These restrictions will continue as long as any member of President Kennedy's immediate family lives."[3]

It has been taken for granted, both by the media and by the Federal Government, that the survivors of John F. Kennedy own the autopsy photographs and X-rays. If, indeed, title to that evidence has passed to the Kennedy family, it has done so without benefit of the prevailing laws that apply to others. The photographs and X-rays were public documents from the moment that they came into existence, and under the law they remain so today. They were created by medical technicians and photographers who were Government employees.[4] Presumably the instruments employed in creating the evidence (the cameras and X-ray equipment), the raw material utilized (the film) and the room in which the exposures were made (the autopsy room at a naval hospital) were all owned by the United States Government.[5] The evidence was created for, among other purposes, use at a forthcoming murder trial.[6] Clearly the mere physical possession of the evidence by the Kennedy family (which appears to have been unsanctioned by law) could not legitimatize that custody. Mere possession is neither tantamount to nor, despite an old adage, equivalent to nine-tenths ownership under the law.

That aspect of the question is no longer at issue, however, for at the present time the Kennedy family has surrendered physical control of the evidence. It now reposes in the National Archives and thus has been properly returned to the Federal Government, which created it and owned it from its inception. Any conditions limiting the use of that material which the Kennedy family might wish to impose upon the United States Government must be considered unenforceable—indeed, under the circumstances, frivolous. That the Administration has made use of the request to suppress the material is not surprising in view of its own history regarding other invaluable evidence in this case, even in the absence of outside inspiration.[7] That the media have so consistently misinformed the public regarding the privilege of the Kennedy family to deny the people's right of access to public property[8] is surprising in view of the general approach taken by the press to such efforts in ordinary circumstances.

William Manchester, in *The Death of a President*, purported to explain the rationale behind this restriction by stating that "because this material is unsightly it will be unavailable until 1971"[9]—at which time presumably it will be less unsightly. In any event, Manchester could not reasonably argue that X-rays could be considered "unsightly."

Although he admitted that he had not seen them himself,[10] Manchester stated flatly that "the X-rays show no entry wound 'below the shoulder' " and that the photographs clearly "reveal that the wound was in the neck."[11] How could Manchester assert this as a fact if he had not had access to the sequestered material? He explained that he had "discussed it with three men who examined it before it was placed under seal. All three carried special professional qualifications."[12] Thus the American people, the majority of whom, according to public opinion polls, had abandoned faith in the Warren Commission's conclusions,[13] were asked by Manchester to share his faith in three unnamed persons.[14] Unlike other published works on the subject, the integrity of which is susceptible to verification through numerous cited references,[15] Manchester's book affords no documentation,[16] and one must depend exclusively upon the author's reliability, which has been shown to be often undeserving of such trust.

In a further plea for confidence in authority, Manchester declared that "the recollections of all doctors present during the autopsy" agree with the location ascribed to the back wound by the Commission.[17] But these "recollections" are contradicted by such hard evidence as the Autopsy Descriptive Sheet,[18] the FBI photographs of President Kennedy's clothing[19] and the Sibert-O'Neill report.[20] These autopsy surgeons have stated that they inadvertently omitted vital corroborative evidence from their finished report,[21] marked an autopsy diagram incorrectly[22] and "never meant to be accurate" in preparing contemporaneous records of their work.[23] They have been characterized as incompetent by prominent pathologists.[24] Moreover, there is no reason to rely upon their "recollections" when the best evidence—the photographs and X-rays—is in the possession of the Government and could easily be made available for inspection by an independent panel of qualified experts.

Dr. Helpern was critical of the Commission's failure to examine the photographs and X-rays before it reached its conclusions.[25] In a published interview, he stated:

> The X-rays of President Kennedy's body . . . were not considered significant enough to the entire investigation to be filed as exhibits to the report. The same holds true of the black and white and the color pictures of the bullet wounds. These were never seen by the Commission members, its staff, or even the autopsy surgeons before the report was finalized. The Commission said it would not "press" for the X-rays and photographs because these would merely "corroborate" the findings of the doctors, and that considerations of "good taste" precluded these from being included. Well, you see, there was nothing that offended "good taste" in the nine X-rays of Governor Connally's body [which were published in Volume XVII of the Commission's evidence].[26]

After the publication of *Rush to Judgment* in 1966, considerable information regarding the possession of the autopsy photographs and X-rays became available for the first time.[27] On October 10, 1966, *U.S. News & World Report* disclosed that "official sources" had given the following account to the magazine:

> Robert F. Kennedy, then U.S. Attorney General and now a U.S. Senator from New York, took charge immediately, and refused to let anyone else see the X rays and pictures. . . . [They] remained under lock and key at Bethesda Naval Hospital until sometime in 1964. Then they were sent to the Secret Service, and turned over to Mrs. Evelyn Lincoln, the late President's longtime secretary. Mrs. Lincoln, at the time, was working on the Kennedy archives.[28]

And on January 14, 1967, the *Saturday Evening Post* quoted a "high FBI official" as having stated that "the autopsy pictures were sequestered by the written order of Attorney General Kennedy, directing the Secret Service not to release any information or material pertaining to the autopsy without his permission."[29]

Nevertheless, although no definitive evaluation may be made until all the principal figures involved have given their version of what transpired, the evidence now available seems to indicate that Chief Justice Earl Warren—and not Senator Kennedy—was personally responsible for the decision to withhold the X-rays and photographs from the Commission which he chaired.[30] Senator Kennedy's office, according to *U.S. News & World Report*, pointed out that the Commission "had not insisted on viewing the pictures."[31]

Arlen Specter was quoted by *The Nation* as having said that he was told by Warren that the Commission had decided "not to press the matter."[32] Edward J. Epstein, who interviewed a number of Commission attorneys,[33] said that while it was generally believed that "Bobby Kennedy had refused to show them [the photographs and X-rays]" to the Commission, "one of the lawyers, Howard Willens, checked his files and found Senator Kennedy never refused. It was Warren who didn't want to see them."[34] Willens had acted as liaison between the Justice Department (then headed by Robert Kennedy) and the Commission,[35] and he was one attorney in a position to know the facts.

Richard Whalen, writing in the *Saturday Evening Post*, cast further light on the matter:

> According to an official of the Treasury Department, the Secret Service did not turn over the autopsy material to the [Kennedy] family until April 26, 1965. Hence, at the time when the pictures might have proved enormously useful, they were still in Government hands, and therefore within reach of the Warren Commission if it had pressed the matter urgently.[36]

If Whalen's source can be credited, the evidence was in the possession of the Government during the entire life of the Warren

Commission and was in fact not dispatched to Robert Kennedy until more than half a year after the Commission had disbanded.[37]

Whalen also disclosed further information about Warren's peculiar sensitivity regarding the medical evidence.[38] "It was Warren who vetoed a long list of questions Specter had prepared for the President's widow," Whalen wrote, "who refused to allow him to be present at her brief questioning, and who directed the deletion from the record of her description of the President's wounds."[39]

The Associated Press offered a curious explanation for the Commission's failure to examine the autopsy material.[40] "Had these photographs been introduced as commission exhibits," the wire service stated, "the commission may have been bound to publish them—as it did with other nonsecret exhibits."[41] Yet the Commission declined to publish many of its exhibits, both secret and "nonsecret."[42] For example, it decided not to reproduce Armstrong Exhibits Nos. 5303 A-H, which it identified as a "series of photographs taken at the Carousel Club."[43] It was absurd of the Associated Press to suggest either that the Commission had published all its "nonsecret exhibits" or that questions of taste might obtain in reference to the publication of X-rays.[44]

Two important governmental figures—the President of the United States and the House Minority Leader—offered amusing *non sequiturs* in response to inquiries regarding the availability of the photographs and X-rays.[45] At a press conference on November 4, 1966, four days after the autopsy material had been placed in the National Archives,[46] President Lyndon B. Johnson was asked "why this material is still not available to competent nongovernment investigators."[47] The President replied that he "wouldn't want to have the garments and the records and everything paraded out in every sewing circle in the country."[48]

Yet as we have observed, no person other than President Johnson had either discussed or considered the ghoulish use and exploitation of the evidence in that fashion. The suggestion and then rejection of such an extravagant possibility, however, should not be permitted to mask the three basic deficiencies that also marred the President's reply. First, it in no way answered the question which was posed by the reporter.[49] Secondly, the President did not explain why such sensitivity did not prevent the Warren Commission from publishing such other intimate but less useful items as a microphotograph of one of Lee Harvey Oswald's pubic hairs[50] and a dental chart showing the condition of Jack Ruby's mother's teeth—on January 15, 1938.[51] I suggest that the latter item would not have been relevant to the Commission's inquiry even if Ruby had bitten

Oswald to death. Thirdly, contrary to President Johnson's contention, the opening of the Archives material to qualified scholars and experts would indeed serve a "good" purpose if not an "official" one: it would quite likely resolve the controversy over President Kennedy's wounds and provide some crucial answers which have been denied to the American people for nearly four years.

Congressman Gerald R. Ford, the House Minority Leader, discussed the X-rays with Richard Warren Lewis and Lawrence Schiller.[52] "The seven members of the Warren Commission are laymen," Ford said.[53]

> We're not medical men. We were either lawyers or civilians not trained in medical practice. Therefore, we were not qualified to take an X ray, look at it and analyze it and come to any sound conclusion. If they had given us the X rays and we had analyzed them, I don't think our judgments would have been sound. What we did, and I think it was the right thing, was to ask technically trained people who could read an X ray to testify under oath.* I must say when one of my children breaks an arm and the doctor shows me the X ray, it doesn't mean very much to me. The doctor knows about the X ray. He can look at it and analyze it and tell you what it means. So, in my judgment, it is not a valid criticism of the Commission that we, as Commission members, didn't personally analyze the X rays. We did the best thing, in my judgment. We got the technically trained people to come and testify under oath as to their opinion on what the X rays meant.[57]

Ford's explanation is a confused melange of inaccuracies, evasions and redundancies. The Commission never heard any "technically trained people . . . come and testify under oath as to their opinion on what the X rays meant."[58] The three autopsy surgeons did testify, of course, but they did not have access to the X-rays or photographs when they were preparing for their appearance, as Commander Humes explicitly stated in his testimony.[59] The question is not only why the X-rays and photographs were not made available to the Commissioners but also why the doctors themselves were unable to secure those documents in preparing for their testimony.[60] In addition, Ford's reasoning fails to take into account the

* Another Commissioner, Hale Boggs of Louisiana, the majority whip of the House of Representatives, made an almost identical statement during a television interview on November 27, 1966.[54] "Of course, the members of the commission themselves are not doctors," Boggs declared.[55] "Looking at them, just looking at X-rays, would not prove anything for me. I don't know how to read medical X-rays. We brought before the commission the man who performed the autopsy. We examined him in great detail."[56]

fact that he was present when other technical evidence—regarding ballistics, for example[61]—was interpreted for the Commissioners by expert witnesses.[62] On many such occasions the physical exhibits themselves were shown to the Commissioners,[63] were explained by "technically trained people"[64] and were subsequently published in the twenty-six volumes of evidence.[65] A jury in any case, criminal or civil, which is composed of laymen, looks at relevant technical evidence whether or not such evidence is fully intelligible without accompanying expert testimony. And, of course, Ford's odd explanation regarding the suppressed evidence could hardly be considered, even by him, to apply to the photographs, which required no expert interpretation.

Some of the Warren Report's champions have advanced other reasons purporting to explain why the X-rays and photographs have not been—or need not be—released for examination by independent experts.[66] For example, an upholder of the Commission's findings identified only as a "well qualified source" was quoted by *The Observer* of London as having said, "We always understood that the trouble with the photographs was that they didn't prove anything conclusively one way or the other—it simply wasn't possible after the surgeon's work at Dallas to show from them the passage of the bullet that was supposed to have gone through the President."[67] It would be very surprising indeed if photographs of the exterior of the President's body could under any circumstances show the path of the bullet once it entered his back. But aside from that point, the "well qualified source" seriously understated the potential value of the autopsy photographs.[68] They could certainly resolve beyond any doubt whether the entry hole was in the President's back "below the shoulders" or in the base of the neck, as the Commission alleged.[69]

41 THE MISSING EVIDENCE

If the suppressed autopsy documents were made available for inspection by nongovernmental investigators, they might shed some light on the unresolved issues regarding the President's throat wound, which was described by the doctors in Dallas—the only physicians to see it before it was extended by the tracheotomy[1]—as a wound of entrance.[2] "If the hole in Kennedy's throat was an entrance wound, caused by a bullet fired from the grassy knoll," asked Charles Roberts, "what became of the bullet?"[3] Perhaps the X-rays could answer that question for Roberts, who had numerous ill-informed or misleading comments to make regarding the throat wound and the testimony relating to it.[4]

Roberts accused me, for example, of misrepresenting in *Rush to Judgment* the statements of Dr. Malcolm Perry,[5] who was widely quoted in the press on November 23, 1963, as having said at a news conference immediately after the President's death that the throat wound was an entrance wound.[6] On what did Roberts base his charge of misrepresentation? "Dr. Perry has since denied making that statement," he declared.[7] I knew of Dr. Perry's denial when I wrote *Rush to Judgment* and accordingly I suggested therein that the Commission "had only to secure, read and then publish a transcript of the press conference" at which Dr. Perry assertedly made his remark in order to ascertain whether or not he had been misquoted.[8] The Commission did not publish such a transcript, I observed,[9]* and "independent efforts to examine the television and radio tapes have been unsuccessful. The three major networks and the local Dallas stations no longer possess them."[11] To the best of my knowledge, this remains as true today as when I wrote those words, more than a year ago.[12]† Yet Roberts, who branded as "an absurd notion" the possibility that the Government or the press willfully issued misleading statements or suppressed relevant information,[15] did not explain, much less mention, the unavailability and apparent disappearance of the tapes of Dr. Perry's press conference.[16]

In *Rush to Judgment* I stated that "the [Dallas] doctors were unanimous about the nature of the throat wound: it was an entrance wound, and all the doctors who expressed an opinion during the days following the assassination described it as such."[17] Roberts called this an "egregious misstatement" and even contended that "the fact is that *none* of the doctors ever made such a finding."[18] (Emphasis in the original.) This allegation is demonstrably false, for if Roberts had only casually perused the third chapter of my book he would have discovered there the names and statements of the physicians in question.[19] For example, as noted on page 52 of *Rush to Judgment*, Dr. Ronald C. Jones stated in a handwritten re-

* On June 26, 1967, Walter Cronkite revealed on CBS-TV that, despite Dr. Perry's later disclaimer, "the transcript of that news conference" confirmed "that Dr. Perry made it sound as if he had a firm opinion" in describing the throat wound as "an entry wound."[10]

† As I have noted in an earlier chapter, a letter dated March 25, 1964, from the director of the Secret Service to the Warren Commission has recently been discovered in the unpublished material in the National Archives.[13] It notes that the tapes of Dr. Perry's statement to the press could not be located.[14]

port dated November 23, 1963, that he had seen "a small hole in anterior midline of neck thought to be a bullet entrance wound."[20] As I have noted above, Dr. Perry told a news conference on November 22 (and was widely quoted in the press as having said) that it was an entrance wound.[21] Other Dallas doctors, including Dr. Charles R. Baxter[22] and Dr. Robert N. McClelland,[23] made similar statements.[24]

Not one doctor who saw the President's throat wound in Dallas on November 22 gave any contemporaneous indication that he believed the hole to have been anything but an entrance wound,[25] and Roberts failed to cite a single physician who could substantiate his irresponsible charge of misrepresentation.[26]

Rather than seeking to conceal his lack of command of the evidence, Roberts seemed almost eager to proclaim it. For example, he alleged that Dr. Charles Carrico was "the only other physician [besides Dr. Perry] to examine the throat wound before Dr. Perry performed the tracheotomy that obliterated its outlines."[27] This statement too is false. At least three other surgeons—Dr. Jones,[28] Dr. Baxter[29] and Dr. Marion T. Jenkins[30]—explicitly testified that they had examined the anterior neck wound before the tracheotomy incision was made.

Another defender of the Warren Report's conclusions, Professor John Kaplan of Stanford University, wrote an attack on the Commission's critics for the Phi Beta Kappa journal *The American Scholar*.[31] In this article, Kaplan alleged that in *Rush to Judgment* I "quote[d] out of context to make it appear that they [the Dallas doctors] thought the wound was an entrance wound because of something in its appearance rather than merely because it was the only wound they saw."[32] The testimony of several of these doctors —Dr. Jones,[33] Dr. Baxter[34] and Dr. McClelland,[35] for example— makes it absolutely clear that they unquestionably did think the wound was an entrance wound because of its appearance. When this error and many of the others with which his article was profusely littered[36] were publicly brought to Kaplan's attention,[37] he proceeded to rewrite the article.[38] In the revised draft, which was published in the *Stanford Law Review* with the remark that it represented a "corrected version" of the earlier essay,[39] all mention of this point regarding the throat wound was omitted[40]—apparently an indication that Kaplan then understood that his original reckless allegation had been without foundation.

Kaplan also alleged in his original article that there was "crucial and irrefutable evidence" that the throat wound was not an entry wound: "the fibers on the front of [President Kennedy's shirt] collar were pushed outward."[41] Although the Commission heard testimony to this effect,[42] that testimony was flatly contradicted by Arlen Specter,[43] who wrote the portion of the Warren Report dealing with the shirt fibers.[44] In an interview published in *U.S. News & World Report*, Specter said, "The fiber on the front of the shirt was inconclusive—it was a slit. You could not determine in which direction the fiber was pushed, nor could the nick on the [President's] tie be used to determine what was the direction of the shot."[45]

Probably the most extraordinary published theory that has been offered to account for the throat wound is the one put forth by Professor Alexander Bickel of Yale.[46] While the evidence suggests that it was an entrance wound[47] and the Warren Commission, evidently for its own purposes, found it to be an exit wound,[48] in Bickel's simplified theorizing there was no throat wound at all.[49] As he constructed the assassination sequence (proposing what he represented as a viable alternative to the single-bullet theory[50]), three shots were fired, all by a lone assassin from the sixth-floor window of the Texas School Book Depository, and the throat wound merely ceased to exist, thus resolving—for Bickel at least—the problem of whether it was an entrance wound or an exit wound.[51] According to Bickel, "the first [bullet] would have lodged in the President's back (later dropping out onto the stretcher), the second would have hit bone in Governor Connally, and—like the third, which went to the President's head—would have broken up, one fragment entering the Governor's thigh, and the rest bouncing up and out of the open car."[52] He goes on to acknowledge that "this theory . . . also raises some questions"; but, he finds, "at least [it] does not clash with the known facts."[53] One might reasonably conclude that some of the known facts evidently are not known to Bickel.

42 THE SINGLE-BULLET THEORY

The single-bullet theory, as mentioned earlier, is the *sine qua non* of the Warren Commission's finding that all the shots were fired by Lee Harvey Oswald using the Mannlicher-Carcano rifle.[1] The Report alleged that its imaginative hypothesis was actually "not necessary to any essential findings of the Commission,"[2] but that second line of defense has now been thoroughly discredited.[3] The efforts of even the most committed of the Commission defenders are now to show that one missile did pass through President Kennedy's body and then caused all Governor Connally's wounds while conceding that the single-bullet theory is indeed essential to the lone assassin theory.[4]*

One outstanding exception appears to be Arlen Specter,[7] who is credited with having formulated the theory in the first place.[8]† On June 26, 1967, on CBS-TV, Dan Rather solicited Specter's views on the subject:[15]

> RATHER: It stated in the Warren Commission Report that belief in the single bullet theory is "not essential" to supporting the conclusion of the Warren Commission Report. Now, can you describe for us any other theory, besides the single bullet theory, that would support the conclusions in the Report?
>
> SPECTER: The Commission concluded that it was probable that one bullet inflicted the wound on the President's neck, and all of the wounds on Governor Connally. But you could have three separate bullets striking under the sequence as we know them. For example, the President could have been struck at frame 186 of the Zapruder film, which is a number given to the Zapruder film. Then Governor Connally could have been struck some 42 frames later, which would be a little over two and a quarter seconds at about frame 228 or 229; and then the third shot could have hit President Kennedy's head at frame 313, which was pretty clearly established. So that it is not

* On June 26, 1967, Walter Cronkite conceded on CBS-TV that "despite its [the Commission's] own words, the single bullet theory is essential to its findings."[5] At the same time, the Associated Press stated, "If . . . the single bullet theory collapses . . . so does the Warren report conclusion that Lee Harvey Oswald alone fired the bullets."[6]

† The almost duplicitous approach by the Commission to this question has misled none of the critics and, as we have seen, few of the defenders either.[9] But one correspondent was evidently awed by the language in which the Commission set its conclusions.[10] "Where there were no final answers," Charles Roberts wrote, "the Commission prudently made no attempt to answer categorically. . . . It did not say flatly that the bullet which pierced President Kennedy's neck also wounded Governor Connally. It said, after prolonged debate, the evidence that it did so was 'very persuasive.'"[11] The Commission, however, with considerably less prudence, stated unequivocally that Oswald fired all the shots from the sixth-floor window of the Book Depository with the Mannlicher-Carcano rifle.[12] That conclusion rests entirely upon the premise that the bullet which struck the Governor first "pierced President Kennedy's neck."[13] To all but the most gullible, the Commission's tergiversation is apparent. The Report's guarded language about the validity of the single-bullet theory does not alter the fact that if the theory was incapable of realization the conclusion that rests upon it is doomed.[14]

> indispensable to have the single bullet conclusion in order to come to the basic finding that Oswald was the sole assassin.[16]

In order for Specter's alternative to be valid within the framework of the Commission's case, one must presume that a number of extremely unlikely, if not almost impossible, circumstances prevailed on November 22, 1963. First, Oswald would have had to fire the first shot (which, in Specter's alternative thesis, finds its mark on President Kennedy's neck[17]) while his view of the President was obstructed by the oak tree.[18] That possibility was analyzed—and discounted as highly implausible, for several reasons—in a previous chapter of this book.[19] Second, the hypothesis requires the presumption that President Kennedy did not begin to react until approximately two seconds after he was hit,[20]* and there is no reason to believe that this was the case.[28]

Most important of all, however, it is very unlikely that a bullet which hit no bone (as the Commission contended was true of the bullet which allegedly passed through the President's neck[29]) would have exited from the limousine without leaving a trace somewhere in the interior of the car.[30] Specter called this point "the single most compelling reason why I concluded that one bullet hit both men."[31] He told *Life* magazine, "Given the trajectory from the Book Depository window, the autopsy, about which I have no doubts, and the FBI report on the limousine ["it concludes that no part of the car's interior was struck by a whole bullet"]: where, if it didn't hit Connally, did that bullet go?"[32]† If Specter sincerely considered it "most compelling" that, in the context of the single-bullet theory, a missile exiting on an undeflected downward trajectory from the

* Assuming that Governor Connally was hit in frame 234 (which he has designated as the point at which he was shot[21]), a previous shot from the Mannlicher-Carcano rifle could conceivably have been fired 42 frames earlier, at frame 192.[22] Prior to the time President Kennedy passed behind a roadside traffic sign and disappeared from Zapruder's view at about frame 207, he showed no sign of having been hit.[23] Lyndal L. Shaneyfelt, the FBI photography expert who scrutinized the Zapruder frames for the Commission,[24] testified that the President's reaction to a wound was "barely apparent" in frame 225, when the President reappeared in Zapruder's film.[25] If the President was hit at frame 192 or before—Specter suggested frame 186 as a likely possibility[26]—then he would be only "barely" reacting approximately two seconds later.[27]

† The key link in Specter's chain of reasoning is, of course, the autopsy report. While he may have "no doubts" about its accuracy[33] (hardly surprising in view of the fact that he authored the Report's chapter endorsing the official autopsy findings[34]), previous portions of this section have demonstrated that grave doubts do indeed exist.[35]

President's throat must have hit either the interior of the limousine or the Governor,[36] then how could he propose in good faith, as a viable alternative to the single-bullet theory, a hypothesis, suggested in the CBS interview, in which the exiting bullet strikes neither the car nor Governor Connally?[37]

Governor Connally testified before the Warren Commission that he was hit between frames 231 and 234 of the Zapruder film.[38] In 1966, asked by *Life* magazine to examine enlarged color slides of the film, the Governor selected 234 as the frame in which he probably was hit.[39]*

Since President Kennedy was hit by frame 225,[43] and Specter believed the same missile had continued forward and struck the Governor in the back,[44] he was required to rebut Connally's statement regarding frame 234. Focusing his attention on frame 230—which is about two-ninths of a second before 234 and slightly more than that after frame 225[45]—Specter told *Life* magazine, "First of all, it looks to me as if his face is wincing [in frame 230], indicating a probability he's been hit."[46] But, according to the publication, "Life's photo interpreters think he looks unharmed [in frame 230], as does Connally himself."[47]

In addition, Specter said, "We're pretty sure from the medical evidence that when Connally was hit, his right wrist was down in his lap. . . . [In] frame 230 the wrist is too high to be hit and throughout the rest of the sequence—all the way until Connally collapses—that wrist stays raised."[48] But *Life* again found Specter's reasoning less than persuasive: "Nor is there any medical evidence, despite Specter's claim, that Connally's right hand was in his lap when he was hit."[49]

Other defenders of the single-bullet theory have sought to explain the Governor's apparently delayed reaction—assuming he was hit by the same bullet which struck the President—by contending that a belated reaction to a bullet impact is a common, if not usual, occurrence.[50] For example, Richard Warren Lewis and Lawrence Schiller declared that unnamed "informed observers have suggested that Connally experienced a delayed reaction to being wounded. The phenomenon is common among those suddenly assaulted."[51] And Charles Roberts was even more emphatic on this point—but no more relevant.[52] "Medical literature and hospital records," Roberts

* This was consistent with the testimony of the physicians who operated on the Governor at Parkland Hospital on November 22.[40] Dr. Robert R. Shaw said he believed the bullet struck in frame "236, give or take 1 or 2 frames."[41] Dr. Charles F. Gregory testified that he felt Governor Connally could have been hit "in frames marked 234, 235, and 236."[42]

asserted, "are crammed with instances of gunshot victims not realizing they were hit for minutes—or even hours—after sustaining their wounds. Or, as Dr. Arthur J. Dziemian, an Army physiologist, put it to the Commission: 'Some people are struck by bullets and do not even know they are hit.' "[53]

It is clear that Lewis, Schiller and Roberts are eager to generalize as broadly as possible on this point, for it enabled them to obfuscate the only relevant issue involved. The matter at hand does not concern "those suddenly assaulted," "medical literature and hospital records," "gunshot victims" or "some people."[54] It concerns John B. Connally, Jr., and it is only by evading any reference to this specific case that these defenders can sustain their argument.[55] Why, for example, did Roberts cite Dr. Dziemian, who never treated Governor Connally, examined his wounds, spoke with the Governor or even discussed the question with the Parkland physicians?[56] It would have been far more enlightening—and germane—to cite the testimony of Dr. Robert R. Shaw, the surgeon who performed the operation on the Governor's chest wound on November 22.[57] Dr. Shaw agreed that it was indeed conceivable in some instances of gunshot injury that "there can be a delay in the sensory reaction."[58] Addressing himself to the type of wound incurred by Governor Connally, however, Dr. Shaw noted that "in the case of a wound which strikes a bony substance such as a rib, usually the reaction is quite prompt."[59]

The controversy over the single-bullet theory, it should be noted, centers around two crucial—but decidedly distinct—questions: Could one bullet have hit both men? If so, could Commission Exhibit 399* have been that bullet?[63] In a masterful display of misrepresentation, Charles Roberts adduced the testimony of three Dallas doctors regarding the first question in an attempt to rebut the arguments of the Commission's critics on the second.[64] After noting that the critics—including myself[65]—had cited the comments of Commander Humes and Lieutenant Colonel Finck to the effect that, in their opinion, Commission Exhibit 399 could not have caused Governor Connally's wrist wound,[66] Roberts stated:

> If this was the opinion of the doctors at Bethesda, who read about Connally's wounds, what about the doctors at Parkland who actually attended the wounded governor? The Commission called three of

* Commission Exhibit 399 is a nearly pristine, undeformed bullet weighing 158.6 grains.[60] Bullets of this type normally weigh 160 or 161 grains before firing.[61] Commission Exhibit 399 was discovered on a stretcher in a corridor at Parkland Hospital on November 22.[62]

them and each, independently, expressed his opinion that the same bullet that traversed Connally's body also caused the wrist and thigh wounds.[67]

Roberts then proceeded to quote each of three surgeons—Shaw, Gregory and Tom Shires—to the effect that he believed a single bullet had caused all the Governor's wounds.[68] Roberts did not produce a word from any one of the three to the effect that he believed that the specific missile to which Humes and Finck had referred—Commission Exhibit 399[69]—could have inflicted all the damage and still retained its almost pristine condition.[70] For example, he quoted Dr. Shaw as having testified that he had "always felt that the wounds of Governor Connally could be explained by the passage of one missile through his chest, striking his wrist and a fragment of it going on into his left thigh. I had never entertained the idea that he had been struck by a second missile."[71] Here Dr. Shaw clearly was asserting his opinion as to whether or not a single bullet could have caused all the Governor's wounds.[72] But Roberts was careless—or careful—enough to omit what the same physician said in a very relevant context—whether or not Commission Exhibit 399 in particular could have caused all the Governor's wounds,[73] the question Roberts was then pretending to explore.[74] On that question Shaw testified, "I feel that there would be some difficulty in explaining all of the [Governor's] wounds as being inflicted by bullet Exhibit 399 without causing more in the way of loss of substance to the bullet or deformation of the bullet."[75]*

Roberts also quoted Dr. Gregory and Dr. Shires as having stated that a single bullet probably caused all Governor Connally's wounds.[77] But again he included that which was irrelevant while omitting that which was germane.[78] Both Dr. Gregory[79] and Dr. Shires[80] found it improbable that the missile which caused the Governor's wounds had first passed through the President. Thus, although they both expressed grave doubts about the plausibility of the single-bullet theory,[81] Roberts selectively quoted from their testimony to create the misleading impression that they actually provided substantiation for it.[82] Moreover, neither Dr. Gregory[83] nor Dr. Shires[84] stated that in his opinion Commission Exhibit 399 could have been the missile which caused all the Governor's wounds.

This example of misrepresentation, however, pales by comparison with Roberts' next effort.[85] Finally turning his attention to the critical issue of whether the metal fragments in Governor Con-

* Immediately following that observation by Dr. Shaw, according to the Commission's published transcript of the hearing, there was a "discussion off the record."[76]

nally's wounds could have come from the 158.6-grain Commission Exhibit 399—which Dr. Shaw found "difficult to believe"[86]—Roberts said:

> As for the reported metal "fragments" in Connally's wounds—which caused Drs. Humes and Finck, at Bethesda, to doubt that Bullet 399 could have inflicted so many wounds and remained intact—Dr. Gregory testified that "on the basis of the metal left behind in Governor Connally's body, as far as I could tell, the missile that struck it could be virtually intact . . ."[87]

An objective investigator interested in ascertaining the whole truth based upon all available evidence would scarcely have chosen to end the quotation from Dr. Gregory in mid-sentence, as Roberts did.[88] The surgeon's full statement was that "on the basis of the metal left behind in Governor Connally's body, as far as I could tell, the missile that struck it could be virtually intact, insofar as mass was concerned, but probably was distorted."[89] Since Commission Exhibit 399 remains in an almost pristine and undistorted condition,[90] the reason for Roberts' omission of the final fragment of the quotation may not be incomprehensible.

Far more significant, however, is the fact that Roberts failed to furnish his readers with the vital information on this particular point.[91] Dr. Gregory testified on two occasions—in Dallas, on March 23, 1964, when he was interrogated by Specter and no Commission member was present;[92] and in Washington on April 21, 1964, when Specter again conducted the examination of the witness, this time in the presence of six of the seven members of the Commission.[93] In his book Roberts elected to cite a portion of Dr. Gregory's testimony from the earlier hearing,[94] although at that time the physician had not seen Commission Exhibit 399, a fact confirmed by a discussion between Dr. Gregory and Senator Richard Russell during the subsequent hearing in Washington.[95]

> RUSSELL: When did you first see this bullet [Commission Exhibit 399], Doctor, the one you have just described in your testimony?
> GREGORY: This bullet?
> RUSSELL: Yes.
> GREGORY: This morning [April 21, 1964], sir.
> RUSSELL: You had never seen it until this morning?
> GREGORY: I had never seen it before this time.[96]

What is significant, therefore, is not what Dr. Gregory said in his first hearing—from which Roberts chose the partial quotation[97] —before he had had a chance to examine the particular missile in question, but rather what he said on April 21 after having seen Commission Exhibit 399 for the first time.[98] On that occasion the following colloquy was recorded:

> Specter: Is there sufficient metallic substance missing from the back or rear end of that bullet [Commission Exhibit 399] to account for the metallic substance which you have described in the Governor's wrist?
>
> Gregory: It is possible but I don't know enough about the structure of bullets or this one in particular, to know what is a normal complement of lead or for this particular missile. It is irregular, but how much it may have lost, I have no idea.[99]

Thus, in his analysis of the evidence relating to Commission Exhibit 399, Roberts' technique was to omit mention of any testimony tending to discredit the single-bullet theory and to select non-representative testimony of those witnesses whom he did choose to quote.[100]*

Roberts then turned his attention to the wound ballistics tests conducted on behalf of the Commission by the United States Army.[103] He stated, "A shot fired into a goat produced, on X-ray examination, a fracture of its eighth rib almost identical to the fracture of Connally's fifth rib—and with little mutilation of the bullet."[104] While it is true that Dr. Alfred G. Olivier, who supervised the test,[105] told the Commission that the damage to the goat carcass was "very similar" to the Connally fracture,[106] it is untrue that there was "little mutilation of the bullet."[107] In the first place, Dr. Olivier testified that "the bullet has been quite flattened."[108] Second, the condition of the test bullet per se is of far less consequence than the matter of how it compared to the condition of Commission Exhibit 399.[109] The photograph of the test bullet published by the Commission[110] confirms Dr. Olivier's assessment of the damage to that missile[111] and shows that it suffered considerably greater mutilation than Commission Exhibit 399,[112] a fact of major importance which Roberts omitted in favor of a more gentle and unrelated generalization.[113]

Arlen Specter also drew invalid conclusions from the wound ballistics tests.[114] In his interview with *U.S. News & World Report*, after describing the various tests that were conducted, Specter de-

* Roberts also failed to mention Dr. Shaw's testimony that "more than three grains of metal" were in the Governor's wrist wound.[101] Could these have come from Commission Exhibit 399, which was missing only 1.4 to 2.4 grains, assuming it weighed the normal 160 or 161 grains before firing?[102]

clared that "all of this, when put together, showed that it was entirely possible" that a 6.5-millimeter bullet could have achieved all that the Commission attributed to Commission Exhibit 399.[115] But, of course, no single test had been undertaken to simulate the entire sequence of collisions.[116] Instead, individual tests, each of which produced damage similar to the Governor's wounds[117] but far greater mutilation to the test bullets than Commission Exhibit 399 displays,[118] were performed.[119] The phrase "when put together"—the key part of Specter's allegation—refers to an event which occurred not in the laboratory under test conditions but rather in Specter's inventive mind, scarcely the best place to determine the probability that the bullet accomplished what it is alleged to have done.*

Time magazine suggested that it was "probable" that Commission Exhibit 399 "had hit both men" because "the wound in Connally's back was oddly large, suggesting that the bullet had begun to wobble and slow down before it struck—presumably because it had just passed through the President's neck."[121] The Warren Report, however, said the Governor's back wound was of "small size,"[122] and in his testimony before the Commission Dr. Shaw stated, "This was a small wound approximately a centimeter and a half [about three-fifths of an inch] in its greatest diameter."[123]

The Warren Report, like its defenders, was very selective in quoting testimony regarding the single-bullet theory.[124] The reader of the Report who is unaware of the testimony and evidence it purports to summarize might well conclude that the Commission's case is a strong one. Had the Commission permitted an attorney to participate in its inquiry as counsel for the deceased defendant, that attorney could have solicited expert testimony from the most reputable pathologists tending to discredit the single-bullet theory. He might well have called, for example, upon Dr. Milton Helpern, who has been quoted earlier in several contexts, or Dr. Cyril H. Wecht, the director of the Institute of Forensic Sciences at the Duquesne University School of Law and the chief forensic pathologist for Allegheny County.

Dr. Helpern declared in a published interview that he "definitely" did not agree that the same missile struck both men.[125] "Now, this bizarre path is perfectly possible," Dr. Helpern said.[126]

* As we have seen in a previous chapter of this book, when CBS-TV attempted to conduct a composite test, under Dr. Olivier's supervision, the results apparently proved that a single bullet could not have passed through the President's body and then caused all the Governor's wounds.[120] See pages 98–102.

> When you are working with bullet wounds, you must begin with the premise that *anything* is possible; but Mr. Specter and the Commission overlooked one important ingredient. The original, pristine weight of this bullet before it was fired was approximately 160 to 161 grains. The weight of the bullet recovered on the stretcher in Parkland Hospital [Commission Exhibit 399] was reported by the Commission as 158.6 grains. This bullet wasn't distorted in any way. I cannot accept the premise that this bullet thrashed around in all that bony tissue and lost only 1.4 to 2.4 grains of its original weight. I cannot believe, either, that this bullet is going to emerge miraculously unscathed, without any deformity, and with its lands and grooves intact.[127] (Emphasis in the original.)

Dr. Wecht discussed the single-bullet theory on CBS-TV on June 26, 1967.[128] He told Dan Rather that "in medicine we always fall back upon the trite expression: we never like to say that something is impossible. I would say that it is highly improbable [that Commission Exhibit 399 hit both men]. I would hesitate, really, to say that it is absolutely 100% impossible, but it is highly improbable. Another one, you see—another one of the very many highly improbables that we are asked to accept by the Warren Commission if we are to accept the validity of their full Report."[129]

Conclusion

THIS is the way a society reacts to a great event that bears within it elements sufficient to expose the full extent of its own stresses and strains. A false decree was issued with such trappings and in such circumstances that it was to be accepted—or the stability of the society was to be brought into question. Those at the controls had evidently decided that their commitment to the untrue explanation was absolute. Representatives of the Congress, the Senate, the judiciary and the various Federal police agencies were induced to become involved.

Liberals—who have by definition questioned the premise upon which the organized artifacts rest and who, alerted by the insight that such probings make visible—became frightened by what they might see. Since their class predominates in what are said to be the responsible media, their reaction was decisive to the Government's early effort to secure broad acceptance for its document. It was not *The National Review* that condemned the critics out of hand and demanded acceptance of the Report; it was the New York *Post*, in a concerted campaign of imprecation replete with editorials, Herblock cartoons and Max Lerner columns. It was not Barry Goldwater and William Buckley, but I. F. Stone and David Susskind. Neither was it the Daughters of the American Revolution that sought to interfere with the investigation of the New Orleans District Attorney; it was the American Civil Liberties Union, which was itself in large part responsible for the inability of Oswald to meet with counsel prior to his death.

In the face of what appeared to be organized hostility but which was certain hostility nevertheless, the dissenters insisted upon being heard. When their voices ended forever the great silence and revealed the Report to be a discredited document to the satisfaction of most Americans, there was but a modest disclaimer, one lacking in a sense of urgency, and one indulged in primarily by those associated with the manufacture of the original document, who stated that their own integrity, having been invested in it, was then at stake. Only when it appeared that an investigation was under way which would not content itself with stating that the Report was in error but that insisted the culpable should be caught and punished was a sense of immediacy, indeed of desperation, engaged.

Engaged also in an unprecedented fashion was almost the entire vast communications industry of America. As we have seen, no segment of society failed to contribute to the myth of the lone assassin. The learned law societies, the academicians, the networks, the newspapers and news magazines, the press services and the police were all well represented. The critics, at first ignored, then denounced, were later to be heeded and accepted, only to be reviled again. One critic complained that Jim Garrison was responsible for the low esteem in which the critics were then being held. Yet Garrison was as responsible for the illness as is a diagnostician who states that he has discovered a fatal disease. The news is universally unpleasant and one may hope that the analysis is erroneous, but the diagnosis cannot be said to have caused the illness.

The society had failed in its efforts to emulate dialectical theology—the truth of the President's death may be unknown to man except as the result of the quasi-divine grace of revelation through the Chief Justice and other leaders. More practical answers to the questions were required. The questions having been raised, there were but two possible responses: the critics had raised questions that deserved serious consideration; or the critics must be dismissed at all costs.

The powerful, as we have seen, have chosen the latter course. The term they most often apply to the doubters is "scavengers." The critics are avaricious; their motivation is greed. This is not so; but even were it so, it would not constitute a fair reply to the serious questions. Indeed, it would constitute no reply at all. But the matter, having been raised so regularly, deserves answer if for no other reason than its persistent presence. He who has read this far and who is acquainted with the gradual and painful stages which led to my full involvement in this matter is in a position to judge my motivation in context.

As for the others—and here I include Mrs. Joseph Field, Penn Jones, Jr., Raymond Marcus, Mrs. Shirley Martin and her family, Sylvia Meagher and Vincent Salandria, all of whom have felt the sting of that charge—they constitute the most devoted and selfless group of men and women I have known. I should be surprised if the combined income derived from their writings on the subject even begins to approach their expenses. Huge sums have been realized by one author: William Manchester, it is said, was transformed into a millionaire. Yet despite that magnificent income, he has not been characterized as a scavenger, no doubt because he supports the Commission's conclusions. Is the term of derogation not seen then to be applied with wondrous inequality to those who have not benefited, while he who has benefited, and knew that he would, is spared? I do not question Manchester's motives, for they disinterest me and I should have no way of satisfying my curiosity did they not. I merely marvel at the discretion of the defenders that exempts the author who earned more from the serialization of his work in one magazine than did all the critics for all the world rights to all their works.

Arlen Specter has again proven that man does not live by bread alone. According to James C. Crumlish, the former District Attorney of Philadelphia and the man who released his young assistant so that he could work as a junior lawyer for the Commission, Specter returned to Philadelphia filled with a sense of his place in history.[1] Said Crumlish of Specter, "He gave me the impression that other people were unwilling or unable to operate the investigation, and that he was running the whole thing."[2] Crumlish added that Specter was "uneasy, uncertain and without complete control of his thinking."[3]

He said that Specter told him, "I don't think anyone will ever believe what we've reported."[4] Specter then changed his political affiliation and ran for the office of district attorney. Although now that the single-bullet theory is widely rejected, Specter is modest about his role in creating it, his political brochures at that time boasted that he had originated the theory.[5] The story of a district attorney who achieves fame, fortune and political power by prosecuting and convicting criminals is part of the story of the big cities in America. Specter, who shortly after his election as District Attorney of Philadelphia became the Republican candidate for Mayor as well, modified the script in one respect—the man he helped to convict was already dead. As is the case with Manchester, Specter has escaped questions directed to his motivation, certainly the charge of scavenger.

As we have observed, the evidence permits a response other than the cry for the critics' heads. For those men of integrity previously more committed to the Report than caution would warrant, a sober call for re-examination of the evidence must constitute a painful although necessary ordeal. The heroes of journalism are not those who crusade for the popular, who attack the weak and who are awarded the much-sought prizes. They are those who calmly assess the evidence; those who do not permit a sense of self to interfere with their professional obligations. They are too few; they are a disappearing breed, if ever they did exist in large numbers.

One such man is Harrison E. Salisbury, an executive and veteran reporter at the *New York Times*. For the first week following the assassination, he directed the news coverage for the *Times*.[6] Subsequently, he wrote an introduction to an edition of the Warren Report.[7] *Rush to Judgment* closed with what could be called a rebuke to Salisbury.[8] This work closes with a salute to him. He has examined the critical works and has concluded that they reveal that the Warren Report cannot be the final word.[9] He has endorsed the proposal that there be an official investigation into the Warren Commission's work.[10] It has been reported that he sought, unfortunately in vain, for an independent inquiry to be conducted by the *New York Times*. In other efforts too, Salisbury has been frank, and thus rendered ineligible for the prize. Yet the prize that eludes us all is an America quite well again, one eager to learn the terrible verities that are our present before they become our history. If they are permitted to fade into the past, without redress, our chance for redemption becomes the more remote.

APPENDIX I*
Letter to Earl Warren (December 17, 1963)

Commission Exhibit No. 2033

MARK LANE
ATTORNEY AT LAW
654 MADISON AVE.
NEW YORK 21, N. Y.
TEMPLETON 8-1000

Rec'd. Pres. Comm
DEC 24 1963

December 17, 1963

Hon. Earl Warren
Justice of the United States Supreme Court
Washington, D.C.

Dear Justice Warren:

As an attorney who witnessed the destruction of almost every right ordinarily available to a person charged with the commission of a crime in the matter of the arrest, interrogation and subsequent killing of Mr. Lee H. Oswald, I felt constrained to comment upon the serious breaches of law and ethics that took place. Accordingly, I drafted an article for publication dealing with these and other related questions. It has been suggested that I submit that article to you for whatever use you may be able to make of it. I submit it herewith.

May I respectfully request that your Commission give consideration to the appointment of defense counsel in order that in your inquiry an advocate zealously protecting his client's rights may be present; an advocate who may examine documents and cross examine witnesses. It would be appropriate, I suggest, that Mr. Oswald, from whom every legal right was stripped, be accorded counsel who may participate with the single purpose of representing the rights of the accused.

Respectfully,

Mark Lane

ML/jo

COMMISSION EXHIBIT NO. 2033

*See page 18.

APPENDIX II*

Letter from J. Lee Rankin (December 30, 1963)

CNS/sw

Dec. 30, 1963

Mark Lane, Esquire
654 Madison Avenue
New York 21, New York

Dear Mr. Lane:

The Commission has asked me to thank you for your letter of December 24, 1963 and the enclosed brief relating to Lee Harvey Oswald. The Commission appreciated your making this material available to it, and in order to minimize any inconvenience to you, we have made a copy and are returning herewith the original to you.

As you know, President Johnson on November 29, 1963 established this Commission to study and report upon all the facts and circumstances relating to the assassination of the late President, John F. Kennedy, and the subsequent killing of the man charged with the assassination. The views contained in your letter will be given appropriate consideration by the Commission prior to the preparation of any final report. I can assure you that the Commission and its staff are determined to implement President Johnson's directive as completely and quickly as possible.

Thank you for your thoughtfulness in writing to the Commission.

Sincerely,

Enclosure

J. Lee Rankin
General Counsel

COMMISSION EXHIBIT No. 2033—Continued

* See page 18.

APPENDIX III*

Letter from J. Lee Rankin (January 23, 1964)

~~Investigation and Evidence~~

LANE Mark
JAN 23 1964

JLR:HPW:al
1/22/64

Mr. Mark Lane
164 West 79th Street
New York, New York

Dear Mr. Lane:

On behalf of the Commission I wish to acknowledge receipt of your recent telegram informing the Commission that you have been retained by Mrs. Marguerite C. Oswald to represent her deceased son.

As you know, the Commission is interested in developing all the pertinent facts relating to the assassination of President John F. Kennedy and the subsequent killing of Lee Harvey Oswald by Jack L. Ruby. Any documentary material which Mrs. Marguerite C. Oswald or others wish to submit to the Commission will receive careful consideration.

The Commission does not believe that it would be useful or desirable to permit an attorney representing Lee Harvey Oswald to have access to the investigative materials within the possession of the Commission or to participate in any hearings to be conducted by the Commission. I can assure you that every effort will be made to ascertain the facts regarding Lee Harvey Oswald's implication in the assassination of President Kennedy as accurately and fairly as possible.

Sincerely,

J. Lee Rankin
General Counsel

Commission Exhibit No. 2033—Continued

* See page 18.

APPENDIX IV*

Graph Showing Speed of Presidential Limousine According to Commission's Evidence

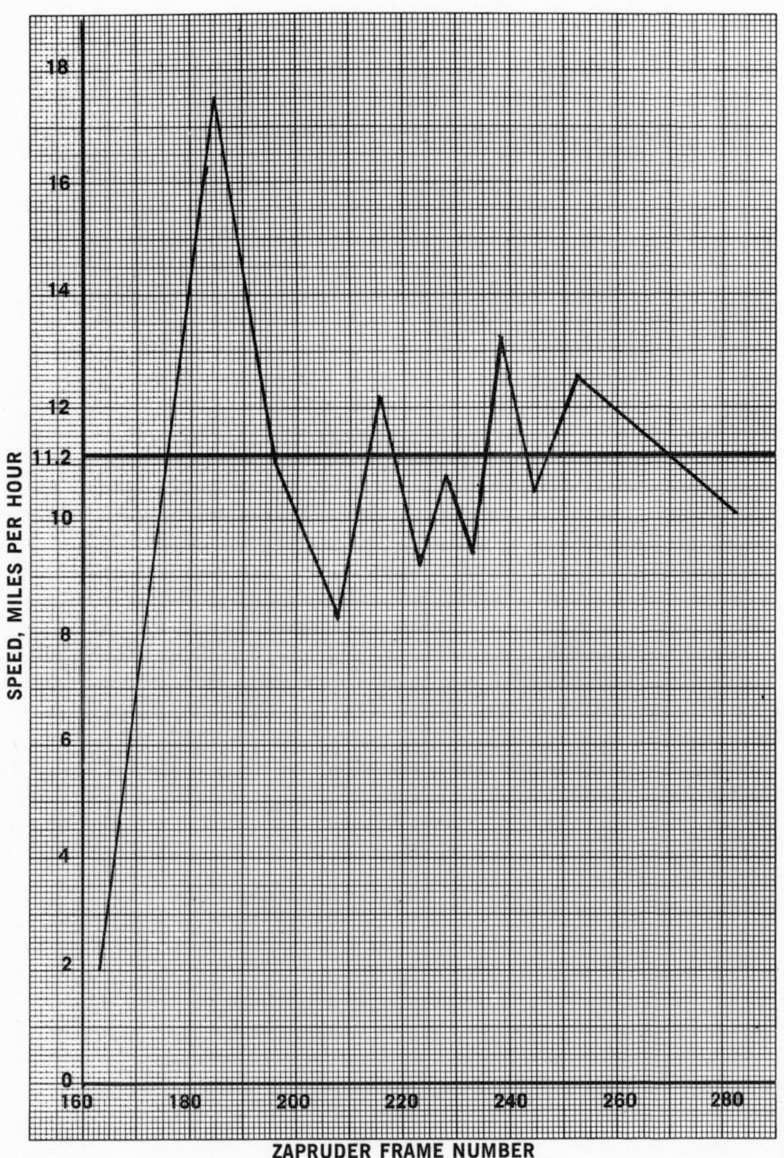

* See page 103.

APPENDIX V*

Letter from Leon R. Brooks, CBS (July 6, 1967)

CBS

Columbia Broadcasting System, Inc.
51 West 52 Street
New York, New York 10019
(212) 765-4321

Leon R. Brooks
Vice President and General Counsel

Dear Mr. Lane:

This is in reply to your telegram of June 28, 1967 to Dr. Stanton, requesting "equal time" to respond to what you describe as "an entirely untruthful and personal attack upon me by CBS," in the broadcast, A CBS NEWS INQUIRY: "The Warren Report, Part IV."

That broadcast was the last of a four-part detailed examination of major questions raised by critics of the Warren Commission Report on the assassination of President John F. Kennedy, reviewing the Commission's findings about events before, during and after the assassination of the President and the murder of Lee Harvey Oswald, and also criticisms of these findings.

Included in the criticisms of the Warren Report considered by the broadcast were questions raised by you. Reference to your position was included in all four broadcasts and you personally appeared on two of the broadcasts, including the one of June 28. Thus, in Part I, reference was made to your challenge of the photograph of Lee Harvey Oswald which showed him with a Mannlicker-Carcano rifle. In Part II reference was made to your book, "Rush To Judgment" and your statement that 58 of the 90 people who were asked about the shots thought they came from the grassy knoll. In Part III, you appeared and were heard to explain your theory that five bullets were fired at President Kennedy from two directions and that, therefore, a conspiracy was involved. In Part IV, reference was made to your book and motion picture of the same name, and you appeared and were heard to say as to the Warren Report, that "there is not an important conclusion which can be supported by the facts and -- this is the problem."

In the course of its Inquiry, CBS News sifted the mass of evidence considered by the Commission and the critics, conducted its own experiments, and conducted separate interviews of certain witnesses, critics and Commission members. In reaching its own conclusions as to the persuasiveness of the Warren Report and of its critics, CBS News agreed with the Report's main findings and, at the same time, agreed that

* See page 119.

certain of the criticisms were not frivolous. For instance, CBS News concluded that the Warren Commission should have insisted on production of the autopsy x-rays and photographs.

Of course, in reaching its conclusion, CBS News differed with some of your criticisms, including some that you expressed on the broadcasts. However, to do so is not to engage in an "untruthful or personal attack." We have reviewed the broadcasts since receipt of your telegram. We find no basis for any charge that the significant viewpoints on any controversial issues of substance were not given in the broadcasts, or that anyone was personally attacked. Accordingly we will not grant your request for time to respond.

Very truly yours,

Leon Brooks

Mr. Mark Lane
860 Lathrop Drive
Stanford, California

July 6, 1967

APPENDIX VI*

Letter from William R. McAndrew, NBC (July 17, 1967)

NBC NEWS

A DIVISION OF NATIONAL BROADCASTING COMPANY, INC.

THIRTY ROCKEFELLER PLAZA, NEW YORK, N.Y. 10020, CIRCLE 7-8300

WILLIAM R. McANDREW
President

July 17, 1967

Mr. Mark Lane
Eight Sixty Lathrop Drive
Stanford University
Stanford, California 94305

Dear Mr. Lane:

I am in receipt of your letter of July 1, 1967, requesting the opportunity to view the unedited interviews used on the program, "The JFK Conspiracy: The Case of Jim Garrison."

As you know, the program was primarily a report on an examination of the methods used by the New Orleans District Attorney's office in its investigation of an alleged conspiracy to assassinate President John F. Kennedy. The statement at the close of the broadcast to which you refer reads: "The filmed testimony you have seen was edited. The unedited film is available to any authorized investigator with a legitimate reason to see it."

NBC News does not generally release to the public material obtained in the course of preparing news programs if such material is not actually broadcast. In this instance, in light of the legitimate interest which official agencies might have in the portion of the interviews not broadcast, we concluded we would provide authorized investigators an opportunity to view the unedited interviews. This offer was made solely for the use of investigators acting on behalf of such agencies and while we can understand your concern and interest, we believe we should continue to confine our offer to official investigations.

Best wishes.

Sincerely yours,

William R. McAndrew

*See page 120.

APPENDIX VII*

Cablegram from Naval Attaché, American Embassy, Moscow (November 3, 1959)

NAVAL MESSAGE — CONFIDENTIAL — NAVY DEPARTMENT

RELEASED BY	DRAFTED BY	EXT NO	COPY NR.

DATE		ROUTED BY	CHECKED BY
3 NOVEMBER 59		HAMNER	RE/HEDIKER

2090

(DATE/TIME GROUP (GCT))

FROM: ALUSNA MOSCOW

TO: CNO

INFO: — Commission Exhibit No. 917 — X-75

PRECEDENCE (ACT) (INFO): FLASH; EMERGENCY; OPERATIONAL IMMEDIATE; PRIORITY; ROUTINE; DEFERRED

ATTENTION INVITED TO AMEMB MOSCOW DISPATCHES 234 DTD 2 NOVEMBER AND 224 DTD 26 OCTOBER CONCERNING THE RENUNCIATION OF US CITIZENSHIP AND REQUEST FOR SOVIET CITIZENSHIP BY LEE HARVEY OSWALD FORMER MARINE AND OSWALD STATED HE WAS RADAR OPERATOR IN MARCORPS AND HAS OFFERED TO FURNISH SOVIETS INFO HE POSSESSES ON US RADAR.

92....ACT

06..60..61..63..IP..BFR..FLAGPLOT..

ADD:FBI..STATE..CIA..CMC..Ø9M..IMMIGRATION NATURALIZATION SERVICE
PER:92 11/Ø4/59/EW/

REPRODUCTION OF THIS DOCUMENT IN WHOLE OR IN PART IS PROHIBITED EXCEPT WITH PERMISSION OF THE ISSUING OFFICE.

CONFIDENTIAL
(When filled in)

OPNAV FORM-2110-4
(REV. 1-58)
DEPT. USE ONLY

PAGE 1 OF 1

A Paraphrase not required except prior to Category "B" encryption. Physically remove all internal references by date-time group prior to declassification.

COMMISSION EXHIBIT 917

* See page 128.

APPENDIX VIII*

Secret Service Report on Interview with Alonzo Hudkins (December 16-17, 1963)

Form No. 1578 (Revised) MEMORANDUM REPORT (7-1-50)

767

UNITED STATES SECRET SERVICE
TREASURY DEPARTMENT

ORIGIN Field | OFFICE Houston, Texas | FILE NO. CO-2-34,030

TYPE OF CASE	STATUS	TITLE OR CAPTION
Protective Research	Closed - Houston (this matter)	Assassination of President Kennedy Lee Harvey Oswald
INVESTIGATION MADE AT: Houston, Texas	PERIOD COVERED: 12/16-17/63	
INVESTIGATION MADE BY: SAIC Lane Bertram		

DETAILS

SYNOPSIS

Interview with Houston Post reporter Alonso H. Hudkins III. He states Oswald reported to be on FBI payroll as an informant, and other information.

DETAILS OF INVESTIGATION

On December 16, Alonso H. Hudkins, reporter, Houston Post, called the office and advised that he was of the opinion that Jack Rubenstein's roommate, George Senator, could possibly have some connection with the murder of Lee Harvey Oswald. He did not appear to have any particular reason for making this suggestion other than when reinterviewed on December 17 he stated that Ruby had a brother and a nephew who formerly worked for Jimmy Hoffa in Detroit, Michigan and he stated it was a "wild guess" that the Hoffa organization could be behind the assassination.

On December 17, Mr. Hudkins advised that he had just returned from a weekend in Dallas, during which time he talked to Allen Sweatt, Chief Criminal Division, Sheriff's Office, Dallas; Chief Sweatt mentioned that it was his opinion that Lee Harvey Oswald was being paid $200 a month by the FBI as an informant in connection with their subversive investigations. He furnished the alleged informant number assigned to Oswald by the FBI as "S172".

Hudkins stated it is significant to him that attorney Milton [Melvin] L. Belli of San Francisco, attorney representing Jack Rubenstein, was listed as an east coast associate on stationery of attorney Ept [Abt] who was the first attorney Lee Harvey Oswald asked to represent him.

He states that Chief Deputy Sheriff Allen Sweatt has copies of this stationery. Sweatt censors all of Ruby's mail.

DISTRIBUTION	COPIES	REPORT MADE BY	DATE
Chief Dallas Houston	Orig & 1 2-cc 1-cc	SPECIAL AGENT	
LB/mts		APPROVED: Lane Bertram, SPECIAL AGENT IN CHARGE	1/3/64

(CONTINUE ON PLAIN PAPER) U. S. GOVERNMENT PRINTING OFFICE 16—61800-1

* See pages 175-176.

APPENDIX IX*

Schematic Drawing Made at Request of Autopsy Surgeons

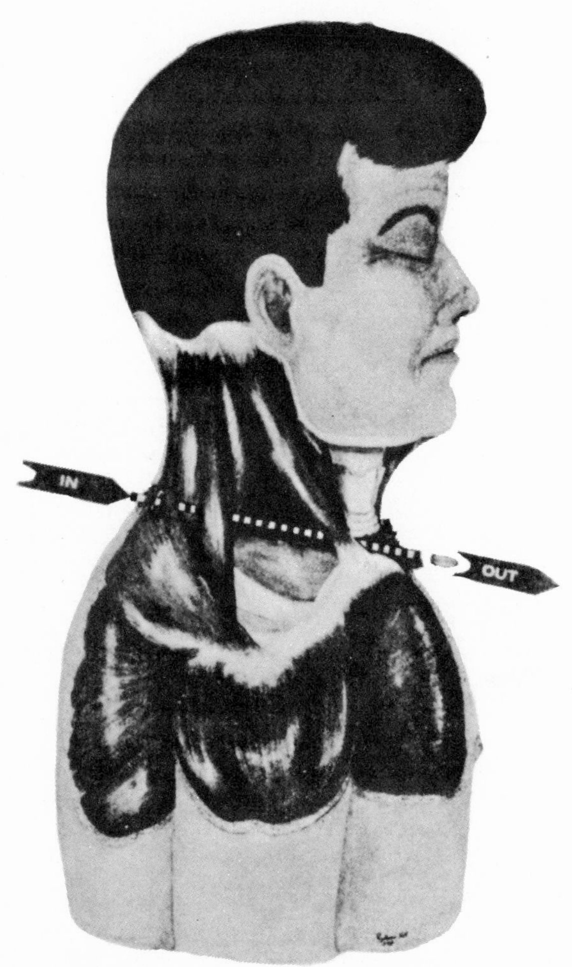

One of the autopsy surgeons, Commander James J. Humes, believed that visual aids were necessary to explain the President's wounds to the Commissioners. The Commission examined three drawings made by an illustrator, one of which is reproduced above, but failed to examine the autopsy photographs and X-rays.

* See page 222.

APPENDIX X*

Autopsy Descriptive Sheet Prepared by Commander James J. Humes

AUTOPSY DESCRIPTIVE SHEET NMS PATH-8 (1-63)

AUTOPSY

NMS # A 63 272 DATE 11-22-63 HR. STARTED________ HR. COMPLETED________

NAME: ________________ RANK/RATE ________

DATE/HOUR EXPIRED: ________ WARD ________ DIAGNOSIS ________

PHYSICAL DESCRIPTION: RACE: ________ Obtain following on babies only:

Height______ in. Weight______ lb. Color Hair______ Crown-rump ______ in. Crown-heel ______ in.

Color eyes______ Pupils: Rt______ mm, Lt.______ mm Circumference: Head______ in., Chest______ in. Abd.______ in.

WEIGHTS: (Grams, unless otherwise specified)

LUNG, RT. 320	KIDNEY, RT. 13?5	ADRENALS, RT. ______
LUNG, LT. 290	KIDNEY, LT. 140	ADRENALS, LT. ______
BRAIN ______	LIVER 150	PANCREAS ______
SPLEEN 90	HEART 350	THYROID ______
THYMUS ______	TESTIS ______	OVARY ______

HEART MEASUREMENTS: A 7.5 cm. P 7 cm. T 12 cm. M 10 cm.

LVM 1.5 cm. RVM .4 cm.

NOTES:

4 cm ; 4 cm ; 6.5 cm ; 3 cm ; 3 cm ; 2 cm ; 3 cm ; 3 cm

ragged, slanting 15 x 6 mm

7 x 4 mm

14 cm from rt acromion

14 cm below tip of rt mastoid process

Scar 15 cm long 2 cm wide

3 cm

Pathologist

COMMISSION EXHIBIT 397—Continued

* See page 222.

APPENDIX XI *
President Kennedy's Shirt and Tie, FBI Exhibit 60

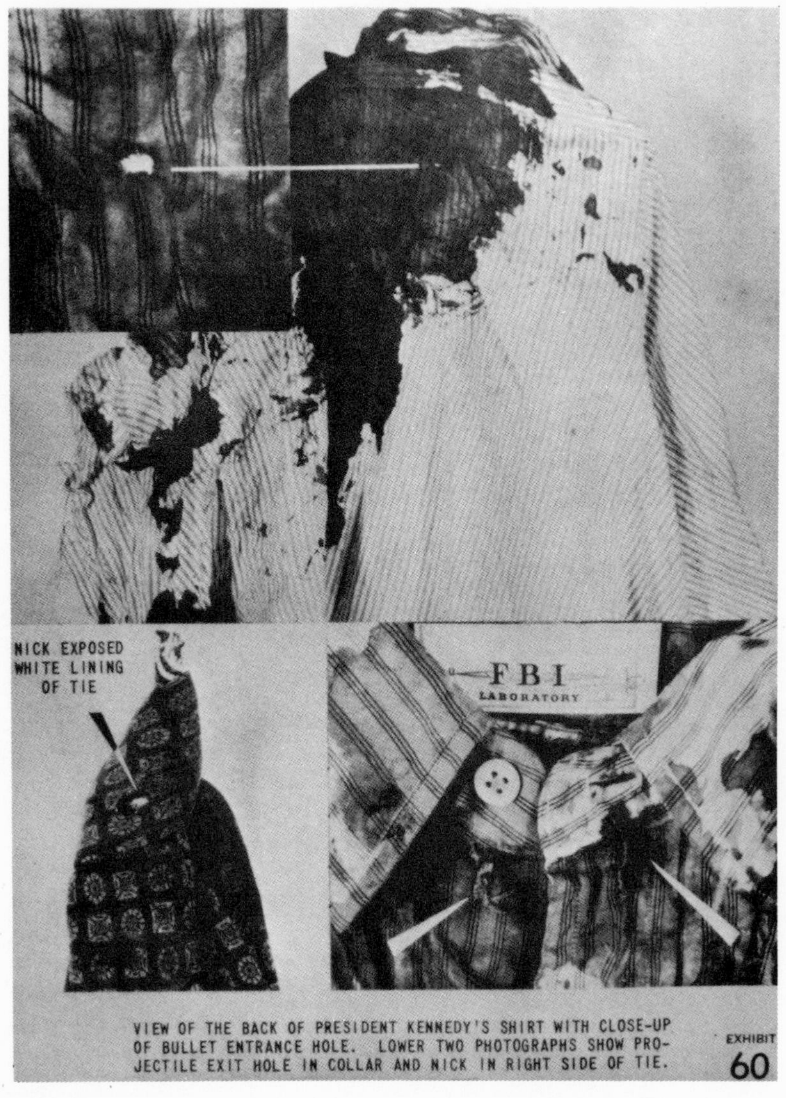

VIEW OF THE BACK OF PRESIDENT KENNEDY'S SHIRT WITH CLOSE-UP OF BULLET ENTRANCE HOLE. LOWER TWO PHOTOGRAPHS SHOW PROJECTILE EXIT HOLE IN COLLAR AND NICK IN RIGHT SIDE OF TIE.

*See page 222.

Citations

The following abbreviated forms of citation are used in the listings below:

References to the *Report of the President's Commission on the Assassination of President John F. Kennedy* (Warren Commission Report) are indicated by the capital letters "WCR" and the page number (e.g., WCR, 107). All such references are to the edition published by the U.S. Government Printing Office (1964).

References to the testimony and exhibits in the 26 volumes of *Hearings Before the President's Commission on the Assassination of President Kennedy* (U.S. Government Printing Office, 1964) are cited as follows: the volume numbers in roman numerals and the page numbers in arabic (e.g., XVII, 357).

References to material not published by the Commission but stored in the National Archives as Commission Documents (Basic Source Materials in Possession of Commission) are cited as "CD" followed by the National Archives file number (e.g., CD 7).

References to *Rush to Judgment* by Mark Lane are cited as "RTJ" followed by the page of the edition published by Holt, Rinehart and Winston (New York, 1966), with the page of the edition published by Fawcett Publications (New York, 1967) in parentheses [e.g., RTJ, 176 (149)].

References to "CBS News Inquiry: 'The Warren Report' " as broadcast over the CBS television network, June 25–28, 1967, are cited as "CBS" followed by the part in roman numerals (I–June 25; II–June 26; III–June 27; IV–June 28) and the page of the official transcript published by the Columbia Broadcasting System, Inc. (New York, 1967) in arabic (e.g., CBS, III, 8).

References to the Associated Press article entitled "The Lingering Shadow: The Warren Report and Its Critics," released June 1967 (and published, e.g., in the San Francisco *Examiner* on June 26, 1967) are cited as "AP" followed by the chapter number in roman numerals (e.g., AP, IV).

References to *The Death of a President* by William Manchester (Harper & Row, New York, 1967) are cited as "Manchester" followed by the page (e.g., Manchester, 93).

References to *The Truth about the Assassination* by Charles Roberts

(Grosset & Dunlap, New York, 1967) are cited as "Roberts" followed by the page (e.g., Roberts, 14).

References to *The Scavengers and Critics of the Warren Report* by Richard Warren Lewis, based on an investigation by Lawrence Schiller (Dell Publishing Co., New York, 1967) are cited as "Lewis & Schiller" followed by the page (e.g., Lewis & Schiller, 21).

Introduction

1. CBS, IV, 20.
2. See, e.g., Harris poll reported in the New York *Herald Tribune* (Paris edition), October 4, 1966; Gallup poll reported in the New York *World Journal Tribune,* January 11, 1967; Harris poll reported in the New York *Post,* May 29, 1967.
3. CBS, IV, 20.
4. RTJ, 398 (340).

PART ONE: THE DISSENT

I • The Death

1 THE FIRST QUESTION

1. *National Guardian,* "A *Guardian* Special: A Lawyer's Brief," December 19, 1963.
2. *The New Republic,* December 21, 1963.
3. *New York Times,* December 19, 1963.
4. *National Guardian,* "A *Guardian* Special: A Lawyer's Brief," December 19, 1963.
5. *Ibid.*

2 THE CALL

1. CBS, IV, 9.

3 REPORTS FROM DALLAS

1. VI, 205-223; XIX, 479, 487; XXII, 838-839; XXV, 853-854.
2. See XXII, 837-838; interview of Charles Brehm by Mark Lane, filmed and tape-recorded in Dallas, March 28, 1966.
3. See *ibid.;* XXII, 837-838.
4. See XIX, 488, 490; XXII, 842-843.
5. VI, 212; see *infra,* p. 187.
6. VI, 207; WCR, 19.
7. XIX, 535-536; XXII, 838.
8. Interview of Charles Brehm by Mark Lane, tape-recorded in Dallas, March 28, 1966.
9. See XIX, 488, 490.
10. II, 42-43; VI, 205-223.
11. WCR, 484, 493.
12. See *id.* at 641.
13. CBS, IV, 16-18.
14. See, e.g., *New York Times,* December 6, 1963.
15. See RTJ, 307-323 (259-273).
16. *New York Times,* November 25, 1963.
17. WCR, 560.
18. November 17, 1966.
19. See Index to Basic Source Materials in possession of Commission, National Archives.
20. See *infra,* pp. 144-145.
21. *New York Times,* November 5, 1966.

II • The Great Silence

4 THE POLICE ARE INTERESTED—IN ME

1. XXIV, 444.
2. *Ibid.*
3. *Id.* at 445.
4. See *ibid.*
5. *Ibid.*
6. *Ibid.*
7. WCR, xiv-xv; see RTJ, 378-380 (321-323).
8. Gerald R. Ford, *Portrait of the Assassin* (New York, 1965), 436.
9. New York *Post,* February 27, 1964.
10. *Ibid.*
11. John Kaplan, "The Assassins," *The American Scholar,* XXXVI (1967), 273.
12. *Ibid.*
13. *Yale Law Journal,* LXXVI (1967), 582.
14. II, 32-33.
15. See *id.* at 56-57.
16. *Id.* at 57.
17. *Ibid.*
18. *Id.* at 57-58.
19. *Id.* at 58.
20. *Ibid.*
21. *Id.* at 60.
22. XXV, 720.
23. *Id.* at 725-726.
24. *Ibid.*
25. *Id.* at 727.
26. V, 555.
27. *Id.* at 556.
28. *Ibid.*
29. *Ibid.*
30. *Ibid.*
31. *Id.* at 556-560.
32. *Id.* at 560.
33. *Id.* at 546-561.
34. *Yale Law Journal,* 582-583.
35. *Id.* at 583.

5 BANNED FOR LIFE

1. Edward Jay Epstein, *Inquest* (New York, 1966), 135.
2. *Ibid.*
3. XXV, 663-669.
4. See *ibid.*
5. See *id.* at 667.
6. *Id.* at 668.
7. *Ibid.*
8. *New York Times,* November 25, 1966.

6 THE DEBATES THAT NEVER OCCURRED

1. Melvin M. Belli, *Dallas Justice* (New York, 1964).
2. *Id.* at 79-80.
3. October 9, 1964.
4. WCR, 235.
5. *People's World,* October 17, 1964.
6. *Ibid.*
7. *Ibid.*
8. *Ibid.*
9. *Ibid.*
10. Manhattan Center, New York City, October 19, 1964.

III • The Response

7 THE MAKING OF A BOOK

1. CD 1, Vol. 1, p. 18
2. See RTJ, 63-66 (51-54).
3. VII, 106-109.
4. *Id.* at 106-107.
5. RTJ, 35 (27).
6. VII, 109.
7. *Id.* at 107.

9 THE MAKING OF A FILM

1. See VI, 239-248.
2. See XV, 388-396.
3. See II, 430-517; III, 1-140.
4. See XIV, 429-487; XV, 321-347.
5. See XI, 224-240.
6. See RTJ, 193-194 (164-165).
7. See VI, 444-454.
8. *Ibid.*
9. WCR, 368-369.
10. *Id.* at 499.
11. See VII, 552-558.
12. XIX, 492.
13. WCR, 495; see RTJ, 32-33 (24-25).
14. See VI, 284-289.
15. *Id.* at 284.
16. *Id.* at 287-288.
17. Interview of Lee Bowers by Mark Lane, filmed and tape-recorded in Arlington, Texas, March 31, 1966.
18. *Ibid.;* see VI, 288.
19. See XII, 225-234.
20. See *infra*, pp. 137-143.
21. *New York Times*, June 3, 1967.
22. *Ibid.*
23. New York *Post*, June 3, 1967.
24. *Ibid.*
25. *Ibid.*
26. *New Yorker*, June 17, 1967.
27. *Ibid.*
28. New York *Daily News*, June 3, 1967.
29. *Ibid.*
30. "The Death of Kennedy," BBC-2, January 29, 1967.

10 A WORLD PREMIERE

1. "The Death of Kennedy," BBC-2, January 29, 1967.
2. *Commentary*, October 1966.
3. WCR, 76.
4. See VI, 244.

PART TWO: THE DEFENDERS

I • CBS News Inquiry

11 TWO DOCUMENTARIES

1. CBS, I, 1-21; CBS, II, 1-20; CBS, III, 1-20; CBS, IV, 1-20.
2. CBS News press release, June 13, 1967.
3. *New York Times*, September 27, 1964.
4. *Variety*, March 29, 1967.
5. *The Random House Dictionary of the English Language* (New York, 1966), p. 937.
6. Docent Hans Villius, University of Stockholm.
7. Edward Jay Epstein, *Inquest* (New York, 1966), 136.
8. *Ibid.*
9. RTJ, 12 (14).
10. *Ibid.*
11. *Ibid.*
12. *Ibid.*
13. WCR, 89-90.
14. CD 678; CBS, II, 9.
15. RTJ, 53 (43).
16. *Ibid.*
17. See, e.g., Roberts, 40-41, 99.
18. CD 678.
19. *Ibid.*
20. CBS, II, 9.
21. *Id.* at IV, 18.
22. *TV Guide*, July 29, 1967.
23. *Newsweek*, July 3, 1967.
24. CBS News press release, June 29, 1967.
25. WCR, 79.
26. See *infra*, pp. 90-92.
27. *TV Guide*, June 24, 1967.
28. Letter from Merrill Panitt to Mark Lane, July 6, 1967.
29. CBS, II, 18-19.
30. *Id.* at III, 17-18; *id.* at IV, 2-3.
31. *Id.* at IV, 8-9.
32. *Id.* at III, 9-17.
33. Boston *Traveler*, April 19, 1967.
34. Letter from Raymond J. Marcus to Leslie Midgley, June 19, 1967.
35. *New York Times*, June 29, 1967.
36. Raymond J. Marcus, *The Bastard Bullet* (Los Angeles, 1966).
37. XIX, 487; XXII, 838-839.
38. See WCR, 108.
39. Letter from Raymond J. Marcus to Leslie Midgley, June 19, 1967.
40. *Ibid.*
41. *Ibid.;* letter from Midgley to Marcus, June 23, 1967.
42. Letter from Marcus to Midgley, June 19, 1967.
43. Letter from Midgley to Marcus, June 23, 1967.
44. This information is contained in an original script prepared by *True* magazine during August 1967 for an article tentatively entitled "New Light on the Second Assassin," to be published subsequently.
45. *New York Times*, June 25, 1967.
46. *Ibid.*

12 DID OSWALD SHOOT THE PRESIDENT?

1. CBS, I, 3-21.
2. *Id.* at I, 3.
3. *Ibid.*
4. *Id.* at I, 4.
5. *Ibid.*
6. *Ibid.*
7. WCR, 127.
8. IV, 281.
9. CBS, I, 4.
10. *Ibid.;* CBS News press release, June 13, 1967.
11. CBS, I, 4.
12. WCR, 127.
13. *Ibid.*
14. See, e.g., New York *World Journal Tribune*, January 22, 1967.
15. CBS, III, 7.
16. *Id.* at III, 7-9.
17. *Id.* at III, 8.
18. *Id.* at III, 7-8.
19. CBS News press release, June 13, 1967.
20. CBS, III, 7-8.
21. *Id.* at III, 8.
22. *Ibid.*
23. *Ibid.*
24. *Id.* at III, 8-9.
25. *Id.* at III, 8.
26. *Newsweek*, March 27, 1967.
27. *Ibid.*
28. *Ibid.*
29. CBS, III, 9.
30. *Id.* at I, 5-6; WCR, 129-137.
31. II, 210-245.
32. *Id.* at 245-251.
33. WCR, 131, 133-134.
34. *Id.* at 133.
35. II, 210-251; RTJ, 142-147 (119-124).
36. CBS, I, 5-6.
37. *Id.* at I, 5.
38. *Ibid.*
39. XXIV, 408-409.
40. *Id.* at 409.
41. *Id.* at 407-408.
42. *Id.* at 408.
43. *Id.* at 407-409.
44. II, 228, 239, 243.
45. *Id.* at 243.
46. CBS, I, 5-6.
47. *Id.* at I, 6.
48. *Ibid.*

49. *Ibid.;* RTJ, 142-147 (119-124).
50. II, 228, 239, 243.
51. CBS, I, 5-6; VI, 376-377.
52. See RTJ, 146 (123).
53. CBS, I, 5-6.
54. RTJ, 142 (120).
55. *Id.* at 142-143 (120).
56. WCR, 129-130.
57. CBS, I, 5.
58. *Ibid.*
59. *Id.* at I, 6.
60. *Id.* at I, 6-7.
61. *Id.* at I, 6-9.
62. *Id.* at I, 7.
63. *Ibid.*
64. CD 5, p. 41.
65. *Ibid.*
66. XXII, 635.
67. CD 5, p. 41.
68. CBS, I, 9.
69. WCR, 63, 144.
70. XXI, 781.
71. *Ibid.*
72. WCR, 147, 149; RTJ, 353-356 (299-302).
73. *Ibid.*
74. CBS, I, 6-9.
75. *Id.* at I, 9; WCR, 149-154.
76. *Id.* at 149-151.
77. *Id.* at 5.
78. *Id.* at 5-6, 149-151.
79. *Id.* at 152-153.
80. *Ibid.;* XXVI, 679.
81. *Ibid.*
82. III, 251.
83. XXVI, 679.
84. *Ibid.*
85. *Ibid.*
86. *Ibid.*
87. See CBS, III, 2.
88. *Id.* at I, 9.
89. *Ibid.*
90. *Id.* at I, 9, 11.
91. *Id.* at I, 9-11.
92. See RTJ, 93 (77); XXVI, 811.
93. WCR, 63-64; II, 190-210; III, 140-161, 184-186, 211.
94. CBS, I, 9-11.
95. *Id.* at I, 9-10.
96. VII, 105-109.
97. III, 291-295.
98. WCR, 79; XIX, 508-509; XXIV, 228.
99. *Ibid.;* VII, 109.
100. WCR, 79, 81, 235, 645.
101. *Ibid.*
102. CBS, I, 9-10.
103. *Ibid.*
104. *Id.* at I, 10.
105. *Id.* at I, 9-10.
106. *Ibid.;* VII, 105-109.

13 CBS IS CONTENTED

1. CBS, III, 1-7.
2. *Id.* at II, 1-20.
3. *Id.* at III, 1.
4. *Id.* at III, 3.
5. *Id.* at III, 1, 3.
6. WCR, 158.
7. *Ibid.*
8. CBS, III, 3.
9. *Ibid.*
10. *Ibid.*
11. *Ibid.;* XXIII, 844.
12. See *id.* at 843-845.
13. CBS, III, 3-4.
14. XXIII, 844, 849-850.
15. *Id.* at 844, 860.
16. *Id.* at 844, 857-858.
17. XVII, 406; CBS, III, 3-4.
18. *Id.* at III, 4.
19. *Ibid.*
20. *Id.* at III, 4-6.
21. *Id.* at III, 5. Callaway identified Oswald at a police line-up on November 22, 1963. See XXIV, 347.
22. CBS, III, 4-6; VI, 444-454.
23. *Id.* at 451-452.
24. WCR, 167.
25. *Id.* at 166-168, 176.
26. CBS, III, 4-6.
27. *Ibid.;* VI, 444-454.
28. CBS, III, 6.
29. *Ibid.*
30. VI, 451-452.
31. *Id.* at 444-454.
32. CBS, III, 6.
33. *Ibid.;* VI, 444-454.
34. CBS, III, 4-6.
35. *Id.* at III, 4, 6.
36. *Ibid.*
37. *Id.* at III, 1-7; WCR, 165-176.
38. *Ibid.*
39. III, 475.
40. *Ibid.*
41. *Id.* at 475, 512.
42. WCR, 171-172.
43. CBS, III, 6.
44. *Ibid.*
45. *Ibid.*
46. *Ibid.*
47. *Id.* at III, 17-18.
48. *Ibid.*
49. *Id.* at III, 18.
50. *Ibid.*
51. See *Ramparts,* June 1967.
52. CBS, III, 18.
53. *Ibid.*
54. *Id.* at III, 18-19.
55. *Id.* at III, 19.
56. *Ibid.*
57. *Ibid.*
58. *Ibid.*
59. *Ibid.*
60. *Ibid.*
61. *Ibid.*

14 AMERICANS ARE CONSPIRACY-MINDED

1. CBS, IV, 12-15.
2. *Id.* at IV, 15.
3. *Ibid.*
4. *Id.* at IV, 12-15.
5. See RTJ, 7 (9).
6. CBS, IV, 15.
7. *Id.* at IV, 16.
8. *Ibid.*
9. *Id.* at IV, 17-18.
10. *Id.* at IV, 17.
11. *Ibid.*
12. *Id.* at IV, 17-18.
13. *Id.* at IV, 17.
14. *Id.* at IV, 17-18.
15. *Id.* at IV, 18.
16. *Ibid.*
17. National Archives, Index of Basic Source Materials in Possession of Commission.
18. *Ibid.*
19. *Ibid.*
20. CBS, I, 13-15.
21. See RTJ, 128n (107n-108n).
22. See, e.g., *New York Times,* June 1, 1964, September 29, 1964, March 14, 1965.
23. *Ibid.*
24. See, e.g., Gallup poll reported in the New York *World Journal Tribune,* January 11, 1967; Harris poll reported in the New York *Post,* May 29, 1967.
25. CBS, IV, 15-20.
26. *New York Times,* June 30, 1967.
27. *Ibid.*
28. *Ibid.*
29. CBS News press release, June 29, 1967.
30. *Ibid.*
31. *Ibid.*
32. *New York Times,* June 29, 1967.
33. *Ibid.*
34. *TV Guide,* July 29, 1967.
35. *Ibid.*
36. CBS, IV, 18.

15 THE SINGLE-BULLET TEST

1. CBS, I, 12-20; CBS, II, 16-17.
2. *Ibid.;* WCR, 19.
3. *Id.* at 193-195; CBS, I, 12-15.
4. *Id.* at I, 15-20; WCR, 96-97.
5. *New York Times,* June 25, 1967.
6. *Ibid.*
7. *Ibid.*
8. WCR, 19, 92-96; XVII, 49.
9. RTJ, 69-80 (56-66).
10. CBS, II, 15.
11. *New York Times,* June 25, 1967.
12. *Ibid.*
13. RTJ, 77-78 (64-65).
14. *Ibid.;* WCR, 580-586.
15. *Ibid.*
16. *Ibid.*
17. See RTJ, 78 (64-65).
18. CBS, II, 16.
19. *Id.* at II, 16-17.
20. *Id.* at II, 16.
21. *Ibid.;* WCR, 106.
22. CBS, II, 16.
23. WCR, 92-93, 531-532.
24. V, 79-80; XVII, 49.
25. CBS, II, 17.
26. *Ibid.*
27. *Id.* at II, 16.
28. *Ibid.*
29. *Id.* at II, 16-17.
30. WCR, 583-584.
31. CBS, II, 16.
32. *Id.* at II, 17.
33. *Ibid.*
34. *Ibid.*
35. *Ibid.*
36. *Id.* at II, 16-17.
37. *Ibid.*
38. *The New Republic,* July 25, 1967.
39. CBS, II, 16-17.
40. WCR, 102-103, 105.

41. CBS, II, 16-17.
42. *Id.* at II, 16.
43. See source cited in Chapter 11, note 44.
44. WCR, 582.
45. See source cited in Chapter 11, note 44.
46. WCR, 582.
47. *Id.* at 582, 584.
48. CBS, II, 16-17.
49. *New York Times,* June 25, 1967.
50. XVII, 849-850; CBS, II, 16-17.
51. *Id.* at II, 13.
52. See source cited in Chapter 11, note 44.
53. *Ibid.*
54. CBS, II, 17.

16 THE RIFLE TEST

1. CBS, I, 13-15.
2. *Id.* at I, 13.
3. *Ibid.*
4. *Id.* at I, 14.
5. *Id.* at IV, 7.
6. WCR, 193-194; III, 441-451.
7. CBS, IV, 7; *id.* at I, 13-15.
8. *Id.* at I, 14.
9. *Ibid.*
10. WCR, 49.
11. *Ibid.*
12. *Ibid.;* CBS, I, 14.
13. *Ibid.*
14. See, e.g., III, 220-221, 266; VI, 233; VII, 440, 487.
15. CBS, I, 14.
16. III, 441-451.
17. See source cited in Chapter 11, note 44.
18. CBS, I, 14.
19. *Ibid.*
20. *Ibid.*
21. *Ibid.*
22. WCR, 191.
23. *Ibid.*
24. *Ibid.*
25. *Id.* at 191, 488.
26. *Id.* at 12-13.
27. *Id.* at 192, 274.
28. *Id.* at 192.
29. *Id.* at 192-193.
30. III, 441-451; XVI, 512.
31. CBS, I, 14.
32. III, 407.
33. *Ibid.*
34. *Ibid.;* CBS, I, 14.
35. *Ibid.*
36. III, 443; XXVI, 104.
37. *Ibid.*
38. III, 443-444.
39. XVI, 512; CBS, I, 13-15.
40. *Id.* at I, 14; XVII, 261-262.
41. See WCR, 102-103.
42. *Id.* at 19.
43. XVII, 261-262.
44. *Ibid.*
45. *Ibid.;* WCR, 193.
46. See source cited in Chapter 11, note 44.
47. WCR, 191-193; CBS, I, 14.
48. *Ibid.;* III, 407.
49. *Id.* at 443; XXVI, 104; CBS, I, 14.
50. *Ibid.;* WCR, 49.
51. CBS, I, 14; see sources cited in note 14.
52. XVII, 261-262; CBS, I, 14.
53. WCR, 117; CBS, I, 14.
54. *Ibid.*
55. *Ibid.*
56. See source cited in Chapter 11, note 44.
57. CBS, I, 14; WCR, 19.
58. CBS, I, 14-15.
59. *Id.* at I, 14.
60. WCR, 191-193.
61. CBS, I, 15.
62. *Ibid.*
63. *Id.* at I, 20.
64. *Id.* at II, 1.
65. *Id.* at III, 1.

17 THE CAMERA TEST

1. CBS, I, 15-20.
2. *Id.* at I, 15-16.
3. *Id.* at I, 16-17.
4. *Id.* at I, 17.
5. *Ibid.*
6. *Ibid.;* WCR, 97.
7. *Ibid.*
8. CBS, I, 17-18.
9. WCR, 97-98.
10. *Id.* at 98.
11. CBS, I, 20.
12. *Id.* at I, 17-18.
13. *Id.* at I, 17, 20.
14. *Id.* at I, 17; *id.* at II, 17, 19.
15. *Id.* at I, 17.
16. XVIII, 10, 13, 17, 24, 27, 58, 72, 79.
17. *Id.* at 13, 17, 24, 58, 79.
18. CBS, I, 15-20.
19. XVIII, 1-80.
20. CBS, I, 18.
21. *Ibid.*
22. *Id.* at I, 15-20.
23. WCR, 97-98.
24. *Ibid.*
25. *Id.* at 98.
26. *Id.* at 111.
27. *Id.* at 105.
28. CBS, I, 15.
29. *Id.* at I, 15, 20.
30. WCR, 117.
31. *Ibid.*
32. *Ibid.*
33. CBS, I, 15, 20.
34. *Id.* at I, 17, 20; V, 153.
35. III, 407.
36. WCR, 97.
37. *Ibid.;* V, 153.
38. CBS, I, 17, 20; WCR, 97.
39. CBS, I, 14.
40. *Id.* at I, 18-20.
41. *Id.* at I, 18
42. WCR, 97.
43. RTJ, 66 (54-55).
44. CBS, I, 18-20.
45. *Ibid.*
46. *Id.* at I, 19.
47. *Ibid.*
48. *Ibid.;* WCR, 97.
49. CBS, I, 20; *id.* at II, 1.
50. *Id.* at I, 18-19.
51. XXV, 576.
52. V, 160.
53. CBS, I, 18-19.
54. *Ibid.;* V, 160.
55. *Ibid.;* XXV, 576.
56. V, 160.
57. *New York Times,* December 8, 1966.
58. *Ibid.;* V, 160; XXV, 576; CBS, I, 20; *id.* at II, 1.
59. *Ibid.*
60. CBS, I, 14-15, 18-20.

18 THE ELECTRIC BULB TEST

1. CBS, II, 6-7.
2. *Id.* at II, 6.
3. RTJ, 55 (44-45).
4. *Ibid.*
5. See, e.g., *Greater Philadelphia Magazine,* August 1966.
6. *Ibid.*
7. *Ibid.*
8. CBS, II, 6.
9. *Id.* at II, 6-7.
10. *Ibid.*
11. *Ibid.*
12. *Id.* at II, 6.
13. *Id.* at II, 6-7.
14. *Ibid.*
15. *Ibid.;* XVIII, 70-75.
16. CBS, II, 6.
17. *Id.* at II, 6-7.
18. *Id.* at II, 6.
19. *Id.* at II, 6-7.
20. *Id.* at II, 7.
21. *Id.* at II, 6-7.
22. *Ibid.*
23. RTJ, 56 (45).
24. VI, 292, 294.
25. *Ibid.;* RTJ, 56 (45); CBS, II, 6-7.
26. *Id.* at II, 7.
27. *Ibid.*
28. *Ibid.*
29. *Id.* at II, 6-7.
30. *Ibid.*
31. *Ibid.*

19 A LOSS OF MORALE

1. CBS, IV, 19.
2. *Ibid.*
3. *Id.* at IV, 19-20.
4. *Id.* at II, 15.
5. *Id.* at III, 19.
6. *Ibid.;* CBS, II, 15.
7. *Id.* at IV, 20.
8. CBS News press release, June 29, 1967.
9. CBS, III, 19.
10. *Ibid.*
11. *Id.* at IV, 8.
12. *Id.* at IV, 9.
13. *Ibid.;* CBS, II, 20.

20 UNEQUAL TIME

1. CBS, IV, 2-3.
2. *Id.* at IV, 3-4.
3. *Id.* at IV, 4.
4. *Ibid.*
5. *Id.* at IV, 3.
6. *Ibid.*
7. WCR, 484; RTJ, 56 (45).
8. *Ibid.*
9. VII, 515-525.
10. *Id.* at 518.
11. See WCR, 108.
12. *Id.* at 19, 108.
13. CBS, IV, 3; *id.* at II, 5.
14. *Id.* at IV, 3-4.
15. *Ibid.*
16. *Ibid.;* RTJ, 56 (45).
17. *Ibid.;* CBS, IV, 3-4.
18. *Ibid.*
19. *Ibid.*

20. *Ibid.;* RTJ, 56 (45).
21. *Ibid.*
22. *Ibid.*
23. *Ibid.*
24. *Ibid.*
25. *Ibid.;* RTJ, 56 (45).
26. CBS, IV, 3-4.
27. Letter from Leon R. Brooks to Mark Lane, July 6, 1967.
28. *Ibid.*
29. *Ibid.*
30. *Ibid.*
31. Letter from Mark Lane to Leon R. Brooks, July 20, 1967.
32. *Ibid.*
33. Letter from Kenneth R. Frankl to Mark Lane, August 14, 1967.
34. "The JFK Conspiracy: The Case of Jim Garrison," NBC-TV, June 19, 1967.
35. NBC-TV, July 15, 1967.
36. "The JFK Conspiracy: The Case of Jim Garrison," NBC-TV, June 19, 1967.
37. Letter from Mark Lane to NBC-TV, June 27, 1967.
38. *Ibid.*
39. Letter from William R. McAndrew to Mark Lane, July 17, 1967.

II • The Advocates

21 THE PRESIDENT AND THE COMMISSIONERS

1. WCR, vii, 471-472.
2. *New York Times,* November 5, 1966.
3. *Ibid.*
4. *Ibid.*
5. *Ibid.*
6. *Ibid.*
7. *Ibid.*
8. *Ibid.*
9. See, e.g., Harris poll reported in the New York *Herald Tribune* (Paris edition), October 4, 1966.
10. *New York Times,* November 5, 1966.
11. San Jose, Calif., *Mercury,* October 6, 1966.
12. *Ibid.*
13. *Ibid.*
14. *Ibid.*
15. *Ibid.;* Edward Jay Epstein, *Inquest* (New York, 1966).
16. San Jose *Mercury,* October 6, 1966; see XVI, 720; XXIV, 445.
17. *Ibid.;* XVI, 720.
18. II, 57.
19. San Jose *Mercury,* October 6, 1966.
20. *Ibid.*
21. See, e.g., *New York Times,* March 6, 1967.
22. *Ibid.*
23. *Ibid.; New York Times,* November, 5, 1966; San Jose *Mercury,* October 6, 1966.

22 JOSEPH A. BALL, ESQ.—ON SCURRILOUS JOURNALISTS

1. December 4, 1964.
2. Meeting at Los Angeles "Town Hall," January 3, 1967. The meeting was broadcast on radio station KRHM-FM, Los Angeles.
3. *Ibid.*
4. *Ibid.*
5. *Ibid.*
6. *Ibid.*
7. *Ibid.*
8. *Ibid.*
9. *Ibid.*
10. *Ibid.*
11. Broadcast on radio station KZSU, Stanford, Calif., June 5, 1967.
12. Statement made at Associated Press Managing Editors convention in San Diego, Calif., November 17, 1966. See transcript in Richmond, Va., *Times-Dispatch,* November 27, 1966.
13. See *infra,* pp. 205-213.
14. XXVI, 811.
15. *Ibid.*
16. See source cited in note 2.
17. *Ibid.;* XXVI, 811.
18. See source cited in note 12.
19. *Ibid.*
20. *Ibid.*
21. *Ibid.*
22. XXIV, 228.
23. See source cited in note 11.
24. WCR, 79, 81, 235, 645.
25. See source cited in note 11.
26. *Ibid.*
27. *Ibid.*
28. See source cited in note 2.
29. RTJ, 473 (393).

23 ALBERT E. JENNER, JR., ESQ.—ON IRRESPONSIBLE AUTHORS

1. Broadcast on WNYC-TV, New York City, December 23, 1966.
2. WCR, 758.
3. *Id.* at 750-751.
4. *Ibid.*
5. *Id.* at 747-748, 770-773.
6. *Id.* at 751.
7. *Id.* at 773-774.
8. XVIII, 115.
9. *Ibid.*
10. *Ibid.*
11. *Ibid.*
12. See source cited in note 1.
13. *Ibid.*
14. *Ibid.*
15. *Ibid.*
16. *Ibid.*
17. *Ibid.;* WCR, 476, 478.
18. See source cited in note 1.
19. *U.S. News & World Report,* October 10, 1966; *Saturday Evening Post,* January 14, 1967; San Jose *Mercury,* October 6, 1966; *New York Times,* November 28, 1966; CBS, IV, 14.
20. *Ibid.*
21. See source cited in note 1.
22. *Ibid.*
23. *Ibid.*
24. *Ibid.*
25. III, 227.
26. *Ibid.*
27. *Id.* at 221, 227.
28. *Id.* at 227.
29. *Id.* at 241-270; see source cited in note 1.
30. III, 246.
31. See source cited in note 1.
32. *Ibid.;* WCR, 149, 151-153.
33. III, 258-262.
34. *Id.* at 260-262.
35. See source cited in note 1.
36. WCR, 153.
37. *Ibid.*
38. *Ibid.*
39. *Ibid.*
40. See *supra,* pp. 89-90; see source cited in note 1.
41. *Ibid.*
42. WCR, 124-125.
43. *Ibid.*
44. *Ibid.*
45. See source cited in note 1.
46. See WCR, 171-174.
47. See source cited in note 1.
48. *Ibid.*
49. *Ibid.*

24 WESLEY J. LIEBELER, ESQ.—A VOCAL SPOKESMAN

1. Edward Jay Epstein, *Inquest* (New York, 1966), xviii, 206.
2. See source cited in Chapter 22, note 11.
3. Lewis & Schiller, 1; John Kaplan, "The Assassins," *Stanford Law Review,* XIX (1967), 1122-1123.
4. *Ibid.*
5. Los Angeles *Times,* October 21, 1966.
6. *Ibid.*
7. See RTJ, 56 (45).
8. *Stanford Daily,* October 18, 1966.
9. See source cited in Chapter 22, note 11.
10. *Ibid.;* see RTJ, 344-346 (291-293).
11. *Ibid.*
12. See source cited in Chapter 22, note 11.
13. *Ibid.*
14. XIX, 535-536.
15. *Id.* at 536.

16. See *supra,* pp. 113-115; CBS, II, 6.
17. *Ibid.*
18. See source cited in Chapter 22, note 11.
19. *Ibid.*
20. *Ibid.*
21. *Ibid.*
22. *Ibid.*
23. *Ibid.*
24. *Ibid.*
25. See *supra,* pp. 83-84.
26. See source cited in Chapter 22, note 11.
27. See RTJ, 29-60 (21-48).
28. See source cited in Chapter 22, note 11.
29. *Ibid.*
30. *Ibid.*
31. *Ibid.*

25 WESLEY J. LIEBELER, ESQ.—A SILENT WITNESS

1. XI, 325-339.
2. WCR, 880.
3. *New York Times,* March 23, 1967.
4. See RTJ, 389-390 (331-332).
5. XI, 326-328.
6. *Id.* at 326.
7. *Ibid.*
8. *Ibid.*
9. *Ibid.*
10. *Ibid.*
11. *Id.* at 328.
12. *Ibid.*
13. *Id.* at 330.
14. *Ibid.*
15. *Ibid.*
16. *Ibid.*
17. *Ibid.*
18. *Id.* at 326-331.
19. *Id.* at 331.
20. *Ibid.*
21. *Ibid.*
22. *Id.* at 334.
23. *Id.* at 325, 334.
24. *Id.* at 334.
25. *Ibid.*
26. *Ibid.*
27. *Id.* at 335.
28. *Id.* at 331.
29. *Id.* at 334.
30. WCR, 325.
31. XI, 331.
32. *Id.* at 337.
33. *Ibid.*
34. *Ibid.*
35. *Ibid.*
36. San Francisco *Examiner,* August 14, 1967.
37. New Orleans *States-Item,* August 3, 1967.
38. *Ibid.*
39. *Ibid.*
40. *Ibid.*
41. *Ibid.*
42. *Ibid.*
43. *Ibid.*
44. XI, 325-339.
45. I, v.
46. *Ibid.*
47. *Ibid.*
48. XI, 339.
49. *Ibid.*
50. *Ibid.*
51. *Ibid.*
52. XVI, vii, 7-8.
53. See WCR, 185-186.
54. *Ibid.;* XI, 294-295.
55. WCR, 185-186.
56. XI, 294-295.
57. *Ibid.*
58. *Ibid.*
59. *Id.* at 295.
60. RTJ, 349-350 (296-297).
61. This confrontation followed a lecture that I had delivered in the fall of 1966 at the University of California at Los Angeles. Liebeler was employed at the law school there, and a short impromptu debate occurred in a public room immediately after the formal lecture. The cited remarks are from a tape recording made on that occasion.
62. See source cited in note 61.
63. *Ibid.*
64. *Ibid.*
65. *Ibid.*
66. New Orleans *States-Item,* August 3, 1967, August 7, 1967.
67. New Orleans *States-Item,* August 7, 1967.
68. San Francisco *Examiner,* August 14, 1967. Andrews' appeal, as previously noted, is pending.
69. Palo Alto, Calif., *Times,* August 14, 1967.
70. *Ibid.*
71. Los Angeles *Times,* August 14, 1967.
72. *Ibid.*
73. ABC-TV News, August 14, 1967.
74. *Ibid.*
75. *Ibid.*
76. *Ibid.*
77. *Ibid.*
78. NBC-TV News (Huntley-Brinkley), August 14, 1967.
79. CBS, III, 16.
80. *Id.* at III, 17.
81. See *id.* at III, 16.
82. CBS-TV News (Cronkite), August 14, 1967.
83. *Ibid.*
84. *Ibid.*
85. *Ibid.*

26 THE VOLUNTEERS

1. New York *Herald Tribune* (Paris edition), November 28, 1966.
2. *Ibid.*
3. *Ibid.*
4. *Ibid.*
5. Dallas *Times Herald,* April 27, 1967.
6. *Ibid.*
7. San Francisco *Sunday Examiner & Chronicle,* November 13, 1966.
8. *Ibid.*
9. *Ibid.*
10. *Ibid.*
11. See WCR, 43, 45-46.
12. See *id.* at 102, 108.
13. See source cited in note 7.
14. See, e.g., XXI, 781-782.
15. See sources cited in notes 7, 14.
16. See source cited in note 7.
17. Palo Alto, Calif., *Times,* June 24, 1967.
18. *Ibid.*
19. See *infra,* pp. 187-250.
20. RTJ, 10 (12).
21. Broadcast on WMCA, New York City, September 30, 1966.
22. *Ibid.*
23. *Ibid.*
24. *Ibid.*
25. *Ibid.*
26. *New York Times,* November 24, 1964.
27. Doubleday edition of the Warren Report, xii.
28. *Id.* at xxvii.
29. *Ibid.*
30. See source cited in note 21.
31. *New York Times,* November 17, 1966.
32. *Ibid.*
33. *Ibid.*
34. XIX, 507; XXIV, 228.
35. WCR, 81-84.
36. See source cited in note 21.
37. WCR, 81.
38. See source cited in note 21.
39. *Ibid.*
40. WCR, 580-586.
41. *Id.* at 30-31, 580-586.
42. *Id.* at 193-194.
43. XVII, 261-262; see source cited in note 21.
44. *Ibid.*
45. WCR, 117, 193.
46. XVII, 261-262; see source cited in note 21.
47. *Ibid.*
48. *Ibid.*
49. WCR, 76-78.
50. See source cited in note 21.
51. WCR, 124-125.
52. See source cited in note 21.
53. WCR, 128-129.
54. See source cited in note 21.
55. WCR, 128-129.
56. See source cited in note 21.
57. WCR, 84, 194.
58. See source cited in note 21.
59. See WCR, 137-141.
60. See source cited in note 21.

III • The Academicians

27 ON PROCEDURE AND PRECEDENT

1. *New York University Law Review,* XL (May 1965).
2. See WCR, 476, 478.
3. See *New York Times,* February 19, 1964.
4. See source cited in note 1.
5. Arthur L. Goodhart, "The Warren Commission from the Procedural Standpoint," *New York University Law Review,* XL (1965), 404.
6. Richard M. Mosk, "The Warren Commission and the Legal Process," *Case & Comment,* LXXII (May-June 1967), 20.
7. See WCR, 480.
8. Mosk, *Case & Comment,* 17.
9. *Ibid.*
10. WCR, xiii.
11. *Ibid.;* Mosk, *Case & Comment,* 17.
12. II, 33.
13. *Ibid.*
14. Goodhart, *New York University Law Review,* 405.
15. *Ibid.*
16. Mosk, *Case & Comment,* 13-20.
17. *Ibid.*
18. *Ibid.*
19. *Id.* at 15.
20. Broadcast on radio station KZSU, Stanford, Calif., June 5, 1967.
21. *Ibid.*
22. See WCR, 476-479.
23. *Id.* at 478-479.
24. *Time,* March 17, 1967.
25. Mosk, *Case & Comment,* 13-20.

28 ARTHUR GOODHART AND THE BAR ASSOCIATION

1. Arthur L. Goodhart, "Three Famous Legal Hoaxes," *The Record of the Association of the Bar of the City of New York,* XXII (1967), 415-437.
2. *Ibid.*
3. *Ibid.*
4. *Id.* at 428-433.
5. *Ibid.*
6. *Ibid.*
7. *Id.* at 428.
8. *Id.* at 429.
9. *Id.* at 415-437.
10. *Id.* at 429.
11. *Id.* at 429-432.
12. *Id.* at 429.
13. *Ibid.;* XIX, 483-484.
14. *Ibid.;* Goodhart, *The Record,* etc., 429.
15. *Ibid.*
16. See XIX, 483-484.
17. WCR, 492, 885.
18. XIX, 483-484.
19. Goodhart, *The Record,* etc., 429.
20. XXIII, 836.
21. Goodhart, *The Record,* etc., 430-431.
22. *Id.* at 430.
23. XXIV, 201.
24. VI, 285-286.
25. *Id.* at 286.
26. RTJ, 31 (23).
27. Goodhart, *The Record,* etc., 430.
28. Interview of Lee Bowers by Mark Lane, filmed and tape-recorded in Arlington, Texas, March 31, 1966.
29. Goodhart, *The Record,* etc., 431.
30. *Ibid.*
31. *Ibid.*
32. *Ibid.*
33. *Ibid.*
34. *Ibid.*
35. VI, 245-246.
36. *Ibid.*
37. VII, 105-109; Goodhart, *The Record,* etc., 431-432.
38. *Ibid.*
39. *Ibid.;* VII, 107, 109.
40. *Id.* at 109.
41. *Id.* at 106-107, 109.
42. *Id.* at 107, 109.
43. *Ibid.*
44. Goodhart, *The Record,* etc., 432.
45. *Ibid.*
46. Interview of James L. Simmons by Mark Lane, filmed and tape-recorded in Mesquite, Texas, March 28, 1966.
47. *Ibid.*
48. *Ibid.*
49. *Ibid.*
50. Goodhart, *The Record,* etc., 432; XXII, 833.
51. *Ibid.*
52. See RTJ, 95-96 (79-80), 102-104 (85-87), 387-390 (330-332).
53. Goodhart, *The Record,* etc., 432.
54. *Ibid.*
55. See RTJ, 40 (31-32).
56. *Id.* at 41-44 (32-35).
57. *Id.* at 46-60 (36-48).
58. Goodhart, *The Record,* etc., 432.
59. *Ibid.*
60. *Ibid.;* see RTJ, 47-48 (37).
61. Goodhart, *The Record,* etc., 433.
62. CBS, II, 9.
63. *Ibid.*
64. *Ibid.*
65. See RTJ, 47 (37).
66. *Ibid.*
67. Goodhart, *The Record,* etc., 433-435.
68. *Id.* at 433.
69. Edward Jay Epstein, *Inquest* (New York, 1966), xviii.
70. Goodhart, *The Record,* etc., 433.
71. *Ibid.*
72. *Ibid.*
73. *Ibid.*
74. *Ibid.*
75. See source cited in Chapter 27, note 20.
76. *Ibid.*
77. Goodhart, *The Record,* etc., 435-437.
78. *Id.* at 435.
79. See RTJ, 273-286 (231-243).
80. Goodhart, *The Record,* etc., 436.
81. *Ibid.*
82. *Ibid.*

29 A LAW JOURNAL'S BONAR

1. *Yale Law Journal,* LXXVI (1967), 581-597.
2. *New York Times,* November 25, 1966.
3. *Yale Law Journal,* 581-597.
4. *Id.* at 582.
5. *Ibid.*
6. RTJ, 90 (75).
7. III, 157.
8. *Yale Law Journal,* 581-597; RTJ, 418-468 (355-380).
9. See III, 157.
10. *Ibid.; Yale Law Journal,* 582.
11. III, 157; RTJ, 90 (75).
12. *Ibid.*
13. Letter from Mark Lane to Marcus Raskin, June 20, 1967.
14. Letter from Marcus Raskin to Mark Lane, July 5, 1967.
15. *Ibid.*
16. John Kaplan, "The Assassins," *The American Scholar,* XXXVI (1967), 271-306; John Kaplan, "The Assassins," *Stanford Law Review,* XIX (1967), 1110-1151.

30 AN AMERICAN SCHOLAR

1. Kaplan, *The American Scholar,* 271-306.
2. *Ibid.*
3. *Ibid.*
4. *Id.* at 300.
5. *Ibid.*
6. Harold Weisberg, *Whitewash* (Hyattstown, Md., 1965).
7. Kaplan, *The American Scholar,* 283.
8. *Ibid.*
9. Harold Weisberg, *Photographic Whitewash* (Hyattstown, Md., 1967), 91.
10. *Ibid.*
11. See *infra,* **pp. 187-250.**
12. Kaplan, *The American Scholar,* 306.
13. *Ibid.*
14. See, e.g., *U.S. News & World Report,* October 10,

1966; *Saturday Evening Post,* January 14, 1967.
15. CBS, IV, 14.
16. Kaplan, *The American Scholar,* 278.
17. *Id.* at 285.
18. RTJ, 81 (67).
19. Public meeting, Stanford, Calif., May 2, 1967.
20. *Ibid.*
21. Kaplan, *The American Scholar,* 279.
22. Public meeting, Stanford, Calif., May 2, 1967.
23. *Ibid.*
24. Kaplan, *The American Scholar,* 281.
25. RTJ, 349 (295-296).
26. *Ibid.*
27. *Ibid.*
28. *Ibid.*
29. Public meeting, Stanford, Calif., May 2, 1967.
30. *Ibid.*
31. Kaplan, *The American Scholar,* 281.
32. Public meeting, Stanford, Calif., May 2, 1967.
33. *Ibid.*
34. *Ibid.*
35. *Ibid.*
36. RTJ, 418-468 (355-380).
37. Kaplan, *The American Scholar,* 278.
38. *Ibid.*
39. Public meeting, Stanford, Calif., May 2, 1967.
40. *Ibid.*
41. Kaplan, *The American Scholar,* 271.
42. Kaplan, *Stanford Law Review,* 1110n.
43. *Id.* at 1110-1151.
44. *Id.* at 1115.
45. RTJ, 398 (339).
46. Kaplan, *Stanford Law Review,* 1115.

IV • The Books

31 WILLIAM MANCHESTER

1. New York *Herald Tribune* (Paris edition), April 8-9, 1967.
2. See Manchester, xi.
3. *Ibid.*
4. *Id.* at 104.
5. *Ibid.*
6. *Id.* at xi.
7. *New York Times,* February 13, 1967.
8. Manchester, 276.
9. *Id.* at 276-277.
10. *Id.* at 278.
11. *Id.* at 93, 568.
12. *Look,* February 21, 1967; see Manchester, 321.
13. *Ibid.; Time,* February 24, 1967.
14. *Ibid.*
15. *Look,* February 21, 1967; Manchester, 325.
16. *Time,* February 17, 1967.
17. *New York Times,* February 13, 1967.
18. *Look,* February 21, 1967.
19. *Time,* February 17, 1967; *New York Times,* February 13, 1967.
20. Manchester, 321, 325.
21. *Id.* at 321.
22. *Id.* at 325.
23. See RTJ, 56 (45).
24. *Ibid.*
25. See Manchester, 150, 154-155, 159, 690.
26. *Ibid.*
27. *Ibid.*
28. *Ibid.*
29. *Id.* at 276.
30. See RTJ, 81-82 (67-68).
31. *Id.* at 82 (68).
32. *Ibid.*
33. *Ibid.*
34. *Ibid.*
35. *Ibid.;* Manchester, 276.
36. *Id.* at 282.
37. See XIX, 113-115; XVII, 228, 230-234.
38. XX, 590.
39. III, 244-245.
40. *Id.* at 245.
41. WCR, 152.
42. Manchester, 159, 278.
43. *Ibid.*
44. *Id.* at 280; WCR, 144.
45. *Ibid.*
46. See RTJ, 83-99 (68-83).
47. Manchester, 280.
48. See WCR, 6-8.
49. *Id.* at 158.
50. Manchester, xii, 283.
51. *Id.* at 283.
52. See WCR, 158.
53. Manchester, 283.
54. *Id.* at 64.
55. *Ibid.*
56. XVIII, 646.
57. Manchester, 369n.
58. *Ibid.*
59. WCR, 668.
60. *Id.* at 294; Manchester, 109.
61. WCR, 294.
62. *Id.* at 297.
63. Manchester, 109.
64. *Id.* at 150-151.
65. WCR, 250-252.
66. Manchester, 150.
67. II, 165-190.
68. *Id.* at 169, 171, 175-176.
69. *Id.* at 175-176.
70. *Id.* at 169, 171.

32 CHARLES ROBERTS

1. Roberts, 27-36.
2. *Ibid.*
3. See *infra,* pp. 187-250.
4. *Ibid.*
5. XVIII, 1-80.
6. *Ibid.*
7. *Id.* at 19.
8. *Ibid.*
9. *Id.* at 89.
10. *Id.* at 19.
11. *Newsweek,* February 6, 1967.
12. *Ibid.*
13. Roberts, 101.
14. *Id.* at 102.
15. *Ibid.;* XVIII, 19; V, 151.
16. XVIII, 1-31.
17. V, 151.
18. *Ibid.*
19. Roberts, 65-76.
20. *Id.* at 70.
21. *Ibid.;* see sources cited in notes 22-23.
22. VII, 594; XV, 703, 744-745; XX, 534; XXI, 25-28, 383-384; XXV, 731.
23. XI, 434-442.
24. See sources cited in notes 22-23; III, 327; Roberts, 69.
25. WCR, 165.
26. See RTJ, 204 (174-175n).
27. Roberts, 69.
28. XXVI, 786-787.
29. *Id.* at 787; Roberts, 98-99.
30. *Id.* at 123-125.
31. See RTJ, 370 (314).
32. *Id.* at 366 (311), 372 (315).
33. Roberts, 123-125; WCR, 327.
34. Roberts, 124.
35. *Id.* at 124-125.
36. *Id.* at 124.
37. *Ibid.*
38. *Ibid.*
39. CD 320, Control No. 767.
40. *Ibid.*
41. *Ibid.*
42. *Look,* July 12, 1966.
43. CD 320, Control No. 767.
44. *Look,* July 12, 1966.
45. WCR, 490.
46. *Look,* July 12, 1966.
47. *Ibid.*
48. WCR, 498.
49. *Id.* at 490, 498.
50. *Ibid.*
51. Roberts, 123-125.
52. *Id.* at 119.
53. *Ibid.*
54. *Ibid.*
55. *Ibid.*
56. *Id.* at 118, 122.
57. *Id.* at 119.

33 THE SCAVENGERS

1. Letter from Charles H. Tillinghast to Mark Lane, July 20, 1967.
2. *Ibid.*
3. Letter from Mark Lane to Charles H. Tillinghast, June 29, 1967.
4. Letter from Mark Lane to John F. Kennedy Memorial Library, June 29, 1967.
5. Letter from Miss Helen Keyes to Mark Lane, July 5, 1967.
6. Letter from Charles H. Tillinghast to Mark Lane, July 20, 1967.
7. *Ibid.*
8. New York *World Journal Tribune,* January 22, 1967.
9. *Ibid.*
10. *Ibid.*
11. *Ibid.* For example, How-

ard L. Brennan was referred to as "H. L. Brennon [*sic*]" and Arlen Specter was called "Arlen Spector [*sic*]."
12. Lewis & Schiller, 64.
13. *Id.* at 77.
14. *Id.* at 65.
15. New York *World Journal Tribune,* January 22, 1967.
16. *Ibid.*
17. *Ibid.*
18. *Ibid.*
19. Lewis & Schiller, 64, 76, 83.
20. *Id.* at 83.
21. *Id.* at 17, 166; WCR, 49.
22. Lewis & Schiller, 84.
23. *Id.* at 48.
24. WCR, 297, 368.
25. Lewis & Schiller, 48.
26. *Ibid.*
27. XIX, 133.
28. Lewis & Schiller, 50.
29. See XXVI, 486.
30. See WCR, 297, 368.
31. See RTJ, 248-259 (210-220).
32. Lewis & Schiller, 50, 200.
33. *Id.* at 39, 50, 200.
34. San Francisco *Chronicle,* December 3, 1963.
35. Lewis & Schiller, 166.
36. *Id.* at 9.
37. *Id.* at 9-11.
38. *Id.* at 12.
39. *Id.* at 11.
40. *Id.* at 12.
41. *Ibid.*
42. WCR, 506.

PART THREE: THE ISSUES

I • The Grassy Knoll

34 PHYSICAL TRACES

1. See II, 42-43; XXV, 853-854.
2. See XVI, 720; XXIV, 445.
3. WCR, 472.
4. See I, ix, 264; XXV, 853-854.
5. *Ibid.;* II, 42-43.
6. *Ibid.*
7. II, 42.
8. XXV, 853-854.
9. II, 32, 42.
10. See, e.g., WCR, 34, 73-75.
11. *Newsweek,* October 5, 1964.
12. *Ibid.*
13. *Time,* May 26, 1967.
14. Roberts, inside front cover.
15. *Ibid.*
16. CBS, II, 20.
17. *U.S. News & World Report,* October 10, 1966.
18. Interview of S. M. Holland by Mark Lane, filmed and tape-recorded in Irving, Texas, March 21, 1966.
19. *Ibid.*
20. *U.S. News & World Report,* October 10, 1966.
21. WCR, 71.
22. VI, 253-256.
23. *Id.* at 248-253.
24. *Id.* at 255-256.
25. *Id.* at 249-250.
26. Interview of James L. Simmons by Mark Lane, filmed and tape-recorded in Mesquite, Texas, March 28, 1966; see source cited in note 18.
27. *U.S. News & World Report,* October 10, 1966.
28. Interview of James L. Simmons by Mark Lane, filmed and tape-recorded in Mesquite, Texas, March 28, 1966.
29. VI, 284-289.
30. *Id.* at 287-288.
31. XIX, 492.
32. *Ibid.;* interview of J. C. Price by Mark Lane, filmed and tape-recorded in Dallas, March 27, 1966.
33. WCR, 495.
34. Edward Jay Epstein, *Inquest* (New York, 1966), 130.
35. *U.S. News & World Report,* October 10, 1966.
36. See VI, 212; XIX, 472, 490; XXIV, 525.
37. VI, 212.
38. XIX, 490.
39. See, e.g., XVIII, 57-69.
40. XXIV, 520.
41. Dallas *Morning News,* November 23, 1963.
42. XIX, 472; XXIV, 525.
43. See, e.g., XIX, 486.
44. WCR, 79, 122-124.
45. CBS, II, 20.
46. *New York Times,* July 23, 1967.
47. *Ibid.*
48. CBS, II, 20.
49. Roberts, 32.
50. Statement made at Associated Press Managing Editors convention in San Diego, Calif., November 17, 1966. See transcript in Richmond, Va., *Times-Dispatch,* November 27, 1966.
51. CBS, III, 18.
52. *Ibid.*
53. *Id.* at II, 3-4; VI, 239-248.
54. CBS, II, 3-4; see source cited in note 18.
55. CBS, II, 4.
56. See source cited in note 18.
57. *Ibid.*
58. VI, 244; interview of S. M. Holland by Mark Lane, filmed and tape-recorded in Dallas, March 23, 1966.
59. *Ibid.*
60. See source cited in note 18.
61. Interview of Lee Bowers by Mark Lane, filmed and tape-recorded in Arlington, Texas, March 31, 1966.
62. VI, 312; VII, 107, 535.
63. VI, 312.
64. VII, 535.
65. *Ibid.*
66. *Ibid.*
67. WCR, 52.
68. CBS, II, 4.
69. See source cited in note 50.
70. VI, 245-246.
71. CBS, II, 4.
72. *Ibid.*
73. See source cited in note 18.
74. See sources cited in notes 28, 76.
75. See source cited in note 28.
76. Interview of Richard C. Dodd by Mark Lane, filmed and tape-recorded in Decatur, Texas, March 24, 1966.
77. John Kaplan, "The Assassins," *The American Scholar,* XXXVI (1967), 279.
78. See VI, 245-246.
79. XXI, 472-483.
80. *Id.* at 475-477.
81. WCR, 116.
82. See XXI, 472-483.
83. Kaplan, *The American Scholar,* 279.
84. John Kaplan, "The Assassins," *Stanford Law Review,* XIX (1967), 1124.
85. *Ramparts,* June 1967.
86. *Ibid.*
87. Kaplan, *The American Scholar,* 271-306; Kaplan, *Stanford Law Review,* 1110-1151.
88. See XVII, 197, 199-200.

35 THE WITNESSES

1. *U.S. News & World Report,* October 10, 1966.
2. *Ibid.*
3. *Ibid.;* see WCR, 76.
4. See source cited in Chapter 34, note 50; Lewis & Schiller, 29-31.
5. See source cited in Chapter 34, note 50.
6. Lewis & Schiller, 29-31.
7. See RTJ, 37 (28).
8. *Ibid.*
9. Roberts, 33.
10. *Ibid.*
11. *Ibid.*
12. *Ibid.;* VI, 245.

13. Roberts, 33.
14. See RTJ, 37 (28), 40 (31).
15. *Id.* at 37 (28).
16. *Ibid.*
17. See *id.* at 36-68 (27-56).
18. *Ibid.*
19. See source cited in Chapter 34, note 18.
20. *Ibid.*
21. *Ibid.*
22. Roberts, 33.
23. See source cited in Chapter 34, note 18.
24. Roberts, 33; VI, 245.
25. *Ibid.*
26. Roberts, 34.
27. WCR, 71.
28. *Ibid.*
29. *Ibid.*
30. *Id.* at 71-72, 76.
31. Roberts, 27-36.
32. WCR, 71-72, 76.
33. Roberts, 27.
34. See WCR, 19.
35. XVIII, 1-80.
36. *Id.* at 70 ff.
37. See Roberts, 27-64.
38. *Id.* at 27.
39. *Id.* at 28.
40. *Ibid.*
41. *Ibid.*
42. See II, 32-61; V, 546-561.
43. II, 42.
44. See *supra*, p. 187.
45. II, 42.
46. Roberts, 28.
47. See RTJ, 29-45 (21-36).
48. *Ibid.*
49. Roberts, 28.
50. XIX, 483-484; see RTJ, 29-30 (21-22).
51. See *id.* at 30-32 (23-24).
52. See *id.* at 32-33 (24-25).
53. Roberts, 28.
54. *Id.* at 29-30.
55. *Ibid.*
56. *Id.* at 29.
57. *Ibid.*
58. *Ibid.*
59. *Id.* at 29-30.
60. *Id.* at 29.
61. RTJ, 29-30 (21-22).
62. *Id.* at 29-31 (21-23).
63. Roberts, 29.
64. RTJ, 29 (22).
65. Roberts, 29.
66. XIX, 483-484.
67. Roberts, 30.
68. *Ibid.*
69. XIX, 454-543.
70. *Id.* at 467-482, 485, 487-501.
71. *Ibid.*
72. *Id.* at 483-484; Roberts, 30.
73. *Ibid.*
74. XIX, 482.
75. *Ibid.*
76. *Ibid.*
77. Roberts, 30.
78. XIX, 477.
79. *Ibid.*
80. *Id.* at 483-484.
81. See RTJ, 37 (28).
82. Roberts, 30.
83. *Ibid.*
84. *Ibid.*
85. XIX, 491.
86. Roberts, 30.
87. *Id.* at 30-34; VI, 284-289.
88. Roberts, 31.
89. RTJ, 31 (23).
90. *Ibid.*; VI, 287; XIX, 483-484.
91. VI, 287.
92. XIX, 483.
93. VI, 287.
94. XIX, 483-484.
95. Roberts, 31.
96. *Ibid.*
97. *Id.* at 31-32.
98. VI, 287-288.
99. See source cited in Chapter 34, note 61.
100. VI, 251.
101. WCR, 71.
102. VI, 251.
103. *Ibid.*
104. *Commentary,* October 1966.
105. *Ibid.*; VI, 251, 287.
106. Roberts, 31-32; *Commentary,* October 1966.
107. RTJ, 32 (24).
108. See source cited in Chapter 34, note 61.
109. *Ibid.*
110. *Ibid.*
111. *Ibid.*
112. *Ibid.*
113. *Ibid.*
114. See, e.g., Roberts, 32-33; Lewis & Schiller, 58-61; Kaplan, *The American Scholar,* 280; Kaplan, *Stanford Law Review,* 1126-1128.
115. Roberts, 33.
116. Kaplan, *The American Scholar,* 280; Kaplan, *Stanford Law Review,* 1126.
117. Roberts, 33.
118. *Ibid.*
119. See source cited in Chapter 34, note 61.
120. RTJ, 32 (24).
121. See sources cited in Chapter 34, note 61, and note 114 *supra.*
122. See source cited in Chapter 34, note 61.
123. Roberts, 14-15, 35.
124. *Id.* at 35.
125. *Ibid.*
126. RTJ, 37, 39 (28, 30).
127. *Id.* at 39 (30).
128. Roberts, 14.
129. VI, 288.
130. See source cited in Chapter 34, note 61.
131. Lewis & Schiller, 31-34.
132. *Id.* at 31-32.
133. XIX, 480.
134. See RTJ, 33-35 (25-26), 40 (31-32).
135. See *id.* at 83-94 (68-78).
136. *Ibid.*; see Lewis & Schiller, 31-32.
137. *Ibid.*; III, 147.
138. Lewis & Schiller, 32.
139. *Id.* at 32-33.
140. *Id.* at 33.
141. WCR, 51; II, 138.
142. *Ibid.*; Lewis & Schiller, 32.
143. *Id.* at 33; II, 138.

36 A PUFF OF SMOKE

1. Lewis & Schiller, 33-34.
2. *Id.* at 34. The photograph is facing page 128.
3. Lewis & Schiller, 34.
4. *Ibid.*; see photograph facing page 128, Lewis & Schiller.
5. *Ibid.*
6. Interview of S. M. Holland by Mark Lane, filmed and tape-recorded in Dallas, March 23, 1966.
7. The showing on BBC television was on January 29, 1967.
8. See RTJ, 40 (31-32).
9. Lewis & Schiller, 34.
10. WCR, 63-64.
11. II, 190-210; III, 140-161, 184-186, 211.
12. Lewis & Schiller, 34.
13. See source cited in Chapter 34, note 50.
14. Kaplan, *The American Scholar,* 279-280; Kaplan, *Stanford Law Review,* 1123-1124.
15. AP, IV.
16. See source cited in Chapter 34, note 50.
17. *Ibid.*
18. Edward Jay Epstein, *Inquest* (New York, 1966), 130.
19. WCR, 118-137, 189-195.
20. XXVI, 811.
21. *Ibid.*; see source cited in Chapter 34, note 50.
22. WCR, 18-19; XXVI, 811.
23. See source cited in Chapter 34, note 50.
24. AP, IV.
25. Kaplan, *The American Scholar,* 279-280; Kaplan, *Stanford Law Review,* 1123-1124.
26. *Id.* at 1124.
27. Lewis & Schiller, 33-34.
28. Kaplan, *Stanford Law Review,* 1124.
29. See RTJ, 37 (28), 40 (31-32).
30. Kaplan, *Stanford Law Review,* 1124.
31. Kaplan, *The American Scholar,* 279.
32. Public meeting, Stanford, Calif., May 2, 1967.
33. Kaplan, *Stanford Law Review,* 1124.
34. Kaplan, *The American Scholar,* 279.
35. Public meeting, Stanford, Calif., May 2, 1967.
36. Kaplan, *Stanford Law Review,* 1124.
37. XXVI, 811.
38. AP, IV.
39. *Ibid.*
40. See RTJ, 40 (31-32).
41. AP, IV.
42. *Ibid.*
43. *Ibid.*
44. *Ibid.*
45. *Ibid.*
46. *Ibid.*
47. See source cited in Chapter 34, note 18.

48. *Ibid.*
49. AP, IV.
50. XIX, 485.
51. AP, IV.
52. *Ibid.*
53. *Ibid.;* RTJ, 40 (31); VI, 226.
54. RTJ, 40 (31).
55. VI, 226.
56. See source cited in Chapter 34, note 61.
57. XIX, 485.
58. *Ibid.*
59. VI, 223-227.
60. See XIX, 485.
61. See, e.g., VIII, 35-38; XV, 709-744.
62. VI, 223-227.
63. *Id.* at 226.
64. XIX, 485.
65. VI, 226-227.
66. *Ibid.*
67. WCR, 492.
68. AP, IV.
69. Kaplan, *Stanford Law Review,* 1124.
70. AP, IV.
71. XXII, 836.
72. *Ibid.*
73. WCR, 490.
74. XXII, 836.
75. *Ibid.*
76. *Ibid.*
77. *Ibid.;* RTJ, 40 (32).
78. *New York Times,* December 9, 1963.
79. *Ibid.*
80. See RTJ, 102-104 (85-87), 387-390 (330-332).
81. See, e.g., *id.* at 95-96 (79-80).
82. See sources cited in notes 80-81.
83. XXII, 836.
84. *Ibid.;* WCR, 490.
85. Kaplan, *Stanford Law Review,* 1124.
86. AP, IV.
87. See sources cited in Chapter 34, note 28, 76.
88. RTJ, 40 (32), 420 (356).
89. *Ibid.*
90. AP, IV.
91. *Ibid.*
92. *Ibid.*
93. *Ibid.;* XXII, 833, 835.
94. AP, IV.
95. See source cited in Chapter 34, note 28.
96. Kaplan, *The American Scholar,* 279; Kaplan, *Stanford Law Review,* 1123-1124.
97. Kaplan, *The American Scholar,* 279.
98. Public meeting, Stanford, Calif., May 2, 1967.
99. XXII, 833.
100. Kaplan, *Stanford Law Review,* 1110n.
101. *Id.* at 1123-1124.
102. *Ibid.;* XXII, 833.
103. See source cited in Chapter 34, note 28.
104. Roberts, 35.
105. *Ibid.*
106. IV, 150-202.
107. VI, 223-231, 236-256.
108. See WCR, 155.
109. *Id.* at 4.
110. Roberts, 35.
111. WCR, 8.
112. IV, 204-205.
113. See II, 181; VI, 288; see source cited in note 6.
114. XIX, 515.
115. *Ibid.*
116. See source cited in Chapter 34, note 61.
117. *Ibid.*
118. *Ibid.*
119. AP, IV.
120. *Ibid.*
121. XXII, 638-639, 845.
122. III, 270-281.
123. XXII, 638.
124. WCR, 485.
125. III, 273.
126. *Id.* at 270-281.
127. AP, IV.
128. *Ibid.;* WCR, 154.
129. *Ibid.*
130. *Id.* at 154, 880.

37 THE PHOTOGRAPHS

1. *New York Times,* May 19, 1967.
2. *Ibid.*
3. See WCR, 96-97; XVIII, 81-83; XXIV, 539.
4. XVIII, 81-83.
5. *New York Times,* November 15, 1966.
6. *Esquire,* December 1966.
7. *Ibid.*
8. *New York Times,* November 15, 1966.
9. Jones Harris.
10. *New York Times,* November 15, 1966.
11. Itek Corporation, *Nix Film Analysis* (Lexington, Mass., 1967), iii.
12. *Ibid.*
13. *New York Times,* May 19, 1967.
14. Itek Corporation, *op cit.,* iv.
15. *Id.* at iii.
16. *New York Times,* May 19, 1967.
17. Letter from Raymond J. Marcus to Leslie Midgley, June 19, 1967.
18. *Ibid.*
19. *Ibid.*
20. *Ibid.*
21. *Ibid.*

II • The New Evidence and the Wounds

38 THE UNDISPUTED FACTS

1. See RTJ, 60-62 (49-50); *New York Times,* November 2, 1966, November 3, 1966, November 5, 1966.
2. CBS, IV, 11.
3. AP, III.
4. CD 7.
5. *New York Times,* November 2, 1966.
6. *New York Times,* November 25, 1966, November 26, 1966; CBS, II, 10-12.
7. See RTJ, 46-80 (36-66); WCR, 3, 18-19, 53-56, 59-60, 85-96.
8. See sources cited in note 7.
9. WCR, 86-87, 108-110; XVIII, 70, 95.
10. See RTJ, 46-55 (36-44), 63-66 (51-54); WCR, 87-92.
11. See, e.g., RTJ, 63-66 (51-54).
12. WCR, 3, 19; Roberts, 48; Manchester, 156.
13. WCR, 3, 19, 60, 97, 98, 105.
14. *Id.* at 19, 543.
15. See *Esquire,* December 1966.
16. *Ibid.*
17. *Ibid.*
18. See RTJ, 46-66 (36-54).
19. See *id.* at 63-66 (51-54); *Esquire,* December 1966.
20. *Ibid.;* see RTJ, 46-55 (36-44).
21. See *id.* at 55-57 (44-46); *Esquire,* December 1966.
22. XVII, 338-339, 347-353.
23. WCR, 19.
24. *Id.* at 19, 56, 92-96.
25. *Id.* at 3, 19, 94-96.
26. *Id.* at 19, 105-107, 109, 117.
27. See *infra,* pp. 241-244.
28. *U.S. News & World Report,* October 10, 1966; CBS, II, 14; Roberts, 53-54.
29. *U.S. News & World Report,* October 10, 1966; CBS, II, 14.
30. *Ibid.*
31. See *infra,* pp. 241-244.
32. CBS, II, 15.
33. AP, III.
34. See, e.g., *Commentary,* October 1966.
35. XVIII, 26 ff.; WCR, 97-98, 105-106; *Life,* November 25, 1966.
36. See sources cited in note 35.
37. See WCR, 96-103, 105-110, 112, 114-115.
38. VII, 569-576; XX, 183.
39. V, 153, 160; XXV, 576.
40. *New York Times,* December 8, 1966.
41. WCR, 97; V, 153, 160.
42. WCR, 97; III, 407.
43. V, 153.
44. WCR, 98.
45. *Ibid.;* XVIII, 18-26.
46. WCR, 98; XVIII, 26.

47. *Id.* at 8, 88; WCR, 101.
48. *Id.* at 98, 100-102; XVIII, 1-19.
49. WCR, 106; V, 170.
50. *Life,* November 25, 1966.
51. WCR, 108-110; XVIII, 70.

39 THE UNDENIABLE EVIDENCE

1. See WCR, 19, 60, 87-89, 105-107.
2. *Id.* at 106.
3. See RTJ, 63-66 (51-54).
4. II, 347-384.
5. XVI, 978-983; WCR, 538-543.
6. CD 7.
7. II, 81, 93, 127, 143.
8. XVII, 45.
9. *New York Times,* November 25, 1966.
10. National Archives, FBI Supplemental Report, January 13, 1964, Exhibit 60.
11. National Archives, FBI Supplemental Report, January 13, 1964, Exhibit 59.
12. See sources cited in notes 4-11; WCR, 19.
13. *Id.* at 52-56.
14. *Id.* at 54.
15. *Id.* at 88-89.
16. *Ibid.*
17. See *Argosy,* July 1967; letter from John Nichols to Mark Lane, August 18, 1966.
18. *Argosy,* July 1967; WCR, 107.
19. *Argosy,* July 1967.
20. *Ibid.*
21. Letter from John Nichols to Mark Lane, August 18, 1966.
22. WCR, 58; VII, 452-453, 468-469.
23. *Ibid.*
24. WCR, 59-60.
25. II, 348-376.
26. *Id.* at 376-377.
27. *Id.* at 377-384.
28. *Id.* at 349; CD 7; *Saturday Evening Post,* January 14, 1967.
29. WCR, 59-60.
30. II, 93-94; XVIII, 727, 729.
31. *Id.* at 723; II, 127.
32. *Id.* at 92-94, 131; CD 7; XVIII, 726-727.
33. *Id.* at 727, 729; CD 7.
34. II, 143; XVIII, 727.
35. CD 7.
36. *Ibid.;* see WCR, 885, 887.
37. *Id.* at 497.
38. *Id.* at 493.
39. *Id.* at 493, 497.
40. See *id.* at 885, 887.
41. CD 7.
42. *Ibid.;* Lewis & Schiller, 114.
43. CD 7.
44. *Ibid.*
45. *Ibid.*
46. WCR, 88-89.
47. *Ibid.*
48. *Id.* at 88.
49. *Ibid.*
50. *Id.* at 89.
51. *Id.* at iv, 88-89.
52. See *Look,* July 12, 1966; *Life,* November 25, 1966; *U.S. News & World Report,* October 10, 1966; II, 368; CD 7.
53. *Ibid.*
54. Roberts, 45-47; Lewis & Schiller, 110-117; Washington *Post,* May 29, 1966.
55. Edward Jay Epstein, *Inquest* (New York, 1966), 130.
56. *Id.* at 49.
57. *Ibid.*
58. *Ibid.;* CD 7; II, 131; Lewis & Schiller, 114.
59. See sources cited in note 58.
60. II, 131.
61. Lewis & Schiller, 114.
62. *Id.* at 113-114.
63. CD 7.
64. See sources cited in note 58.
65. Roberts, 46.
66. *Ibid.;* II, 131.
67. Roberts, 46.
68. *Ibid.*
69. *Ibid.;* see sources cited in note 52.
70. WCR, 88-89.
71. See sources cited in note 52.
72. II, 368.
73. *Look,* July 12, 1966.
74. *Ibid.*
75. Epstein, *op. cit.,* 130; WCR, 88-89.
76. *U.S. News & World Report,* October 10, 1966.
77. *Ibid.*
78. See sources cited in note 52.
79. *Ibid.*
80. *Ibid.*
81. *Ibid.*
82. *Life,* November 25, 1966.
83. XVII, 48.
84. II, 373.
85. CBS, II, 12.
86. *Ibid.;* II, 348-376.
87. *U.S. News & World Report,* October 10, 1966.
88. *Ibid.*
89. *Saturday Evening Post,* January 14, 1967.
90. WCR, 538-543.
91. CD 7.
92. XVII, 45.
93. National Archives, FBI Supplemental Report, January 13, 1964, Exhibits 59-60.
94. XVII, 45; *New York Times,* November 25, 1966.
95. WCR, 89.
96. XVII, 45; *New York Times,* November 25, 1966.
97. *Ibid.;* Roberts, 48; CBS, II, 10-11; AP, III.
98. *Ibid.*
99. CD 7.
100. II, 81, 127, 143.
101. *Id.* at 81.
102. *Id.* at 127.
103. *Id.* at 143.
104. National Archives, FBI Supplemental Report, January 13, 1964, Exhibits 59-60.
105. AP, III.
106. See RTJ, 63-64 (52), 66 (54).
107. *Id.* at 66 (54).
108. AP, III.
109. WCR, 98, 105, 111.
110. *Id.* at 98.
111. *Id.* at 105.
112. *Id.* at 111.
113. *New York Times,* November 25, 1966.
114. *Ibid.*
115. *Argosy,* July 1967.
116. *Ibid.*
117. *Ibid.*
118. *Ibid.*
119. CBS, II, 10-11.
120. *Id.* at II, 11.
121. *Argosy,* July 1967.
122. *Ibid.*
123. Letter from John Nichols to Mark Lane, August 18, 1966.
124. CBS, II, 10-11.
125. XVII, 45.
126. XVI, 977.
127. CBS, II, 11.
128. *Ibid.; New York Times,* November 25, 1966; II, 373.
129. *Id.* at 349-350.
130. *Id.* at 347, 349-350; XVI, 977; CBS, II, 11.
131. II, 347, 350.
132. *Id.* at 350.
133. *Ibid.*
134. AP, III.
135. *Ibid.*
136. *Ibid.*
137. Manchester, 432.
138. AP, III.
139. *Saturday Evening Post,* January 14, 1967.
140. WCR, 59-60.
141. *New York Times,* November 3, 1966.
142. *Argosy,* July 1967.
143. National Archives, FBI Supplemental Report, January 13, 1964, Exhibit 60.
144. *Ibid.;* see XVII, 25-26.
145. See source cited in note 143; WCR, 92.
146. *Ibid.;* XVII, 45; see sources cited in notes 113, 143.
147. CD 7; WCR, 92; see source cited in note 143.
148. WCR, 3, 92; see source cited in note 143.
149. See WCR, 91-92.
150. AP, III; Lewis & Schiller, 120-122.
151. AP, III; WCR, 92.
152. *Ibid.*
153. AP, III.
154. WCR, 59-60, 538.
155. Roberts, 49.
156. XVII, 23-26; see sources cited in note 104.
157. *Ibid.*

40 THE BEST EVIDENCE

1. *New York Times,* November 2, 1966.
2. *New York Times,* November 3, 1966.
3. *Ibid.*
4. II, 349; CD 7; *Saturday Evening Post,* January 14, 1967.
5. See sources cited in note 4.
6. *New York Times,* November 3, 1966.
7. See, e.g., RTJ, 128n (107n-108n).
8. See, e.g., *New York Times,* November 2, 1966, November 3, 1966.
9. Manchester, 156n.
10. *Look,* February 7, 1967.
11. Manchester, 157n.
12. *Id.* at 156n.
13. See, e.g., Gallup poll reported in the New York *World Journal Tribune,* January 11, 1967; Harris poll reported in the New York *Post,* May 29, 1967.
14. Manchester, 156n-157n.
15. See, e.g., RTJ, 418-468 (355-380); WCR, 817-879.
16. See Manchester, xi.
17. *Id.* at 157n.
18. II, 348-384; XVII, 45.
19. See sources cited in Chapter 39, note 104; II, 348-384.
20. *Ibid.;* CD 7.
21. AP, III.
22. *Ibid.; New York Times,* November 25, 1966.
23. CBS, II, 11.
24. *Argosy,* July 1967; letter from John Nichols to Mark Lane, August 18, 1966.
25. *Argosy,* July 1967.
26. *Ibid.*
27. See, e.g., *U.S. News & World Report,* October 10, 1966; *Saturday Evening Post,* January 14, 1967.
28. *U.S. News & World Report,* October 10, 1966.
29. *Saturday Evening Post,* January 14, 1967.
30. *Ibid.; The Nation,* July 11, 1966; Lewis & Schiller, 117-118.
31. *U.S. News & World Report,* November 14, 1966.
32. *The Nation,* July 11, 1966.
33. Edward Jay Epstein, *Inquest* (New York, 1966), xviii.
34. Lewis & Schiller, 117-118.
35. WCR, v.
36. *Saturday Evening Post,* January 14, 1967.
37. *Ibid.;* WCR, vii.
38. *Saturday Evening Post,* January 14, 1967.
39. *Ibid.*
40. AP, III.
41. *Ibid.*
42. See, e.g., XIX, vi, xii.
43. *Id.* at vi.
44. AP, III.
45. *New York Times,* November 5, 1966; Lewis & Schiller, 118.
46. *New York Times,* November 2, 1966.
47. *New York Times,* November 5, 1966.
48. *Ibid.*
49. *Ibid.*
50. XVII, 330.
51. XXII, 395.
52. Lewis & Schiller, 118.
53. *Ibid.*
54. *New York Times,* November 28, 1966.
55. *Ibid.*
56. *Ibid.*
57. Lewis & Schiller, 118.
58. *Ibid.;* II, 347-384; see WCR, 483-500.
59. II, 347-384; see *id.* at 349-350.
60. *Ibid.*
61. See, e.g., III, 451-515.
62. *Ibid.;* IV, 1-56, 358-383.
63. *Ibid.;* III, 451-515.
64. *Ibid.*
65. See, e.g., III, 451-515; XVII, 264-280.
66. See, e.g., *The Observer* (London), October 16, 1966; *The Nation,* July 11, 1966.
67. *The Observer* (London), October 16, 1966.
68. *Ibid.*
69. CD 7; WCR, 19.

41 THE MISSING EVIDENCE

1. WCR, 88-91.
2. See RTJ, 46-55 (36-44).
3. Roberts, 43.
4. *Id.* at 37-50.
5. *Id.* at 39-44.
6. *New York Times,* November 23, 1963; San Francisco *Chronicle,* November 23, 1963; New York *Daily News,* November 23, 1963; CBS, II, 9.
7. Roberts, 41.
8. RTJ, 53 (43).
9. *Ibid.*
10. CBS, II, 9.
11. RTJ, 53 (43).
12. See *ibid.*
13. CD 678.
14. *Ibid.*
15. Roberts, 99-100.
16. See *id.* at 37-50.
17. RTJ, 47-48 (37).
18. Roberts, 41.
19. See RTJ, 46-55 (36-44).
20. *Id.* at 52 (41-42); XX, 333.
21. See sources cited in note 6.
22. See RTJ, 52 (42); VI, 42.
23. *Id.* at 37; *The New Republic,* December 21, 1963; see RTJ, 51-52 (40-41).
24. See sources cited in notes 22-23; *New York Times,* November 23, 1963.
25. See RTJ, 46-55 (36-44).
26. Roberts, 41-44.
27. *Id.* at 42.
28. VI, 53-54.
29. *Id.* at 41-42.
30. *Id.* at 47-48.
31. John Kaplan, "The Assassins," *The American Scholar,* XXXVI (1967), 271-306.
32. *Id.* at 281.
33. VI, 54.
34. *Id.* at 42.
35. *Id.* at 37.
36. See *supra,* pp. 161-166.
37. Public meeting, Stanford, Calif., May 2, 1967.
38. John Kaplan, "The Assassins," *Stanford Law Review,* XIX (1967), 1110-1151.
39. *Id.* at 1110n.
40. *Id.* at 1110-1151.
41. Kaplan, *The American Scholar,* 281.
42. V, 61.
43. *U.S. News & World Report,* October 10, 1966.
44. Edward Jay Epstein, *Inquest* (New York, 1966), 130; WCR, 91-92.
45. *U.S. News & World Report,* October 10, 1966.
46. *Commentary,* October 1966.
47. See RTJ, 46-55 (36-44).
48. WCR, 3, 19.
49. *Commentary,* October 1966.
50. *Ibid.*
51. *Ibid.*
52. *Ibid.*
53. *Ibid.*

42 THE SINGLE-BULLET THEORY

1. See CBS, II, 15; AP, III.
2. WCR, 19.
3. See CBS, II, 15; AP, III.
4. *Ibid.;* CBS, II, 15.
5. *Ibid.*
6. AP, III.
7. *U.S. News & World Report,* October 10, 1966; CBS, II, 14.
8. *Ibid.*
9. *Id.* at II, 15; AP, III; WCR, 19.
10. Roberts, 26.
11. *Ibid.*
12. WCR, 18-19.
13. See Roberts, 26.
14. See *supra,* pp. 241-242.
15. CBS, II, 14.
16. *Ibid.*
17. *Ibid.*
18. WCR, 98, 100-102.
19. See *supra,* pp. 109-110.
20. CBS, II, 14; V, 157.
21. *Life,* November 25, 1966.
22. *Ibid.;* V, 153.
23. *Id.* at 151; WCR, 98; XVIII, 1-19.
24. V, 138-165, 176-178.
25. *Id.* at 157.
26. CBS, II, 14.
27. *Ibid.;* V, 157, 160.
28. See WCR, 105.
29. *Id.* at 106.
30. *Id.* at 105.

31. *Life,* November 25, 1966.
32. *Ibid.*
33. *Ibid.*
34. Epstein, *op. cit.,* 130; WCR, 85-92.
35. See *supra,* pp. 229-232.
36. *U.S. News & World Report,* October 10, 1966; *Life,* November 25, 1966; CBS, II, 14.
37. *Ibid.*
38. IV, 145.
39. *Life,* November 25, 1966.
40. IV, 114, 128.
41. *Id.* at 114.
42. *Id.* at 128.
43. WCR, 98; XVIII, 26.
44. *U.S. News & World Report,* October 10, 1966; *Life,* November 25, 1966; CBS, II, 14.
45. XVIII, 26, 28, 30; WCR, 97.
46. *Life,* November 25, 1966.
47. *Ibid.*
48. *Ibid.*
49. *Ibid.*
50. See, e.g., Roberts, 63-64; Lewis & Schiller, 135.
51. *Ibid.*
52. Roberts, 63-64.
53. *Ibid.*
54. *Ibid.;* Lewis & Schiller, 135.
55. *Ibid.*
56. *Ibid.;* WCR, 580-581.
57. IV, 101-117.
58. *Id.* at 116.
59. *Ibid.*
60. XVII, 49; WCR, 95.
61. *Ibid.;* III, 430.
62. WCR, 79-81; see RTJ, 79-80 (65-66).
63. See *id.* at 74-79 (61-65).
64. Roberts, 55-56.
65. See RTJ, 76-77 (63-64).
66. Roberts, 55.
67. *Ibid.*
68. *Id.* at 55-56.
69. II, 374-376, 382; XVII, 49.
70. Roberts, 55-56.
71. *Id.* at 55.
72. VI, 91.
73. IV, 114.
74. Roberts, 55.
75. IV, 114.
76. *Ibid.*
77. Roberts, 55-56.
78. *Ibid.;* IV, 127; VI, 110.
79. IV, 127.
80. VI, 110.
81. *Ibid.;* IV, 127.
82. Roberts, 55-56.
83. IV, 117-129; VI, 95-104.
84. *Id.* at 104-113.
85. Roberts, 55-56.
86. IV, 113.
87. Roberts, 56.
88. *Ibid.;* VI, 99.
89. *Ibid.*
90. XVII, 49.
91. Roberts, 56; IV, 123; VI, 99.
92. *Id.* at 95-104.
93. IV, 101, 117-129.
94. Roberts, 56.
95. IV, 23.
96. *Ibid.*
97. Roberts, 56.
98. IV, 121, 123.
99. *Id.* at 121.
100. Roberts, 55-56.
101. *Ibid.;* IV, 113.
102. WCR, 95.
103. See *id.* at 580-586; Roberts, 56-57.
104. *Id.* at 57.
105. WCR, 580; V, 74-90.
106. *Id.* at 79.
107. *Id.* at 80; Roberts, 57.
108. V, 80; XVII, 849.
109. *Id.* at 49, 849.
110. *Id.* at 849.
111. V, 80.
112. XVII, 49, 849.
113. Roberts, 57.
114. *U.S. News & World Report,* October 10, 1966.
115. *Ibid.*
116. WCR, 580-586.
117. V, 79, 81.
118. XVII, 49, 849-850.
119. WCR, 580-586.
120. CBS, II, 16-17.
121. *Time,* September 16, 1966.
122. WCR, 92.
123. IV, 104.
124. See WCR, 107, 109.
125. *Argosy,* July 1967.
126. *Ibid.*
127. *Ibid.*
128. CBS, II, 17-18.
129. *Id.* at II, 18. In the transcript of the program released by CBS, this statement is incorrectly attributed to Dr. William F. Enos.

Conclusion

1. *Philadelphia Inquirer,* November 25, 1966.
2. *Ibid.*
3. *Ibid.*
4. *Ibid.*
5. *Ibid.*
6. *The Progressive,* November 1966.
7. The edition published by Bantam Books (New York, 1964).
8. RTJ, 398 (339-340).
9. *The Progressive,* November 1966.
10. *Ibid.*

Index